The Poems of Shakespeare

Edited with an Introduction
and Notes by

George Wyndham

ATLANTIC

PUBLISHERS & DISTRIBUTORS (P) LTD

Published by
ATLANTIC
PUBLISHERS & DISTRIBUTORS (P) LTD
7/22, Ansari Road, Darya Ganj, New Delhi-110002
Phones : +91-11-40775252, 23273880, 23275880, 23280451
Fax : +91-11-23285873
Web : www.atlanticbooks.com
E-mail : orders@atlanticbooks.com

Branch Office
5, Nallathambi Street, Wallajah Road, Chennai-600002
Phones : +91-44-64611085, 32413319
E-mail : chennai@atlanticbooks.com

First published 1898

Printed in India at Nice Printing Press, A-33/3A, Site-IV, Industrial Area, Sahibabad, Ghaziabad, U.P.

Contents

INTRODUCTION

THE TEXT

of his life, and then subtract so much as may be due to these. He was born[1] at the very heart of this island in Stratford-on-Avon, a town in the ancient Kingdom of Mercia—the Kingdom of the Marches—whose place-names still attest the close and full commingling of Angle with Celt.[2] And he was born—April 22nd or 23rd, 1564—full eighty years after Bosworth Field, by closing the Middle Age, had opened a period of national union at home, and had made room and time for a crowd of literary and artistic influences from abroad. He was, therefore, an Englishman in the wider extension of that inadequate term; and he lived when every insular characteristic flared up in response to stimulants from the Renaissance over-sea. For nationality is not fostered by seclusion, but dwindles, like a fire, unless it be fed with alien food. By parentage he was heir to the virtues and traditions of diverse classes. His mother, Mary Arden, daughter of a small proprietor and 'gentleman of worship,' could claim descent from noble stocks, and that in an age when good blood argued a tradition of courtesy among its inheritors as yet unprized by other ranks. But, though something of Shakespeare's gentleness and serenity may be traced to his mother's disposition, it is—with Shakespeare as with Dickens[3]—the father, John, who strikes us the more sharply, with the quainter charm of a whimsical temperament. John was the eldest son of Richard, tenant of a forest farm at Snitterfield, owned by Robert Arden of Wilmcote, the aforesaid 'gentleman of worship.' But John had a dash of the adventurer, and dreamed of raising the family fortunes to a dignity whence they had declined.[4] So he left the little farm behind him in 1551, and, shifting his base of operations some three or four miles to Stratford, he there embarked his capital

1. Among many sources of information let me acknowledge my special indebtedness to Professor Dowden, Mr. Robert Bell, and above all, the late Thomas Spencer Baynes. (*Shakespeare Studies*. Longmans, Green and Co., 1894.)
2. Cf. the Rev. Stopford Brooke's *History of Early English Literature*, and T.S. Baynes, who quotes J.R. Green and Matthew Arnold.
3. The parallel was noted first—but only in talk—by the late R.L. Stevenson. He was keenly alive (I am told) to its possibilities, which, indeed, are encouraging enough.
4. Griffin Genealogy. *Times*, October 14, 1895.

of hope in a number of varied enterprises[1]: with such success, that in six years he could pretend to the hand of Mary Arden, the heiress of his father's landlord. Like Micawber, he counted on 'something turning up' in a market town; and, although his career was marked from the very outset by a happy-go-lucky incuriousness,[2] at first he was not disappointed. He becomes a burgess, or town-councillor, probably at Michaelmas 1557, High Bailiff in 1568, Chief Alderman in 1571; purchasing house property, and making frequent donations to the poor. His high heart and his easy good-nature won him wealth and friends; but they landed him at last in a labyrinth of legal embarrassments, so that the family history becomes a record of processes for debt, of mortgages and sales of reversionary interests. In 1578 he obtains relief from one-half of the aldermanic contribution to military equipment; and, again, he is altogether excused a weekly contribution of fourpence to the poor. In the same year he mortgages his estate of the Asbies for forty pounds, and his sureties are sued by a baker for his debt of five pounds. In 1579 he sells his interest in two messuages at Snitterfield for four pounds. In 1586 his name is removed from the roll of Aldermen because he 'doth not come to the halles when they are warned, nor hath done for a long time.' And in 1592 his affairs have sunk to so low an ebb that—curiously enough—with Fluellen and Bardolph for companions in misfortune, he 'comes not to church for fear of process for debt.'[3] Yet poverty and sorrow

1. He is described in the register of the Bailiff's Court for 1556 as a 'glover,' but according to tradition he was also a butcher, wool-stapler, corn-dealer, and timber-merchant.
2. He was fined in 1552 for not removing the household refuse which had accumulated in front of his house, and in 1558 for not keeping his gutter clean. Some argue, but not very plausibly, that every record or tradition which they hold derogatory to Shakespeare or his father, is to be referred to others of the same name.
3. Some have held this plea a pretext to cover recusancy: and, from Malone downwards, the best authorities have conjectured in John Shakespeare one of the many who at that time had no certitude of, perhaps no wish for, a definite break and a new departure in religion. The Rev. T. Carter, however, has argued (*Shakespeare, Puritan and Recusant*), 1897, that John Shakespeare and William, were Puritans. Such conscription of the dead to the standards of religious factions may well seem unnecessary in any case. Applied to the Poet of All

Lost, the *Midsummer Night's Dream* and the *Two Gentlemen of Verona*, the *Venus* and the *Lucrece*, and the *Sonnets*. They are of that sweet and liquid utterance, which conveys long trains of images caught so freshly from Nature that, like larks in cages, they seem still to belong to the fields and sky.

Our loss is great indeed if an impertinent solicitude for Shakespeare's morals, an officious care for his reputation as a creator of character, lead us to pass over *Titus Andronicus*, or to lend, in the other early plays, a half-reluctant ear to his 'enchanting song' and his succession of gracious images. But that loss, great as it is in the Plays, is greater and more gratuitous in the Poems, which belong to the same phase of his genius, and yield it a more legitimate expression. The liquid utterance by every character of such lovely imagery as only a poet can see and seize may be, and is most often, out of place in a drama: since it delays the action, falsifies the portraiture, and carries the audience from the scene back to the Playwright's boyhood in the Warwickshire glades. But in a poem it is the true, the direct, the inevitable revelation of the artist's own delight in Beauty. And it is too much to ask of those who drink in this melody without remorse from the Plays, that they shall sacrifice the Poems also to the fetish of characterisation, or shall mar their enjoyment of the Sonnets with vain guesses at a moral problem, whose terms no man has been able to state. Let those, who care for characterisation only, avoid the Poems and stick to the Plays: even as they neglect Chaucer's *Troilus* for his *Prologue* to *The Canterbury Tales*. Each must satisfy his own taste; but, if there be any that dwell overfondly (as it seems to others) on the sweetness of Shakespeare's earlier verse, let them remember that he too dwelt with a like fondness on Chaucer's long lyric of romantic love. The *Troilus* must certainly have been a part of Shakespeare's life, else he could never have written the opening to the Fifth Act of his *Merchant of Venice*:—

> 'The moon shines bright; in such a night as this
> When the sweet wind did gently kiss the trees
> And they did make no noise, in such a night
> Troilus methinks mounted the Troyan walls
> And sigh'd his soul toward the Grecian tents
> Where Cressid lay that night.'

He had stood with the love-sick Prince through that passionate vigil on the wall, and had felt the sweet wind 'increasing in his face.' And if Shakespeare, 'qui après Dieu créa le plus,' found no cause in the *Prologue* for slighting the *Troilus*, surely we, who have created nothing, may frankly enjoy his Poems without disloyalty to his Plays?

Of course, to the making of these Poems, as to the making of every work of art, there went something of the author's personal experience, something of the manner of his country and his time; and these elements may be studied by a lover of Poetry. Yet only that he may better appreciate the amount superadded by the Poet. The impression which the artist makes on his material, in virtue of his inspiration from Beauty, and of his faculty acquired in the strenuous service of Art, must be the sole object and reward of artistic investigation. For the student of history and the lover of art are bound on diverse quests. The first may smelt the work of art in his crucible, together with other products of contemporary custom and morality, in order to extract the ore of historic truth. But for the second to shatter the finished creations of art in order to show what base material they are made of—surely this argues a most grotesque inversion of his regard for means and end? To ransack Renaissance literature for parallels to Shakespeare's verse is to discover, not Shakespeare's art but, the common measure of poetry in Shakespeare's day; to grope in his Sonnets for hints on his personal suffering is but to find that he too was a man, born into a world of confusion and fatigue. It is not, then, his likeness as a man to other men, but his distinction from them as an artist, which concerns the lover of art. And in his Poems we find that distinction to be this: that through all the vapid enervation and the vicious excitement of a career which drove some immediate forerunners down most squalid roads to death, he saw the beauty of this world both in the pageant of the year and in the passion of his heart, and found for its expression the sweetest song that has ever triumphed and wailed over the glory of loveliness and the anguish of decay.

II—BOYHOOD IN WARWICKSHIRE

To measure the amount in these Poems which is due to Shakespeare's art, let us consider the environment and accidents

Introduction

I—THE CHARACTERISTICS OF SHAKESPEARE'S POEMS

Modern critics have found it convenient to preserve the classification of poetry which their predecessors borrowed from the ancients at the Revival of Learning. But, in order to illustrate his theory, each has been forced to define anew such terms as 'lyric,' 'elegiac,' 'epic,' and the terms, in consequence of these repeated attempts, have at last ceased to be definite. Now, despite this shifting indefiniteness, when we say of any poetry that it is lyrical and elegiac, we are understood to mean that it deals with emotion rather than with doctrine or drama; and further, that its merit lies, not so much in the exclusive delineation of any one emotional experience as, in the suggestion, by beautiful imagery and musical sound, of those aspirations and regrets which find a voice but little less articulate in the sister-art of music. Narrowing the definition, we may say that the best lyrical and elegiac poetry expresses, by both its meaning and its movement, the quintessence of man's desire for Beauty, abstracted from concrete and transitory embodiments. The matter in such poetry is of 'Beauty that must die'; the method, a succession of beautiful images flashed from a river of pleasing sound. It is the effect of an art which appeals to the mind's eye with a lovely and vivid imagination, and to the mind's ear with a melody at all times soft and (since Beauty dwells with Sadness) at many times pathetic.[1]

1. Mr. Bagehot seems to deny this when he says (*Hartley Coleridge*) that with 'whatever differences of species and class the essence of lyrical poetry remains in all identical; it is designed to express, and when successful does express, some one mood, some single sentiment, some

To illustrate one art by another is often to lose, in the confusion of real distinction, most of the gain won by comparing justly; yet, at the risk of that loss, it may be said of lyrical and elegiac poetry that it stands to other poetry, and to all speech, in some such relation as that of sculpture to architecture. And this is particularly true of Shakespeare's Poems. Marble may be used for many ends, and in all its uses may be handled with a regard for Beauty; but there comes a Phidias, possessed beyond others with the thirst for Beauty, and pre-eminent both in perception and in control of those qualities which fit marble for expressing Beauty to the mind through the eye. He is still unsatisfied by any divided dedication; and so, in the rhythmic procession of a frieze, he consecrates it to Beauty alone. At other times he may be the first of architects, an excellent citizen at all. The Poems of Shakespeare may be compared to the Frieze of the Parthenon, insomuch as both are works in which the greatest masters of words and of marble that we know have exhibited the exquisite adaptation of those materials to the single expression of Beauty. Other excellences there are in these works—excellences of truth and nobility, of intellect and passion; and we may note them, even as we must note them in the grander achievement of their creators: even as we may, if we choose, find much to wonder

isolated longing in human nature.' I doubt it. On the contrary the essence of lyrical, certainly of elegiac poetry, consists in the handling of sentiment and emotion to suggest infinity, not unity, not the science of psychology but, the mysticism of desire. The emotion may sometimes be isolated for the sake of more effectively contrasting its definiteness with the vast aspiration it engenders. A lyrical poet, for instance, would be content to echo the single note of a curlew, but only because it suggests a whole moorland: the particular moorland, that is, over which one bird is flying, and therewith the flight of all birds, once a part of religion, over all moorlands in all ages. Such a poem, if it were successful, would give, not only the transient mood of a single listener but, all the melancholy and all the meaning and all the emotion without meaning that have ever followed the flight of a lonely bird over a waste place. Mr. Bagehot knows this, for he goes on thus:—'Hence lyrical poets must not be judged literally from their lyrics: they are discourses; they require to be reduced into the scale of ordinary life, to be stripped of the enraptured element, to be clogged with gravitating prose.' And why is this to be done? 'To judge the poet.' Exactly! But why judge the poet instead of enjoying the poem?

at or to revere in the lives of their creators. But in these things of special dedication we must seek in the first place for the love of Beauty perfectly expressed, or we rebel against their authors' purpose. Who cares now whether Phidias did, or did not, carve the likeness of Pericles and his own amidst the mellay of the Amazons? And who, intent on the exquisite response of Shakespeare's art to the inspiration of Beauty, need care whether his Sonnets were addressed to William Herbert or to another? A riddle will always arrest and tease the attention; but on that very account we cannot pursue the sport of running down the answer, unless we make a sacrifice of all other solace. Had the Sphinx's enigma been less transparent, it must have wrecked the play of Sophocles, for the minds of the audience would have stayed at the outset: much in the manner of trippers to Hampton Court who spend their whole time in the Maze. Above all, must the mind be disencumbered, clean, and plastic, when, like a sensitive plate, it is set to receive the impression of a work of art.

But are Shakespeare's Poems works of art? Can the *Venus and Adonis*, the *Lucrece*, and the *Sonnets* be received together as kindred expressions of the lyrical and elegiac mood? These questions will occur to every one acquainted with the slighting allusions of critics to the Narrative Poems, or with the portentous mass of theory and inference which has accumulated round the Sonnets. For to find these Poems and certain of these Sonnets so received we must turn back, over three hundred years, to one of Shakespeare's contemporaries. Francis Meres, in his *Palladis Tamia*, a laboured but pleasing 'comparative discourse' of Elizabethan poets and the great ones of Italy, Greece, and Rome, wrote thus:—'As the soule of Euphorbus was thought to live in Pythagoras, so the sweete wittie soule of Ovid lives in mellifluous and honey-tongued Shakespeare, witness his *Venus and Adonis*, his *Lucrece*, his sugred sonnets among his private friends.' Meres, therefore, was the first to collect the titles or to comment on the character of Shakespeare's Poems. But although, since 1598, he has had many successors more competent than himself, and though nearly all have quoted his saying, not one has followed his example of reviewing the three works together and insisting on their common characteristic. The Poems, indeed, have but rarely been printed hand in hand (so to speak) and apart from the Plays. This strange omission did not follow, as I think, on any deliberate judgment: it was, rather, the accidental outcome of the greater interest aroused by the Plays. The Poems were long eclipsed; and critics, even when they turned to them again, were still thinking of the Plays—were rather seeking in the Poet for the man hid in the Playwright than bent on esteeming the loveliness of Shakespeare's lyrical art. For this purpose the Sonnets showed the fairer promise: so the critics have filled shelves with commentaries on them, scarcely glancing at the *Venus* and the *Lucrece*; and, even in scrutinising the Sonnets, they have been so completely absorbed in the personal problems these suggest as to discuss little except whether or how far they reveal the real life of the man who, in the Plays, has clothed so many imaginary lives with the semblance of reality. The work done in this field has been invaluable on the whole. It is impossible to over-praise Mr. Tyler's patience in research, or to receive with adequate gratitude the long labour of Mr. Dowden's love. Yet even Mr. Dowden, when he turns from considering Shakespeare's art in the Plays, and would conjure up his soul from the Sonnets, cannot escape the retribution inseparable from his task. This probing in the Sonnets after their author's story is so deeply perplexed an enterprise as to engross the whole energy of them that essay it: so that none bent on digging up the soil in which they grew has had time to count the blossoms they put forth. Some even (as Gervinus) have been altogether blinded by the sweat of their labour, holding that the 'Sonnets, æsthetically considered, have been over-estimated' (Shakespeare, *Commentary*, 452). He writes much of Shakespeare's supposed relation to Southampton; but 'for the elegancy, facility, and golden cadence of poetry, *caret*.' Yet we know from Meres and others that Shakespeare impressed his contemporaries, during a great part of his life, not only as the greatest living dramatist but also, as a lyrical poet of the first rank. Thus in 1598 Richard Barnfield, after praising Spenser, Daniel, and Drayton[1]:—

1. '*A Remembrance of some English Poets*: Poems in Divers Humors,' printed with separate title-page at the end of *The Encomion of Lady Pecunia*, 1598. Michael Drayton in his *Matilda*, 1594-1596, after referring to

'And *Shakespeare* thou, whose hony-flowing Vaine
(Pleasing the World) thy Praises doth obtaine.
Whose *Venus* and whose *Lucrece*, (sweet, and chaste)
Thy Name in fame's immortall Booke have plac't
Live ever you, at least in Fame live ever:
Well may the Body dye, but Fame dies never':—

and thus John Weever in 1599 (*Epigrammes in the Oldest Cut and Newest Fashion*):—

'Honie-tong'd Shakespeare, when I saw thine issue,
  I swore Apollo got them and none other,
Their rosie-tainted features cloth'd in tissue,
  Some heaven-born goddesse said to be their mother;
Rose-checkt *Adonis* with his amber tresses,
  Fair fire-hot *Venus* charming him to love her,
Chaste *Lucretia*, virgine-like her dresses,
  Prowd lust-stung Tarquine seeking still to prove her....

Now, these tributes were paid at a time when lyrical poetry was the delight of all who could read English. In one year (1600) three famous anthologies were published—*England's Helicon*, that is, *England's Parnassus*, and *Belvedere, or the Garden of the Muses*; and, something more than a year later, the author of the *Returne from Parnassus* writes this of Shakespeare, when he reaches him in his review of the poets whose lyrics were laid under contribution for the *Belvedere*:—

Ingenioso. William Shakespeare.
Judicio. Who loves Adonis' love, or Lucre's rape,
  His sweeter verse containes hart robbing life,
  Could but a graver subject him content,
  Without loves foolish languishment.

Discounting somewhat from the academical asperity of his judgment, you find Shakespeare still regarded well into the Seventeenth Century[1] as a love poet whose siren voice could steal men's hearts.

In gauging the æsthetic value of a work of art we cannot always tell 'how it strikes a contemporary'; and, even when

Daniel's *Rosamond*, refers to Shakespeare's *Lucrece*. It is interesting to note that the reference is cut out of all subsequent editions.

1. Dated by Arber.

we can, it is often idle to consider the effect beside maturer judgments. But when, as in the case of these Poems, later critics have scarce so much as concerned themselves with æsthetic value, we may, unless we are to adventure alone, accept a reminder of the artist's intention from the men who knew him, who approved his purpose, and praised his success. To Francis Meres, living among poets who worshipped Beauty to the point of assigning a mystical importance to its every revelation through the eye, it was enough that Shakespeare, like Ovid, had wrought an expression for that worship out of the sound and the cadence of words, contriving them into harmonies haunted by such unexplained emotion as the soul suffers from beautiful sights. We need not set Meres as a critic beside, say, Hazlitt. But when Hazlitt quarrels with the Narrative Poems because they are not realistic dramas, and when Gervinus takes the Sonnets for an attempt at autobiography, baulked only by the inherent difficulty of the Sonnet form, it may be profitable to reconsider the view of even the euphuist Meres. Still, none can be asked to accept that view without some warning of the risk he runs. To maintain, with Meres, that Shakespeare's Poems, including the Sonnets, are in the first place lyrical and elegiac, is to court a hailstorm of handy missiles. Hazlitt—who, to be sure, would none of Herrick,—denounced the Narrative Poems for 'ice-houses'; and Coleridge's ingenious defence—that their wealth of picturesque imagery was Shakespeare's substitute for dramatic gesture—is almost as damaging as Hazlitt's attack. The one states, the other implies, that they were awkward attempts at Drama, mere essays at the form in which the author was afterwards to find his vocation. And when we come to the Sonnets, the view of Meres, and of all who agree with Meres, draws a hotter fire: not only from those who push the personal theory to its extreme conclusion, treating the Sonnets as private letters written to assuage emotion with scarce a thought for art, but also from those who vigorously deny that any Sonnet can be lyrical. Yet the hazard must be faced; for the *Venus*, the *Lucrece*, and the *Sonnets* are, each one, in the first place lyrical and elegiac. They are concerned chiefly with the delight and the pathos of Beauty, and they reflect this inspiration in their forms: all else in them, whether of personal experience or contemporary art, being mere raw material and conventional trick, exactly as important to these works of Shakespeare as the existence of quarries at Carrara and the inspiration from antique marbles newly discovered were to the works of Michelangelo. It is easy to gauge the relative importance in Shakespeare's work between his achievement as an artist and his chances as a man. For that relative importance is measured by the chasm which sunders his work from the work of contemporaries labouring under like conditions; and if his Sonnets have little in common with Constable's, his narrative verse has still less in common with (say) Marston's *Pygmalion*.

Unless this view be admitted there is no excuse for republishing the Narrative Poems with the Sonnets: we can take down the Plays, or study, instead of the Sonnets, such conclusions upon Shakespeare's passionate experience as the commentator has been able to draw. And many of us do this, yielding to the bias of criticism deflected from its proper office by pre-occupation with matters outside the mood of æsthetic delight. But the mistake is ours, and the loss, which also is ours, is very great. The nature of it may be illustrated from that which comes upon the many who shrink from reading the earliest of Shakespeare's Plays, or read it only in search of arguments against his authorship. Starting from the improbable conjecture, that the character of an author may be guessed from the incidents he chooses to handle, critics have either alluded to *Titus Andronicus* with an apology, or have denied it to be Shakespeare's.[1] But, read without prejudice or without anxiety to prove that Shakespeare could not have chosen the theme of Mutilation for the spring of unspeakable pathos, the play in no wise 'reeks of blood,' but, on the contrary, is sweet with the fragrance of woods and fields, is flooded with that infinite pity whose serene fountains well up within the walls of an hospital. It is true that Lavinia suffers a worse fate than Philomela in Ovid's tale; that her tongue is torn out, lest it should speak her wrong; that her hands are cut off, lest they should

1. Dowden, *Shakespeare, His Mind and Art*, pp. 54-55. Gerald Massey, *Shakespeare's Sonnets and His Private Friends*, p. 851. Halliwell-Phillipps, *Outlines*, i. 79.

write it. But mark the *treatment* of these worse than brutalities. Thus speaks Marcus of her hands (ii. 4):—

> 'Those sweet ornaments,
> Whose circling shadows Kings have sought to sleep in,
> And might not gain so great a happiness
> As have thy love.'

And again:—

> 'O, had the monster seen those lily hands
> Tremble, like aspen-leaves, upon a lute,
> And make the silken strings delight to kiss them,
> He would not then have touched them for his life!'

And of her tongue (iii. 1):—

> 'O, that delightful engine of her thoughts,
> That blabb'd them with such pleasing eloquence,
> Is torn from forth its pretty hollow cage
> Where, like a sweet melodious bird, it sung
> Sweet varied notes, enchanting every ear.'

Who can listen to these lines or to those which tell how

> 'Fresh tears
> Stood on her cheeks, as doth the honey-dew
> Upon a gather'd lily almost wither'd,'

and yet conclude that 'if any portions of the Play be from his hand, it shows that there was a period in Shakespeare's authorship when the Poet had not yet discovered himself'? In the same scene, hark to the desolate family:—

> 'Behold our cheeks
> How they are stain'd, as meadows yet not dry
> With miry slime left on them by a flood':—

and consider that daughter's kiss which can avail her father nothing:—

> 'Alas, poor heart, that kiss is comfortless
> As frozen water to a starved snake.'

These passages are stamped with the plain sign-manual of Shakespeare: not the creator who, living in the world, fashioned Hamlet and Falstaff and Lady Macbeth, but the lyrical poet, bred in Arden Forest, who wrote *Romeo and Juliet* and *Love's Labour's*

Time, it is repugnant and absurd. As to John, Mr. Carter's contention is found to rest on certain entries in the municipal accounts of Stratford-on-Avon. These show that images were defaced by order of the Town Council in the year 1562-63, and that vestments were sold in 1571. Now, John Shakespeare filled a small office during the first, and the important post of Chief Alderman during the second, of these two years. In order to gauge how nearly such transactions may point to every member of the Town Council, who did not repudiate them, having been a Puritan, it is necessary to consider the attitude of most Englishmen towards questions or ritual at that time. According to Green and other received authorities it was an attitude of uncertainty, 'To modern eyes,' Green writes (*History of the English People*, ii. 308), 'the Church under Elizabeth would seem little better than a religious chaos.' After ten years of her rule 'the bulk of Englishmen were found to be "utterly devoid of religion," and came to church "as to a May game."' It is therefore difficult or, as I hold, impossible to determine from the action of individuals upon questions of ritual, and still more so from their inaction, whether they were Puritans, loyal supporters of the last new State Religion, or Church-Papists, viz.:—those who conformed in public and heard mass at home. But apart from such points, which can hardly be determined, Mr. Carter puts himself out of court on two broad issues. (1) He makes John a Puritan, and chronicles his application for coat-armour (p. 177) without comment. Contrast 'Lenvoy to the Author' by Garter Principal King of Arms, prefixed to Guillim's *Display of Heraldrie* 1610:—

> '*Peevish* Precisenesse, *loves no* Heraldry,
> Crosses *in Armes*, *they hold* Idolatry....
> *Shortly no difference twixt the* Lord *and* Page.
>
> Honours, Recusants' (*i.e.* puritan recusants.) '*doe so multiply*,
> *As Armes, the* Ensignes *of* Nobility,
> *Must be laid downe; they are too glorious*' (boastful)
> '*Plaine idle shewes, and superstitious:*
> Plebeian *basenesse doth them so esteeme.*
>
> "Degrees *in bloud, the steps of pride and scorne,*
> *All* Adam's *children, none are Gentle borne:*
> Degrees *of state, titles of* Ceremony:"
> Brethren *in* Christ, *greatnesse is* tyranny:
> O *impure* Purity *that so doth deeme!*'

and Guillim's own opinion:— 'the *swans purity* is too *Puritanicall*, in that his featters and outward appearance he is all white, but inwardly his body and flesh is very blacke.' (2) He omits the introduction of stage plays into Stratford under John Shakespeare's auspices, and asserts (p. 189) that 'Puritans of the days of Elizabeth had not the abhorrence of the stage which the corruptions of Charles II.'s reign neither tamed his ambition nor sealed up his springs of sentiment. Through the lean years he persists in appealing to the Heralds' College for a grant of arms[1]; and in 1579, being reduced to the straitest expedients, he still pays an excessive sum for the bell at his daughter's funeral. It was not altogether from Shakespeare's own experience, but also, we may think, from boyish memories of this kindly and engaging Micawber that he was afterwards to draw his unmatched pictures of thriftless joviality. From him, also, Shakespeare may well have derived his curious knowledge of legal procedure and of the science of heraldry, for his father contested some sixty lawsuits, and applied, at least three times, for coat-armour. But the father, if he squandered his inheritance, left him an early love and understanding of the stage. 'The best companies in the Kingdom constantly visited Stratford during the decade of Shakespeare's active youth from 1573 to 1584'[2]: thanks, I cannot but think, to the taste and instigation of Shakespeare's sire; for we first hear of stage plays during the

called forth.' Let me quote the Corporation of London in 1575:—'To play in plague-time increases the plague by infection: to play out of plague-time calls down the plague from God' (Fleay, *History of the Stage*, p. 47):—and William Habington, a devout Catholic, writing in 1634, when Prynne had just lost his ears for attacking Players in *Histrio-mastix*:—

'Of this wine should *Prynne*
Drinke but a plenteous glasse, he would beginne
A health to *Shakespeare's* ghost.'
Castara, Part ii., *To a Friend*.

Mr. Carter's attempt to incarcerate Shakespeare in the 'prison-house of Puritanism' rests on too slender a basis to stand unless buttressed by new, and not very convincing, accounts of the principal movements and characters of the time. For example, he makes James I. a hero of Puritanism, in the face of his declarations:—'A Scottish Presbytery as well fitteth with Monarchy as God and the Devil,' and his threat against the Puritans:—'I will make them conform, or I will harry them out of the land!'

1. Conceded in 1596 and extended in 1599. Some dispute this. But the arms of 1596 appear on Shakespeare's monument. *Cf.* the drafts of Grants of Coat-Armour proposed to be conferred on John Shakespeare, from original MSS. preserved at the College of Arms. (Halliwell-Phillipps, *Outlines*, ii. pp. 56, 61.)
2. Baynes, p. 67.

year in which he was High Bailiff, or Mayor, and we know that, during his year of office, he introduced divers companies to the town, and, doubtless, in accordance with custom, inaugurated their performances in the Guild-hall.

From the known facts of John Shakespeare's extraction and career we may infer the incidents of his son's boyhood: the visits to the old home at high seasons of harvest and sheepshearing; the sports afield with his mother's relations; the convivial gatherings of his father's cronies; and certain days of awe-struck enchantment when the Guild-hall resounded to the tread and declamation of Players. But in the first years all these were incidental to the regular curriculum of Stratford Grammar-School—still to be seen in the same building over the Hall. Fortunately we know what that curriculum was, and a bound is set to speculation on the nature and extent of the schooling Shakespeare had. From the testimony of two forgotten books,[1] Mr. Baynes has pieced together the method of teaching in use at grammar-schools during the years of Shakespeare's pupilage; and his theory is amply and minutely confirmed by many passages in the Plays.[2] Shakespeare went to school at seven, and, after grinding at Lily's *Grammar*, enjoyed such conversation in Latin with his instructors as the Ollendorfs of the period could provide. The scope and charm of these 'Confabulationes pueriles' may be guessed from his sketch in *Love's Labour's Lost*:—

> *Sir Nathaniel.* 'Laus Deo, bone intelligo.'
> *Holophernes.* 'Bone! bone for bene. Priscian a little scratched; 'twill serve.'
> *Sir Nathaniel.* 'Videsne quis venit?'
> *Holophernes.* 'Video et gaudeo.'[3]

1. John Brinsley's *Ludus literarius, or Grammar Schoole,* 1612 (Brinsley was master of the Ashby-de-la-Zouche Grammar-School for 16 years), and Charles Hoole's *A New Discovery of the Old Art of Teaching School,* etc. This book, though of later date—Hoole was born in 1610—has its own interest; since the author was head-master of a school at Rotherham closely resembling the Stratford School in 'its history and general features.'—(Baynes.)
2. Baynes, *Shakespeare Studies*, pp. 147-249: '*What Shakespeare Learnt at School.*'
3. I preserve Theobald's emendation. In one of the manuals, '*Familiares Colloquendi Formulae in usum Scholarum concinnatae,*' Mr Baynes

And from Holophernes his 'Fauste precor. Old Mantuan, old Mantuan! who understandeth thee not, loves thee not,' we may infer that the pupil did not share the pedagogic admiration for the Eclogues of the monk, Mantuanus.[1]

But when, with Æsop's fables, these in their tum had been mastered, the boy of twelve and upwards was given his fill of Ovid, something less of Cicero, Virgil, Terence, Horace, and Plautus, and, perhaps, a modicum of Juvenal, Persius, and Seneca's tragedies; and of these it is manifest, from the Poems and the early Plays,[2] that Ovid left by far the most profound impression in his mind. But his studies were cut short. At fourteen[3] he was taken from school, doubtless to assist his father amid increasing difficulties, and we have a crop of legends suggesting the various callings in which he may have laboured to that end.[4] None of these legends can be proved, but none is impossible in view of his father's taste for general dealing and of the random guidance he is likely to have given his son. After four and a half years of such hand-to-mouth endeavour, sweetened, we may guess, by many a holiday in the forest and derelict deer-park at Fulbrook,[5] Shakespeare, in December 1582, being yet a lad of eighteen, married Anne Hathaway, his senior by eight years,

---

has found, 'Who comes to meet us? *Quis obviam venit?* He speaks false Latin, *Diminuit Prisciani caput*; 'Tis barbarous Latin, *Olet barbariem*.' *Cf*. Holofernes:- 'O, I smell false Latin, "dunghill" for unguem.'

1. From Michael Drayton's epistle in verse to Henry Reynolds—*Of Poets and Poesy*—1627, we gather that his poetic aspirations survived the same youthful ordeal:—

   'For from my cradle (you must know that) I
   Was still inclined to noble Poesie;
   And when that once *Pueriles* I had read,
   And newly had my Cato construéd....
   And first read to me honest *Mantuan*.'
2. *Cf*. in particular *Love's Labour's Lost* and *Titus Andronicus*.
3. Rowe, 1709·
4. Rowe makes him a dealer in wool, on the authority of information collected by Betterton; Aubrey (before 1680) a school-master, and elsewhere a journeyman butcher, which is corroborated by the Parish Clerk of Stratford, born 1613. To Malone's conjecture, that he served in an Attorney's office, I will return.
5. The property of an attainted traitor, 'sequestered, though not administered by the Crown.'—Baynes, as above, p. 80.

daughter to the tenant of Shottery Farm. This marriage may, or may not, have been preceded in the summer by a betrothal of legal validity[1]: his eldest child, Susannah, was born in May 1588. But in either case the adventure was of that romantic order which is justified by success alone, and such success must have seemed doubtful when twins were born in February 1585. About this period of youth, 'when the blood's lava and the pulse a blaze,' may be grouped the legends of the drinking-match between rival villages at Bidford, and of the deer-slaying resented by Sir Thomas Lucy. Mr. Baynes places this latter exploit at Fulbrook; and, if he be right, Sir Thomas's interference was unwarranted, and may have been dictated by Protestant bigotry against Shakespeare for his kinship with the Ardens of Parkhall, who stood convicted of a plot against the Queen's life.[2] We know little of these years; but we know enough to approve Shakespeare's departure in search of fortune. For at Stratford, frowned on by the mighty and weighed down with the double burden of a thriftless father and his own tender babes, there was nothing for him but starvation.

III—ADVENT TO LONDON: LETTERS AND THE STAGE

To London, then, he set out on some day between the opening of 1585 and the autumn of 1587, looking back on a few years of lad's experience and forward to the magical unknown. And to what a London! Perhaps the first feature that struck him, re-awaking old delights, was the theatres on both banks of Thames. It may even be that he rode straight to one of these houses—(one built by James Burbage, himself a Stratford man)—and that, claiming the privilege of a fellow-townsman, he enrolled himself forthwith in the company of the Earl of Leicester's players.[3] It is likelier than not; for Burbage can hardly have built, not this later structure but, *the* 'Theater,' twenty years earlier, for

1. Mr. Halliwell-Phillipps argues that it was. There is no evidence either way.
2. Certain indications, each slight in itself, taken together point to some sympathy on Shakespeare's part with the older faith. The Rev. Richard Davies in notes on Shakespeare, made before the year 1708, says 'he dyed a Papist.'
3. Baynes. Fleay holds that Shakespeare joined the company at Stratford and travelled with it to London.

a first home of the drama in London, without receiving the congratulations, perhaps the advice, of Shakespeare's father, in those old prosperous aldermanic days, when every strolling company might claim a welcome from the Mayor of Stratford; and the probability is increased by the presence of two other Stratford men, Heminge and Greene, in the same company. In Blackfriars, also, and near the theatres, stood the shop of Thomas Vautrouillier, publisher, and here Shakespeare found another acquaintance: for Richard Field served the first six years of his apprenticeship (1579-1585) with Vautrouillier, and Richard was the son of 'Henry ffielde of Stratford uppon Aven in the countye of Warwick, tanner,' whose goods and chattels had once, we know, been valued by the Poet's father and two other Stratfordians.[1] Now, about the time of Shakespeare's advent to London, Richard Field married Jaklin, the daughter or widow[2] of Vautrouillier, and succeeded to the *émigré's* business. The closeness of the connexion is confirmed by our knowledge that Field printed the first three editions of *Venus* (1593, 1594, 1596) and the first *Lucrece* (1594). But Field also printed Puttenham's *Arte of English Poesie* (1589), and, in 'a neat brevier Italic,' fifteen books of Ovid's *Metamorphosis*. In 1595, again, he printed his fine edition, the second,[3] of North's *Plutarch*, following it up with others in 1603, 1607, 1612. Without companioning Mr. William Blades[4] so far as to infer that Shakespeare worked as a printer with Field, we cannot miss the significance of his friend's having given to the world the Latin poem which left so deep an impression on Shakespeare's earlier lyrical verse, and that English translation from Amyot's *Plutarch*, out of which he quarried the material of his Greek and Roman plays.

1. *Diet. Nat. Biog*. Richard Field. Arber, transcript, ii. 93.
2. In 1588 he married, says Ames, 'Jaklin, d. of Vautrollier' (*Typographical Antiquities*, ed. Herbert, ii. 1252) and succeeded him in his house 'in the Black Friers, neer Ludgate.' Collier quotes the marriage register—R. Field to Jacklin, d. of Vautrilliam 12 Jan. 1588. It is stated, however, in a list of master-printers included in the 'Stationers' Register' (transcript, iii. 702) that Field married Vautrouillier's widow, and succeeded him in 1590.
3. The first was published by Vautrouillier in 1579.
4. *Shakespeare and Typography*, 1877.

When Shakespeare came to London, then, he found in Blackfriars a little colony of his fellow-townsmen caught up in the two most pronounced intellectual movements of that day: the new English Drama and the reproduction, whether in the original or in translation, of classical masterpieces. We know nothing directly of his life during the next five years. There is the tradition that he organised shelter and baiting for the horses of the young gallants, who daily rode down to the Theatres after their midday meal; and there is the tradition that he paid one visit to Stratford every year.[1] Yet it is easy to conjecture the experience of a youth and a poet translated from Warwickshire to a London rocking and roaring with Armada-patriotism and the literary fervour of the 'university pens.' All the talk was of sea-fights and new editions: Drake and Lyly, Raleigh and Lodge, Greene and Marlowe and Grenville were names in every mouth. The play-houses were the centres, and certain young lords the leaders, of a confused and turbulent movement appealing with a myriad voices to the lust of the eye and the pride of life. In pure letters Greene's *Menaphon* (1589), Lodge's *Rosalynd*[2] (1590), were treading on the heels of Lyly's later instalments of *Euphues*; and Sidney's *Arcadia*,[3] long known in MS, was at last in every hand. The first three books of *The Faery Queen* were brought over from Ireland, and were published in the same year. Poetry, poetical prose, and, for the last sign of a literary summer, even criticism of the aim and art of poetry—as Webb's *Discourse of English Poetrie* (1586), Puttenham's *Arte of English Poesie* (1589), and Sidney's *Apologie for Poetrie*[4]—all kept pouring from the press. But the Play was the thing that chiefly engaged the ambition of poets, and took the fancy of young lords. The players, to avoid the statute which penalised their profession, were enrolled as servants of noblemen, and this led, directly, to relations, founded on their common interest, between the patron who protected a company and the poet who wrote for it. Indirectly it led to much freedom of access between nobles who, though

1. Aubrey (before 1680).
2. Where Shakespeare found the germ of *As You Like It*.
3. Begun 1580, published 1590.
4. Not published till 1595, but written perhaps as early as 1581.

not themselves patrons, were the friends or relatives of others that were, and the leading dramatists and players. Noblemen are associated with Poets, *i.e.* Playwrights, in contemporary satires. In Ben Jonson's *Poetaster,* for example, Cloe, the wife of a self-made man, asks, as she sets out for the Court: 'And will the Lords and the Poets there use one well too, lady?' These artistic relations often ripened into close personal friendships: Ben Jonson, for example, left his wife to live during five years as the guest of Lord Aubigny;[1] and Shakespeare's friendships with Southampton and William Herbert are so fully attested as to preclude the omission of all reference to their lives from any attempt at reconstituting the life of Shakespeare. Doubtless they arose in the manner I have suggested. In 1599[2] we read 'the Lord Southampton and Lord Rutland came not to the Court; the one doth very seldom; they pass away the time in London, merely in going to plays every day'; and from Baynard's Castle to the Blackfriars Theatre was but a step for Pembroke's son, William Herbert, 'the most universally beloved and esteemed of any man of his age.'[3] Shakespeare wrote to Southampton:—'The love I dedicate to your lordship is without end';[4] and we know, apart from any inference deduced from the Sonnets, that William Herbert also befriended our poet. His comrades dedicated the Folio (1623) after his death to William Herbert and his brother Philip, as 'the most incomparable paire of brethren,' in memory of the favour with which they had 'prosequuted' both the Plays 'and their Authour living.' Shakespeare was the friend of both Southampton and Herbert; and in his imagination, that mirror of all life, the bright flashes and the dark shadows of their careers must often have been reflected.

1. Esme Stewart, Lord Aubigny, Duke of Lennox (*cf.* Jonson's *Epigrams*, 19, and the dedication of *Sejanus*). 'Five years he had not bedded with her, but had remained with my lord Aulbany,' *Drummond's Conversations*, 13, quoted by Fleay.
2. Letter from Rowland White to Sir Robert Sidney. Rowe, on the authority of Sir William Davenant, states that Southampton once gave Shakespeare £1000. The story, if it be true, probably refers to an investment in the Blackfriars Theatre.
3. Clarendon.
4. Dedication of *Lucrece*.

IV—POLITICS OF THE STAGE

Southampton was scholar, sailor, soldier, and lover of letters.[1] Born in 1573, he graduated at sixteen as a Master of Arts at St. John's College, Cambridge.[2] At twenty-four he sailed with Essex as captain of the *Garland*, and, attacking thirty-five Spanish galleons with but three ships, sank one and scattered her fellows. And for his gallantry on shore in the same year (1597), he was knighted in the field by Essex before Villa Franca, ere 'he could dry the sweat froth his brows, or put his sword up in the scabbard.'[3] Now, in 1598 Essex was already out of favour with the Queen—she had been provoked to strike him at a meeting of the Council in July; but he was popular in London, and had come, oddly enough, to be looked on as a deliverer by Papists and Puritans both. In April 1599 he sailed for Ireland, accompanied by Lord Southampton; and we need not surmise, for we know, how closely Shakespeare followed the fortune of their arms. In London, 'the quick forge and working-house of thought,' Shakespeare weaves into the chorus to the Fifth Act of his *Henry V*. a prophetic picture of their victorious return:—

> 'Were now the general of our gracious empress,
> As in good time he may, from Ireland coming,
> Bringing rebellion broachéd on his sword,
> How many would the peaceful city quit
> To welcome him!'

The play was produced in the spring of that year, but its prophecy went unfulfilled. Essex failed where so many had failed before him; and, being censured by the Queen, replied with impertinent complaints against her favours to his political opponents, Cecil, Raleigh, and that Lord Cobham who had two years earlier

1. Qui in primo aetatis flore praesidio bonarum literarum et rei militaris scientia nobilitatem communit, ut uberiores fructus maturiore aetate patriae et principi profundat.'—Camden's *Britannia*, 8vo, 1600, p. 240.
2. Southampton was admitted a student in 1585 (aet. 12). Note that Tom Nash, who in after years 'tasted the full spring' of Southampton's liberality (*Terrors of Night*, 1594) matriculated at the same College in 1582, and ever cherished its memory:—'Loved it still, for it ever was and is the sweetest nurse of knowledge in all that university' (*Lenten Stuff*).
3. Gervois Markham, *Honour in its Perfection*, 4to, 1624.

taken umbrage at Shakespeare's *Henry IV*.[1] In September he returned suddenly from a futile campaign, and on Michaelmas Eve, booted, spurred, and bespattered, he burst into the Queen's chamber, to find her with 'her hair about her face.'[2] He was imprisoned and disgraced, one of the chief causes of Elizabeth's resentment being, as she afterwards alleged, 'that he had made Lord Southampton general of the horse contrary to her will.'[3] For Southampton was already under a cloud. He had presumed to marry Elizabeth Vernon without awaiting the Queen's consent, and now, combining the display of his political discontent with the indulgence of his passion for the theatre, he, as I have said, is found avoiding the Court and spending his time in seeing plays. The combination was natural enough, for theatres were then, as newspapers are now, the cock-pits of political as of religious and literary contention. Rival companies, producing new plays, or 'mending' old ones each month, and almost each week, were quick to hail the passing triumphs, or to glose the passing defeats of their chosen causes. Whilst high-born ladies of the house of Essex besieged the Court clad in deep mourning,[4] and the chances of his being forgiven were canvassing among courtiers wherever they assembled, Dekker in *Patient Grissel* (1599), Heywood in his *Royal King and Loyal Subject*,[5] hinted that probation, however

1. *Infra*.
2. Rowland White to Sir Robert Sidney, Michaelmas day, 1599.
3. *Ibid*., 25th October 1599.
4. Rowland White, *passim*.
5. I venture to date this play 1600, although printed much later, on the following grounds:—(1) It was published with an apology for the number of its 'rhyming lines,' which pleaded that such lines were the rage at the date of its first production, though long since discarded in favour of blank verse and 'strong lines.' The plea would hardly tally with a later date. (2) The allusion to Dekker's *Phaethon*, produced 1598, and re-written for the Court, 1600, points to Heywood's play having been written whilst Dekker's, referred to also in Jonson's *Poetaster*, 1601, was attracting attention. In *Poetaster*, iv. 2, Tucca calls Demetrius, who is Dekker, Phaethon. (3) The passage of Heywood's play in which this allusion occurs is significant:—

   '*Prince*. The Martiall's gone in discontent, my liege.
   King. Pleas'd, or not pleas'd, if we be England's King,
   And mightiest in the spheare in which we move,
   Wee 'll shine along this *Phaethon* cast down.'

remorseless, might be but the prelude to a loftier honour. Now, just at this time there occurs a strange reversal in the attitudes of the Court and the City towards the Drama. One Order of Council follows another,[1] enjoining on the Mayor and Justices that they shall limit the number of play-houses; but the City authorities, as a rule most Puritanical, are obstinately remiss in giving effect to these decrees. Mr. Fleay attributes this waywardness to a jealous vindication of civic privileges: I would rather ascribe it to sympathy with Essex, 'the good Earl.' The City authorities could well, had they been so minded, have prevented the performance of *Richard II.*, with his deposition and death, some 'forty times' in open streets and houses, as Elizabeth complained;[2] and, indeed, it is hard to account for the Queen's sustained irritation at this drama save on the ground of its close association with her past fears of Essex.[3] Months after the Earl's execution, she exclaimed to Lambard:—'I am Richard the Second, knowe yee not that?'[4] And we have the evidence of Shakespeare's friend and colleague, Phillips, for the fact that *Richard II.*, was performed by special request of the conspirators on the eve of their insane rising[5]

This trial of the Marshal, who is stripped of all his offices and insignia, seems moulded on the actual trial of Essex in June 1600, as described by Rowland White in a letter to Sir Robert Sidney of June 7th, 1600:—'The poore Earl then besought their Honors, to be a meane unto her Majestie for Grace and Mercy; seeing there appeared in his offences no Disloyalty towards Her Highness, but Ignorance and Indiscretion in hymself. I heare it was a most pitifull and lamentable sight, to see hym that was the Mignion of Fortune, now unworthy of the least Honor he had of many; many that were present burst out in tears at his fall to such misery.' A writer (probably Mr. R. Simpson) in *The North British Review,* 1870, p. 395, assigns Heywood's play to 1600.

1. June 22, 1600. March 10, 1601. May 10, 1601. December 31, 1601. Quoted by Fleay.
2. Nichols, iii. 552.
3. *Cf.* Elizabeth to Harrington:—'By God's Son I am no Queen; this man is above me.'
4. Halliwell-Phillipps, *Outlines,* ii. 359. Lambard, August 1601, had opened his *Pandecta Rotulorum* before her at the reign of Richard II.
5. 'Examination of Augustyne Phillypps servant unto the Lord Chamberleyne, and one of his players,' quoted by Halliwell-Phillipps,

(February 7, 1601)—that act of folly, which cost Essex his head and Southampton his liberty during the rest of Elizabeth's reign.

But if Shakespeare's colleagues, acting Shakespeare's Plays, gave umbrage to Essex's political opponents in *Henry IV.*, applauded his ambition in *Henry V.*, and were accessories to his disloyalty in *Richard II.*, there were playwrights and players ready enough to back the winning side. Henslowe, an apparent time-server, commissioned Dekker to re-write his *Phaethon* for presentation before the Court (1600), with, it is fair to suppose, a greater insistence on the presumption and catastrophe of the 'Sun's Darling'; and Ben Jonson, in his *Cynthia's Revels* (1600), put forth two censorious allusions to Essex's conduct. Indeed the framework of this latter play, apart from its incidental attacks on other authors, is a defence of 'Cynthia's' severity. Says Cupid (i. 1):—'The huntress and queen of these groves, Diana, in regard of some black and envious slanders hourly breathed against her for divine justice on Actæon...hath...proclaim'd a solemn revels, which (her godhead put off) she will descend to grace.' The play was acted before Elizabeth, and contains many allusions to the 'Presence.' After the masque, Cynthia thanks the masquers (v. 3):—

> 'For you are they, that not, as some have done,
> Do censure us, as too severe and sour,
> But as, more rightly, gracious to the good;
> Although we not deny, unto the proud,
> Or the profane, perhaps indeed austere:
> For so Actæon, by presuming far,
> Did, to our grief, incur a fatal doom....
> Seems it no crime to enter sacred bowers
> And hallow'd places with impure aspect.'

In 1600, such lines can only have pointed to Essex-Actæon's mad intrusion into the presence of a Divine Virgin. In 1601 if, as some hold, these lines were a late addition, the reference to Essex's execution was still more explicit.

We know that Essex had urged the Scotch King, our James I., to enforce the recognition of his claim to the succession by a

---

Outlines, ii. 360. Phillips died, 1605, leaving by will 'to my fellow William Shakespeare, a thirty shillings piece of gold.'

show of arms,[1] and that James 'for some time after his accession considered Essex a martyr to his title to the English crown.'[2] Mr. Fleay points out[3] that 'Lawrence Fletcher, comedian to His Majesty,' was at Aberdeen in October 1601, and that Fletcher, Shakespeare, and the others in his company, were recognised by James as his players immediately after his accession (1603).[4] The title-page of the first *Hamlet* (1603: entered in the Stationers' Registers, July 26, 1602) puts the play forward 'as it hath beene diverse times acted by his Highnesse servants in the Cittie of London; as also in the two Universities of Cambridge and Oxford, and *elsewhere*.' Mr. Fleay, therefore, to my thinking, proves his case:[5] that Shakespeare's company was travelling in 1601 whilst Ben Jonson's *Cynthia* was being played by the children of the Chapel. In the light of these facts it is easy to understand the conversation between Hamlet and Rosencrantz, Act ii. 2, which, else, is shrouded in obscurity:—

> '*Hamlet.* What players are they?
>
> *Rosencrantz.* Even those you were wont to take such delight in, the tragedians of the *City*.
>
> *Hamlet.* How chances it they travel? Their residence, both in reputation and profit, was better both ways.
>
> *Rosencrantz.* I think their inhibition comes by means of the late innovation.
>
> *Hamlet.* Do they hold in the same estimation they did when I was in the City? are they so followed?
>
> *Rosencrantz.* No, indeed they are not.
>
> *Hamlet.* How comes it? Do they grow rusty?
>
> *Rosencrantz.* Nay, their endeavour keeps in the wonted pace; but there is, sir, an *eyrie of children*, little eyases that

1. *Queen Elizabeth*, E.S. Beesley.
2. *Criminal Trials*, L.E.K. i. 394; quoted by Fleay.
3. *History of the Stage*, 136.
4. The license is quoted by Halliwell-Phillipps in full, *Outlines*, ii. 82.
5. Mr. Sidney Lee (*Dic. Nat. Biog.* 'Shakespeare'), objects that there is nothing to indicate that Fletcher's companions in Scotland belonged to Shakespeare's company. This hardly touches the presumption raised by the fact that 'Fletcher, *Comedian to His Majesty*,' *i.e.* to James as King of Scotland in 1601, was patented with Shakespeare, Burbage, and others, as the 'King's servants' on James's accession to the English throne in 1603.

> cry out on the top of question and are most *tyrannically* clapped for't: these are now the fashion, and so berattle the common stages—so they call them—that many wearing rapiers are afraid of goose-quills, and dare scarce come thither.... Faith, there has been much to do on both sides, and the nation holds it no sin to tarre them to controversy; there was for a while no money bid for argument unless the poet and the player went to cuffs on the question....[1]
>
> *Hamlet.* Do the boys carry it away?
>
> *Rosencrantz.* Ay, that they do, my lord; Hercules and his load too.'[2]

The collection of such passages; Shakespeare's professed affection for Southampton; his silence when so many mourned the Queen's death, marked (as it was) by a contemporary: all these indications tend to show that Shakespeare shared in the political discontent which overshadowed the last years of Elizabeth's reign. But it is safer not to push this conclusion, and sufficient to note that the storms which ruined Essex and Southampton lifted at least a ripple in the stream of Shakespeare's life.[3]

V—THE COURT AND NOBLE PATRONS

To turn from Southampton to Shakespeare's other noble patron, is to pass from the hazards of war and politics to the lesser triumphs and disasters of a youth at Court. Many slight but vivid pictures of Herbert's disposition and conduct, during the first two years of his life at Court, are found in the intimate letters of Rowland White to Herbert's uncle, Sir Robert Sidney. 'My Lord Harbert'—so he invariably styles him—'hath with much a doe brought his Father to consent that he may live at *London*, yet not before next spring.' This was written 19th April 1597, when Herbert was but seventeen. During that year a project was mooted between Herbert's parents and the Earl of Oxford for his marriage with Oxford's daughter, Bridget Vere,

1. See *infra* on the personal attacks in *Cynthia's Revels* and *Poetaster*.
2. I.e. the Globe Theatre.
3. I shall not pursue the further vicissitudes of Southampton's adventurous career, for the last of Shakespeare's Sonnets was written almost certainly before the Queen's death or soon after.

aged thirteen.[1] It came to nothing by reason of her tender years, and Herbert, in pursuance of a promise extracted from a father confined by illness to his country seat, came up to town, and thrust into the many-coloured rout, with all the flourish and the gallantry, and something also of the diffidence and uneasiness, of youth. You catch glimpses of him: now, a glittering figure in the medley, watching his mistress, Mary Fitton, lead a masque before the Queen, or challenging at the Tournay in the valley of Mirefleur[2]—an equivalent for Greenwich, coined for the nonce, since both place and persons must be masked after the folly of the hour; and again you find him sicklied with ague and sunk in melancholy—the Hamlet of his age, Gardiner calls him—seeking his sole consolation in tobacco.

I cannot refrain from transcribing Rowland White's references in their order, so clean are the strokes with which he hits off Herbert, so warm the light he sheds on the Court that surrounded Herbert. 4th August 1599:—'My lord Harbert meanes to follow the camp and bids me write unto you, that if your self come not over, he means to make bold with you and send for *Bayleigh*'—Sir Robert Sidney's charger—'to Penshurst, to serve upon. If you have any armor, or Pistols, that may steede him for himself only, he desires he may have the Use of them till your own Return.' 11th August 1599:—'He sent to my lady'—('Sidney's sister, Pembroke's mother')—'to borrow *Bayleigh*. She returned this Answer, that he shall have it, but conditionally, that if you come over or send for yt to Flushing he may restore yt, which he agrees to.' 18th August 1599:—'My Lord Harbert hath beene away from Court these 7 Daies in *London*, swagering yt amongest the Men of Warre, and viewing the Maner of the Musters.' 8th September 1599:—'My lord Harbert is a continuall Courtier, but doth not follow his Business with that care as is fit; he is to cold in a matter of such Greatness.' 12th September 1599:—'Now that my lord Harbert is gone, he is much blamed for his cold and weak manner of pursuing her Majestie's Favor, having had so good steps

1. Mr. Tyler, *Shakespeare's Sonnets*, p. 45, quotes the Rev. W.A. Harrison and the original letters, discovered by him, which prove the existence of this abortive contract.
2. This name belongs to 1606; in 1600, however, he also jousted at Greenwich.

to lead him unto it. There is want of spirit and courage laid to his charge, and that he is a melancholy young man.' September 13, 1599:—'I hope upon his return he will with more lisse[1] and care undertake the great matter, which he hath bene soe cold in.'[2] On the 20th September 1599, White perceives 'that Lord Nottingham would be glad to have Lord Harbert match in his house'—i.e. marry his daughter. This, then, is the second project of marriage entertained on Herbert's behalf. On Michaelmas Day, White describes Essex's return, and you gather from many subsequent letters how great was the commotion caused by his fall. 'The time,' he writes, September 30th, 'is full of danger,' and 11th October:—'What the Queen will determine with hym is not knowen; but I see little Hope appearing of any soddain liberty.' Meanwhile Herbert steers clear of the eddies, and prosecutes his cause with greater energy. Whilst Southampton is a truant at the play, 'My lord Harbert' (11th October), 'is at Court, and much bound to her Majestie for her gracious Favor, touching the Resignation of the office of Wales.' Herbert, indeed, seems to have been favoured by all the Court faction, including even Sir Robert Cecil, the chief enemy of Essex and, therefore, of Southampton. November 24, 1599:—'My lord Harbert is exceedingly beloved at Court of all men.' And 29th November 1599, '9000 (Herbert) is very well beloved here of all, especially by 200 (Cecil) and 40 who protest in all places they love him.' In the same letter, '9000 (Herbert) is highly favoured by 1500 (the Queen) for at his departure he had access unto her, and was private an Houre; but he greatly wants advise.' On 28th December 1599, we find him sick with ague, and again, 5th January 1600:—'My Lord Harbert is sick of his tertian ague at Ramesbury.' On the 12th January 1600 we have the first notice of Mary Fitton:—'Mrs Fitton is sicke, and gone from Court to her Father's.' 19th January 1600:—'My lord Harbert coming up towards the Court, fell very sicke at Newberry, and was forced to goe backe again to Ramisbury. Your pies,' White continues, exhibiting the solicitude

1. Fr. Liesse=Gaiety.
2. About this time his father underwent an operation for the stone, and, if he had died under it, his place in Wales would have gone to the Earl of Worcester or the Earl of Shrewsbury. Herbert was to secure the reversion to himself.

of uncle and mother alike for the young courtier, 'were very kindly accepted there, and exceeding many Thankes returned. My Lady Pembroke desires you to send her speedely over some of your excellent Tobacco.'[1] 24th January 1600:—Herbert has 'fallen to have his ague again, and no hope of his being here before Easter.' 26th January 1600:—He complains 'that he hath a continuall Paine in his Head, and finds no manner of ease but by taking of Tobacco.' The mother's care extended even to the lady, Mary Fitton, whom her son was soon to love—supposing, that is, that he did not love her already. 21st February 1600:—'My lady goes often to my Lady Lester, my Lady Essex and my Lady Buckhurst, where she is exceeding welcome; she visited Mrs. Fitton, that hath long bene here sicke in London.' But her son was soon to recover. 26th February 1600:—'My lord Harbert is well again; they all remove upon Saturday to Wilton to the races; when that is ended, my Lord Harbert comes up.' 22nd March 1600:—'My lord Harbert is at Court and desires me to salute you very kindly from him. I doubt not but you shall have great comfort by him and I believe he will prove a great man in Court. He is very well beloved and truly deserves it.'

But some of the love he won brought danger in its train. The next two references, describing the marriage of Mistress Anne Russell to 'the other Lord Herbert,' viz., Lord Worcester's son, picture a masque in which Mrs. Fitton played a conspicuous part before the eyes of her young lover. 14th June 1600:—'There is a memorable mask of 8 ladies; they have a straunge Dawnce newly invented; their attire is this: Each hath a skirt of cloth of silver, a rich wastcoat wrought with silkes, and gold and silver, a mantell of Carnacion Taffete cast under the Arme, and there Haire loose about their shoulders, curiously knotted and interlaced. These are the maskers, My Lady Doritye, Mrs. Fitton, Mrs. Carey, Mrs. Onslow, Mrs. Southwell, Mrs. Bes Russell, Mrs. Darcy and my lady Blanche Somersett. These 8 daunce to the musiq Apollo bringes, and there is a fine speech that makes mention of a ninth,'—of course the Queen—'much to her Honor and Praise.' The ceremony was 'honored by Her Majestie's Presence,' and a

1. Tobacco was first introduced by Nicot as a sovereign remedy against disease.

sennight later we hear how all passed off. 23rd June 1600:—'After supper the maske came in, as I writ in my last; and delicate it was to see 8 ladies soe pretily and richly attired. Mrs. Fitton leade, and after they had donne all their own ceremonies, these 8 Ladys maskers choose 8 ladies more to daunce the measures. Mrs. Fitton went to the Queen, and wooed her to daunce; her Majesty asked what she was; *Affection*, she said. Affection! said the Queen. *Affection* is false. Yet her Majestie rose and daunced.'... 'The bride was lead to the Church by Lord Harbert,' and 'the Gifts given that day were valewed at £1000 in Plate and Jewels at least.' Nine months later Mrs. Fitton bore Herbert an illegitimate child; but meanwhile he pursued his career as a successful courtier. 8th August 1600:—'My lord Harbert is very well thought of, and keapes company with the best and gravest in Court, and is well thought of amongst them.' The next notice, in the circumstances as we know them, is not surprising. 16th August 1600:—'My lord Harbert is very well. I now heare litle of that matter intended by 600 (Earl of Nottingham) towards hym, only I observe he makes very much of hym; but I don't find any Disposition at all in this gallant young lord to marry.'

With the next we come to Herbert's training for the tournament, and gather something of his relations with the learned men whom his mother had collected at Wilton to instruct him in earlier years. Mr. Sandford had been his tutor, sharing that office, at one time, with Samuel Daniel, the poet and author of the *Defence of Rhyme*. 26th September 1600:—'My Lord Harbert resolves this yeare to shew hymselfe a man at Armes, and prepared for yt; and because it is his first tyme of runninge, yt were good he came in some excellent Devize, I make it known to your lordship that if you please to honor my lord Harbert with your advice; my feare is, that Mr. Sandford will in his Humor, persuade my lord to some pedantike Invention.' Then, 18th October 1600:—'My lord Harbert will be all next weeke at Greenwich, to practice at Tylt. He often wishes you here. Beleve me, my lord, he is a very gallant Gentleman and, indeed, wants such a Frend as you are neare unto him.' Again, 24th October 1600:—'Lord Harbert is at Greenwich practicing against the Coronation (?)'; and, 30th October 1600:—'My lord Harbert is practicing at Greenwich, I sent him word of this; he leapes, he dawnces, he singes, he gives cownterbusses, he makes his Horse runne with more speede; he thanckes me, and meanes to be exceeding merry with you this winter in Baynard's Castel, when you must take Phisicke.' The rest is silence; for Rowland White, the intimate, the garrulous, is succeeded in the Sidney Papers by duller correspondents, who attend more strictly to affairs of state, and the issue of Herbert's intrigue is learned from other sources. But before I draw on them, let me set Clarendon's finished picture of Herbert[1] by the side of these early thumbnails:—'He was a man very well bred, and of excellent parts, and a graceful Speaker upon any subject, having a good proportion of Learning, and a ready Wit to apply it, and enlarge upon it: of a pleasant and facetious humour, and a disposition affable, generous, and magnificent.... Yet his memory must not be Flatter'd, that his virtues, and good inclinations may be believ'd; he was not without some allay of Vice, and without being clouded with great Infirmities, which he had in too exorbitant a proportion. He indulged to himself the Pleasures of all kinds, almost in all excesses. To women, whether out of his natural constitution, or for want of his domestick content and delight (in which he was most unhappy, for he paid too dear for his Wife's Fortune, by taking her Person into the bargain) he was immoderately given up. But therein he likewise retain'd such power, and jurisdiction over his very appetite, that he was not so much transported with beauty, and outward allurements, as with those advantages of the mind, as manifested an extraordinary wit, and spirit, and knowledge, and administered great pleasure in the conversation. To these he sacrificed Himself, his precious time, and much of his fortune. And some, who were nearest his trust and friendship, were not without apprehension, that his natural vivacity, and vigour of mind begun to lessen and decline by those excessive Indulgences.' In time he filled nearly all the greater offices of the Court, and 'died of an Apoplexy, after a full and chearful supper,' in 1630, leaving no children from his marriage, but a debt of £80,000 on his estate.[2]

1. *History of the Rebellion*, ed. 1705, vol. 1. book i. p. 57.
2. *Court and Times of Charles I.*, ii. 73.

I have lingered over William Herbert, who, excepting Southampton, received more dedicatory verses from poets, who were also playwrights, than any other noble of his time; for, whether or not he was the 'only begetter' of Shakespeare's Sonnets, he was certainly Shakespeare's friend, and one of the brightest particles in the shifting kaleidoscope of Court and Stage. Though now one company and now another was *inhibited*, the Court and Theatre were never in closer contact than during the last years of Elizabeth's reign, when at Christmas and Twelfth Night a play was almost invariably acted by request 'in the Presence.' Two companies of players were the servants of the highest officers at the Court, the Lord Chamberlain and the Lord Admiral. And the Lord Admiral was that Earl of Nottingham who 'made very much' of Herbert and desired him for a son-in-law.[1] The Theatre was dignified by the very trick of majesty, and the Court transfigured by the spirit of masquerade. Davies tells of Shakespeare in a 'Kingly part,' picking up a glove let drop by Gloriana's self, with the gag:—

> 'And though now bent on this high embassy,
> Yet stoop we to take up our cousin's glove.'

The tradition that Shakespeare played these parts is persistent, and I cannot doubt that his allusion to himself was obvious to his audience when he puts into Hamlet's mouth these words:—'He that plays the King shall be welcome; his majesty shall have tribute of me.'[2]

---

1. We have a pretty picture of his kindness to Herbert's little cousin in another letter of Rowland White to Sir R. Sidney. April 26th, 1600:—'All your children are in Health, the 3 greater, and little Mr. Robert, were at Court, and in the Presence at St. George's Feast, where they were much respected. I brought up Mr. Robert, when the Knights were at dinner; who plaied the wagg soe pretily and boldly that all tooke Pleasure in him, but above the rest, my lord Admirall, who gave him sweet meats and he prated with his Honor beyond measure.'
2. Personal allusions were the sauce of every play. Cf. Jonson's *Cynthia's Revels* (1600) Act v. 2:—

   '*Amorphus*. Is the perfume rich in this jerkin?

   Perfumer. Taste, smell; I assure you, sir, pure benjamin, the only spirited scent that ever awaked a Neapolitan nostril.'

It is almost certain that Mary Fitton, the Queen's Maid of Honour, was on intimate terms with the players in the Lord Chamberlain's (Shakespeare's) Company; for Kempe, who played the Clown's part, seems to have dedicated to her the account of his famous *Morris to Norrviche*,[1] as he writes, 'to shew my duety to your honourable selfe, whose favour (among other bountifull frends) makes me (despight of this sad world) judge my hart corke and my heeles feathers.' Such an intimacy is intrinsically probable from her relations with Herbert, who 'prosecuted Shakespeare with his favour,' from the custom of the age, and above all from her own fantastic disposition. Elsewhere you read[2] that 'in the tyme when that Mrs. Fytton was in great favour, and one of her Majestie's maids of honor (and during the tyme yt. the Earle of Pembroke[3] favoured her), she would put off her head tire and tucke upp her clothes, and take a large white cloak, and march as though she had bene a man to meete her lover, William Herbert.' The inspiration of Shakespeare's laughter-loving heroines in doublet and hose need not, then, have come exclusively from boys playing in women's parts.[4]

But there are shadows in the hey-day pageantry of this Court which borrowed the trappings and intrigues of the Stage, and something of its tragedies also. In 1601 Southampton is arrested, and Essex dies on the scaffold for the criminal folly of the Rising. In the same spring William Herbert is disgraced and imprisoned, because Mary Fitton is to bear him a child, and he

---

Jonson is constantly called 'Benjamen' (Bengemen) in Henslowe's *Diary*.

1. Entered at Stationers' Hall, 22nd April 1600. The dedication, it is true, gives 'Anne,' almost certainly in error, for Mary Fitton. Anne, so far as we know, was never a Maid of Honour, and can hardly have been one in 1600 since she had married Sir John Newdigate in 1585. See W. Andrews, *Bygone Cheshire*, p. 150. He quotes Rev. W.A. Harrison.
2. In a document (assigned by Mr. Tyler after a pencil note on it to Oct. 1602). *Domestic Addenda*, Elizabeth, vol. xxxiv. Mary Fitton suffered from hysteria (*Gossip from a Muniment Room*, 1897, p. 27).
3. Herbert succeeded, 1601.
4. Marston. *Sat*. ii. (1598):—

   'What sex they are, since strumpets breeches use,
   And all men's eyes save Lynceus can abuse.'

'utterly renounceth all marriage.'[1] In truth 'twas a dare-devil age

1. Mr. Tyler (*Shakespeare's Sonnets*, 1890, p. 56) quotes (1) the postscript of a letter, February 5, 1601, from Sir Robert Cecil to Sir George Carew:—'We have no news but that there is a misfortune befallen Mistress Fitton, for she is proved with child, and the Earl of Pembroke, being examined, confesseth a fact, but utterly renounceth all marriage. I fear they will both dwell in the Tower awhile, for the Queen hath vowed to send them thither' (*Calendar of Carew MSS.*). (2) A letter in the Record Office from Tobie Matthew to Dudley Carleton, March 25, 1601:—'I am in some hope of your sister's enlargement shortly, but what will happen with the Erle I cannot tell' (W.E.A. Axon in William Andrews' *Bygone Cheshire*, 1895). In 1606(?) Mary's mother writes:—'I take no joye to heer of your sister, nore of that boy, if it had pleased God when I did hear her, that she hade bene beried, it hade saved me from a gret delle of sorow and gryffe, and her ffrom shame, and such shame as never have Cheshyre Woman; worse now than evar, wright no more of her.'—*Ibid.* Tyler quotes a document of the late Rev. F.C. Fitton copied by his father (b. 1779) from a MS. by Ormerod, author of he *History of Cheshire*, containing this entry:—

Capt. Lougher =	Mary Fitton =	Capt. Polwhele
1st husband	Maid of Honour had one bastard by Wm. E. of Pembroke, and two bastards by Sir Richard Leveson, Kt.	2nd husband

This entry is confirmed, though the order of Mary Fitton's marriages is reversed, by an extract, communicated by Lord de Tabley to the Rev. W.A. Harrison, from 'a very large (elephant) folio of *Cheshire Genealogies* with coloured arms, thus:—

Sir Edward ffitton of Gawesworth

Captaine =	Mary =	Captaine	This Mary Fitton had by Will. Herbert Earle of Pembroke a bastard. And also by Sir Richard Lusan she had two bastard daughters.
Lougher	ffitton	Polewheele	
2 husb.	mayd of honour	i. husband	

Some years later Mary's mother writes to her daughter Anne that Polewhele 'is a veri knave, and taketh the disgrace off his wyff and all her ffryndes to make the world thynk hym worthy of her and that she dessarved no better.' Also about 1606-07 Mary's aunt, wife of Sir Francis Fitton, denounces her niece as 'the vyles woman under the sun.' Mary was baptized at Gawesworth, June 24, 1578, so that her of large morals and high spirits. Sir Nicholas l'Estrange reports that when Sir William Knollys lodged 'at Court, where some of the ladyes and maydes of Honour us'd to friske and hey about in the next room, to his extreme disquiete a nights, though he often warned them of it; at last he getts in one night at their revells, strips off his shirt, and so with a payre of spectacles on his nose and Aretine in his hand, comes marching in at a posterne door of his owne chamber, reading very gravely, full upon the faces of them.' He enjoyed his joke: 'for he fac'd them and often traverst the roome in this posture above an houre.' As the coarse web of Elizabethan embroidery shows beneath the delicate ornament and between the applied patches of brilliant colour, so in the manners of Elizabeth's Court does a texture, equally coarse, run visibly through the refinements of learning and the bravery of display. Even in the amusements of the Queen, who read Greek and delighted in Poetry, do we find this intermingling of the barbarous, of the 'Gothic' in the contemptuous application of that byword, and also of that unconscious humour which we read into archaic art. 'Her Majesty is very well,' writes Rowland White (12th May 1600); 'this Day she appointes to see a *Frenchman* doe Feates upon a Rope, in the Conduit Court. To-morrow she hath commanded the Beares, the Bull and the Ape, to be baited in the Tiltyard. Upon Wednesday she will have solemne Dawncing.' An archaic smile is graven on the faces above the ruff of this Renaissance Cynthia, and our Ninth Muse is also our 'Good Queen Bess,' own daughter to 'Bluff King Hal.' Sometimes she proceeded somewhat drastically to adjust her several diversions:—'On 25th July 1591 the Privy Council wrote to the Lord Mayor directing the suppression of plays on Sundays and on Thursdays, because it interfered with bear-baiting, which was maintained for Her Majesty's pleasure, 'if occasion require.'[1] This singular ground was but one, and certainly the least, of many, for interfering with the Theatres. They shut automatically whenever the number of plague-cases reached a statutory limit; and they were closed, I

age was 22-23 in March 1601. *Cf.* also Lady Newdigate-Newdegate's *Gossip from a Muniment Room*, 1897.

1. Fleay: from Chalmers's *Apology*, p. 379.

have surmised, for political reasons, and also, more than once, for handling religious controversies.

VI—MARTIN MARPRELATE AND RELIGIOUS CONTROVERSY

Soon after Shakespeare's advent, the Martin Marprelate controversy, begun in 1588, overflowed from the press[1] to the stage.[2] Shakespeare, without doubt, saw Martin, the pseudonymous *persona* of the Reformers, caricatured by their antagonists, with a cock's comb, an ape's face, a wolf's belly, and a cat's claws,[3] the better to scratch the face of Divinity;[4] he also saw 'blood and humour' taken from him, on the very boards[5] perhaps, of the theatre in which he played. These astounding products of religious intolerance, coupled with the prevailing taste for mountebank bear-fighting, led to the staying of all plays in the City by the Lord Mayor (Harte) at the instance of Lord Walsingham[6] acting on representations from Tilney, Master of the Revels. The Admiral's players and Lord Strange's—i.e., Shakespeare and his colleagues—were summoned and inhibited. But Lord Strange's company contumaciously shifted its venue, and played that afternoon at the Cross Keys; so two of the players were committed to the Counter and prohibited till further orders.[7] On the death of Ferdinando Lord Strange, Shakespeare and his colleagues joined the Chamberlain's Company.[8] And, in July 1597,

1. The pamphlets are alluded to by Shakespeare. Nash, in *Strange News*, etc., January 12, 1593, p. 194, mentions Lyly's *Almond for a Parrot*, and bids Gabriel (Harvey) *respice funem*. Cf. *Comedy of Errors*, iv. 4:— Dro. E. Mistress, *Respice funem*, or rather, the prophecy like the parrot, 'Beware the rope's end.'—FLEAY.
2. Before August 1589. Arber, *Introduction to Martin Marprelate*. Fleay, *History of the Stage*, p. 92.
3. Lyly's *Pap with a Hatchet*, about September 1589.—Arber.
4. Nash, *Pasquil's Return*, October 1589.
5. Nash, *Countercuffe to Martin Junior*, August 1589.
6. Fleay.
7. Lyly, *Pap with a Hatchet*, September 1589:—'Would these comedies (against Martin) might be allowed to be played that are penned.'—Fleay, *The English Drama*, ii. 39.
8. Mr. Fleay, in his Index lists of Actors, places Shakespeare in Leicester's Company, 1587-89; in Lord Strange's, 1589-93; in the Chamberlain's, 1594-1603. From his list of Companies it appears that on the death

they, with other companies, were again in difficulties, probably of a like origin. The Privy Council, acting on a letter from the Lord Mayor, directed the Justices of Surrey and Middlesex 'nerest to London' to prohibit all plays 'within London or about the city,' and to 'pluck down' the theatres: alleging 'the lewd matters handled on the stage' as the first ground for such action.[1] The city fathers had complained that the theatres tempted their apprentices to play truant; but the 'matters handled on the stage' must have counted for as much, or more, in fostering their puritanical opposition.

High among the causes of offence to the ultra-protestant faction at this time, I must reckon the name first given to the Sir John Falstaff of Shakespeare's *Henry IV*.—viz., Sir John Oldcastle; for Sir John Oldcastle, Lord Cobham, had died a Protestant martyr, burned for Lollardy by Henry v. Some traces of this initial offence survive in the revised version, published in quarto, the first part in 1598, the second in 1600. Thus (Part I. 1. ii.):—

> '*Falstaff*. And is not my hostess of the tavern a most sweet wench?
>
> *Prince*. As the honey of Hybla, my old lad of the Castle.'

In Part II. 1. ii. line 113 the Quarto, instead of the *Fal.* given later in all the Folios, prefixes *Old.* to Falstaff's speech.[2] In II. iii. 2. Shallow is made to say:—'Then was Jack Falstaff, now Sir John, a boy and Page to Thomas Mowbray, Duke of Norfolk'—a

---

of Henry Carey, Lord Hunsdon, July 22, 1596, who had been Chamberlain since 1585, George Carey, Lord Hunsdon, took over the Company under his own name until, on the 27th April 1597, he succeeded Lord Chamberlain Brook, who died the 5th of the preceding March. He kept on the Company as Chamberlain from then till 1603.

1. Halliwell, *Illustrations*, p. 21, quoting 'Registers of the Privy Council.' On the death of Lord Chamberlain Brook (*cf.* Note 5) and succession of George Carey, Lord Hunsdon, this action was annulled, and his players took possession of the Curtain.
2. Theobald concluded that 'the play being printed from the Stage manuscript, Oldcastle had been all along alter'd into Falstaff, except in this single place, by an oversight, of which the printers not being aware, continued the initial traces of the original name.' Malone rejects this conclusion, but the evidence against him is decisive.

post actually filled by the historical Oldcastle.[1] In the Epilogue to Part II. the old name is explicitly withdrawn:—'Falstaff shall die of a sweat, unless already a' be killed with your hard opinions; for Oldcastle died a martyr, and this is not the man.' The whole transaction is set forth by Fuller in a passage which I have not seen quoted.[2] In his life of John Fastolfe, Knight, he writes:—'To avouch him by many arguments valiant, is to maintain that the sun is bright, though since the *Stage* hath been over bold with his memory, making him a *Thrasonical Puff*, and emblem of *Mock-valour*. True it is Sir *John Oldcastle* did first bear the brunt of the one, being made the *make-sport* in all plays for a *coward*. It is easily known out of what *purse* this black *peny* came. The *Papists* railing on him for a *Heretick*, and therefore he must also be a *coward*, though indeed he was a *man of arms, every inch of him*, and as valiant as any in his age. Now as I am glad that Sir *John Oldcastle is put out*, so I am sorry that Sir *John Fastolfe* is *put in*, to relieve his memory in this base service, to be the *anvil* for every *dull wit* to strike upon. Nor is our Comedian[3] excusable by some alteration of his name, writing him Sir *John Falstafe* (and making him the *property of pleasure* for King *Henry* the Fifth, to abuse) seeing the *vicinity* of sounds intrench on the memory of *that worthy Knight*, and few do heed the *inconsiderable difference* in spelling of their name.'

But the matter does not end here. Shakespeare's name appears on the title-page of another play, also published in quarto in the same year, 1600:—

'The first part
of the true and hono-
rable history, of the life of
Sir John Old-castle, the good
Lord Cobham.
As it hath bene lately acted by the Right
honorable the Earle of Notingham

1. Boaz, *Shakspere and his Predecessors*, 1896, p. 260.
2. *The History of the Worthies of England*, published posthumously by Fuller's son, 1662. This passage in the account of Norfolk must have been written less by a great deal than forty years after Shakespeare's death.
3. Shakespeare, without a doubt. *Cf.* Fuller's account of him, *infra*.

Lord High Admirall of England
his servants.
Written by William Shakespeare
London, printed for T.P.
1600.'

Now, Shakespeare did not write this play,[1] and his name only appears on certain copies. It has, accordingly, been urged that his name was added to enhance the value of a pirated edition. Yet I find it hard to believe that any one can have hoped to palm off such a play as Shakespeare's. It was written for and acted by the rival Company (the Admiral's) during the run of Shakespeare's *Henry IV.*, abnormally prolonged during several years, off and on, by the popularity of this very character. It is also, in fact and on the face of it, a protestant pamphlet, written specifically in reply to Shakespeare's abuse of Oldcastle's name. This is apparent from the Prologue, the significance of which has not, I believe, been noted:—

'The *doubtfull Title* (Gentlemen) prefixt
Upon the Argument we have in hand,
May breed suspence, and wrongfully disturbe
The peacefull quiet of your settled thoughts.
To stop which scruple, let this breefe suffice.
It is no pamper'd Glutton we present,
Nor aged Counsellor to youthful sinne;
But one, whose vertue shone above the rest,
A valiant martyr, and a vertuous Peere,[2]
In whose true faith and loyalty exprest
Unto his Soveraigne, and his Countries weale:
We strove to pay that tribute of our love

1. We know from Henslowe's *Diary* that it was written by M(ichael) D(rayton) A(nthony) M(onday), Hathway and Wilson, who were paid in full, £10, October 16, 1599, with a gift of 10s. for the first playing in November.—Fleay, *History of the Stage*, p. 108.
2. The astounding inaccuracy of Mr. Carter (*Shakespeare: Puritan and Recusant*) may be illustrated as above from his handling of this subject. He attributes this line to Shakespeare, and gives it to the *Merry Wives*! In the same paragraph, p. 144, he gives the early use of the name *Oldcastle* to the *Merry Wives* instead of *Henry IV.*, and the phrase, 'Oldcastle died a martyr, and this is not the man' also to the *Merry Wives* instead of to the *Epilogue, II. Henry IV.*

Your favours merit: let *faire Truth be grac'd*
Since forg'd invention former time defac'd.'

The villain and principal character of the Play, which follows to 'grace fair truth,' is a Priest who turns highwayman for his leman's sake, robs the King in a scene inverted from Prince Hal's escapade, is discovered, in dicing against him, through staking a stolen angel which the King had marked, commits murder, and is finally hanged in chains. The addition of Shakespeare's name to a missile so violently retorted against his handiwork may well be but an insolent device, for which there are many analogues in the controversial amenities of the time.[1]

VII—THE UNIVERSITY PENS

If there be dark shadows in the life of the Court, there are shadows, also dark enough, in the other brilliant world of letters. Greene starves in a garret (September 1592). Marlowe, his *Hero and Leander* yet unpublished, is stabbed to death in a tavern brawl (1593). And, apart from the squalid tragedy of their deaths, these great men of letters were literary Mohocks in their lives. There are few parallels to the savage vindictiveness of the Marprelate controversy, and the men who could wield such weapons were ever ready to lay them with amazing truculence about the shoulders of any new adventurer into the arena of their art. Shakespeare came in for his share of the bludgeoning from the outset. The swashing blows of Tom Nash, in his address 'To the Gentlemen students of both Universities' (prefixed to Greene's *Menaphon*, 1589)[2] whistled suspiciously near his head, and must, at least, have been aimed at some of his new colleagues.[3] And they

1. *E.g.* Jonson having attacked Dekker in *The Poetaster*, a play into which he introduces himself as Horace, Dekker retorted in *Satiromastix* by lifting one of Jonson's characters, Tucca, the better to rail at Jonson, again under his self-chosen name of Horace.
2. Dated by Ed. Arber.
3. *Ibid.* 'It is a common practice now a daies amongst a sort of shifting comparisons, that runne through every arte and thrive by none, to leave the trade of noverint (i.e. attorney) whereto they were borne, and busie themselves with the indevors of Art, that could scarcelie latinise their necke-verse (to claim benefit of clergy) if they had neede; yet English Seneca read by candle night yeeldes manie good sentences, as *Bloud is a beggar*, and so foorth; and if you intreate him faire on

are but a part of the general attack delivered by the 'University pens' upon the actors and authors of the new Drama:—'Who (mounted on the stage of arrogance) think to outbrave better pens

a frostie morning, he will affoord you whole *Hamlets*, I should say handfulls of tragical speaches.' Mr. Arber has argued that this passage does not refer to Shakespeare, (1) because *his* play of *Hamlet* was not yet written, (2) because it applies only to translators. On the other hand (1) the earlier *Hamlet*, referred to here and in Dekker's *Satiromastix*, was acted by Shakespeare's colleagues, and may have been retouched by him before he produced the two versions attributed to his authorship—if indeed the Quarto of 1603 can be called a separate version, and be not a pirated edition made from shorthand notes. (2) Although the whole passage refers to translators, this and other incidental remarks are clearly directed against the new drama. *Titus Andronicus* is ascribed by Mr. Dowden to the preceding year, and is said by Baynes to reflect the form of Seneca's later plays. Out of four plays acted by Shakespeare's company, June 3-13, 1594, three bear the titles of plays afterwards ascribed to him, viz., *Andronicus*, *Hamlet*, *The Taming of the Shrew* (Fleay, *History of the Stage*, p. 97). Many other plays with titles afterwards borne by plays indubitably rewritten by Shakespeare, were acted even earlier. Fleay and Dowden agree substantially in placing *Love's Labour's Lost*, *Love's Labour Won* (*Much Ado about Nothing*), *Comedy of Errors*, *Romeo and Juliet*, *Two Gentlemen of Verona*, three parts of *Henry VI.*, *All's Well that Ends Well*, *Troylus and Cressida*, *The Jealous Comedy* (*Merry Wives of Windsor*), and *Twelfth Night* in the early years, 1588-93. Without even considering the date at which Shakespeare may be called sole author of a play (for that is a wholly different question), we may infer that his practice of adding touches to the stock MSS. of his company was one which grew with the popular success attending it. If that be so, an attack in 1589 on a play, afterwards appropriated to Shakespeare, cannot be said to miss him.

The extensive habit of anonymity and collaboration in the production of plays shows that they were regarded simply as the property of the company, and were paid in full when the authors received their fee. The profits were shared: *cf.* Tucca to Histrio, the *impresario*, after the exhibition of acting by his two boys:—'Well, now fare thee well, my honest penny-biter: commend me to seven shares and a half, and remember to-morrow. If you lack a service—(i.e. a patron whose service should protect against the statute)—you shall play in my name, rascals; but you shall buy your own cloth, and I'll have two shares for my countenance.' It was a matter of business, and remained so until the fame of certain authors led to publication. Drayton's Plays of which he was sole author have all perished.

with the swelling bombast of a bragging blank verse.' 'Players avant'[1] was their war-cry; and, when Greene himself utters it, he does not leave the reference in doubt. In a *Groat's Worth of Wit Bought with a Million of Repentance* (1592) he warns Marlowe, Peele, and Lodge, his particular friends in the fraternity of 'ballet makers, pamphleteers, press-haunters, boon pot-poets, and such like,'[2] to beware of players:—'Those puppets, who speak from our mouths, those anticks garnisht in our colours.... Yes,' he goes on, 'trust them not; for there is an upstart crow, beautified in our feathers, that, with his *tiger's heart wrapt in a players hide*,[3] supposes he is as well able to bombast out a blank verse as the best of you, and being an absolute *Johannes fac totum*, is, in his own conceit, the only Shakescene in a country.'

You find the same attitude towards players in *The Return from Parnassus*.[4] Acting is the 'basest trade,' (iv. 5), and again (v. 1):—

'Better it is mongst fiddlers to be chiefe,
Than at plaiers trenchers beg reliefe.'

Such is the conclusion of the two Scholars in the play after exhausting every expedient to win a livelihood by their learning. They go on to attack 'those glorious vagabonds,'

'That carried earst their fardels on their backes,'

grudging them their 'coursers,' and 'Sattan sutes,'[5] 'and pages,' since

'With mouthing words that better wits had framed,
They purchase lands, and now Esquires are made.'

The last shot must surely have been aimed at Shakespeare, who had procured a grant of arms for his father in 1599, and had purchased 107 acres of arable for £320 in 1602. But the date of this Play is uncertain: Mr. Arber argues for January in that year,

1. From a poem by Thomas Brabine, gent.; also appended to Greene's *Menaphon*.
2. Lodge: *cf.* W. Raleigh, *The English Novel*.
3. A line parodied from the 3rd *Henry VI.*: 'Recently revised, if not originally written, by Shakespeare.'—Baynes, 105.
4. Acted by the students of St. John's College, Cambridge.
5. 'Satin suits' is one of the catchwords in the duel between Jonson and Dekker.—*Infra*.

and this would cast doubt on the reference. On the other hand, Burbage and Kempe, Shakespeare's colleagues, are introduced in their own persons (iv. 5), when Kempe thus trolls it off:—'Few of the University pen plaies well, they smell too much of that writer *Ovid*, and that writer *Metamorphosis*, and talke too much of *Proserpina* and *Juppiter*. Why, heres our fellow Shakespeare puts them all downe, I and Ben Jonson too. O, that Ben Jonson is a pestilent fellow, he brought up Horace giving the Poets a pill,[1] but our fellow *Shakespeare* hath given him a purge that made him beray his credit.' Controversy has raged round this passage; but it seems certain (a) that, in common with the whole scene, it is an ironical reflection on the ignorance and the social success of the players; and (b) that it refers to Dekker's *Satiromastix* or *The Untrussing of the Humorous Poet*. This play, in which Dekker retorted upon *The Poetaster*, was published in 1602; but, of course, it had before been presented 'publickly by the Lord Chamberlaine his servants, and privately by the Children of Paules.'[2]

VIII—THE POETOMACHIA

Of more importance than all the 'paper warres in Paules Church-yard' was this famous campaign fought out upon the stage—the Poetomachia[3] in which Dekker and Jonson were protagonists. As distinguished from the onslaught of the 'university pens,' it was a civil war, involving most of the leading playwrights and actors. It raged for years;[4] we know that Shakespeare must have been in the thick of it; and if it be impossible to say for certain on which side he was ranged, it is easy to hazard a guess.

Of his attitude towards Jonson we know little. There is the tradition that he introduced him to the stage; there is the fact that he acted in his plays—in *Every Man in His Humour*, 1598,

1. Viz., in *The Poetaster*, v. i.
2. Title-page.
3. Dekker's address '*To the World*' prefixed to *Satiromastix*.
4. Jonson, as the Author, in the 'Apology' appended to *The Poetaster*:—

'Three years
They did provoke me with their petulant styles
On every stage.'

immediately before the Poetomachia, and in *Sejanus*, 1604, soon after it; there is Fuller's account of the 'wit combats' between them;[1] there is the tradition that Shakespeare entertained Jonson and Drayton at Stratford on the eve of his death.[2] Against these

1. *The History of the Worthies of England, endeavoured by Thomas Fuller, D.D.* Published, unfinished, by 'the author's orphan, John Fuller,' in 1662. From its bulk we may judge that it occupied many years of Thomas Fuller's life, so that it brings his account of Shakespeare fairly close to the date of his death (1616), and well within the range of plausible tradition. I quote the whole passage for its quaintness:—'William Shakespeare was born at Stratford on Avon in this county (Warwick) in whom three eminent Poets may seem in some sort to be compounded. 1. *Martial* in the *warlike* sound of his Sur-name (whence some may conjecture him of a Military extraction), *Hasti-vibrans* or *Shake-spear*. 2. *Ovid*, the most *natural* and *witty* of all Poets, and hence it was that Queen Elizabeth coming into a Grammar-school made this extempore verse:—

   'Persias *a Crab-staffe, Bawdy* Martial, Ovid *a fine wag.*'

   3. Plautus, who was an exact Comædian, yet never any scholar, as our *Shake-spear* (if alive) would confess himself. Adde to all these, that though his Genius generally was *jocular*, and inclining him to *festivity*, yet he could (when so disposed) be *solemn* and *serious*, as appears by his tragedies, so that *Heraclitus* himself (I mean if secret and unseen) might afford to smile at his Comedies, they were so *merry*, and *Democritus* scarce forbear to smile at his Tragedies, they were so *mournfull*.

   'He was an eminent instance of the truth of that Rule, *Poeta non fit, sed nascitur, one is* not *made*, but *born* a Poet. Indeed, his learning was very little, so that as *Cornish diamonds* are not polished by any lapidary, but are pointed and smoothed even as they are taken out of the Earth, so *Nature* itself was all the *art* which was used upon him.

   'Many were the *wit-combates* betwixt him and *Ben Jonson*, which two I behold like a *Spanish Great Gallion*, and an *English Man of War*; Master Jonson (like the former) was built far higher in learning, *solid*, but *slow* in his performances. *Shake-spear* with the *English Man of War*, lesser in *bulk*, but lighter in *sailing*, could turn with all tides, tack about and take advantage of all winds, by the quickness of his Wit and Invention. He died Anno Domini 16...and was buried at *Stratford* upon *Avon*, the Town of His Nativity.'

2. Shakespeare, Drayton, and Ben Jonson 'had a merry meeting, and it seems drank too hard, for Shakespeare died of a fever there contracted.'—*Diary* of Ward, Vicar of Stratford, bearing the date 1662.

proofs of good-fellowship there is the conjecture,[1] founded on Kempe's speech quoted above, that Shakespeare had a hand in the production of Dekkers *Satiromastix*[2] and, perhaps, played William Rufus in it. Of Jonson's attitude towards Shakespeare we know more, but the result is ambiguous. We have the two poems in *Underwoods*—the second, surely, the most splendid tribute ever paid by one poet to another? But, then, we have Jonson's conversations with Drummond of Hawthornden, in which he spared Shakespeare as little as any, laying down that he 'wanted art and sometimes sense.' We have, also, the strong tradition that Jonson treated Shakespeare with ingratitude. This may have sprung from the charge of malevolence preferred against Jonson, so he tells us himself, by Shakespeare's comrades (*Discoveries*: 'De Shakespeare nostrat'). 'I remember,' he says, 'the players have often mentioned it as an honour to Shakespeare, that in his writing (whatsoever he penned) he never blotted out a line. My answer hath been, Would he had blotted a thousand, which they thought a malevolent speech.' In this passage we probably have Jonson's settled opinion of Shakespeare, the artist and the man. He allows 'his excellent phantasy, brave notions and gentle expressions wherein he flowed,' but, he qualifies, 'with that facility, that sometimes it was necessary he should be stopped.' He admits that 'his wit was in his own power,' but adds:—'Would the rule of it had been so too, many times he fell into those things could not escape laughter.' As arrogant as men (and scholars) are made, Jonson found some of Shakespeare's work 'ridiculous'; but he was honest, and when he says, 'I loved the man, and do honour his memory, on this side idolatry, as much as any,' we must believe him. But we are not to infer with Gifford that Drummond misrepresented Jonson, or that Jonson, during the Poetomachia, did not trounce Shakespeare for rejecting, with success, the Jonsonian theory of the Drama.

Gifford, to minimise the authority of Drummond's report, denounces that Petrarchan for a 'bird of prey'; but his whole apology for Ben Jonson is a piece of special pleading too violent and too acerb to command much confidence. He is very wroth

1. T. Tyler and R. Simpson.
2. Acted by his Company, the Lord Chamberlain's.

with the critics of the eighteenth century, who had scented an attack on Shakespeare in the Prologue to Jonson's *Every Man in His Humour*. But what are the facts? The Play, in which Shakespeare had acted (1598), is published (1600) without the Prologue. A revised version is published with the Prologue in 1616, but, as Mr. Fleay has proved[1] from internal references to the 'Queen' and 'Her Majesty' that version must also have been acted before Elizabeth's death (1603), and he adds an ingenious argument for assigning its production to the April of 1601.[2] In the added Prologue Jonson denounces the 'ill customs of the age' in neglecting the Unities. He 'must justly hate' to 'purchase' the 'delight' of his audience by the devices of those who

> 'With three rusty swords,
> And help of some few foot and half-foot words,
> Fight over York and Lancaster's long jars,
> And in the tiring-house bring wounds to scars'

With his usual complacency:—

> 'He rather prays you will be pleas'd to see
> One such to-day, as other plays should be;
> Where neither chorus wafts you o'er the seas,' etc. etc.

Without referring these two gibes specifically to Shakespeare's *Henry VI*. ii. and iii., and *Henry V*. (although the second describes what the chorus in *Henry V*. was actually doing at the time[3]), or the remaining lines to other plays from his hand, it is clear that the whole tirade is an attack in set terms on the kind of play which Shakespeare wrote, and which the public preferred before Jonson's.[4] The attack is in perfect accord with Jonson's reputation

1. *The English Drama*, vol. i. p. 358.
2. iii. 2, Bobadil says:—'To-morrow's St. Mark's day.' It appears from Cob's complaint that the play was acted on a Friday. *Cf*. Jonson's *Bartholomew Fair*, 1614:—'Tales, Tempests and such like drolleries.'
3. Fleay, *ibid*.
4. *Cf*. the copy of verse by Leonard Digges (floruit 1617-35) 'evidently written,' says Halliwell-Phillipps, 'soon after the opening of the second Fortune Theatre in 1623:—

> 'Then some new day they would not brooke a line,
> Of tedius (though well laboured) *Catiline*,
> *Sejanus* was too irksome; they prize the more
> Honest Iago, or the jealous Moore.

for militant self-sufficiency, and, if he made friends again with Shakespeare, he also made friends again with Marston. Dekker wrote thus of him:—''Tis thy fashion to flirt ink in every man's face; and then to crawle into his bosome.'[1]

In the Poetomachia Dekker and Marston were the victims of Jonson's especial virulence, which spared neither the seaminess of an opposite's apparel nor the defects in his personal appearance; but it is hard to say whether they or he began it. Drummond in his *Conversations* attributes the beginning of Jonson's quarrel with Marston to Marston's having 'represented him on the stage in his youth given to venery'; and in Dekker's *Patient Grissel* (1599), in which Chettle had a hand, Emulo may be Jonson; for the taunt at his thin legs:—'What's here? laths! Where's the lime and hair, Emulo?':—is of a piece with innumerable jests at the expense of Jonson's scragginess[2] and his early work at bricklaying. Jonson, at any rate, did not reserve his fire till 1601, though in his apology to *The Poetaster* he suggests that he did:—

> 'Three years
> They did provoke me with their petulant styles
> On every stage.'

It was in 1599 that he began the practice of staging himself and his fellows: himself as a high-souled critic, his fellows as poor illiterates whose foibles it was his duty to correct. As Asper in *Every Man out of His Humour* (1559), as Crites[3] in *Cynthia's Revels* (1600), as Horace in *The Poetaster* (1601), he professes a lofty call to reform the art and manners of his age. This was too much for rivals in a profession in any case highly competitive, and rendered the more precarious by the capricious inhibition of the Companies for which its members wrote. It was hard when their own men were 'travelling'[4] or idle, on account of the

He goes on to say that Jonson's other plays, *The Fox* and *The Alchemist*, even when acted 'at a friend's desire...have scarce defrai'd the seacole fire'; when 'let but Falstaffe come,' Hal, Poins, or 'Beatrice and Benedicke,' and 'loe, in a trice the cock-pit, galleries, boxes, all are full.'

1. *Satiromastix*.
2. He got fat in later life.
3. Criticus in an earlier version.
4. *E.g.* Shakespeare's Company in 1601.—Fleay.

Plague or for having offended the authorities, to be lampooned by 'the children of the Chapel' playing Jonson's pieces before the Queen. And at last in *Satiromastix* (1602), Dekker gave as good as he got, through the mouth of the Tucca he had borrowed from Jonson:—'No, you starv'd rascal, thou 't bite off mine eares then, thou must have three or foure suites of names, when like a lousie Pediculous vermin th'ast but one suite to thy backe; you must be call'd *Asper*, and *Criticus*, and *Horace*, thy tytle's longer in reading than the stile a the big Turkes: Asper, Criticus, Quintus, Horatius, Flaccus.'

Between the opening in 1599 and the end in 1602, the wordy war never relaxes. Jonson staged Marston in *Every Man out of His Humour* (1599) as Carlo Buffone[1]:—'a public, scurrilous and profane jester...a good feast-hound and banquet-beagle,' whose 'religion is railing and his discourse ribaldry'; and, in *Satiromastix*, Dekker suggests that Jonson-Horace, if at a tavern supper he 'dips his manners in too much sauce,' shall sit for a penalty 'a th' left hand of *Carlo Buffon*.' Jonson-Crites in *Cynthia's Revels* (1600) attacks Hedon-Dekker and Anaides-Marston (iii. 2):—

> 'The one a light, voluptuous reveller,
> The other a strange, arrogating puff,
> Both impndent and arrogant enough.'

Dekker retorts by quoting the lines in *Satiromastix*; while Marston parodies them in *What You Will*.[2] In *The Poetaster* (1601) Jonson-Horace administers pills to Demetrius Fannius-Dekker and Crispinus[3] (or Cri-spinas or Crispin-ass)-Marston, so that they vomit on the stage such words in their vocabulary as offended his purist taste. Dekker in *Satiromastix*, 'untrusses the Humorous poet,' i.e. tries Horace-Jonson, and condemns him to wear a wreath of nettles until he swears, among other things, not to protest that he would hang himself if he thought any man could write Plays as well as he; not 'to exchange compliments

1. Fleay rejects this attribution, but he is alone in his opinion.
2. Published 1607, 'written shortly after the appearance of *Cynthia's Revels*.' A.H. Bullen. Introduction to Works of John Marston, 1887. Acted 1601.—Fleay.
3. Juvenal's 'Ecce iterum Crispinus'—a notorious favourite of Domitian.

with Gallants in the Lordes roomes, to make all the house rise up in Armes, and to cry that's Horace, that's he, that's he, that's he, that pennes and purges Humours and diseases'; nor, when his 'playes are misse-likt at Court,' to 'crye Mew like a Pussecat,' and say he is glad to 'write out of the Courtier's Element.' In all these Plays acute literary criticism is mingled with brutal personal abuse. Thus, for sneering at seedy clothes and bald or singular heads,[1] Horace is countered with his bricklaying and his coppered 'face puncht full of oylet-holes, like the cover of a warming pan.' One might hastily infer that Jonson was the life-long enemy at least of Dekker and Marston. Yet it was not so. Dekker had collaborated with him on the eve of these hostilities,[2] though for the last time. Marston's shifting alliances are merely bewildering: the very man whom he libels at one time he assists, at another, in libelling a third. Outraged (you would think) by Jonson's reiterated onslaughts, and conscious of equally outrageous provocation and retort, in 1604 he plasters *Sejanus* with praise; but next year, after the failure of that Play, he hits it, so to say, when it is down.[3] Between the two pieces of attention he collaborates with Jonson and Chapman in producing

1. *Tucca*. 'Thou wrongst heere a good honest rascall Crispinus, and a poor varlet Demetrius Fannius (brethren in thine owne trade of Poetry); thou sayst Crispinus' sattin dublet is reveal'd out heere, and that this penurious sneaker is out of elboes.'—*Satiromastix*.
   Sir Vaughan. 'Master Horace, Master Horace...then begin to make your railes at the povertie and beggerly want of hair.' Follows a mock heroic eulogy of hair by Horace, thirty-nine lines in length.—*Ibid*.
   Tucca. 'They have sowed up that broken seame-rent lye of thine that Demetrius is out at Elbowes, and Crispinus is out with sattin.'—*Ibid*.
2. Dekker and Jonson are paid for '*Page of Plymouth*, Aug. 20 and Sept. 2, 1599. Dekker, Jonson, and Chettle for *Robert* 2, *King of Scots*,' Sept. 3, 15, 16, 27, 1599—Henslowe's *Diary*, quoted by Fleay.
3. Preface to *Sophonisba*:—'Know that I have not laboured in this poem to tie myself to relate anything as an historian, but to enlarge everything as a poet. To transcribe authors, quote authorities and translate Latin prose orations into English blank verse, hath, in this subject, been the least aim of my studies':—an obvious blow at *Sejanus*.

Eastward Ho.[1] He, certainly, was no friend to Shakespeare;[2] for when *The Metamorphosis of Pigmalion*, his 'nasty' copy of *Venus and Adonis*—the epithet is his own—failed as a plagiarism, he had the impudence (*Scourge of Villainy*, vi.) to declare it a parody, written to note

> 'The odious spot
> And blemish that deforms the lineaments
> Of modern Poesy's habiliments.'

Yet he must have sided with Shakespeare now and then. As we shall see.

But amidst the welter and confusion of this embroilment, it is possible to discern, if not a clear-cut line between opposed forces, at least a general grouping about two standards. There was the tribe of Ben, with Jonson for leader, and Chapman for his constant,[3] Marston for his occasional, ally. And, to borrow the war-cries of 1830, there was opposed to this Classical army a Romantic levy, with Shakespeare, Dekker, and Chettle among its chiefs. Where much must be left to surmise, we know that Chettle once went out of his way to befriend Shakespeare, apologising handsomely for Greene's onslaught in *A Groat's Worth of Wit*, and contrasting him favourably with Marlowe; and that Dekker, as we gather from Kempe's speech in *The Return from Parnassus*,

---

1. In which Warton (*History of English Poetry*, iv. 276, ed. 1824) discovers many 'satirical parodies' of Shakespeare. Gifford replies; but Gertrude's parody of Ophelia's song, iii. 2, is a hard nut for the apologist, not to insist on the name—Hamlet—given to a footman who is accosted by Potkins with a 'S'foot, Hamlet, are you mad?'
2. He harps on one of Shakespeare's lines,
   'A man, a man, a kingdom for a man.'
   The first line of Sat. vii. *The Scourge of Villainy* (1598).
   'A fool, a fool, a fool, my coxcomb for a fool.'
   Parasitaster.
   'A boat, a boat, a full hundred marks for a boat.'
   Eastward Ho.
3. Jonson in his Conversations with Drummond said that 'he loved Chapman.' They were imprisoned together for satirising James First's Scotch Knights in *Eastward Ho*, but Chapman turned in his old age. One of his latest poems arraigns Ben for his overweening arrogance.

found Shakespeare an ally in his war against Jonson.[1] We know, too, from Henslowe's *Diary*, that Dekker and Chettle collaborated in April and May 1599, on a play called *Troilus and Cressida*,[2] and, from the Stationers' Registers, that a play with that name was acted by the Lord Chamberlain's servants (Shakespeare's Company) on February 7, 1603. May we not have herein the explanation of Shakespeare's *Troilus*, in which he caricatures the manners and motives of everybody in the Greek (i.e. the Classic) tents?[3] This play and the allusions to rival poets in the Sonnets are the two deepest mysteries of Shakespeare's work. But if we accept the division of forces which I have suggested, a gleam of light may fall on both. It is reasonable to suppose that Shakespeare, who habitually vamped old Plays, took the Dekker-Chettle play for the staple of his own; and, if he did, the satirical portions of his *Troilus and Cressida*, so closely akin to the satire of *Satiromastix*, may be a part of Dekker's attack on Chapman, Jonson, and Marston. Chapman's *Shield of Achilles* and his '*Seaven Bookes of the Iliades of Homere, Prince of*

1. Some find an allusion to this in Jonson's dialogue acted, only once, at the end of *The Poetaster* in place of an Author's apology, which the Authorities had suppressed:—

   'What they have done 'gainst me,
   I am not moved with: if it gave them meat
   Or got them clothes, 'tis well; that was their end,
   Only amongst them, I am sorry for
   Some better natures, by the rest so drawn
   To run so vile a line.'
2. *Trojelles and Cressida*. Also in *Patient Grissel*, October 1599.
3. Shakespeare's Play was published in 1609, *apparently* in two editions: (1) with 'As it was acted by the King's Majestie's servants at the Globe (the title of Shakespeare's Company after 1603); and (2) with a preface stating that the Play had never been 'Stal'd with the Stage.' But the two editions are 'absolutely identical,' even the Title-page being printed from the same forme.—*Preface to Cambridge Shakespeare*, vol. vi. This mystification does not affect the overmastering presumption that Shakespeare's Play, published in 1609, and acted by his company between 1603-09, was the Play, or a re-written version of the Play, acted by his Company in 1603. The presumption that the 1603 Play was founded on that of Dekker and Chettle is also strong. Dekker's *Satiromastix* was played by Shakespeare's Company in 1601.

Poets'[1] appeared in 1598, the year before the Dekker-Chettle *Troilus*, and were prefaced by arrogant onslaughts, repeated again and again, upon 'apish and impudent braggarts,'[2] men of 'loose capacities,' 'rank riders or readers who have no more souls than bur bolts': upon all, in short, who prefer '*sonnets* and lascivious ballads' before 'Homerical poems.'[3] If this suggestion be accepted, we have Shakespeare, a Trojan, abetting the Trojan Dekker against Chapman, an insolent Greek. Shakespeare's play, and Dekker's of 1599, if, as I have surmised, it was the sketch which Shakespeare completed, were founded, ultimately, on the mediæval romance into which the French Trouvère, Benoit de Sainte-Maure, first introduced the loves of Troilus and Briseida, *Roman de Troie* (1160)—afterwards imitated by Boccaccio, Guido delle Colonne, Chaucer and Caxton (*Recuyell of the Histories of Troy*).[4] In this traditional story, adapted to flatter a feudal nobility, which really believed itself the seed of Priam, Hector is the hero, treacherously murdered by Achilles. In *Lucrece* there is no attack on the Greeks, but Dekker, who calls London Troynovant (*Seven Deadly Sins*, 1607), and the Romantic School generally, resented the rehabilitation of Homer's credit—Chaucer had called him a liar—involving, as it did, the comparative disgrace of their hero: all the more that the new glorification of the Greeks came from arrogant scholars, who presumed on their knowledge of the Greek language to rail at the ignorance and to reject the art of their contemporaries and predecessors. That Shakespeare did so abet Dekker against Chapman is a theory more in harmony with known facts than Gervinus' guess that Shakespeare, chagrined by the low moral tone of Homer's heroes, felt it incumbent on him to travesty their action. Minto and Mr. Dowden find in Chapman the rival

1. Books 1, 2, and 7-11 inclusive. The copy in the British Museum bears the autograph, 'Sum Ben Jonsonii.'
2. Preface to the Reader. Folio.
3. 'To the Understander,' *Shield of Achilles*. His deepest concern is lest he should be thought a 'malicious detractor of so admired a poet as Virgil.'—*Epistle dedicatory to the Earl Marshal, Ibid.*
4. Ker, *Epic and Romance*, p. 378, traces Shakespeare's 'dreadful sagittary,' *Troilus and Cressida*, v. v. 14) back to Benoit's 'Il ot o lui un saietaire Qui moult fu fels et deputaire.'

poet of Shakespeare's Sonnets—(I should prefer to say one of the rival poets)—and this falls in with the theory. The banter of Ben Jonson (Ajax) in the Play is more obvious, and pushes, even beyond reasonable supposition, the view, which I submit, that much of Shakespeare's version was written by him during the Poetomachia. Many of the plainest attacks and counterbuffs of that war are in the Epilogues and Prologues to the Plays involved in it. The Speaker of the Epilogue to *Cynthia* (1600) will not 'crave their favour' of the audience, but will 'only speak what he has heard the maker say':—

> 'By God 'tis good, and if you like 't, you may.'

As Envy descends slowly, in the Introduction to *The Poetaster* (1601), the Prologue enters 'hastily in armour,' and replies to censures provoked by this bragging challenge:—

> 'If any muse why I salute the stage
> An *armed* Prologue; know, 'tis a dangerous age,
> Wherein who writes, had need present his scenes
> Forty-fold proof against the conjuring means
> Of base detractors and illiterate apes....
> Whereof the allegory and hid sense
> Is, that a well erected *confidence*
> Can fright their pride and laugh their folly hence.
> Here now, put case our author should once more,
> Swear that his play was good; he doth implore
> You would not argue him of arrogance.'

Marston's Epilogue, added, I imagine, to his *Antonio and Mellida*[1] (1601), says:—'Gentlemen, though I remain an *armed* Epilogue, I stand not as a *peremptory challenger of desert*, either for him that composed the Comedy, or for us that acted it'; and, at the lips of the Prologue to Shakespeare's *Troilus*, the jest runs on—

> 'Hither am I come
> A Prologue *arm'd*, but not in *confidence*
> Of Author's pen or actor's voice....'

I venture to call this Prologue Shakespeare's, for other lines in it, as those on the Trojan Gates:—

1. It is satirised in *The Poetaster* (1601); so that both may have been on the boards together.

'With massy staples,
And corresponsive and fulfilling bolts':—

are to me *audibly* his.[1] Shakespeare, I hold, wrote this Prologue, and wrote it while the Prologue to *The Poetaster* was still a fresh object for ridicule.[2] That Thersites in Shakespeare's *Troilus* stood for Marston can hardly be doubted. When Agamemnon says ironically (I. iii. 72):—

'We are confident
When rank Thersites opes his *mastic*[3] jaw
We shall hear music':—

the allusion to Marston, who had signed himself 'Therio *mastix*' to the prose *Envoy* of his *Scourge of Villainy*, is patent.[4] More: apart from this punning taunt there is no parallel for the foul railing of Thersites' every speech outside the persistent blackguardism of Marston's *Satires* and *Scourge of Villainy*.

Did Shakespeare join elsewhere with his own hand in the Poetomachia? The question arises when we reflect that the Plays

1. Mr. Fleay, *Chronicles of the English Drama*, ii. 190, holds the authorship of the Prologue very doubtful. But this is a question not of evidence but of ear.
2. Fleay, *Ibid.*, i. 366:—'Whoever will take the trouble to compare the description of Crites (Jonson) by Mercury in *Cynthia's Revels*, ii. 1, with that of Ajax by Alexander in *Troilus and Cressida*, i. 2, will see that Ajax is Jonson.' But he is inconsistent. *Ibid.*, ii. 189:—'The setting up of Ajax as a rival to Achilles shadows forth the putting forward of Dekker by the King's men to write against Jonson his *Satiromastix*,' so that Ajax = Dekker, Achilles = Jonson. This inconsistency does not invalidate his conclusion that rival playwrights are satirised, and in many other passages of *Troilus*, the 'guying' of the Greek Commander by Patroclus to amuse Achilles (I. iii. 140-96):—

   'And with ridiculous and awkward action
   Which, Slanderer, he imitation calls,
   He pageants us':—

   and the 'guying' of Ajax by Thersites (undoubtedly Marston) also to amuse Achilles (III. iii. 266-92), are not to be explained unless as portions easily recognisable at the time of the general 'guying' in the Poetomachia.
3. Rowe suggested *mastiff*; Boswell *mastive*.
4. Fleay, again inconsistently, refers this line to Dekker, *History of the Stage*, 106, and to Marston, *Chronicle of the English Drama*, i. 366.

contributed to it by Jonson, Marston, and Dekker fairly bristle with personalities: recognised by the key which Dekker supplied in *Satiromastix*. Of all Shakespeare's characters, Pistol is the one in which critics have especially scented a personal attack; and some have thought that Marlowe was the victim. But Marlowe never wrote as Pistol is made to speak; whilst Marston generally, and particularly in the Satire (*Scourge* vi.) to which I have already alluded, writes in the very lingo of the Ancient. Urging that his nasty *Pigmalion* was in truth but a reproach upon *Venus and Adonis*, he says, and the accent is familiar:—

> 'Think'st thou that genius that attends my soul,
> And guides my fist to scourge magnificos,
> Will deign my mind be rank'd in Paphian shows?':—

Indeed, when we remember the 'wit combats' at the Mermaid, in which these pot companions and public antagonists—Carlo Buffone cheek by jowl with Asper—rallied each other on their failings, and Jonson's anecdote[1] that he had once 'beaten Marston and taken his *pistol* from him,' it is pleasant to imagine that the name of Shakespeare's scurrilous puff was the nickname of Jonson's shifty ally.[2] For in considering this wordy war, it is necessary to remember that the fight was, in the main, a pantomime 'rally,' in which big-sounding blows were given and returned for the amusement of the gallery. Captain Tucca, the character borrowed from *The Poetaster* to set an edge on Dekker's retort, speaks the Epilogue to *Satiromastix*, and begs the audience to applaud the piece in order that Horace (Jonson) may be obliged

1. Drummond's *Conversations*.
2. Jonson comments on some such adventure in his *Epigrams*, lxviii.—On Playwright:—

> 'Playwrit convict of public wrongs to men,
> Takes *private beatings*, and begins again.
> Two kinds of valour he doth shew at once;
> Active in 's brain, and passive in his bones.'

The Quarto of Shakespeare's *Henry V.* was published in 1600. Pistol is beaten in it, as Thersites is beaten in *Troilus*. Pistol uses the fustian word 'exhale'; so does Crispinus in *Poetaster* (noted by Fleay). Pistol's 'Fetch forth the lazar kite of Cresides kinde' is reminiscent of *Troilus*, produced the year before. Pistol's 'What, have we Hiren here' is a mock quotation from an early play of which Marston makes use more than once.

to reply once again. Half in fun and half in earnest did these ink-horn swash-bucklers gibe each other over their cups, and trounce each other on the boards. Yet behind all the chaff and bustle 'of that terrible Poetomachia lately commenced between Horace the Second and a band of lean-witted poetasters,'[1] there was a real conflict of literary aims; and in that conflict Shakespeare took the part of the Romantics, upon whose ultimate success the odds were, in Dekker's nervous phraseology, 'all Mount Helicon to Bun-hill.'[2] Without seeking further to distinguish the champions, it is sufficient to know that Shakespeare was an actor and a playwright throughout the alarums and excursions of these paste-board hostilities, whose casualties, after all, amounted but to the 'lamentable merry murdering of Innocent Poetry.'[3]

IX—SHAKESPEARE'S SHOP

In examining the relation between the lyrics which Shakespeare wrote and the environment of his life, it was impossible to overlook this controversy which must have lasted longer and bulked larger than any other feature in that life.[4] For Shakespeare, the man, was in the first place an actor and a playwright bound up in the corporate life of the Company to which he belonged. We are apt to reconstruct this theatric world, in which he had his being, fancifully: from his Plays rather than from the Plays of his contemporaries, and from the few among his Plays which are our favourites, just because they differ most widely from theirs. But his world of everyday effort and experience was not altogether, as at such times it may seem to us, a garden of fair flowers and softly sighing winds and

1. Address 'To the World' prefixed to *Satiromastix*. The author thanks Venusian Horace for the 'good words'—detraction, envy, snakes, adders, stings, etc.—which he gives him. They are taken from the Prologue to *The Poetaster.*
2. 'To the World' prefixed to *Satiromastix*.
3. Dekker, Epilogue to *Satiromastix*. In the thick of the fray, 1601, Jonson, Chapman, Marston, and Shakespeare each contributed a poem on *The Phoenix and the Turtle* to Robert Chester's *Love's Martyr*!
4. The *Venus* and *Lucrece* were written, of course, years before the Poetomachia; but, unless we accept the improbable view that Shakespeare brought his *Venus* with him from Stratford, both were written under conditions to which the Poetomachia gives a clue.

delicate perfumes, nor altogether a gorgeous gallery of gallant inventions: it was also garish, strident, pungent; a Donnybrook Fair of society journalists, a nightmare of Gillray caricature. 'A Gentleman,' you read, 'or an honest Citizen, shall not sit in your pennie-bench Theatres with his squirrel by his side cracking nuttes; nor sneake into a Taverne with his Mermaid; but he shall be satyr'd, and epigram'd upon, and his humour must run upo' the Stage: you'll ha *Every Gentleman in 's humour*, and *Every Gentleman out on 's humour*.'[1] Shakespeare tells the same story, when he makes *Hamlet* say of the players:—'They are the abstract and brief chronicles of the time: after your death you were better to have a bad epitaph than their ill report while you live.'[2] Note that he speaks of the actors, not the playwrights: though much of their satire turned on size of leg, scantness of hair, pretensions to gentility and seediness of apparel in well-known individuals veiled under transparent disguises. Far more obvious even than such lampooning was the actors' 'guying' of persons and types which we see reflected in *Troilus*[3] and enacted in *Cynthia's Revels*. The actor playing Crites (v. 3) takes off every trick of speech and gesture in the person whom he caricatures, for, says Hedon:—'Slight, Anaides, you are mocked'; and again, in the Induction, one of the three children who play it borrows the Prologue's cloak, and mimics, one after another, the gallants who frequent the theatre; so that here is the 'genteel auditor' to the life, with his 'three sorts of tobacco in his pocket,' swearing—'By this light'—as he strikes his flint, that the players 'act like so many

1. Dekker's *Satiromastix*. In his address '*To the World*' he instances Captain Hannam as the living prototype taken for *Tucca* by Jonson. In the earlier Marprelate plays (*circa* 1589) Nash's antagonist, Gabriel Harvey, was put on the stage. Aubrey, before 1680, wrote that 'Ben Jonson and he (Shakespeare) did gather humours of men daily wherever they came.'
2. *Hamlet*, 11. ii. 501. Fleay, *History of the Stage*, p. 160:—'1601, May 10, the Council writes to the Middlesex Justices complaining that the players at the Curtain represent on the stage 'under obscure manner, but yet in such sort as all the hearers may take notice both of the matter and the persons that are meant thereby': certain gentlemen that are yet alive.
3. I. iii. 140-96. III. iii. 266-292. *Cf. supra.*

wrens' and, as for the poets—'By this vapour'—that 'an 'twere not for tobacco the very stench of them would poison' him.

We can picture from other sources both the conditions of Shakespeare's auditors and the upholstering of his stage. Dekker,[1] describing 'how a gallant should behave himself at a playhouse,' writes of the groundling who masked the view of the 'prentices:—'But on the very rushes where the comedy is to dance, yea, under the state of Cambyses himself, must our feathered estridge, like a piece of ordnance, be planted valiantly (because impudently) beating down the mews and hisses of the opposed rascality.' The dignity of 'Cambyses state' may be guessed from Henslowe's list[2] of grotesque properties—'Serberosse (Cerberus') three heads; Ierosses (Iris') head and rainbow; 1 tomb of Dido; 1 pair of stairs for Fayeton (Phaethon) and his 2 leather antic's coats' and 'the city of Rome(!).' 'The galant in gorgeous apparel, his jerkin 'frotted' with perfumes, 'spikenard, opoponax, ænanthe,'[3] the 'Court-mistress' in 'Satin cut upon six taffetaes,' the 'prentice and harlot viewed these plays, farced with scurrilous lampoons, and rudely staged on rushes, through an atmosphere laden with tobacco and to an accompaniment of nut-cracking and spitting. This was Shakespeare's shop, the 'Wooden O' into which he crammed

> 'the very casques
> That did affright the air at Agincourt,'[4]

and in which, year after year, he won fame and wealth and rancorous envy from defeated rivals.

We catch a last note of detraction, in *Ratseis' Ghost* (1605-06), wherein the phantom hightobyman advises a strolling Player to repair to London:—'There thou shalt learn to be frugal (for players were never so thrifty as they are now about London), and to feed upon all men; to let none feed upon thee; to make thy hand a stranger to thy pocket, thy heart slow to perform thy tongue's promise; and when thou feelest thy purse well lined, buy thee some place of lordship in the country, that, growing

1. *Gull's Horn-Book.*
2. Quoted by Fleay, *History of the Stage*, 114.
3. *Cynthia's Revels.*
4. Chorus to *Henry V*. i.

weary of playing, thy money may then bring thee to dignity and reputation: then thou needest care for no man; no, not for them that before made thee proud with speaking their words on the stage.' 'Sir, I thank you,' quoth the Player, 'for this good council: I promise you I will make use of it, for I have heard, indeed, of some that have gone to London very meanly and have come in time to be exceeding wealthy.' It is significant, almost conclusive, to know that Shakespeare's name appeared on the roll of the King's Players for the last time in 1604 and that in 1605 he purchased an unexpired term (thirty years) in the lease of tithes, both great and small, in Stratford: thus securing an addition to his income equal to at least £350[1] a year of our money.

X—LAST DAYS AND DEATH

Behind this life of business, on and for the stage, Shakespeare, as the friend of young noblemen, saw something of the Court with its gaiety and learning and display, ever undermined by intrigue, and sometimes eclipsed by tragedy. He was impeded in his art by controversies between puritans, churchmen, and precisians, and exercised in his affection for those who to their own ruin championed the old nobility against the growing power of the Crown. As a loyal citizen of London, he must have grieved at her sins and diseases, over which even Dekker, the railing ruffler of *Satiromastix*, wailed at last in the accents of a Hebrew prophet:—'O *London*, thou art great in glory, and envied for thy greatness; thy Towers, thy Temples, and thy Pinnacles stand upon thy head like borders of fine gold, thy waters like frindges of silver hang at the hemmes of thy garments. Thou art the goodliest of thy neighbours, but the prowdest, the welthiest, but the most wanton. Thou hast all things in thee to make thee fairest, and all things in thee to make thee foulest; for thou art attir'd like a Bride, drawing all that looke upon thee, to be in love with thee, but there is much harlot in thine eyes'...so 'sickness was sent to breathe her unwholesome ayres into thy nosthrills, so that thou, that wert before the only Gallant and Minion of the world, hadst in a short time more diseases (than a common harlot hath) hanging upon thee; thou suddenly becamst the by-

1. Baynes.

talke of neighbors, the scorne and contempt of Nations.'[1] Thus Dekker in 1606; and, in the next year, Marston, who equalled him in blatant spirits and far excelled him in ruffianism, left writing for the Stage, and entered the Church!

These are aspects of Shakespeare's environment which we cannot neglect in deciding how much or how little of his lyrical art he owed to anything but his own genius and devotion to Beauty. Least of all may we first assume that his art reflects his environment, and then, inverting this imaginary relation, declare it for the product of a golden age which never existed. Yet, thanks to modern idolatry of naked generalisations, it is the fashion to throw Shakespeare in with other fruits of the Renaissance, acknowledging the singularity of his genius, but still labelling it for an organic part of a wide development. And in this development we have been taught to see nothing but a renewal of life and strength, of truth and sanity, following on the senile mystifications of an effete Middle Age. The theory makes for a sharp definition of contrast; but it is hard to find its justification either in the facts of history or in the opinions of Shakespeare's contemporaries, who believed that, on the contrary, they lived in an epoch of decadence. In any age of rapid development there is much, no doubt, that may fitly be illustrated by metaphors drawn from sunrise and spring; but there are also aspects akin to sunset and autumn. The truth seems to be that at such times the processes of both birth and death are abnormally quickened. To every eye life becomes more coloured and eventful daily; but it shines and changes with curiously mingled effects: speaking to these of youth and the hill-tops, and to those of declension and decay.

In 1611 Shakespeare withdrew to Stratford-on-Avon.[2] Of his life in London we know little at first hand. But we know enough of what he did; enough of what he was said to have done; enough of the dispositions and the lives of his contemporaries; to imagine very clearly the world in which he worked for some

1. *The Seven Deadly Sins of London* (1606).
2. Baynes argues that he left London in 1608. He ceased writing for the stage in 1611, and disposed of his interest in the Globe and Blackfriars Theatres probably in that year.

twenty-three years. He lived the life of a successful artist, rocked on the waves and sunk in the troughs of exhilaration and fatigue. He was befriended for personal and political reasons by brilliant young noblemen, and certainly grieved over their misfortunes. He was intimate with Southampton and William Herbert, and must surely have known Herbert's mistress, Mary Fitton. He suffered, first, rather more than less from the jealousy and detraction of the scholar-wits, the older University pens, and then, rather less than more, from the histrionic rivalry of his brother playwrights. He was himself a mark for scandal,[1] and he watched the thunder clouds of Politics and Puritanism gathering over the literature and the drama which he loved.[2] Yet far away from the dust and din of these turmoils he bore the sorrows, and prosecuted the success of his other life at Stratford. His only son, Hamnet, died in 1596. His daughter, Susannah, married, and his mother, Mary Arden, died in 1608, and in the same year he bestowed his name on the child of an old friend, Henry Walker. Through all these years, by lending money and purchasing land, he built up a fortune magnified by legend long after his death. And in the April of 1616 he died himself, as some have it, on his birthday. He 'was bury'd on the north side of the chancel, in the great Church at Stratford, where a monument is plac'd on the wall. On his grave-stone underneath is:—

> "Good friend, for Jesus' sake, forbear
> To dig the dust inclosed here.

1. Sir W. Davenant boasted that he was Shakespeare's son:—'When he was pleasant over a glass of wine with his most intimate friends' (Aubrey's *Lives of Eminent Persons*. Completed before 1680). *Cf.* Halliwell-Phillipps' *Outlines*, ii. 43. And there is that story of the trick the poet played on Burbage: which might hail from the *Decameron*. See John Manningham's *Diary*, 13th March 1601-02.
2. Warton, *Hist. of Eng. Poetry* (1824), iv. 320. 'In 1599...Marston's *Pygmalion*, Marlowe's *Ovid*, the *Satires* of Hall and Marston, the epigrams of Davies and the Caltha poetarum, etc., were burnt by order of the prelates, Whitgift and Bancroft. The books of Nash and Harvey were ordered to be confiscated, and it was laid down that no plays should be printed without permission from the Archbishop of Canterbury, nor any "English Historyes" (novels ?) without the sanction of the Privy Council.'

Blest be the man that spares these stones,
And curst be he that moves my bones."'[1]

This slight and most imperfect sketch, founded mainly on impressions brought away from the study of many noble portraits, is still sufficient to prove how little the Poems owe, even remotely, to the vicissitudes of an artist's career. Of the wild woodland life in Arden Forest, of boyish memories and of books read at school, there is truly something to be traced in echoes from Ovid and in frequent illustrations drawn from sport and nature. But of the later life in London there is little enough, even in the Sonnets that tell of rival poets and a dark lady, and nothing that points so clearly to any single experience as to admit of definite application. For in Shakespeare's Poems, as in every great work of art, single experiences have been generalised or, rather, merged in the passion which they rouse to a height and a pitch of sensitiveness immeasurable in contrast with its puny origins. The volume and the intensity of an artist's passion have led many to believe that great artists speak for all mankind of joy and sorrow. But to great artists the bliss and martyrdom of man are of less import, so it seems, than to others. The griefs and tragedies that bulk so largely in the lives of the inapt and the inarticulate are—so far as we may divine the secrets of an alien race—but a small part of the great artist's experience: hardly more, perhaps, than stimulants to his general sense of the whole world's infinite appeal to sensation and consciousness.

XI—THE DETACHMENT OF SHAKESPEARE'S POEMS

Shakespeare's Poems are detached by the perfection of his art from both the personal experience which supplied their matter and the artistic environment which suggested their rough-hewn form. Were they newly discovered, you could tell, of course, that they were written in England, and about the end of the Sixteenth Century: just as you can tell a Flemish from an Italian, a Fourteenth from a Sixteenth Century picture; and every unprejudiced critic has said of the Sonnets that they 'express

1. Rowe, 1709.

Shakespeare's own feelings in his own person.'[1] That is true. But it is equally true, and it is vastly more important, that the Sonnets are not an Autobiography. In this Sonnet or that you feel the throb of great passions shaking behind the perfect verse; here and there you listen to a sigh as of a world awaking to its weariness. Yet the movement and sound are elemental: they steal on your senses like a whisper trembling through summer-leaves, and in their vastness are removed by far from the suffocation of any one man's tragedy. The writer of the Sonnets has felt more, and thought more, than the writer of the *Venus* and the *Lucrece*; but he remains a poet—not a Rousseau, not a Metaphysician—and his chief concern is still to worship Beauty in the imagery and music of his verse. It is, indeed, strange to find how much of thought, imagery, and rhythm is common to *Venus and Adonis* and the *Sonnets*, for the two works could hardly belong by their themes to classes of poetry more widely distinct—(the first is a late Renaissance imitation of late Classical Mythology; the second a sequence of intimate occasional verses)—nor could they differ more obviously from other poems in the same classes. Many such imitations and sequences of sonnets were written by Shakespeare's contemporaries, but among them all there is not one poem that in the least resembles *Venus and Adonis*, and there are but few sonnets that remind you, even faintly, of Shakespeare's. And just such distinctions isolate *The Rape of Lucrece*. By its theme, as a romantic story in rhyme, it has nothing in common with its two companions from Shakespeare's hand; but it is lonelier than they, having indeed no fellow in Elizabethan poetry and not many in English literature. Leaving ballads on one side, you may count the romantic stories in English rhyme, that can by courtesy be called literature, upon the fingers of one hand. There are but two arches in the bridge by which Keats and Chaucer communicate across the centuries, and Shakespeare's *Lucrece* stands for the solitary pier. Yet, distinct as they are from each other in character,

1. Mr. Dowden:—'With Wordsworth, Sir Henry Taylor, and Mr. Swinburne; with François-Victor Hugo, with Kreyssig, Ulrici, Gervinus, and Hermann Isaac; with Boaden, Armitage Brown, and Hallam; with Furnivall, Spalding, Rossetti, and Palgrave, I believe that Shakespeare's Sonnets express his own feelings in his own person.' So do Mr. A.E. Harrison and Mr. Tyler.

these three things by Shakespeare are closely united in form by a degree of lyrical excellence in their imagery and rhythm which severs them from kindred competitors: they are the first examples of the highest qualities in Elizabethan lyrical verse. No poet of that day ever doubted that 'poesie dealeth with *Katholon*, that is to say with the universall consideration,'[1] or that of every language in Europe their own could best 'yeeld the sweet slyding fit for a verse.'[2] But in these three you find the highest expression of this theory and this practice alike: a sense of the mystery of Beauty profound as Plato's, with such a golden cadence as no other singer has been able to sustain.

XII—VENUS AND ADONIS

Venus and Adonis was published in 1593, the year of Marlowe's death, and was at once immensely popular, editions following one hard upon another, in 1594, 1596, 1599, 1600, and (two editions) 1602. Shakespeare dedicated his poem to Lord Southampton, and called it 'the first heir of his invention.' There is nothing remarkable in his choice of a metre—the 'staffe of sixe verses' (ab ab cc); for four years earlier Puttenham (?) had described it (*The Arte of English Poesie*, 1589) as 'not only *most usual*, but also very pleasant to th' eare.' We need not, then, suppose that Shakespeare borrowed it exclusively from Lodge. He may have been guided in his choice. For Lodge had interwoven a short allusion to *Adonis'* death into his *Scylla's Metamorphosis*, also published in 1589 and written in this staff of six. But Lodge's melody is not Shakespeare's:—

> 'Her dainty hand addressed to claw her dear,
> Her roseal lip allied to his pale cheek,
> Her sighs, and then her looks, and heavy cheer,
> Her bitter threats, and then her passions meek:
> How on his senseless corpse she lay a-crying,
> As if the boy were then but now a-dying':—

and, indeed, Shakespeare's poem is, in all essentials, utterly unlike Lodge's *Scylla*, Marlowe's unfinished *Hero and Leander*, Drayton's *Endymion and Phœbe*, and Chapman's *Ovid's Banquet*

1. Sidney, *Apologie for Poetrie*.
2. *Ibid*.

of Sense. Still less does it resemble the earlier adaptations from Ovid's *Metamorphosis*, as Thomas Peend's '*Salmacis and Hermaphroditus*' (1565):—

> 'Dame Venus once by Mercurye
> Comprest, a chylde did beare,
> For beauty farre excellyng all
> That erst before hym weare.'

It borrows from, or lends to, Henry Constable's *Sheepheards Song* scarce a phrase,[1] and the same may be said still more emphatically of its relation to Spenser's five stanzas[2] on 'The Love of *Venus* and her Paramoure,' and to Golding's Ovid. Briefly, it has nothing to do either with studious imitations of the Classics or with the 'rhyme doggerel' that preceded them, for it throws back to the mediæval poets' use of Ovid: to Chrétien de Troyes, that is, the authors of the *Roman de la Rose*, and Chaucer, who first steeped themselves in the *Metamorphosis*, and then made beautiful poems of their own by the light of their genius in the manner of their day. Sometimes you may trace the extraction of an image in Shakespeare's verse back and up the mediæval tradition. Thus (Sonnet cxix.):—

> 'What potions have I drunke of syren teares
> Distill'd from lymbecks.'

Thus Chaucer (*Troilus*, iv.):—

---

1. *The Sheepheard's Sang of Venus and Adonis*. First published in *England's Helicon*, 1600: it may have been written before Shakespeare's *Adonis*. The bare theme, which is not to be found in Ovid, of Venus's vain soliciting and of Adonis's reluctance, is alluded to in Marlowe's *Hero and Leander*:—

   > 'Where Venus in her naked glory strove
   > To please the careless and disdainful eyes
   > Of proud Adonis, that before her lies':—

   and in Robert Greene's pamphlet, *Never Too Late* (1590):—

   > 'Sweet *Adon*, dar'st not glance thine eye
   > (*N'oseres vous, mon bel amy?*)
   > Upon thy Venus that must die?
   > *Je vous en prie*, pitty me:
   > *N'oseres vous, mon bel*, mon bel,
   > *N'oseres vous, mon bel amy?*'

2. *Faerie Queene*, iii. 1, 34-38.

'This Troilus in tearës gan distill
As licour out of allambick full fast.'

And thus the *Roman de la Rose* (l. 6657):—

'Por quoi donc en tristor demores?
Je vois maintes fois que tu plores.
Cum alambic sus alutel.'

But with greater frequency comes the evidence of Shakespeare's loving familiarity with Ovid whose effects he fuses: taking the reluctance of Adonis from *Hermaphroditus* (*Metamorphosis*, iv.); the description of the boar from Meleager's encounter in viii.; and other features from the short version of *Venus and Adonis* which Ovid weaves on to the terrible and beautiful story of Myrrha (x.).[1] In all Shakespeare's work of this period the same fusion of Ovid's stories and images is obvious. Tarquin and Myrrha are both delayed, but, not daunted, by lugubrious forebodings in the dark; and *Titus Andronicus*, played for the first time in the year which saw the publication of *Venus and Adonis*, is full of debts and allusions to Ovid. Ovid, with his power of telling a story and of eloquent discourse, his shining images, his cadences coloured with assonance and weighted with alliteration; Chaucer, with his sweet liquidity of diction, his dialogues and soliloquies—these are the 'only true begetters' of the lyric Shakespeare. In these matters we must allow poets to have their own way: merely noting that Ovid, in whom critics see chiefly a brilliant man of the world, has been a mine of delight for all poets who rejoice in the magic of sound, from the dawn of the Middle Ages down to our own incomparable Milton.[2] His effects of alliteration:—

'Corpora Cecropidum pennis pendere putares;
Pendebant pennis....
Vertitur in volucrem, cui stant, in vertice cristae':—

his gleaming metaphors, as of Hermaphroditus after his plunge:—

'In liquidis translucet aquis; ut eburnea si quis
Signa tegat claro, vel candida lilia, vitro':—

1. *Cf. Le Roman de la Rose*. Chap. cvii. follows the order of Ovid's Tenth Book, passing from Pygmalion to 'Mirra' and adding ll. 21992, 'Li biaus *Adonis* en fu nés.'
2. Mackail on 'Milton's Debt to Ovid.' (*Latin Literature*, 142.) *Cf.* Ker, *Epic and Romance*, 395.

are the very counterpart of Shakespeare's manner in the Poems and the Play which he founded in part on his early love of the *Metamorphosis*.

But in *Titus Andronicus* and in *Venus and Adonis* there are effects of the open air which hail, not from Ovid but, from Arden:—

'The birds chant melody on every bush;
The snake lies rolled in the cheerful sun;
The green leaves quiver with the cooling wind,
And make a chequer'd shadow on the ground':—

Thus the Play (ii. 3), and thus the Poem:—

'Even as the wind is hush'd before it raineth...
Like many clouds consulting for foul weather.'

Indeed in the Poem, round and over the sharp portrayal of every word and gesture of the two who speak and move, you have brakes and trees, horses and hounds, and the silent transformations of day and night from the first dawn till eve, and through darkness to the second dawn so immediately impressed, that, pausing at any of the cxcix. stanzas, you could almost name the hour. The same express observation of the day's changes may be observed in *Romeo and Juliet*. It is a note which has often been echoed by men who never look out of their windows, and critics, as narrowly immured, have denounced it for an affectation. Yet a month under canvas, or, better still, without a tent, will convince any one that to speak of the stars and the moon is as natural as to look at your watch or an almanack. In the *Venus* even the weather changes. The Poem opens soon after sunrise with the ceasing of a shower:—

'Even as the sun with purple colour'd face,
Had ta'en his last leave of the weeping morn.'

But by the 89th Stanza, after a burning noon, the clouds close in over the sunset. 'Look,' says Adonis:—

'The world's comforter with weary gate
His day's hot task hath ended in the west,
The owl (night's herald) shrieks, 'tis very late,
The sheep are gone to fold, birds to their nest,
And coal-black clouds, that shadow heaven's light,
Do summon us to part and bid good-night.'

The next dawn is cloudless after the night's rain:—

'Lo here the gentle lark, weary of rest,
From his moist cabinet mounts up on high,
And wakes the morning, from whose silver breast
The sun ariseth in his majesty;
Who doth the world so gloriously behold,
That cedar tops and hills seem burnisht gold.'

Beneath these atmospheric effects everything is clearly seen and sharply delineated:—

'The studded bridle on a ragged bough
Nimbly she fastens.'

And when the horse breaks loose:—

'Some time he trots, as if he told the steps.'

Then the description of a hunted hare (stanzas 114-18):—

'Sometimes he runs along a flock of sheep
To make the cunning hounds mistake their smell....

By this poor Wat far off upon a hill
Stands on his hinder legs with listening ear....
Then shalt thou see the dew-bedabbled wretch
Turn and return, indenting with the way;
Each envious briar his weary legs doth scratch,
Each shadow makes him stop, each murmur stay':—

howbeit a treasure of observation, is no richer than that other of the hounds which have lost their huntsman:—

'Another flap-mouth'd mourner, black and grim,
Against the welkin, vollies out his voice,
Another and another, answer him,
Clapping their proud tails to the ground below,
Shaking their scratch-ears, bleeding as they go.

The illustrations from nature:—

'As the dive-dapper peering through a wave
Who being lookt on, ducks as quickly in...

As the snail whose tender horns being hit
Shrinks backward in his shelly cave with pain':—

are so vivid as to snatch your attention from the story; and when you read that 'lust' feeding on 'fresh beauty,'

> 'Starves and soon bereaves
> As caterpillars do the tender leaves,'

the realism of the illustration does violence to its aptness. It is said that such multiplicity of detail and ornament is out of place in a classic myth. But Shakespeare's Poem is not a classic myth. Mr. Swinburne contrasts it unfavourably with Chapman's *Hero and Leander*, in which he finds 'a small shrine of Parian sculpture amid the rank splendour of a tropical jungle.' Certainly that is the last image which any one could apply to *Venus and Adonis*. Its wealth of realistic detail reminds you rather of the West Porch at Amiens. But alongside of this realism, and again as in Mediæval Art, there are wilful and half-humorous perversions of nature. When Shakespeare in praise of Adonis' beauty says that

> 'To see his face, the lion walked along
> *Behind some hedge*, because he would not fear him,'

or that

> 'When he beheld his shadow in the brook,
> The fishes spread on it their golden gills,'

you feel that you are still in the age which painted St. Jerome's lion and St. Francis preaching to the birds. But you feel that you are half way into another. The poem is not Greek, but neither is it Mediæval: it belongs to the debatable dawntime which we call the Renaissance. There is much in it of highly charged colour and of curious insistence on strange beauties of detail; yet, dyed and dædal as it is out of all kinship with classical repose, neither its intricacy nor its tinting ever suggests the Aladdin's Cave evoked by Mr. Swinburne's Oriental epithets: rather do they suggest a landscape at sunrise. There, too, the lesser features of trees and bushes and knolls are steeped in the foreground with crimson light, or are set on fire with gold at the horizon; there, too, they leap into momentary significance with prolonged and fantastic shadows; yet overhead, the atmosphere is, not oppressive but, eager and pure and a part of an immense serenity. And so it is in the Poem, for which, if you abandon Mr. Swinburne's illustration, and seek another from painting, you may find a more fitting counterpart in the Florentine treatment of classic myths: in Botticelli's *Venus*, with veritable gold on the goddess's hair and on the boles of the pine trees, or in Piero di Cosima's *Cephalus and Procris*, with its living animals at gaze before a tragedy that tells much of Beauty and nothing of Pain. Shakespeare's Poem is of love, not death; but he handles his theme with just the same regard for Beauty, with just the same disregard for all that disfigures Beauty. He portrays an amorous encounter through its every gesture; yet, unless in some dozen lines where he glances aside, like any Mediæval, at a gaiety not yet divorced from love, his appeal to Beauty persists from first to last; and nowhere is there an appeal to lust. The laughter and sorrow of the Poem belong wholly to the faery world of vision and romance, where there is no sickness, whether of sentiment or of sense. And both are rendered by images, clean-cut as in antique gems, brilliantly enamelled as in mediæval chalices, numerous and interwoven as in Moorish arabesques; so that their incision, colour, and rapidity of development, apart even from the intricate melodies of the verbal medium in which they live, tax the faculty of artistic appreciation to a point at which it begins to participate in the asceticism of artistic creation. 'As little can a mind thus roused and awakened be brooded on by mean and indistinct emotion, as the low, lazy mist can creep upon the surface of a lake while a strong gale is driving it onward in waves and billows':—thus does Coleridge resist the application to shift the venue of criticism on this Poem from the court of Beauty to the court of Morals, and upon that subject little more need be said. How wilful it is to discuss the moral bearing of an invitation couched by an imaginary Goddess in such imaginative terms as these:—

> 'Bid me discourse, I will inchant thine eare,
> Or like a Fairie, trip upon the greene,
> Or like a Nymph, with long disheveled heare,
> Daunce on the sands, and yet no footing seene!'

As well essay to launch an ironclad on 'the foam of perilous seas in fairylands forlorn.'

When Venus says, 'Bid me discourse, I will inchant thine ear,' she instances yet another peculiar excellence of Shakespeare's lyrical art, which shows in this Poem, is redoubled in *Lucrece*, and in the Sonnets yields the most perfect examples of human speech:—

> 'Touch but my lips with those fair lips of thine,
> Though mine be not so fair, yet are they red....
> Art thou ashamed to kiss? Then wink again,
> And I will wink, so shall the day seem night....'

These are the fair words of her soliciting, and Adonis's reply is of the same silvery quality:—

> 'If love have lent you twenty thousand tongues,
> And every tongue more meaning than your own,
> Bewitching like the wanton mermaid's songs,
> Yet from mine ear the tempting tune is blown....'

And, as he goes on:—

> 'Lest the deceiving harmony should run
> Into the quiet closure of my breast':—

you catch a note prelusive to the pleading altercation of the Sonnets. It is the discourse in *Venus and Adonis* and *Lucrece* which renders them discursive. And indeed they are long poems, on whose first reading Poe's advice, never to begin at the same place, may wisely be followed. You do well, for instance, to begin at Stanza cxxxvi. in order to enjoy the narrative of Venus' vain pursuit: with your senses unwearied by the length and sweetness of her argument. The passage hence to the end is in the true romantic tradition: Stanzas cxl. and cxli. are as clearly the forerunners of Keats, as cxliv. is the child or Chaucer. The truth of such art consists in magnifying selected details until their gigantic shapes, edged with a shadowy iridescence, fill the whole field of observation. Certain gestures of the body, certain moods of the mind, are made to tell with the weight of trifles during awe-stricken pauses of delay. Venus, when she is baffled by 'the merciless and pitchy night,' halts

> 'amazed as one that unaware
> Hath dropt a precious jewel in the flood,
> Or stonisht as night wanderers often are,
> Their light blown out in some mistrustfull wood.'

She starts like 'one that spies an adder'; 'the timorous yelping of the hounds appals her senses'; and she stands 'in a trembling extasy.'

Besides romantic narrative and sweetly modulated discourse, there are two rhetorical tirades by Venus—when she 'exclaimes on death'[1]:—

'Grim grinning ghost, earth's-worme, what dost thou meane
To stifle beautie and to steale his breath,' etc.:—

and when she heaps her anathemas on love:—

'It shall be fickle, false and full of fraud,
Bud, and be blasted in a breathing while;
The bottome poyson, and the top ore-strawed
With sweets, that shall the truest sight beguile,
The strongest bodie shall it make most weake,
Strike the voice dumbe, and teach the foole to speake':—

and in both, as also in Adonis's contrast of love and lust:—

'Love comforteth, like sunshine after raine,
But lust's effect is tempest after sunne,
Love's gentle spring doth always fresh remaine,
Lust's winter comes ere summer halfe be donne;
Love surfets not, lust like a glutton dies:
Love is all truth, lust full of forged lies':—

you have rhetoric, packed with antithesis, and rapped out on alliterated syllables for which the only equivalent in English is found, but more fully, in the great speech delivered by Lucrece.[2] The seed of these tirades, as of the dialogues and the gentle soliloquies, seems derived from Chaucer's *Troilus and Criseyde*; and in his *Knight's Tale* (lines 1747-58) there is also a foreshadowing of their effective alliteration, used—and this is the point—not as an ornament of verse, but as an instrument of accent. For example:—

'The helmës they to-hewen and to-shrede;
Out brest the blood, with sternë stremës rede.
With mighty maces the bonës they to-breste;
He thurgh the thikkeste of the throng gon threste,' etc.

This use of alliteration by Shakespeare, employed earlier by Lord Vaux:—

1. I retain the early spelling, as something of the rhetorical force depends on the sounds it suggests.
2. In denunciation of Night, Opportunity, and Time (lines 764-1036).

'Since death shall dure till all the world be waste'[1]:—

and later by Spenser[2]:—

'Then let thy flinty heart that feeles no paine,
Empierced be with pitiful remorse,
And let thy bowels bleede in every vaine,
At sight of His most sacred heavenly corse,
So torne and mangled with malicious forse;
And let thy soule, whose sins His sorrows wrought,
Melt into teares, and grone in grieved thought':—

is not to be confused with 'the absurd following of the letter amongst our English so much of late affected, but now hist out of Paules Church yard';[3] for it does not consist in collecting the greatest number of words with the same initial, but in letting the accent fall, as it does naturally in all impassioned speech, upon syllables of cognate sound. Since in English verse the accent is, and by Shakespeare's contemporaries was understood to be, 'the chief lord and grave Governour of Numbers,'[4] this aid to its emphasis is no less legitimate, and is hardly less important, than is that of rhyme to metre in French verse: we inherit it from the Saxon, as we inherit rhyme from the Norman; both are essential elements in the poetry built up by Chaucer out of the ruins of two languages. But Shakespeare is the supreme master of its employment: in these impassioned tirades he wields it with a naked strength that was never approached, in the Sonnets with a veiled and varied subtlety that defies analysis. There are hints here and there in the *Venus* of this gathering subtlety:—

'These blew-vein'd violets whereon we leane
Never can blab, nor know not what we meane...
Even as a dying coale revives with winde...
More white and red than doves and roses are.'

But apart from the use of cognate sounds, which makes for emphasis without marring melody, in many a line there also

1. *Paradise of Dainty Devices*, 1576.
2. *An Hymne of Heavenly Love* (September 1596).
3. Campion, *Observations in the Art of English Poesy*, 1602.
4. S. Daniel's *Defence of Ryme*, 1603:—'Though it doth not strictly observe long and short sillables, yet it most religiously respects the accent.'—*Ibid*. *Cf*. Sidney's *Apologie*:—'Wee observe the accent very precisely.'

lives that more recondite sweetness, which plants so much of Shakespeare's verse in the memory for no assignable cause:—

> 'Scorning his churlish drum and ensinge red....
> Dumbly she passions, frantikely she doteth....
> Showed like two silver doves that sit a billing....
> Leading him prisoner in a red-rose chaine....
> Were beautie under twentie locks kept fast,
> Yet love breaks through and picks them all at last....
> O learne to love, the lesson is but plaine
> And once made perfect never lost again.'

Herein a cadence of obvious simplicity gives birth to an inexplicable charm.

I have spoken of Shakespeare's images, blowing fresh from the memory of his boyhood, so vivid that at times they are violent, and at others wrought and laboured until they become conceits. You have 'No fisher but the ungrown fry forbears,' with its frank reminiscence of a sportsman's scruple; or, as an obvious illustration, 'Look how a bird lies tangled in a net'; or, in a flash of intimate recollection:—

> 'Like shrill-tongu'd tapsters answering everie call,
> Soothing the humours of fantastique wits':—

the last, an early sketch of the 'Francis' scene in *Henry IV.*, which, in quaint juxtaposition with 'cedar tops and hills' of 'burnisht gold,' seems instinct with memories of John Shakespeare and his friends, who dared not go to church. But, again, you have conceits:—

> 'But hers (eyes), which through the crystal tears gave light,
> Shone like the Moone in water seen by night';

'A lilie prison'd in a gaile of snow'; and 'Wishing her cheeks were gardens ful of flowers. So they were dew'd with such distilling showers.' But, diving deeper than diction, alliteration, and rhythm: deeper than the decoration of blazoned colours and the labyrinthine interweaving of images, now budding as it were from nature, and now beaten as by an artificer out of some precious metal: you discover beneath this general interpretation of Phenomenal Beauty, a gospel of Ideal Beauty, a confession of faith in Beauty as a principle of life. And note—for the coincidence is vital—that these, the esoteric themes of *Venus and Adonis*, are the essential themes of the *Sonnets*. In Stanza xxii.:—

> 'Fair flowers that are not gathered in their prime
> Rot and consume themselves in little time':—

and in Stanzas xxvii., xxviii., xxix., you have the whole argument of Sonnets i.-xix. In Stanza clxxx.:—

> 'Alas poore world, what treasure hast thou lost,
> What face remains alive that's worth the viewing?
> Whose tongue is musick now? What canst thou boast,
> Of things long since, or any thing insuing?
> The flowers are sweet, their colours fresh, and trim,
> But true sweet beautie liv'd, and di'de with him':—

you have that metaphysical gauging of the mystical importance of some one incarnation of Beauty viewed from imaginary standpoints in time; which was afterwards to be elaborated in Sonnets xiv., xix., lix., lxvii., lxviii.; civ.; cvi. And in Stanza clxx.:—

> 'For he being dead, with him is beautie slaine,
> And beautie dead, blacke Chaos comes again':—

you have the succinct *credo* in that incarnation of an Ideal Beauty, of which all other lovely semblances are but 'shadows' and 'counterfeits,' which was to find a fuller declaration in Sonnets xxxi. and liii., and xcviii.

But in Shakespeare's Poems the beauty and curiosity of the ceremonial ever obscure the worship of the god; and; perhaps, in the last stanza but one; addressed to the flower born in place of the dead Adonis and let drop into the bosom of the Goddess of Love, you have the most typical expression of those merits and defects which are alike loved and condoned by the slaves of their invincible sweetness:—

> 'Here was thy father's bed, here in my brest,
> Thou art the next of blood, and 'tis thy right,
> So in this hollow cradle take thy rest,
> My throbbing hart shall rock thee day and night;
> There shall not be one minute in an houre
> Wherein I will not kiss my sweet love's floure.'

Here are conceits and a strained illustration from the profession of law; but here, with these, are lovely imagery and perfect diction and, flowing through every line, a rhythm that rises and falls softly, until, after a hurry of ripples, it expends itself in the three last retarding words.

XIII—THE RAPE OF LUCRECE

The Rape of Lucrece was published in 1594, and was dedicated in terms of devoted affection to Lord Southampton. It was never so popular as the *Venus*, yet editions followed in 1598, 1600, 1607, 1616, 1624, and 1632[1]; and its subsequent neglect remains one of the enigmas of literature. It is written in the seven-lined stanza borrowed by Chaucer from Guillaume de Machault, a French poet, whose talent, according to M. Sandras[2] was 'essentiellement lyrique.' The measure, indeed, is capable of the most heart-searching lyrical effects. Chaucer chose it, first for his *Compleint unto Pité* and, more notably, for his *Troilus and Criseyde*; in 1589 Puttenham (?) had noted that 'his meetre Heroicall is very grave and stately,' and, was 'most usuall with our auncient makers'; Daniel had used it for his *Rosamund*, published four years before *Lucrece*, Spenser for his *Hymnes*, published the year after. The subject lay no further than the form from Shakespeare's hand. He took it from Ovid's *Fasti.*[3] Mr. Furnivall has argued that he may also have read it in Livy's brief version of the tragedy, or in *The Rape of Lucrece*, from William Painter's *The Palace of Pleasure* (1566), where, he notes, 'Painter is but Livy, with some changes and omissions.' Warton, *History of English Poetry* (1824, iv. 241-42), cites 'A ballet the grevious complaynt of Lucrece,' 1568; 'A ballet of the death of Lucreessia,' 1569; and yet another of 1576. He adds:—'Lucretia was the grand example of conjugal fidelity throughout the Gothic Ages.' That is the point. Shakespeare took the story from Ovid, with the knowledge that Chaucer had drawn on the same source for the Fifth Story in his *Legend of Good Women*, just as Chaucer had taken it from Ovid, with the knowledge that its

1. Two others of 1596 and 1602 have been cited but never recovered.
2. *Etude sur G. Chaucer*, 1859.
3. Book ii. line 721 *et seq.*

appositeness had been consecrated before 1282 in chapter l. of *Le Roman de la Rose*:—

'Comment Lucrece par grant ire
Son cuer point, derrompt et dessire
Et chiet morte sur terre adens,
Devant son mari et parens.'

And Shakespeare must certainly have been familiar with the allusion to it in North's *Plutarch*, as with the passage in Sidney's *Apologie*, where a painting of *Lucrecia* is imagined to illustrate the art of those who are 'indeed right Poets' as distinguished from the authors of religious or of moral and metaphysical verse. This passage, save where it suffers from the constraint of an apologetic attitude, stands still for a sound declaration of the ethics of art; and in Shakespeare's day, when such questions were canvassed as freely as in our own, it may well have determined his choice.

But speculation on the literary origins of a poem is idle when the poem is in itself far worthier attention than all the materials out of which it has been contrived—the more so when of these the literary origins are the most remote and the least important. Shakespeare, indeed, owes more to the manner of Chaucer's *Troilus* than to the matter of his *Lucretia*, or of its original in Ovid. For in treating that story the two poets omit and retain different portions: Chaucer, on the whole, copying more closely paints on a canvas of about the same size, whereas Shakespeare expands a passage of 132 lines into a poem of 1855. Chaucer omits Ovid's note rendered by Shakespeare's

'Haply that name of chaste unhap'ly set
This bateless edge on his keen appetite.'

He also omits Lucretia's unsuspecting welcome of Tarquin, making him '*stalke*' straight into the house 'ful theefly.' Shakespeare retains the welcome, and reserves the phrase, 'Into the chamber wickedly he *stalks*,' for a later incident. On the other hand, Chaucer renders the passage, 'Tunc quoque jam moriens ne non procumbat honeste, respicit,' somewhat quaintly:—

'And as she fel adown, she cast her look
And of her clothës yit she hedë took,
For in her falling yit she haddë care
Lest that her feet or swichë thing lay bare':—

and Shakespeare omits it. Both keep the image of the lamb and the wolf, together with Lucretia's *flavi capilli*, which are nowhere mentioned by Livy.

In the *Lucrece*, as in the *Venus*, you have a true development of Chaucer's romantic narrative; of the dialogues, soliloquies, and rhetorical bravuras which render Books iv. and v. of his *Troilus* perhaps the greatest romance in verse. And yet the points of contrast between the *Lucrece* and the *Venus* are of deeper interest than the points of comparison, for they show an ever-widening divergence from the characteristics of Mediæval romance. If the *Venus* be a pageant of gesture, the *Lucrece* is a drama of emotion. You have the same wealth of imagery, but the images are no longer sunlit and sharply defined. They seem, rather, created by the reflex action of a sleepless brain—as it were fantastic symbols shaped from the lying report of tired eyes staring into darkness; and they are no longer used to decorate the outward play of natural desire and reluctance, but to project the shadows of abnormal passion and acute mental distress. The Poem is full of nameless terror, of 'ghastly shadows' and 'quick-shifting antics.' The First Act passes in the 'dead of night,' with 'no noise' to break the world's silence 'but owls' and wolves' death-boding cries,' nor any to mar the house's but the grating of doors and, at last, the hoarse whispers of a piteous controversy. The Second shows a cheerless dawn with two women crying, one for sorrow, the other for sympathy. There are never more than two persons on the stage, and there is sometimes only one, until the crowd surges in at the end to witness Lucrece's suicide. I have spoken for convenience of 'acts' and a 'stage,' yet the suggestion of these terms is misleading. Excepting in the last speech and in the death of Lucrece, the Poem is nowhere dramatic: it tells a story, but at each situation the Poet pauses to survey and to illustrate the romantic and emotional values of the relation between his characters, or to analyse the moral passions and the mental debates in any one of them, or even the physiological perturbations responding to these storms and tremors of the mind and soul. When Shakespeare describes Tarquin's stealthy approach:—

'Night wandering weazels shriek to see him there;
They fright him, yet he still pursues his fear':—

or Lucrece shrinking from the dawn:—

'Revealing day through every cranny spies
And seems to point her out where she sits weeping':—

or Collatine's attempt at railing when he is inarticulate with wrath:—

'Yet some time "Tarquin" was pronounced plain
But through his teeth, as if the name he tore':—

his method is wholly alien from the popular methods of our own day. Yet would they be rash who condemned it out of hand.

The illustration of gesture, and of all that passes in the mind, by the copious use of romantic imagery constitutes an artistic process which is obviously charged with sensuous delight, and is in its way not less realistic than the dramatic method which has superseded it. The hours of life, which even ordinary men and women expend in selfish sensation and a fumbling, half-conscious introspection, far outnumber the hours in which they are clearly apprized of eventful action and speech between themselves and their fellows; and in men of rarer temperament life often becomes a monodrama. The dramatic convention is also but a convention with its own limitations, staling by over-practice into the senseless rallies of a pantomime or the trivial symbols of a meagre psychology. The common-place sayings and doings of the puppets are meant by the author to suggest much; and, when they are duly explained by the critics, we may all admire the reserved force of the device. But it remains a device. In the romantic narratives of Chaucer, Shakespeare, and Keats, with their imaginative illustrations of the mind's moods and their imaginative use of sights and sounds accidental to moments of exacerbated sensation, you have another device which portrays, perhaps more truly, the hidden mysteries of those temperaments whose secrets are really worth our guessing. It is at least worth while to watch an artist, who has shown the inevitable acts and words of any one man in any one situation, at work within upon the accompanying sequence of inevitable sensations and desires. And sometimes, too, from the analysis of emotion in the *Lucrece* you catch a side-light on the more subtle revelation in the Sonnets:—

> 'O happiness, enjoy'd but of a few,
> And if possest, as soon decayed and done
> As is the morning's silver melting dew
> Against the golden splendour of the sun!
> The aim of all is but to nurse the life
> With honour, wealth and ease, in waning age;
> And in this aim there is such thwarting strife
> That one for all or all for one we gage;
> As life for honour in fell battle's rage;
> Honour for wealth; and oft that wealth doth cost
> The death of all, and all together lost.
> What win I if I gain the thing I seek?
> A dream, a breath, a froth of fleeting joy,
> Who buys a minute's mirth to wail a week
> *Or sells eternity to get a toy?*'

Vanitas vanitatum! Besides this philosophy of pleasure, there is also a pathos in *Lucrece* which is no wise Mediæval. The Poem is touched with a compassion for the weakness of women, which is new and alien from the Trouvère convention of a knight who takes pity on a damsel:—

> 'Their gentle sex to weep are often willing;
> Grieving themselves to guess at others' smarts,
> And then they drown their eyes, or break their hearts...
>
> Though men can cover crimes with bold stern looks,
> Poor women's faces are their own fault's books.'

Then let

> 'No man inveigh against the withered flower,
> But chide rough winter that the flower hath kill'd:
> Not that devour'd, but that which doth devour
> Is worthy blame.'

But in spite of so much that is new in the *Lucrece*, there is no absolute break between it and the *Venus*: the older beauties persist, if they persist more sparsely, among the fresh-blown. As ever in Shakespeare's earlier work, there are vivid impressions of things seen:—

'You mocking birds, quoth she, your tunes entomb
Within your hollow swelling feather'd breasts...

Ay me! the bark peel'd from the lofty pine,
His leaves will wither, and his sap decay...
As lagging fouls before the Northern blast.'

As through an arch the violent roaring tide
Outruns the eye that doth behold his haste,
Yet in the eddy boundeth in his pride
Back to the strait that forced him on so fast...

Illustrations are still drawn from sport:—

'Look, as the full fed hound or gorged hawk
Unapt for tender smell or speedy flight.'...

There are, as ever, conceits:—

'Without the bed her other fair hand was,
On the green coverlet; whose perfect white
Showed like an April daisy on the grass...'

'And now this pale swan in her watery nest
Begins the sad dirge of her certain ending':—

and there are, as I have said, tirades of an astonishing rhetorical force, passages which, recited by an English Rachel, would still bring down the house. As the denunciations of Night:—

'Blind muffled bawd! dark harbour of defame!
Grim cave of death! whispering conspirator':—

of Opportunity:—

'Thy secret pleasure turns to open shame,
Thy private feasting to a public fast,
Thy smoothing titles to a ragged name:
Thy sugard tongue to bitter wormwood tast:
Thy violent vanities can never last':—

and of Time:—

'Eater of youth, false slave to false delight,
Base watch of woes, sin's pack-horse, vertue's snare':—

whose glory it is:—

'To ruinate proud buildings with thy hours
And smear with dust their glitt'ring golden towers...
To feed oblivion with decay of things.'

The form of these tirades is repeated from the *Venus*, but their music is louder, and is developed into a greater variety of keys, sometimes into the piercing minors of the more metaphysical Sonnets:—

> 'Why work'st thou mischief in thy pilgrimage?
> Unless thou could'st return to make amends.
> One poor retiring minute in an age
> Would purchase thee a thousand thousand friends....
>
> Thou ceaseless lackey to eternity!'

This last apostrophe is great; but that in *Lucrece* there should be so many of the same tremendous type, which have escaped the fate of hackneyed quotation, is one of the most elusive factors in a difficult problem:—

> 'Pure thoughts are dead and still
> While Lust and Murder wake to stain and kill....
>
> His drumming heart cheers up his burning eye....
>
> Tears harden lust, though marble wears with raining....
>
> Soft pity enters at an iron gate....
>
> Unruly blasts wait on the tender spring,
> Unwholesome weeds take root with precious flowers,
> The adder hisses where the sweet birds sing,
> What virtue breeds, iniquity devours.'

These, for all their strength and sweetness, might conceivably have been written by some other of the greater poets. But these:—

> 'And dying eyes gleam'd forth their ashy lights....
>
> 'Tis but a part of sorrow that we hear:
> Deep sounds make lesser noise than shallow fords,
> And sorrow ebbs, being blown with wind of words....
>
> O! that is gone for which I sought to live,
> And therefore now I need not fear to die....
>
> For Sorrow, like a heavy hanging bell,
> Once set on ringing with his own weight goes':—

these, I say, could have been written by Shakespeare only. They may rank with the few which Arnold chose for standards from the poetry of all ages; yet by a caprice of literary criticism they are never quoted, and are scarce so much as known.

XIV—THE SONNETS AND SONNETEERING

The fate of Shakespeare's Sonnets has been widely different from the fate of his Narrative Poems. The *Venus* and the *Lucrece* were popular at once, and ran through many editions: the Sonnets, published in 1609, were not reprinted until 1640, and were then so effectually disguised by an arbitrary process of interpolation, omission, re-arrangement, and misleading description as to excite but little attention, until in 1780 Malone opened a new era of research into their bearing on the life and character of Shakespeare. Since then the tables have been turned. For while the *Venus* and the *Lucrece* have been largely neglected, so many volumes, in support of theories so variously opposed, have been written on this aspect of the Sonnets, that it has become impossible even to sum up the contention except by adding yet another volume to already overladen shelves.

The controversy has its own interest; but that interest, I submit, is alien from, and even antagonistic to, an appreciation of lyrical excellence. I do not mean that the Sonnets are 'mere exercises' written to 'rival' or to 'parody' the efforts of other poets. Such curiosities of criticism are born of a nervous revulsion from conclusions reached by the more confident champions of a 'personal theory'; and their very eccentricity measures the amount of damage done, not by those who endeavour, laudably enough, to retrieve a great lost life but, by those who allow such attempts at biography to bias their consideration of poems which we possess intact. If, indeed, we must choose between critics, who discover an autobiography in the Sonnets, and critics, who find in them a train of poetic exhalations whose airy iridescence never reflects the passionate colours of this earthy, then the first are preferable. At least their theory makes certain additions which, though dubious and defective, are still additions to our guesses at Shakespeare the man; whereas the second subtracts from a known masterpiece its necessary material of experience and emotion. But we need not choose: the middle way remains of accepting from the Sonnets only the matter which they embody and the form which they display.

Taking them up, then, as you would take up the *Lucrece* or another example of Shakespeare's earlier work, there is nothing to note in their metrical form but the perfection of treatment by which Shakespeare has stamped it for his own. They were immediately preceded by many sonnet-sequences: by so many, indeed, that Shakespeare could hardly have taken his place at the head of his lyrical contemporaries without proving that he, too, could write sonnets with the best of them. Sidney's *Astrophel and Stella* (written 1581-84) had been published in 1591—(when Tom Nash was constrained to bid some other 'Poets and' Rimers to put out their 'rush candles,' and bequeath their 'crazed quaterzayns' to the chandlers—for 'loe, here hee cometh that hath broek your legs')—with the sonnets of 'sundry other noblemen and gentlemen' appended, among them twenty-eight by S(amuel) D(aniel), nineteen of which were afterwards reprinted in his *Delia*; the next year H(enry) C(onstable) published twenty, afterwards reprinted in his *Diana*; in 1593 B. Barnes published *Parthenophil and Parthenope,* containing a hundred and four (besides madrigals, odes, and eclogues); and in 1594 W. Percy, to whom this gathering had been dedicated, riposted in twenty, 'to the fairest Cœlia,' which touch the nadir of incompetence. But in the same memorable year three other sequences appeared, whose excellence and fame rendered an attempt in this form almost obligatory upon any one claiming to be a poet: H(enry) C(onstable)'s *Diana*, with 'divers quatorzains of honourable and learned personages,'—notably, eight by Sidney, afterwards appended to the Third Edition of the *Arcadia*; Samuel Daniel's *Delia*, consisting of fifty-five;[1] and Michael Drayton's Idea's *Mirrour*, fifty-one strong, augmented to fifty-nine in 1599 and eventually (1619) to sixty-three. Then in 1595 Spenser published his *Amoretti* (written 1592(?)), and in 1596 R. L(inche) his *Diella* and B. Griffin his *Fidessa*. I name these last because an example from R. Linche:—

> 'My mistress' snow-white skin doth much excell
> The pure soft wool Arcadian sheep do bear':—

will show what inept fatuity co-existed with the highest flights of Elizabethan verse; and because the third number in *Fidessa*[2] was

1. Nineteen of which had appeared, *cf. supra*.
2. Griffin was almost certainly one of Shakespeare's connexions by marriage. See 'Shakespeare's Ancestry,' *The Times*, Oct. 14, 1895.

reprinted by Jaggard in the *Passionate Pilgrim* (1599), together with other pieces stolen from Shakespeare and Barnefield. The publication of such a medley attests the well-known fact that Elizabethan sonnets were handed about in ms. for years among poetical cliques, and, as W. Percy complains, 'were committed to the Press' without the authors' knowledge, although 'concealed... as things privy' to himself.[1] It is also worth noting that the Elizabethans I have named, who signed their sonnet-sequences sometimes only with initials, often transfigured them by additions, omissions, and re-arrangings prior to republication; and this was especially the practice of Daniel and Drayton, whose sonnets, it so happens, offer the closest points of comparison to Shakespeare's. That two of Shakespeare's should have been published with the work of others in 1599, and afterwards, with slight variations, as units in a fairly consecutive series, is quite in the manner of the time. There is no mention of *Delia* in all the twenty-eight appended by Daniel to *Astrophel and Stella*[2]; but nineteen of these were interpolated into the later sequence, which bears her name, yet mentions it in thirteen only out of fifty-five. To glance at Drayton's *Idea* is to be instantly suspicious of another such mystification. The poem begins:—

> 'Into these loves, who but for Passion looks,
> At this first sight here let him lay them by':—

and the author goes on to boast that he sings 'fantasticly' without a 'far-fetched sigh,' an 'Ah me,' or a 'tear.' Yet the sixty-first in the completed series (1619) is that wonderful sob of supplication for which Drayton is chiefly remembered:—

> 'Since there's no help, come, let us kiss and part!'

Only by the use of the comparative method can we hope to recover the conditions under which sonnets were written and published in Shakespeare's day. A side-light, for instance, is thrown on the half good-natured, half malicious rivalry between the members of shifting literary cliques, from the fact that Shakespeare, Chapman, Marston, and Jonson all contributed

---

1. W. Percy to the Reader.
2. Sonnet xiii. opens thus:—
   'My *Cynthia* hath the waters of mine eyes.'

poems on the Phœnix to Rob. Chester's *Love's Martyr* (1601),[1] and that sonnets on the same subject occur in Daniel's additions to *Astrophel* (Sonnet iii.), and in Drayton's *Idea* (Sonnet xvi.). All six poets are suspected, and some are known, to have been arrayed from time to time on opposed sides in literary quarrels; yet you find them handling a common theme in more or less friendly emulation. I fancy that many of the coincidences between the Sonnets of Shakespeare and those of Drayton, on which charges of plagiarism have been founded, and by whose aid attempts have been made to fix the date of Shakespeare's authorship, may be explained more probably by this general conception of a verse-loving society divided into emulous coteries. Mr. Tyler adduces the conceit of 'eyes' and 'heart' in Drayton's xxxiii. (Ed. 1599), and compares it to Shakespeare's xlvi. and xlvii. (1609); but it appears in Henry Constable. Again, he instances Drayton's illustration from a 'map' in xliii.[2]; but, perhaps by reason of the fashionable interest in the New World, the image was a common one: Daniel employs it in his *Defence of Ryme*. And if Drayton, in this sonnet, 'strives to eternize' the object of his affection in accents echoed by Shakespeare, Daniel does the like in his l.:—

> 'Let others sing of Knights and Palladins
> In aged accents, and untimely words,' etc.:—

with a hit at Spenser that only differs in being a hit from Shakespeare's reference in cvi.:—

> 'When in the chronicle of wasted time
> I see descriptions of the fairest wights
> And beauty making beautiful old rhyme
> In praise of ladies dead and lovely Knights.'

Of course it differs also in poetic excellence; yet many chancing on Daniel's later line:—

> 'Against the dark and Time's consuming rage':—

might mistake it for one by the mightier artist. Drayton, like Shakespeare, upbraids some one, whom he compares to the son—and the sex is significant—'of some rich penny-father,' for wasting his 'Love' and 'Beauty,' which Time must conquer,

1. See Note IV. on *The Sonnets*.
2. Ed. 1599=xliv. of 1619.

'on the unworthy' who cannot make him 'survive' in 'immortal song.'[3] And the next number sounds familiar, with its curious metaphysical conceit of identity between the beloved one and the poet who sings him.[4] If any one had thought it worth his while to investigate the biographical problems of Drayton's obviously doctored *Idea*, he would have found nuts to crack as hard as any in Shakespeare's Sonnets. It is best, perhaps, to take Sidney's advice, and to 'believe with him that there are many misteries contained in Poetrie, which of purpose were written darkely.' At any rate, the ironic remainder of the passage throws a flood of light on the extent to which the practice of *immortalising* prevailed:—'Believe' the poets, he says, 'when they tell you they will make you immortal by their verses,' for, thus doing, 'your name shall flourish in the Printers' shoppes; thus doing, you shall bee of kinne to many a poetical preface; thus doing, you shall be most fayre, most rich, most wise, most all, you shall dwell upon superlatives.'[5]

Shakespeare's Sonnets, then, belong to a sonneteering age, and exhibit many curious coincidences with the verse of his friends and rivals. But his true distinction in mere metrical form, apart from finer subtleties of art, consists in this: that he established the quatorzain as a separate type of the European Sonnet; he took as it were a sport from the garden of verse, and fixed it for an English variety. The credit for this has been given to Daniel; but the attribution cannot be sustained. For Daniel sometimes hankered after the Petrarchan model, though in a less degree than any other of Shakespeare's contemporaries: he travels in Italy,[6] contrasts his Muse with Petrarch's,[7] imitates his structure,[8] and strains after feminine rhymes. Shakespeare alone selected the English quatorzain, and sustained it throughout a sonnet-sequence.[9] Even the merit of invention claimed for Daniel must

3. Sonnet x. Ed. 1619.
4. *Cf.* Shakespeare's xxxix., xlii., lxii.
5. Sidney, *Apologie*.
6. *Delia*, xlvii., xlviii.
7. *Ibid.*, xxxviii.
8. *Ibid.*, xxxi. and xxxiii. and x. of the Sonnets appended to *Arcadia*.
9. Sidney and Drayton frequently copy French and Italian models. Spenser's linked quatrains are neither sonnets nor quatorzains: they represent an abortive attempt to create a new form.

be denied him. When Shakespeare makes Slender say[1]:—'I had rather than forty shillings I had my book of songs and sonnets here':—he refers to *Tottel's Miscellany*, published in 1557. But the numbers by the Earl of Surrey in that anthology were written many years earlier, and in the Eighth of his Sonnets there printed, you will find as good a model for Shakespeare's form as any in Daniel's *Delia*:—

'Set me whereas the sunne doth parche the grene
Or where his beames do not dissolve the yse:
In temperate heate where he is felt and sene:
In presence prest of people madde or wise.
Set me in hye, or yet in lowe degree:
In longest night, or in the shortest daye:
In clearest skye, or where clowdes thickest be:
In lusty youth, or when my heeres are graye.
Set me in heaven, in earth or els in hell,
In hyll, or dale, or in the fomyng flood:
Thrall, or at large, alive where so I dwell:
Sicke or in health: in evyll fame or good.
Hers will I be, and onely with this thought
Content my selfe, although my chaunce be nought.[2]

The theme is borrowed from Petrarch; but the form is Surrey's, who used it in nine out of his fourteen sonnets, and essayed the Petrarchan practice in but one. By this invention he achieved a sweetness of rhythm never attained in any strict imitation of the Italian model until the present century. His sonnet is the true precursor of Shakespeare's, and it owes—directly—little more than the number of its lines to France and Italy: being founded on English metres of alternating rhymes, with a final couplet copied by Chaucer from the French two centuries before.

The number of sonnet-sequences published in the last decade of the Sixteenth Century, during which Shakespeare lived at London in the midst of a literary movement, raises a presumption in favour of an early date for his Sonnets, published in 1609; and this presumption is confirmed by the publication of two of them

1. *Merry Wives of Windsor*, i. i.
2. 'Form and favour' in Shakespeare's Sonnet cxxv., 'golden tresses' in his lxviii. may also be echoes of Surrey.

in *The Passionate Pilgrim* (1599). We know from civ. that three years had elapsed since he first saw the youth to whom the earlier Sonnets were addressed; and the balance of internal evidence, founded whether on affinities to the plays or on references to political and social events affecting Shakespeare as a dramatist and a man,[1] points to the years 1599-1602 as the most probable period for their composition.[2] Further confirmation of an almost decisive character has been adduced by Mr. Tyler.[3] But I pass his arguments, since they are based, in part, on the assumption that the youth in question was William Herbert; and, although Mr. Tyler would, as I think, win a verdict from any jury composed and deciding after the model of Scots procedure, his case is one which cannot be argued without the broaching of many issues outside the sphere of artistic appreciation.

XV—SONNET-GROUPS

Had Shakespeare's Sonnets suffered the fate of Sappho's lyrics, their few surviving fragments would have won him an equal glory, and we should have been damnified in the amount only of a priceless bequest. But our heritage is almost certainly intact: the Sonnets, as we find them in the Quarto of 1609, whether or not they were edited by Shakespeare, must so far have commanded his approval as to arouse no protest against the form in which they appeared. It would have been as easy for him to re-shuffle and re-publish as it is impossible to believe that he could so re-shuffle and re-publish, and no record of his action survive. Taking the Sonnets, then, as published in their author's lifetime, you discover their obvious division into two Series:—in the First, one hundred and twenty-five, closed by an Envoy of six couplets, are addressed to a youth; in the Second, seventeen out of twenty-eight are addressed to the author's mistress, and the others comment, more or less directly, on her infidelity and on his infatuation. Most critics—indeed all not quixotically compelled to reject a reasonable view—are agreed that the order in the First

1. *Cf.* Sonnet lxvi.:—'And art made tongue-tied by authority':—with the edict of June 1600, inhibiting plays and playgoers.
2. See Note iii. on *The Sonnets*.
3. Introduction to the 'Shakespeare Q., No. 30' and *Shakespeare's Sonnets*. London, D. Nutt, 1890.

Series can scarce be bettered; and that within that Series certain Groups may be discerned of sonnets written at the same time, each with the same theme and divided by gaps of silence from the sonnets that succeed them. There is also substantial agreement as to the confines of the principal Groups; but between these there are shorter sequences and even isolated numbers, among which different critics have succeeded in tracing a greater or lesser degree of connexion. The analogy of a correspondence, carried on over years between friends, offers perhaps the best clue to the varying continuity of the First Series. There, too, you have silences which attest the very frequency of meetings, with silences born of long absence and absorption in diverse pursuits; there, too, you have spells of voluminous writing on intimate themes, led up to and followed by sparser communications on matters of a less dear importance. The numbers seem to have been chronologically arranged; and, that being so, the alternation of continuous with intermittent production shows naturally in a collection of poems addressed by one person to another at intervals over a period of more than three years.

There are seven main Groups in the First Series:—

Group A, i.-xix.:—The several numbers echo the arguments in *Venus and Adonis*, Stanzas xxvii.-xxix. They are written ostensibly, to urge marriage on a beautiful youth, but, essentially, they constitute a continuous poem on Beauty and Decay. That is the subject, varied by the introduction of two subsidiary themes; the one, philosophic, on immortality conferred by breed:—

> 'From fairest creatures, we desire increase
> That thereby beauty's *Rose* might never die':—

the other, literary, on immortality conferred by verse:—

> 'My love shall in my verse ever live young.'

This line is the last of the sonnet which serves as an envoy to the Group. Here follow Sonnets xx.-xxi., xxii., xxiii.-xxiv., xxv.: occasional verses written, playfully or affectionately, to the youth who is now dear to their author. In giving the occasional sonnets I bracket only those which are obviously connected and obviously written at the same time.

Group B, xxvi.-xxxii.:—A continuous poem on absence, dispatched, it may be, in a single letter, since it opens with a formal address and ends in a full close. In this group there are variations on the disgust of separation and the solace of remembered love; but it is a poem and not a letter—turning each succeeding emotion to its full artistic account.

Group C, xxxiii.-xlii.:—The first of the more immediately personal garlands. The writer's friend has wronged him by stealing his mistress's love. The counterpart to this group, evidently written on the same theme and at the same time, will be found in the Second Series (cxxxiii.-cxliv.), addressed in complaint to the writer's mistress, or written in comment on her complicity in this wrong. The biographical interest of this Group has won it an undeserved attention at the expense of others. Many suppose that all the Sonnets turn on this theme, or, at least, that the loudest note of passion is here sounded. But this is not so. Of all ten three at the most can be called tragic. These are xxxiv.—but it arises out of the lovely imagery of xxxiii.; xxxvi., but it ends:—

> 'I love thee in such sort
> As thou being mine, mine is thy good report';

and xl., but it ends:—'Yet we must not be foes.' xxxiii. is indeed beautiful, but the others return to the early theme of mere immortalising, or are expressed in abstruse or playful conceits which make it impossible to believe they mirror a soul in pain. They might be taken for designed interpolations, did they not refer, by the way, to a sorrow, or misfortune, not to be distinguished from the theme of their fellows. Knowing what Shakespeare can do to express anguish and passion, are we not absurd to find the evidence of either in these Sonnets, written, as they are, on a private sorrow, but in the spirit of conscious art?

> 'If my slight Muse do please these curious days
> The pain be mine, but thine shall be the praise.'—xxxviii.

Here follow xliii., xliv.-xlv., xlvi.-xlvii.-xlviii., xlix., l.-li., lii., connected or occasional pieces on mere absence. Then liii.-liv., and lv. return to the theme of immortalising. The first two are steeped in Renaissance Platonism; while the last (as Mr. Tyler has shown) does but versify a passage in which Meres quotes Ovid and Horace (1598): it seems to be an Envoy.

Group D, lvi.-lxxiv.:—The Poet writes again after silence:—'Sweet love, renew thy force.' The first three are occasioned by a voluntary absence of his friend; but that absence, unexpectedly prolonged, inspires a mood of contemplation which, becoming ever more and more metaphysical, is by much removed from the spirit of the earlier poem on absence (*Group B*, xxvi.-xxxii.) with its realistic handling of the same theme. In lix. the poet dwells on the illusion of repeated experience, and speculates on the truth of the philosophy of cycles:—

> 'If there be nothing new, but that which is
> Hath been before, how are our brains beguiled.'

In lx. he watches the changing toil of Time:—

> 'Like as the waves make towards the pebbled shore
> So do our minutes hasten to their end.'

In lxi. he gazes into the night at the phantasm of his absent friend, and thus leads up to a poem in three parts (lxii.-lxv., lxvi.-lxx., lxxi.-lxxiv.) on Beauty that Time must ruin, on the disgust of Life, and on Death. These nineteen numbers, conceived in a vein of melancholy contemplation, are among the most beautiful of all, and are more subtly metaphysical than any, save only cxxiii., cxxiv., cxxv. There follow lxxv., lxxvi., lxxvii.

Group E, lxxviii.-lxxxvi., is the second of a more immediate personal interest. It deals with rival poets and their meretricious art—especially with one Poet who by 'the proud full sail of his great verse' has bereft the writer of his friend's admiration. The nine are written in unbroken sequence and are playful throughout, suggesting no tragedy.

But in *Group F*, lxxxvii.-xcvi., the spirit of the verse suddenly changes: the music becomes plangent, and the theme of utter estrangement is handled with a complete command over dramatic yet sweetly modulated discourse. The Group is, indeed, a single speech of tragic intensity, written in elegiac verse more exquisite than Ovid's own. Here the First Series is most obviously broken, and xcvii. xcviii.-xcix. emphasise the break. They tell of two absences the first in late summer (xcvi.), the second in the spring. They are isolated from the Group which precedes, and the Group which follows them, and they embrace an absence extending, at least, from early autumn in one year to April in the next. The first is of great elegiac beauty, the second of curious metaphysical significance; the third seems an inferior, perhaps a rejected, version of the second.

Group G, c.-cxxv., opens after a great silence:—'Where art thou, Muse, that thou forget'st so long':—and the poet develops in it a single sustained attack on the Law of Change, minimising the importance of both outward chances and inward moods. Once more taking his pen, he invokes his Muse (c.) 'to be a satire to Decay,' to bring contempt on 'Time's spoils,' and to 'give fame faster than Time wastes Life.' True, he argued against this in *Group E*: deprecating (lxxxii.) 'strained touches of rhetoric' when applied to one 'truely fair' and, therefore, 'truely sympathized' by 'true plain words': maintaining (lxxxiii.) that silence at least did not 'impair beauty,' and disparaging (lxxxv.) 'comments of praise richly compiled.' But now he puts this same defence into the mouth of his Muse, making her argue in turn (ci.) that Truth and Beauty, which both 'depend on' his Love, need no 'colour' and no 'pencil' since 'best is best, if never intermixed.' Yet he bids her 'excuse not silence so,' since it lies in her to make his love 'outlive a guilded tomb,' and 'seem long hence as he shows now.' In this Group, as in earlier resumptions, the music is at first imperfect. But it soon changes, and in cii. the apology for past silence is sung in accents sweet as the nightingale's described. There are marked irregularities in the poetic excellence of the Sonnets: which ever climbs to its highest pitch in the longer and more closely connected sequences. This is the longest of all: a poem of retrospect over a space of three years to the time when 'love was new, and then but in the spring.' In its survey it goes over the old themes with a soft and silvery touch: Beauty and Decay, Love, Constancy, the Immortalising of the Friend's beauty conceived as an incarnation of Ideal Beauty viewed from imaginary standpoints in Time. And interwoven with this re-handling, chiefly of the themes in the First and Fourth Groups, is an apology (cix.-cxii., cxvii.-cxx., cxxii.) for a negligence on the Poet's part of the rites of friendship, which he sets off (cxx.) against his Friend's earlier unkindness:—'*That you were once unkind, befriends me now.*' This apology offers the third, and only other, immediate reference to Shakespeare's personal experience; and, on these sonnets, as on those which treat of the Dark Lady and the Rival Poet, attention has been unduly concentrated. They seem founded on episodes and moods necessarily incidental to the life which we know Shakespeare must have led. To say that he could never have slighted his art as an actor:—

> 'Alas, 'tis true I have gone here and there
> And made myself a motley to the view...
>   My nature is subdued
> To what it works in like the dyer's hand':—

and then to seek for far-fetched and fantastic interpretations, is to evince an ignorance, not only of the obloquy to which actors were then exposed, and of the degradations they had to bear, but also of human nature as we know it even in heroes. Wellington is said to have wept over the carnage at Waterloo; the grossness of his material often infects the artist, and 'potter's rot' has its analogue in every profession. This feeling of undeserved degradation is a mood most incident to all who work, whether artists or men of action: an accident, real but transitory, which obliterates the contours of the soul, and leaves them intact, as a fog swallows the Town without destroying it.

In cxxi. there is a natural digression from this personal apology to reflexions cast on Shakespeare's good name. In cxxii. the apology is resumed with particular reference to certain tablets, the gift of the Friend, but which the Poet has bestowed on another. He takes this occasion to resume the main theme of the whole group by pouring contempt on '*dates*' and '*records*' and '*tallies* to *score* his dear love': the tablets, though in fact given away, are still 'within his brain, full charactered, beyond all date even to Eternity.' Thus does be lead up directly to the last three sonnets (cxxiii., cxxiv., cxxv.), which close this 'Satire to Decay,' and with it the whole series (i.-cxxv.). They are pieces of mingled splendour and obscurity in which Shakespeare presses home his metaphysical attack on the reality of Time; and the difficulty, inherent in an argument so transcendental, is further deepened by passing allusions to contemporary events and persons, which many have sought to explain, with little success. Here follows an Envoy of six couplets to the whole Series.

The Second Series shows fewer traces of design in its sequence than the First. The magnificent cxxix. on 'lust in action' is wedged between two: one addressed to Shakespeare's mistress and one descriptive of her charm; both playful in their fancy. cxlvi. to his soul, with its grave pathos and beauty, follows on a foolish verbal conceit, written in octosyllabic verse; while cliii. and cliv. are contrived in the worst manner of the French Renaissance on the theme of a Greek Epigram.[1] But the rest are, all of them, addressed to a Dark Lady whom Shakespeare loved in spite of her infidelity, or they comment on the wrong she does him. It cannot be doubted that they were written at the same time and on the same subject as the sonnets in Group C, xxxiii.-xlii., or that they were excluded from that group on any ground except that of their being written to another than the Youth to whom the whole First Series is addressed. Like the numbers in Group C, they are alternately playful and pathetic; their diction is often as exquisite, their discourse often as eloquent. But sometimes they are sardonic and even fierce:—

> 'For I have sworn thee fair and thought thee bright,
> Who art as black as hell, as dark as night.'

XVI—THEMES OF THE SONNETS

The division of the Sonnets into two Series and a number of subsidiary Groups, springs merely from the author's actual experiences, which were the occasions of their production, and from the order in time of those experiences. But the poetic themes suggested by such experiences and their treatment by Shakespeare belong to another sphere of consideration. They derive—not from the brute chances of life which, in a man not a poet, would have suggested no poetry, and, to a poet not Shakespeare, would have dictated poetry of another character and a lesser perfection, but—from Shakespeare's inborn temperament and acquired skill, both of selection and execution. These poetic themes are comparatively few in number, and recur again and again in the several Groups. Some are more closely connected with the facts of Shakespeare's life; others embody the general experience of man; others, again, detached, not only from the life of Shakespeare

1. Dowden, 1881.

but, from the thought of most men, embody the transcendental speculations of rare minds which, at certain times and places—in Socratic Athens and in the Europe of the Renaissance—have commanded a wide attention. Follows a tabulation.

(1) Themes personal to Shakespeare:—

His Friend's Error. Group C, xxxiii.-xlii., xciv.-xcvi., cxx. cxxxiii.-cxxxv.
The Dark Lady. Group C, and the Second Series, cxxvii.-clii.
His Own Error. xxxvi., cx., cxii., cxvii.-cxxii.
His Own *Misfortune.* xxv., xxix., xxxvii., cxi.
The Rival Poets . xxl, xxxii. Group E, lxxviii.-lxxxvi., and (as I hold) lxvii., lxviii., lxxvi., and cxxv.

That there were more Rival Poets than one is evident from lxxviii. 3:—

'Every alien pen hath got my use,
And under thee their poesy disperse':—

and from lxxxiii. 12:—

'For I impair not beauty, being mute
When others would give life.'

And among these others who still sing, while the Poet is himself silent, two are conspicuous:—

'There lives more life in one of your fair eyes
Than *both your poets* can in praise devise.'

(2) Themes which embody general experience:—

Love. xx.-xxxii., xxxvii., xliii.-lii., lvi., lxiii., lxvi., lxxi., lxxii., lxxv., lxxxvii., xcii, xcvi., cii., cv., cxv.-cxvi.
Absence. Group B, xxvi.-xxxi., xxxix., xliii.-lii., lvii., lviii., xcvii., xcviii.
Beauty and Decay. Group A, i.-xix., xxii., lxxvii.

At times this Theme is treated in a mood of contemplation remote from general experience—as in liv., lv., lx., lxiii.-lxv.—and, thus handled, may serve, with two Themes, derived from it:—

Immortality by Breed. i.-xiv., xvi., xvii.
Immortality by Verse. xv., xvii.-xix., xxxviii., liv., lv., lx., lxv., lxxiv., lxxxi., c., cl., cvii.:—

for a transition to (3) Themes which are more abstruse and demand a more particular examination.

Identity with his Friend:—

xx. 'My glass shall not persuade me I am old
So long as youth and thou are of one date....
For all that beauty that doth cover thee
Is but the seemly raiment of my heart....'

xxxix. 'What can mine own praise to mine own self bring?
And what is 't but mine own when I praise thee?...'

xlii. 'But here 's the joy: my friend and I are one....'

lxii. ''Tis thee, myself that for myself I praise,

Painting my age with beauty of thy days....'

cxii. (See Note.)

cxxxiii. 'Me from my self thy cruel eye hath taken
And my next self (his friend) thou harder hast ingrossed'...

cxxxiv. 'My self I 'll forfeit, so that other mine
Thou wilt restore.'

The conceit of Identity with the person addressed is but a part of the machinery of Renaissance Platonics derived, at many removes, from discussions in the Platonic Academy at Florence. Michelangelo had written in 1553:—'If I yearn day and night without intermission to be in Rome, it is only in order to return again to life, which I cannot enjoy without the soul'[1]—viz., his friend.

The Idea of Beauty.

In xxxvii. 'That I...by a part of all thy glory live' is a '*Shadow*,' cast by his Friend's excellence, which yet 'doth such *substance* give' that 'I am not lame, poor, nor despised.' In xxxi. all whom the Poet has loved and 'supposed dead'—'love and all Love's loving parts'—are not truly dead, 'but things removed that hidden in there lie'—viz.—in the Friend's bosom:—

'Their images I lov'd I view in thee,
And thou, all they, hast all the all of me.'

The mystical confusion with and in the Friend of all that is beautiful or lovable in the Poet and others, is a development from the Platonic theory of the Idea of Beauty: the eternal type of which all beautiful things on earth are but shadows. It is derived

1. J.A. Symonds' translation.

by poetical hyperbole from the Poet's prior identification of the Friend's beauty with Ideal Beauty. The theory of Ideal Beauty was a common feature of Renaissance Poetry throughout Europe. Du Bellay had sung it in France fifty years before Shakespeare in England:—

> 'Là, O mon âme, au plus haut ciel guidée,
> Tu y pourras recognoistre l'idée
> De la beauté qu'en ce monde j'adore.'

We need not infer that Shakespeare studied Du Bellay's verse or the great *corpus* of Platonic poetry in Italy. Spenser, who translated some of Du Bellay's sonnets at seventeen, had touched the theory in his *Hymne of Heavenly Beautie* (1596):—

> 'More faire is that (heaven), where those *Idees* on hie
> Enraungèd be, which *Plato* so admired':—

and had set it forth at length in his *Hymne in Honour of Beautie* (1596):—

> '*What time this world's great Workmaister* did cast
> To make all things such as we now behold,
> It seems that he before his eyes had plast
> A goodly Paterne....
>
> That wondrous Paterne...
> Is perfect *Beautie*, which all men adore....
>
> How vainely then do ydle wits invent,
> That *Beautie* is nought else but mixture made
> Of colours faire....
>
> Hath white and red in it such wondrous power,
> That it can pierce through th'eyes unto the hart...?
>
> That *Beautie* is not, as fond men misdeeme,
> An outward shew of things that only seeme....
>
> But that faire lampe...
> ...is heavenly born(e) and cannot die,
> Being a parcell of the purest skie....
>
> Therefore where-ever that thou doest behold
> A comely corpse, with beautie faire endowed,
> Know this for certaine, that the same doth hold
> A beauteous soul....'

Mr. Walter Raleigh has pointed out to me that Spenser and Shakespeare must have been familiar with Hoby's translation of Baldassare Castiglione's *Il Cortegiano*, published in 1561.[1] Indeed Spenser in his *Hymne in Honour of Beautie* does but versify the argument of Hoby's admirable Fourth Book. 'Of the *beawtie*,' Hoby writes, 'that we meane, which is onlie it that appeereth in bodies, and especially in the face of man...we will terme it *an influence of the heavenlie bountifulness*, the whiche for all it stretcheth over all thynges that be created (like the light of the Sonn) yet when it findeth out a face well proportioned, and framed with a certein livelie agreement of severall colours, and set forth with lightes and shadowes, and with an orderly distance and limites of lines, therinto it distilleth itself and appeereth most welfavoured, and decketh out and lyghtneth the subject, where it shyneth with a marveylous grace and glistringe (like the sonne beames that strike against a beautiful plate of fine golde wrought and sett with precyous jewelles).'

In Hoby's exposition the beauty of the human face is the best reflector of the Heavenly Beauty which, like the sunlight, is reflected from all things—from the 'world,' the 'heaven,' the 'earth,' the 'sun,' the 'moon,' the 'planets,'—from 'fowls,' 'trees,' 'ships,' 'buildings'—even from the 'roof of houses': so that 'if under the skye where there falleth neyther haile nor rayne a mann should builde a temple without a reared ridge, it is to be thought, that it coulde have neyther a sightly showe nor any beawtie. Beeside other thinges therefore, it giveth great praise to the world, in saying that it is beawtifull. It is praised, in sayinge, the beawtifull heaven, beawtifull earth, beawtifull sea, beawtifull rivers, beawtifull wooddes, trees, gardeines, beawtifull cities, beawtifull churches, houses, armies. In conclusion this comelye and holye beawtie is a wonderous settinge out of everie thinge. And it may be said that *Good and beawtifull* be after a sort

1. '*The Courtyer* of Count Baldessar Castilio divided into foure bookes. Very necessary and profitable for yonge Gentilmen and Gentilwomen abiding in Court, Palaice or Place, done into Englyshe by Thomas Hoby. Imprinted at London by Wyllyam Seres at the signe of the Hedghogge, 1561.' *Cf.* 'Adieu, my true court-friend: farewell my dear Castilio':—where *Malevole* addresses *Bilioso*.—Marston's *The Malcontent*, i. i. 302.

one selfe thinge, especiallie in the bodies of men: of the beawtie whereof the nighest cause (I suppose) is the beawtie of the soule: the which as a partner of the right and heavenlye beawtie, maketh sightly and beawtifull what ever she toucheth.' Plato's theory of Beauty had been ferried long before from Byzantium to Florence, and had there taken root, so that Michelangelo came to write:—

'Lo, all the lovely things we find on earth,
Resemble for the soul that rightly sees
That source of bliss divine which gave us birth:
Nor have we first-fruits or remembrances
Of heaven elsewhere. Thus, loving loyally,
I rise to God, and make death sweet by thee.'[1]

And from Italy young noblemen, accredited, to Italian courts or travelling for their pleasure, had brought its influence to France and England. So you have Spenser's *Hymne*; Drayton harping on *Idea*[2]; and Barnfield (1595) apostrophising the sects:—

'The Stoicks thinke (and they come neere the truth)
That vertue is the chiefest good of all,
The Academicks on *Idea* call.'

Shakespeare must have read Spenser's *Hymn* and Hoby's *Courtyer*, in which Plato, Socrates, and Plotinus are all instanced: the phrase—*genio Socratem*—applied to him in the epitaph on his monument attests his fondness for Platonic theories; he was conversant with these theories, and in the Sonnets he addressed a little audience equally conversant with them; it is, therefore, not surprising that he should have borrowed their terminology. In some sonnets he does so, but the *Sonnets* are not, therefore, as some have argued, an exposition of Plato's theory or of its

1. J.A. Symonds's translation. The great body of Platonic poetry did not pass without cavil even in Italy, for thus does the Blessed Giovenale Ancina state the defence and his reply:—'Mi rispose per un poco di scudo alla difesa, non esser cio tenuto ivi per lascivo, ne disonesto amore, se ben vano, e leggiero, ma *Platonico*, civile, modesto, con simplicita, e senza malitia alcuna, e per consequente poi honesto, gratioso, e comportabile. Al che sogginusi io subito, non amor *Platonicoy* nò, ma si ben veramente *Plutonico*, civè Satanico, e Infernale.' *Nuove Laudi Ariose della Beatissima Virgine*. Rome. 1600.
2. On the title-page of *The Shepherd's Garland*, 1593; *Ideas Mirrour*, 1594, etc.

Florentine developments. Shakespeare in certain passages does but lay under contribution the philosophy of his time just as, in other passages, he lays under contribution the art and occupations of his time, and in others, more frequently, the eternal processes of Nature. His *Sonnets* are no more a treatise of philosophy than they are a treatise of law. So far, indeed, is he from pursuing, as Spenser did pursue, a methodical exposition of the Platonic theory that he wholly inverts the very system whose vocabulary he has rifled. The Friend's beauty is no longer Hoby's 'plate of fine gold,' which reflects Eternal Beauty more brilliantly than aught else. For a greater rhetorical effect it becomes in Shakespeare's hand itself the very archetypal *pattern* and *substance* of which all beautiful things are but *shadows*.[1]

In i. the Poet urges the youth to marry, 'That thereby Beauty's *Rose*[2] might never die':—

> xiv. '*Truth and Beauty* shall together thrive
> If from thy self to store thou would'st convert:
> Or else of thee this I prognosticate,
> Thy end is *Truth's* and *Beauty's* doom and date.'
>
> xix. His is 'Beauty's *pattern* to succeeding men.'
>
> liii. 'What is your *substance*, whereof are you made
> That millions of strange *shadows* on you tend?
> Since every one hath, every one, one shade,
> And you, but one, can every *shadow* lend.'

The beauty of Adonis is such a *shadow*, so is the beauty of Helen: the 'spring of the year...doth *shadow* of your beauty show...and you in every blessed shape we know. In all external grace you have some part.' And in xcviii. 'The lily's white, the deep vermilion in the rose' are:—

> 'But figures of delight, drawn after you, you *pattern* of all those,'
>
> 'As with your *shadow* I with these did play.'
>
> *The Truth of Beauty.*

1. 'Shadow' (Lat. *umbra*) was the term of art in Renaissance Platonism for the Reflexion of the Eternal Type. Giordano Bruno discoursed in Paris '*De Umbris Idearum*.'
2. See Note on Typography of the Quarto (1609).

The theme of the Idea of Beauty, of his friend's beauty as the incarnation of an eternal type, is often blended with another metaphysical theme—The Truth of Beauty, e.g. in xiv. (*supra*). liv.:—*Truth* is an ornament which makes '*Beauty*' seem more beauteous. Here the Poet seems to equivocate on the double sense, moral and intellectual, of our word Truth, comparable to the double sense of our word Right, if, indeed, this be altogether a confusion of thought arising from poverty of language, and not a mystical perception by poets of some higher harmony between the Beautiful, the Good, and the True. Goethe wrote:—*Das Schöne enthält das Gute*; and Keats:—

> 'Beauty is Truth, Truth Beauty, that is all
> Ye know on earth and all ye need to know.'

Many hold this for madness, but if that it be, it has been a part of the 'divine madness' of poets since they first sang—'the most excellent of all forms of enthusiasm (or possession)';[1] and Shakespeare, when he handles the Truth of Beauty, does so almost always with but a secondary allusion, or with no allusion at all, to his Friend's constancy. He argues that the Idea of Beauty, embodied in his Friend's beauty, of which all other beautiful things are but shadows, is also Truth: an exact coincidence with an 'eternal form' to which transitory presentments do but approximate. Plato wrote:—'Beauty alone has' any such manifest image of itself: 'so that it is the clearest, the most certain of all things, and the most lovable,'[2] and Shakespeare (*Lucrece*, ll. 29-30):—

> 'Beauty itself doth of itself persuade
> The eyes of men without an orator.'

Thus, in lxii., the Poet looks in the glass and thinks:—

> 'No face so gracious is as mine,
> No shape so *true*, no *truth of such account*.'

And why is his shape so *true* and the *truth* of it so important? Because, reverting to the theme of *Identity*, his shape is that of the Friend's beauty:—

1. Plato's *Phœdrus*. *Plato and Platonism*, Pater, 156.
2. Plato's *Phœdrus*. *Plato and Platonism*, Pater, 158.

> ''Tis thee (myself) that for myself I praise,
> Painting my age with *beauty* of thy days....'

Again in ci.:—

> 'O Truant Muse, what shall be thy amends
> For thy neglect of *truth* in *beauty* dyed?
> Both *truth* and *beauty* on my love depends.'

And the Poet makes his Muse reply:—

> '*Truth* needs no colour with his colour fixt,
> *Beauty* no pencil *beauty's truth* to lay:
> But best is best, if never intermixt.'

False Art Obscures the Truth of Beauty.

In this last passage the Poet resumes an argument, put forward in earlier numbers, that the beauty of his Friend, being true, can only suffer from 'false painting' and 'ornament.' While so defending Beauty, which is Truth, from the disfigurement of false ornament, Shakespeare compares the false art of the Rival Poets, who also sing his Love, with the common practices of painting the cheeks[1] and wearing false hair[2]:—

> xxi. 'So is it not with me as with that Muse,
> Stirred by a painted beauty to his verse,
> Who heaven itself for *ornament* doth use,
> And every fair with his fair doth rehearse....
> O let me *true* in love but *truly* write,
> And then believe me my love is as *fair*
> As any mother's child.'

---

1. *Cf.* Richard Barnfield, *The Complaint of Chastitie*, 1594. An obvious echo of the tirades in Shakespeare's *Lucrece*. He writes of many:—

   > 'Whose lovely cheeks (with rare vermillion tainted)
   > Can never blush because their faire is painted.'

   > 'O faire—foule tincture, staine of Women-kinde,
   > Mother of Mischiefe, Daughter of Deceate,
   > False traitor to the Soule, blot to the Minde,
   > Usurping Tyrant of true Beautie's seate;
   > Right Coisner of the eye, lewd Follie's baite,
   > The flag of filthiness, the sinke of Shame,
   > The Divell's dey, dishonour of thy name.'

2. *Cf.* Bassanio's speech, *Merchant of Venice*, iii. 2:—'The world is still deceived by ornament.'

In lxvii. all these themes are brought together:—

> 'Why should *false painting* immitate his cheek
> And steal dead seeing of his living hue?
> Why should poor *Beauty* indirectly seek
> Roses of *skaddow*, since his Rose is *true*?'

In lxviii. 'His cheek is the map of days out-worn, before the golden tresses of the dead...were shorn away...to live a second life on second head':—

> 'And him as for a map doth nature store
> To shew *false art* what Beauty was of yore.'

Here 'false art' cannot refer, at any rate exclusively, to the actual use of fucuses and borrowed locks, for when the theme is resumed (lxxxii.), the illustration of 'gross painting' is directly applied to the 'false art' of the Rival Poets:—

> 'When they have devized
> What strained touches Rhetoric can lend,
> Thou, *truly fair*, wert *truly* sympathised
> In *true* plain words, by thy true telling friend.
> And their *gross painting* might be better used
> Where cheeks need blood, in thee it is abused.'

lxxxiii. continues:—

> 'I never saw that you did *painting* need,
> And therefore to your fair no *painting* set....
> Their lives more life in one of your fair eyes
> Than both your *Poets* can in *praise* devize.'

And in lxxxiv.:—

> 'Who is it that says most, which can say more.
> Than this rich praise, that you alone are you.'

This 'false painting' is the 'false art' of the Rival Poets in lxxxv., their 'praise richly compiled,' their 'golden quill' and 'precious phrase by all the Muses filed.'

Imaginary Standpoints in Time.

The Poet views this *Ideal Beauty* of his friend from *Imaginary Standpoints in Time*. He looks back on it from an imaginary future (civ.), and tells the 'Age unbred, Ere you were born was Beauty's summer dead.' He looks forward to it from the past, and, the descriptions of the fairest wights in the Chronicle of wasted Time (cvi.) shew him that

> 'Their antique pen would have exprest
> Even such Beauty as you master now.'

So all their 'praises are but prophesies.' Sometimes, with deeper mysticism, he all but accepts the *Illusion of Repeated Experience* for a truth of Philosophy. 'If there be nothing new, but that which is, hath been before' (lix.), then might 'Record with a backward look

> Even of five hundred courses of the sun
> Show me your image in some antique book.'

For his Friend's beauty is more than a perfect type prophesied in the past: it is a re-embodiment of perfection as perfection was in the prime:—

> lxvii. 'O, him she (Nature) stores, to show what wealth she had
> In days *long since* before these last so bad...'

> lxviii. 'And him as for a map doth Nature store
> To shew false art what Beauty was *of yore*.'

The Unreality of Time.

Since this Ideal Beauty is true, is very Truth, it is independent of Time, and eternal; it, with the love it engenders, is also independent of accident, and is unconditioned:—

> cvii. 'Eternal love in love's fresh case
> Weighs not the dust and injury of age,
> Nor gives to necessary wrinkles place,
> But makes antiquity for aye his page....'

> cxvii. 'Love 's not Time's fool, though rosy lips and cheeks
> Within his bending sickle's compass come.'

Thus does the whole Series culminate in an *Attack on the Reality of Time.*—cxxiii., cxxiv., cxxv. are obscure to us; yet they are written in so obvious a sequence, and with so unbroken a rhythmical swing, as to preclude the idea of extensive corruption in the text. They must once have been intelligible. Some attempts at elucidation have been made by fixing on single words, such as 'state' (cxxiv. 1) and 'canopy' (cxxv. 1), and then endeavouring to discover an allusion to historical events or to the supposed nobility of the person to whom the verses were addressed. But these attempts dissemble the main drift of the verses' meaning, which is clearly directed, at least in cxxiii. and cxxiv., against the reality and importance of Time. In c., which opens this Group (c.-cxxv.), the Poet has bidden his Muse to 'make Time's spoils despised everywhere.' In cxvi. he has declared that Love is an eternal power, of a worth unknown, but immeasurably superior to the accidents of Time. In lix. he has urged that even our thoughts may be vain repetitions of a prior experience:—

> 'If there be nothing new, but that which is
> Hath been before, how are our brains beguiled
> Which labouring for invention bear amiss,
> The second burthen of a former child?'

And here, in a magnificent hyperbole, he asserts that 'pyramids' (1, 2) built up by Time with a might which is 'newer' by comparison to his own changelessness, are, for all their antiquity, but 'new dressings' of sights familiar to ante-natal existence:—

> 'Our dates are brief and therefore we admire
> What thou dost foist upon us that is old.'

So far there is fairly plain sailing, but the ensuing Lines 7, 8, constitute a real crux:—

> 'And rather make them born(e) to our desire
> Than think that we before have heard them told':

Assuming these lines to refer to 'what' Time 'foists upon us,' the second implies that we ought to recognise the old things foisted upon us by Time for objects previously known, but that we 'prefer to regard them as really new'—as just 'born'—(Tyler), and 'specially created for our satisfaction' (Dowden). The explanation is not satisfactory, though probably the best to be got from the assumed reference. But (1) this reference of 'them' to 'what,' followed by a singular 'that is,' can hardly be sustained grammatically, and (2) it scarce makes sense. Shakespeare cannot have intended that we admire things for their age while 'we regard them as really new.' I suggest that the plural 'them' refers grammatically to the plural 'dates,' and that the word usually printed 'born'[1] in line 7, had best be printed 'borne' as it is in the Quarto[2] (= '*bourn*'). We make our brief dates into a bourn or limit to our desire (*cf.* 'confined doom,' cvii. 4) instead of recollecting that 'we have heard them told' (= *reckoned*) 'before.' There is but a colon in the Quarto after Line 8. And the third Quatrain continues to discuss dates (= *registers*, Line 9, and *records*, Line 11). In Line 11 Shakespeare denies the absolute truth both of Time's records and the witness of our senses:—

'For thy records and what we see doth lie.'

The sonnet, in fact, does but develop the attack of the one before it (cxxii.), in which he declares that the memory of his Friend's gift 'shall remain beyond all *date* even to Eternity; that such a '*record*' is better than the 'poor retention' of tablets; and that he needs no '"*tallies*" to "*score*" his dear love.'

In cxxiv. Line 1:—'If my dear love were but the child of *State*':—'State' may contain a secondary allusion (as so often with Shakespeare) to the dignity of the person addressed; but its primary meaning, continuing the sense of the preceding sonnet, and indeed of all the numbers from c., is 'condition' or 'circumstance.' (*Cf.* 'Interchange of *state* and *state* itself confounded to decay,' lxiv.; and 'Love's great *case*' in cviii.). If his Love were the child of circumstance it might be disinherited by any chance result of Fortune; but on the contrary, 'it was builded far from *accident*.' And '*accident*,' as were '*case*' and '*State*,' is also a term of metaphysic: his Love belongs to the absolute and unconditioned, to Eternity and not to Time. In developing the idea of mutations in fortune, Shakespeare glances aside at some contemporary reverse in politics or art which we cannot decipher. It may have been the closing of the Theatres, the censorship of Plays, the imprisonment of Southampton or of Herbert. No one can tell, nor does it matter, for the main meaning is clear: namely, that this absolute Love is outside the world of politics, which are limited by Time, and count on leases of short numbered hours; but in itself is 'hugely politic,' is an independent and self-sufficing State. In the couplet:—

1. Printed so first by Gildon, and accepted by subsequent editors.
2. *Borne* (French), and in *Hamlet*, Folio 1623 and Quarto.

'To this I witness, call the fools of time
Which die for goodness, who have lived for crime':—

some find an allusion to the merited execution of Essex, popularly called 'the good Earl.' But the probability is that Shakespeare sympathised with Essex and those of the old nobility who were jealous of the Crown. And, again, it is simpler to take the lines as a fitting close to the metaphysical disquisition, and to see in them a rebuke of those who are so much the slaves of Time and its dates as to imagine that a moment of repentance cancels the essential iniquity of their lives.

cxxv. is even more obscure. Yet the sense, to my mind, again seems clearer if we dismiss the theory that Shakespeare is here dwelling exclusively on the dignity of the person he addresses. Most of the sonnets, in the First Series, handle the themes of an Ideal Beauty incarnate in a mortal body, yet saved from decay by the immortality which verse confers; of the need that such verse should truly express the Truth and Beauty of its object; and of Love and Constancy which transcend the limitations of Time. Since cxxv. comes at the end of the peroration to the last twenty-six Sonnets, which are all retrospective, and immediately before the Envoy, it seems to me only reasonable to read it in the light of its immediate predecessors and of the principal themes recurring throughout the whole Series.

The search for direct allusions to life in the Sonnets distracts us from the truth, that the selection of their themes was based quite as much upon current philosophy and artistic tradition as upon any actual experience. Something of all is involved, and we should lose sight of none. The poetry of Europe was steeped in Platonism, and, since the *Trionf* of Petrarch, the 'Triumph of Time' and his ultimate defeat had been a common theme in many forms of art, especially in the Tapestries of Arras introduced into great English houses during the Sixteenth Century:—

'The wals were round about apparelléd
With costly cloths of *Arras* and of *Tours*.'

Faerie Queen, iii. i, 34.

Shakespeare wrote out of his own experience, but also under these influences of contemporary Art and Philosophy. And here, pursuing the earlier themes, he asks if it were ought to him, holding his views, to worship the outward show of Beauty with external homage, or, as I interpret Lines 3, 4, to win eternity by the mere form of his verse. This interpretation of 3-4 is borne out by the second quatrain. We have in it, as I submit, a recurrence to his attacks on the styles of poetry which he deprecated in the 'false painting' of lxvii.; the 'false art' of lxviii.; the '*compounds* strange' of lxxvi.; the 'strained touches of rhetoric' and 'gross painting' of lxxxii.; the 'comments of praise richly compiled' of lxxxv. These are the 'compounds sweet' of Line 7, for which dwellers on form and favour pay too much rent. 'That you are you' (lxxxiv.) is all that needs to be said, for (lxxxiii.):—

> 'There lives more life in one of your fair eyes
> Than both your poets can in praise devise.'

Therefore he tenders his '*oblation poor but free*, which is not *mixed with seconds*.'

That last word—'seconds'—has been a stumbling-block for more than a century, thanks to Steevens. His note runs thus:—'I am just informed by an old lady that *seconds* is a provincial term for the *second kind of flour*, which is collected after the smaller bran is sifted. That our author's oblation was pure, *unmixed with baser matter*, is all that he meant to say.' But may not *seconds* mean 'assistants' and refer to the collaboration of the Two Poets in lxxxiii.? It can hardly mean 'baser matter'; since the contrast is between an offering humble, poor, and without art, and some other offering presumably rich and artificial, such as the verse of the Rival Poets criticised in the group concerned with their efforts. As for Line 13, 'Hence thou suborned *Informer*,' I have argued elsewhere[1] that the words in italics with capitals are not accidents of printing. This word of violent apostrophe refers to some person whose identity was obvious to the object of Shakespeare's verse, and if, as I have tried to show, these Sonnets belong to one sequence, it may be compared to the 'frailer spies' of cxxi.

1. Note on typography of the Quarto (1609).

XVII—IMAGERY

Imagery.—These poetic themes are figured and displayed throughout the *Sonnets* by means of an Imagery which, as in *Venus* and *Lucrece*, is often so vividly seized and so minutely presented as to engross attention to the prejudice of the theme. Indeed, at some times the poet himself seems rather the quarry than the pursuer of his own images—as it were a magician hounded by spirits of his summoning. Conceits were a fashion, and Shakespeare sometimes followed the fashion; but this characteristic of his lyrical verse is rather a passive consequence of such obsession than the result of any deliberate pursuit of an image until it become a conceit. Put 'his' for 'her' and, in *Lucrece* he, himself, describes the process:—

> 'Much like a press of people at a door,
> Throng *his* inventions which shall go before.'

The retina of his mind's eye, like a child's, or that of a man feverish from the excitement of some high day, is as it were a shadow-sheet, on which images received long since revive and grow to the very act and radiancy of life. A true poet, it is tritely said, ever remains a child, but especially in this, that his vision is never dulled. The glass of the windows through which he looks out on the world is never ground of set purpose that his mind may the better attend to business within. And to a poet, as to a child, the primal processes of the earth never lose their wonder. So the most of Shakespeare's images are taken from Nature, and then are painted—but the word is too gross to convey the clarity of his art—in so transparent an atmosphere as to seem still a part of Nature, showing her uses of perpetual change. In the *Sonnets* we watch the ceaseless *Passing of the Year*:—

> civ. 'Three winters cold
> Have from the forests shook three summers' pride;
> Three beauteous springs to yellow autumn turn'd;
> In process of the seasons have I seen,
> Three April perfumes in three hot Junes burn'd....'

> v. 'Sap check'd with frost and lusty leaves quite gone....'

> xii. '...lofty trees...barren of leaves
> Which erst from heat did canopy the herd....'

xiii. '...the stormy gusts of winter's day
And barren rage of death's eternal cold....'

lxxiii. 'That time of year thou may'st in me behold
When yellow leaves, or none, or few, do hang
Upon those boughs which shake against the cold,
Bare ruin'd choirs, where late the sweet birds sang':—

or, in a narrower cycle we follow the *Decline of Day*:—

xxxiii. 'Full many a glorious morning have I seen
Flatter the mountain-tops with sovereign eye,
Kissing with golden face the meadows green,
Gilding pale streams with heavenly alchymy;
Anon permit the basest clouds to ride
With ugly rack on his celestial face,
And from the forlorn world his visage hide,
Stealing unseen to west with this disgrace...

lxxiii. 'In me thou see'st the twilight of such day
As after sunset fadeth in the west;
Which by and by black night doth take away
Death's second self, that seals up all the rest.'

Taine insists, perhaps too exclusively, on the vivid imagery of Shakespeare's verse; Minto and Mrs. Meynell, perhaps too exclusively, on the magic of sound and association which springs from his unexpected collocation of words till then unmated. The truth seems to lie in a fusion of the two theories. When Shakespeare takes his images from Nature, the first excellence is predominant; the second, when he takes them from the occupations of men.

Often, in the Sonnets, he illustrates his theme with images from *Inheritance*,[1] or *Usury*,[2] or the *Law*;[3] and then his effects

1. i. 'tender heir.' ii. 'by succession.' iv, 'legacy'; 'bequest.'
2. iv. 'usurer.' vi. 'usury'; 'loan.' xxxi. 'tears' are 'interest of the dead.'
3. xiii. lease; determination. xviii. lease; date. xxx. sessions; summon. xlvi. defendant's plea; title; impannelled; quest; tenants; verdict. xlix. 'And this my hand against myself uprear,' viz., in taking an oath. lxxiv. arrest; trial. lxxxvii. charter; bonds; determinate; patent; misprision; judgment. cxx. fee; ransoms. cxxvi. audit; quietus, 'a technical term for the acquittance which every Sheriff (or accountant) receives on selling his account, at the Exchequer.' The frequency of these terms in the Sonnets and Plays led Malone to conclude that Shakespeare must

are rather produced by the successful impressment of technical terms to the service of poetry than by the recollections they revive of legal processes:—

> 'When to the *sessions* of sweet silent thought
> I *summon* up remembrance of things past.'

Among such occupations he draws also upon *Journeys* (l.); *Navigation* (lxxx., lxxxvi., cxvi.):—

> 'O, no! it is an ever-fixed mark (sea-mark)
> That looks on tempests and is never shaken;
> It is the star to every wandering bark':—

Husbandry (iii.); *Medicine* (cxviii.); Sieges (ii.):—

> 'When forty winters shall *besiege* thy brow
> And dig deep *trenches* in thy beauty's *field*':—

and a *Courtier's Career* (vii., cxiv.):—

> xxxiii. 'Full many a glorious morning have I seen
> *Flatter* the mountain-tops with *sovereign* eye....'
>
> xxv. 'Great princes' *favourites* their fair leaves spread
> But as the marygold at the sun's eye':—

and this last was of a more striking application than now in the days of Elizabeth or James. He draws also on the arts of *Painting* (frequently), of *Music* (viii., cxxviii.), of the *Stage* (xxiii.); on the *Dark Sciences*:—

> xv. 'Whereon the stars in secret influence comment.'
>
> cvii. 'The mortal moon hath her eclipse endured,
> And the sad augurs mock their own presage'—
>
> xiv. 'Not from the *stars* do I my judgement pluck,
> And yet, methinks, I have *Astronomy*' (Astrology):—

so *prognosticating* from his friend's 'eyes'; on *Alchemy* (xxxiii.), and *Distillation* (vi., liv.):—

> v. 'Then were not summer's *distillation* left
> A liquid prisoner pent in walls of glass....'

---

at one time have been an attorney. If so, we may the better believe that Ben Jonson intended Ovid for Shakespeare in *The Poetaster*, i. i:—'Poetry! Ovid, whom I thought to see the pleader, became Ovid the play-maker!' *Ibid.*, '*Misprize!* ay. marry, I would have him use such words now.... He should make himself a style out of these.' And *passim*.

> cxix. 'What *potions* have I drunk of Syren tears
> *Distill'd* from lymbecks (alembics) foul as hell within.'—

When, as in these examples, he takes his illustrations from professions and occupations, or from arts and sciences, his magic, no doubt, is mainly verbal; but it springs from immediate perception (as in the case of annual and diurnal changes), when his images are taken from subtler effects of sensuous appreciation, be it of *Shadows*; of the *Transparency of Windows* (iii., xxiv.); of *Reflections in Mirrors* (iii., xxii., lxii., lxxvii., ciii.), or of *Hallucinations in the Dark*:—

> xxvii. 'Save that my soul's imaginary sight
> Presents their shaddow to my sightless view,
> Which, like a jewell hung in ghastly night,
> Makes black night beauteous....'
>
> xliii. 'When in dead night thy fair imperfect shade
> Through heavy sleep on sightless eyes doth stay!'
>
> lxi. 'Is it thy will thy image should keep open
> My heavy eyelids to the weary night?'

And this source of his magic is evident also, when, as frequently, he makes use of *Jewels* (xxvii., xxxiv., xlviii., lii., lxv., xcvi.);—*Apparel* (ii., xxvi., lxxvi.);—the *Rose* (i., xxxv., liv., lxvii., xcv., xcix., cix.);—the *Grave* (i., iv., vi., xvii., xxxi., xxxii., lxxi., lxxii, lxxvii., lxxxi.);—*Sepulchral Monuments* (lv., lxxxi., cvii.);—the *Alternation of Sunshine with Showers* (xxxiii., xxxiv.);—the *Singing of Birds* (xxix.), and their *Silence* (xcvii., cii.). *Realism* is the note of these imaginative perceptions, as it is when he writes:—

> xxxiv. ''Tis not enough that through the cloud thou break
> To dry the rain on my storm-beaten face....'
>
> xxiii. 'As an imperfect actor on the Stage,
> Who with his fear is put beside his part....'
>
> l. 'The beast that bears me, tired with my woe
> Plods dully on....'
>
> lx. 'Like as the waves make towards the pebbled shore....'
>
> lxxiii. 'When yellow leaves, or none, or few do hang
> Upon those boughs':—

when he instances the '*Dyer's Hand*' (cxi.) and the '*crow that flies in heaven's sweetest air*' (lxx.)—a clue to carrion—or when he captures a vivid scene of nursery comedy:—

> cxliii. 'Lo, as a careful housewife runs to catch
> One of her feather'd creatures broke away,
> Sets down her babe, and makes all swift despatch
> In pursuit of the thing she would have stay;
> Whilst her neglected child holds her in chase,
> Cries to catch her whose busy care is bent
> To follow that which flies before her face,
> Not prizing her fair infant's discontent.'

In all such passages the magic springs from imaginative observation rather than from unexpected verbal collocutions. And, while this observation is no less keen, the rendering of it no less faithful, than in the earlier Lyrical Poems, *Conceits*, though still to be found, are fewer:—e.g., of the *Eye and Heart* (xxiv., xlvi., xlvii.); Of the *Four Elements*—earth, air, fire, water (xliv., xlv.); and of the *taster to a King* (cxiv.).

XVIII—ELOQUENT DISCOURSE

Eloquent Discourse.—On the other hand the Eloquent Discourse of the earlier Poems becomes the staple of the *Sonnets* and their highest excellence. It is for this that we chiefly read them:—

> xxxvi. 'Let me confess that we two must be twain
> Although our undivided loves are one....'
>
> xl. 'Take all my loves, my love, yea, take them all;
> What hast thou then more than thou hadst before?...'
>
> cxxxix. 'O call me not to justify the wrong
> That thy unkindness lays upon my heart....'
>
> cxl. 'Be wise as thou art cruel; do not press
> My tongue-tied patience with too much disdain;
> Lest sorrow lend me words, and words express
> The manner of my pity-wanting pain.
> If I might teach thee wit, better it were,
> Though not to love, yet, love to tell me so....
> For if I should despair, I should grow mad,
> And in my madness might speak ill of thee.'

The last, addressed to the Dark Lady, are, it may be, as eloquent as any addressed to the Youth, but they lack something of those others' silvery sadness:—

lxxi. 'No longer mourn for me when I am dead,
Than you shall hear the surly sullen bell,
Give warning to the world that I am fled
From this vile world, with vilest worms to dwell:
Nay, if you read this line, remember not
The hand that wrote it; for I love you so,
That I in your sweet thoughts would be forgot,
If thinking of me then should make you woe.
O, if, I say, you look upon this verse
When I perhaps compounded am with clay,
Do not so much as my poor name rehearse,
But let your love even with my life decay;
  Lest the wise world should look into your moan,
  And mock you with me after I am gone.

lxxii. 'O, lest the world should task you to recite
What merit lived in me that you should love,
After my death, dear love, forget me quite,
For you in me can nothing worthy prove;
Unless you would devise some virtuous lie,
To do more for me than mine own desert,
And hang more praise upon deceaséd I
Than niggard truth would willingly impart:
O, lest your true love may seem false in this,
That you for love speak well of me untrue,
My name be buried where my body is,
And live no more to shame nor me nor you.
  For I am sham'd by that which I bring forth,
  And so should you, to love things nothing worth.'

xc. 'Then hate me when thou wilt; if ever, now;
Now while the world is bent my deeds to cross,
Join with the spite of fortune, make me bow,
And do not drop in for an after-loss:
Ah! do not when my heart hath scap'd this sorrow,
Come in the rearward of a conquer'd woe;
Give not a windy night a rainy morrow,
To linger out a purpos'd overthrow.

If thou wilt leave me, do not leave me last,
When other petty griefs have done their spite;
But in the onset come; so shall I taste
At first the very worst of fortune's might;
  And other strains of woe, which now seem woe,
  Compar'd with loss of thee will not seem so.'

XIX—VERBAL MELODY

Verbal Melody.—The theme of xc. is a sorrow which has, I suppose, been suffered, at one time or another, by most men: it is hackneyed as dying. Yet the eloquence is peerless. I doubt if in all recorded speech such faultless perfection may be found, so sustained through fourteen consecutive lines. That perfection does not arise from any thought in the piece itself, for none is abstruse; nor from its sentiment, which is common to all who love, and suffer or fear a diminution in their love's return; nor even from its imagery, though the line, 'Give not a windy night a rainy morrow,' holds its own against Keats's 'There is a budding morrow in midnight,' which Rossetti once chose for the best in English poetry. It arises from perfect verbal execution: from diction, rhythm, and the just incidence of accentual stresses enforced by assonance and alliteration. The charm of Shakespeare's verbal surprise—e.g., 'a lass unparalleled,' 'multitudinous seas,' instanced by Mrs. Meynell—once noted, is readily recognised, but much of his Verbal Melody defies analysis. Yet some of it, reminding you of Chaucer's 'divine liquidness of diction, his divine fluidity of movement'[1]:—

'Feel I no wind that soúneth so like peyne
It séith "Alás! why twýnned be we tweýne"':—

or of Surrey:—

'The gólden *gift* that nature did thee gëve
To *f*asten *f*rendes, and *f*ede them at thy will
With *f*orm and *f*avour, taught me to beléve
How thou art m*á*de to shew her gr*éa*test skill:—

may be explained by that absolute mastery he had over the rhythmical use of our English accent. Mr. Coventry Patmore has

1. Matthew Arnold.

justly observed[1] that 'the early poetical critics'—notably Sidney and Daniel—'commonly manifest a much clearer discernment of the main importance of rhyme and *accentual stress*, in English verse, than is to be found among later writers.' And this because, as he goes on to say, 'the true spirit of English verse appears in its highest excellence in the writings of the poets of Elizabeth and James.' If we neglect *Quantity*, that is to say the duration of syllables, whose sum makes up an equal duration for each line—and we must neglect it, for, except in the classical age of Greece, and of Rome in imitation of Greece, no language observes so constant a quantity for its syllables as to afford a governing element in verse—we find in English verse *Rhyme* and *Accentual Stress* or *Ictus*. Now, *Rhyme*, but falteringly nascent in Folk-song before his day, was fully acclimatised by Chaucer from French, which has no emphatic accents, at a time when French was the natural tongue of the cultured in England. In a language without emphatic accents, or exact quantity, Rhyme was, and Rhyme is, a necessity to mark off and enforce the only constant element, viz., *Metre* or the number of syllables in each line. But in the homely and corrupt English of Chaucer's day, and side by side with the Court poetry, another poetry persisted, which was based exclusively upon the accentual stresses natural to northern languages. And it persisted down even to Shakespeare's day. We find so curious and artful a metrist as Dunbar pursuing both traditions:—Chaucer's rhymed 'staff of seven' and the unrhymed, alliterative verse of *Piers Plowman*. Dunbar died, c. 1513 (as some think, at Flodden). But after his voice was silenced we have a contemporary poem on the battle—*Scottish Field*[2]:—

> There was girding forth of guns, with many great stones;
> Archers uttered out their arrows and eagerly they shotten;
> They proched us with spears and put many over;
> That the blood outbrast at their broken harness.
> There was swinging out of swords, and swapping of heads,
> We blanked them with bills through all their bright armour,
> That all the dale dinned of the derf strokes:—

1. *Essay on English Metrical Law.*
2. Cited by Ker with the reference:—Ed. Robson, Chetham Society, 1855, from the Lyme ms.; ed. Furnivall and Hales, *Percy Folio Manuscript*, 1867.

and editions of *Piers Plowman* were published in 1551 and 1561, showing a continuous appreciation of our indigenous but archaic mode. In that mode the major accents fall on syllables either consonantal or of cognate sound. This was no device of mere artifice: the impassioned speech of any Englishman becomes charged with stresses so heavy as to demand syllables of kindred sound on to which they may fall, and the demand is met unconsciously, since otherwise the weight of the accent would interrupt and shatter the flow of discourse. The heavy beat at the end of a French line and the heavy accents in an English line must be met and supported in the first case by Rhyme, in the second, by syllables similarly produced. Shakespeare, in the Sonnets, whilst revelling in the joy of Rhyme, handed down from the French origin of English verse and confirmed by the imitation of Italian models, also turned the other and indigenous feature of English verse to the best conceivable advantage. No other English poet lets the accent fall so justly in accord with the melody of his rhythm and the emphasis of his speech, or meets it with a greater variety of subtly affiliated sounds.

This may be illustrated from any one of the more melodious and, therefore, the more characteristic Sonnets. Take the First:—

1. From *f*ai*r*est *Crea*tures we desi*re* i*ncrease*
2. That thereby beauty's *R*ose might never *Die*
3. But as the *Ri*per should by *T*ime *d*ecease
4. His *t*ender h*e*ir might b*ear* his memory.
5. But thou con*trac*ted to thine own *bright eyes*
6. *F*eed'st thy light's *f*lame with sel*f*-substantial *f*uel
7. Making a *f*amine where a*b*undance *lies*,
8. T*hy*self thy *f*oe to thy sweet self *too crue*l
9. Th*ou* that art n*ow* the world's fresh *o*rnament
10. And *o*nly h*er*ald to the *g*audy spri*ng*
11. With*in* thine own *bu*d *bu*riest thy con*ten*t
12. And *ten*der ch*url* ma*k*'st wa*st*e in niggarding
13. P*i*ty the w*o*r*l*d or else this *gl*utton *be*
14. To *eat* the world's due by the gr*a*ve and *th*e*e*:—

and you observe (1) the use of kindred sounds, of alliteration or of assonance or of both, to mark the principal stresses in any one line:—e.g., Line 1, *Crea*tures and in*crea*se, where both are used; Line 3, *Ri*per and T*i*me; Line 4, *heir* and b*ear*; Line 5, con*tra*cted and *bright*; Line 99 T*hou* and *now*:—and (2), and this is most characteristic, the juxtaposition of assonantal sounds where two syllables consecutive, but in separate words, are accented with a marked pause between them:—E.g., Line 5, bright *eyes*; Line 8, *too* cr*ue*l; Line 11, b*ud* b*u*riest; Line 12, m*ak*'st w*a*ste. Mr. Patmore points out[1] that 'ordinary English phrases exhibit a great preponderance of emphatic and unemphatic syllables in consecutive couples,' and our eighteenth century poets; absorbed in Metre and negligent of varied Rhythm, traded on this feature of our tongue to produce a number of dull iambic lines by the use of their banal trochaic epithets, 'balmy,' 'mazy,' and the rest. Shakespeare constantly varies his Rhythm in the Sonnets, and frequently by this bringing of two accented syllables together, with a pause between. But, when he does so, he ensures a correct delivery by affiliating the two syllables in sound, and prefixing to the first a delaying word which precludes any scamping of the next ensuing accent:—E.g. 'own,' before 'bright eyes'; 'self' before 'too cruel'; 'churl' before 'mak'st waste.' *Cf.* 'Earth' before 'sings hymns' in xxix. 12; and xv. 8, 'and *wear their brave state* out of memory.'

It is by this combination of Accent with Rhyme that Shakespeare links the lines of each quatrain in his Sonnets into one perfect measure. If you except two—'Let me not to the marriage of true minds,' and 'The expense of spirit in a waste of shame'—you find that he does not, as Milton did afterwards, build up his sonnet, line upon line, into one monumental whole: he writes three lyrical quatrains, with a pronounced pause after the second and a couplet after the third. Taking the First Sonnet once more, you observe (3) The binding together of the lines in each quatrain by passing on a kindred sound from the last, or most important, accent in one line to the first, or most important, in the next:—E.g. from 2 to 3, from D*ie* to *Ri*per by assonance; from 3 to 4, from *T*ime to *T*ender by alliteration; from 6 to 7, from *F*uel to *F*amine; from 7 to 8, from *F*amine... *lies* to Thyself...*Foe*; from 9 to 10, from *Or*nament to H*er*ald;

1. *Essay on English Metrical Law.*

from 11 to 12, from con*tent* to *ten*der; from 13 to 14, from *be* to *ea*t. *Cf*. lx. lines 6, 7:—

> '*Cr*awls to maturity wherewith being *cr*own'd
> *Cr*ooked eclipses 'gainst his glory fight.'

and cviii. 9, 10:—

> 'So that eternal love in love's fresh *case*
> *Weighs* not the dust.'

In a Petrarchan sonnet any such assonance, if it embraced the rhyme, would prove a blemish, but in the Shakespearian quatorzain it is a pleasant and legitimate accessory to the general binding together of the quatrain. Most subtle of all is the pent-up emphasis brought to bear on *Rose* in i. 2—a word not easily stressed—by the frequency of R's in the first line and their absence till *Rose* is reached in the second. (4) For a further binding together of the quatrain the Rhyme, or last syllable, though not accented, is often tied by assonance to the first syllable, though not accented, of the next line:—E.g. i. lines 3, 4, decease—H*is*; lines 7, 8, l*ies*—t*hy*self; lines 10, 11, Spr*ing*—*within*, lines 12, 13, niggard*ing*—P*i*ty. Shakespeare's effects of alliteration, apart from this use of them for the binding together of the quatrain, are at some times of astonishing strength:—

> lxv. 7, 8. 'When rocks impregnable are not so *st*out
> Nor ga*tes* of *ste*el so *st*rong but Time decays':—

and at others of a strange sweetness:—

> ix. 5. 'The *w*orld *w*ill be thy *w*idow and still *weep*.'

Again, at others he uses the device antithetically in discourse:—

> xxxix. 10. 'Were it not thy *sour leisure* gave *sweet leave*':—

and his rhythm is at all times infinitely varied:—

> xix. 14. 'My love shall in my verse *ev*er live long....'
>
> xxxiii. 7. 'And from the *forlorn world* his visage hide....'
>
> lxxxvi. 4. 'Making their *tomb* the *womb* wherein they grew....'
>
> xi. 10. 'Harsh, featureless, and rude, *barrenly* perish.'

Apart from all else, it is the sheer beauty of diction in Shakespeare's Sonnets which has endeared them to poets. The passages, which I have quoted to other ends, must abundantly have proved this. Yet let me add these:—

v. 5, 6. 'For never-resting time leads summer on
To hideous winter, and confounds him there.'

xvii. 7-12. 'The age to come would say, This Poet lies,
Such heavenly touches ne'er touch'd earthly faces.
So should my papers, yellowed with their age,
Be scorn'd, like old men of less truth than tongue,
And your true rights be termed a poet's rage,
And stretchéd metre of an antique song.'

xviii. 1-4. 'Shall I compare thee to a summer's day?
Thou art more lovely and more temperate:
Rough winds do shake the darling buds of May
And summer's lease hath all too short a date.'

xlviii. 10, 11. 'Save where thou art not, though I feel thou art
Within the gentle closure of my breast.'

liv. 5, 6. 'The canker-blooms have all as deep a die
As the perfuméd tincture of the roses.'

lx. 9, 10. 'Time doth transfix the flourish set on youth,
And delves the parallels in beauty's brow.'

lxiv. 5, 6. 'When I have seen the hungry ocean gain
Advantage on the kingdom of the shore.'

lxv. 1-4. 'Since brass, nor stone, nor earth, nor boundless sea,
But sad mortality o'ersways their power,
How with this rage shall beauty hold a plea,
Whose action is no stronger than a flower?'

lxxxix. 8. 'I will acquaintance strangle, and look strange.'

xciv. 9, 10. 'The summer's flower is to the summer sweet,
Though to itself it only live and die.'

xcvii. 1-4. 'How like a winter hath my absence been,
From thee, the pleasure of the fleeting year!
What freezings have I felt, what dark days seen!
What old December's bareness everywhere.'

xcvii. 12-14. 'And thou away, the very birds are mute:
Or, if they sing, 'tis with so dull a cheer,
That leaves look pale, dreading the winter's near.

xcviii. 9, 10. 'Nor did I wonder at the lily's white,
Nor praise the deep vermilion in the rose.'

cv. 1. 'Let not my love be call'd idolatry.'

cxxxii. 5, 6. 'And truly not the morning sun in heaven
Better becomes the gray cheeks of the East.'

cxlii. 5, 6. 'Or, if it do, not from those lips of thine
That have profaned their scarlet ornaments.'

cxlvi. 13, 14. 'So shalt thou feed on death, that feeds on men,
And death once dead, there's no more dying then.'

XX—CONCLUSION

It matters nothing to Art that Titian may have painted his Venus from the Medici's wife: Antinous gave the world a Type of Beauty to be gazed at without a thought of Hadrian. But the case is not altered when the man who rejoices or suffers is also the man who labours and achieves. It matters nothing to Art that Luca Signorelli painted the corpse of his beloved son, and it is an open question if Dante loved indeed a living Beatrice. Works of perfect Art are the tombs in which artists lay to rest the passions they would fain make immortal. The more perfect their execution, the longer does the sepulchre endure, the sooner does the passion perish. Only where the hand has faltered do ghosts of love and anguish still complain. In the most of his Sonnets Shakespeare's hand does not falter. The wonder of them lies in the art of his poetry, not in the accidents of his life; and, within that art, not so much in his choice of poetic themes as in the wealth of his Imagery, which grows and shines and changes: above all, in the perfect execution of his Verbal Melody. That is the body of which his Imagery is the soul, and the two make one creation so beautiful that we are not concerned with anything but its beauty.—G.W.

P.S.—Let me here acknowledge my great debt to Mr. W.E. Henley for his constant help in the preparation of this Edition. But for his persuasion I should never have attempted a task which, but for his encouragement, I could never have accomplished.

Venus and Adonis

'Vilia miretur vulgus; mihi flavus Apollo
Pocula Castalia plena ministret aqua.'

TO THE

RIGHT HONOURABLE HENRE WRIOTHESLEY,

Earle of Southampton, and Baron of Titchfield.

Right Honourable,—I know not how I shall offend in dedicating my unpolisht lines to your Lordship, nor how the worlde will censure mee for choosing so strong a proppe to support so weak a burthen: onelye, if your Honour seeme but pleased, I account my selfe highly praised, and vowe to take aduantage of all idle houres, till I have honoured you with some grauer labour. But if the first heire of my inuention proue deformed, I shall be sorie it had so noble a god-father, and neuer after eare so barren a land, for feare it yeeld me still so bad a haruest. I leaue it to your Honourable suruey, and your Honor to your heart's content; which I wish may always answere your owne wish and the world's hopefull expectation.—Your Honor's in all dutie,

William Shakespeare.

Venus and Adonis

I

Even as the sun with purple-colour'd face
Had ta'en his last leave of the weeping morn,
Rose-cheek'd Adonis hied him to the chace;
Hunting he loved, but love he laugh'd to scorn; 4
  Sick-thoughted Venus makes amain unto him,
  And like a bold-faced suitor 'gins to woo him.

II

'Thrice-fairer than myself,' thus she began, 7
'The field's chief flower, sweet above compare,
Stain to all Nymphs, more lovely than a man,
More white and red than doves or roses are; 10
  Nature that made thee, with herself at strife,
  Saith that the world hath ending with thy life.

III

'Vouchsafe, thou wonder, to alight thy steed, 13
And rein his proud head to the saddle-bow;
If thou wilt deign this favour, for thy meed
A thousand honey secrets shalt thou know: 16
  Here come and sit, where never serpent hisses,
  And being set, I'll smother thee with kisses:

IV

'And yet not cloy thy lips with loath'd satiety, 19
But rather famish them amid their plenty,

Making them red, and pale, with fresh variety;
Ten kisses short as one, one long as twenty:
  A summer's day will seem an hour but short,
  Being wasted in such time-beguiling sport.'

V

With this she seizeth on his sweating palm,
The precedent of pith and livelihood,
And trembling in her passion, calls it balm,
Earth's sovereign salve, to do a goddess good:
  Being so enraged, desire doth lend her force
  Courageously to pluck him from his horse.

VI

Over one arm the lusty courser's rein,
Under her other was the tender boy,
Who blush'd, and pouted in a dull disdain,
With leaden appetite, unapt to toy;
  She red and hot as coals of glowing fire,
  He red for shame, but frosty in desire.

VII

The studded bridle on a ragged bough
Nimbly she fastens:—O, how quick is love!—
The steed is stallèd up, and even now
To tie the rider she begins to prove:
  Backward she push'd him, as she would be thrust,
  And govern'd him in strength, though not in lust.

VIII

So soon was she along as he was down,
Each leaning on their elbows and their hips:
Now doth she stroke his cheek, now doth he frown,
And 'gins to chide, but soon she stops his lips;
  And kissing speaks, with lustful language broken,
  'If thou wilt chide, thy lips shall never open.'

IX

He burns with bashful shame, she with her tears
Doth quench the maiden burning of his cheeks;
Then with her windy sighs and golden hairs
To fan, and blow them dry again she seeks:
  He saith she is immodest, blames her miss;
  What follows more she murders with a kiss.

X

Even as an empty eagle, sharp by fast,
Tires with her beak on feathers, flesh, and bone,
Shaking her wings, devouring all in haste,
Till either gorge be stuff'd or prey be gone;
  Even so she kiss'd his brow, his cheek, his chin,
  And where she ends she doth anew begin.

XI

Forced to content, but never to obey,
Panting he lies and breatheth in her face;
She feedeth on the steam as on a prey,
And calls it heavenly moisture, air of grace;
  Wishing her cheeks were gardens full of flowers,
  So they were dew'd with such distilling showers.

XII

Look, how a bird lies tangled in a net,
So fast'ned in her arms Adonis lies;
Pure shame and aw'd resistance made him fret,
Which bred more beauty in his angry eyes:
  Rain added to a river that is rank
  Perforce will force it overflow the bank.

XIII

Still she entreats, and prettily entreats,
For to a pretty, ear she tunes her tale;
Still is he sullen, still he lours and frets,

Twixt crimson shame and anger ashy-pale;
Being red, she loves him best; and being white,
Her best is better'd with a more delight.

XIV

Look how he can, she cannot choose but love;
And by her fair immortal hand she swears,
From his soft bosom never to remove,
Till he take truce with her contending tears,
Which long have rain'd, making her cheeks all wet;
And one sweet kiss shall pay this comptless debt.

XV

Upon this promise did he raise his chin,
Like a dive-dapper peering through a wave,
Who, being look'd on, ducks as quickly in;
So offers he to give what she did crave;
But when her lips were ready for his pay,
He winks, and turns his lips another way.

XVI

Never did passenger in summer's heat
More thirst for drink than she for this good turn:
Her help she sees, but help she cannot get;
She bathes in water, yet her fire must burn:
'O, pity,' 'gan she cry, 'flint-hearted boy!
'Tis but a kiss I beg; why art thou coy?

XVII

'I have been woo'd, as I entreat thee now,
Even by the stern and direful god of war,
Whose sinewy neck in battle ne'er did bow,
Who conquers where he comes in every jar;
Yet hath he been my captive and my slave,
And begg'd for that which thou unask'd shalt have.

XVIII

'Over my Altars hath he hung his lance,
His batter'd shield, his uncontrolléd crest,
And for my sake hath learn'd to sport and dance,
To toy, to wanton, dally, smile and jest,
  Scorning his churlish drum and ensign red,
  Making my arms his field, his tent my bed.

XIX

'Thus he that overruled I overswayéd,
Leading him prisoner in a red-rose chain:
Strong-temper'd steel his stronger strength obeyéd,
Yet was he servile to my coy disdain.
  O, be not proud, nor brag not of thy might,
  For mast'ring her that foil'd the god of fight!

XX

'Touch but my lips with those fair lips of thine,—
Though mine be not so fair, yet are they red—
The kiss shall be thine own as well as mine:
What seest thou in the ground? hold up thy head:
  Look in mine eye-balls, there thy beauty lies;
  Then why not lips on lips, since eyes in eyes?

XXI

'Art thou ashamed to kiss? then wink again,
And I will wink; so shall the day seem night;
Love keeps his revels where there are but twain;
Be bold to play, our sport is not in sight:
  These blue-vein'd violets whereon we lean,
  Never can blab, nor know not what we mean.

XXII

'The tender spring upon thy tempting lip
Shows thee unripe; yet mayst thou well be tasted:
Make use of time, let not advantage slip;

Beauty within itself should not be wasted: 130
Fair flowers that are not gather'd in their prime
Rot and consume themselves in little time.

XXIII

'Were I hard-favour'd, foul, or wrinkled-old, 133
Ill-nurtured, crooked, churlish, harsh in voice,
O'erworn, despiséd, rheumatic and cold,
Thick-sighted, barren, lean, and lacking juice, 136
Then mightst thou pause, for then I were not for thee;
But having no defects, why dost abhor me?

XXIV

'Thou canst not see one wrinkle in my brow; 139
Mine eyes are grey and bright and quick in turning;
My beauty as the spring doth yearly grow,
My flesh is soft and plump, my marrow burning; 142
My smooth moist hand, were it with thy hand felt,
Would in thy palm dissolve, or seem to melt.

XXV

'Bid me discourse, I will enchant thine ear, 145
Or, like a Fairy, trip upon the green,
Or, like a Nymph, with long dishevell'd hair,
Dance on the sands, and yet no footing seen: 148
Love is a spirit all compact of fire,
Not gross to sink, but light, and will aspire.

XXVI

'Witness this Primrose bank whereon I lie; 151
These forceless flowers like sturdy trees support me;
Two strengthless doves will draw me through the sky,
From morn till night, even where I list to sport me: 154
Is love so light, sweet boy, and may it be
That thou shouldst think it heavy unto thee?

XXVII

'Is thine own heart to thine own face affected? 157
Can thy right hand seize love upon thy left?
Then woo thyself, be of thyself rejected:
Steal thine own freedom, and complain on theft. 160
  Narcissus so himself himself forsook,
  And died to kiss his shadow in the brook.

XXVIII

'Torches are made to light, jewels to wear, 163
Dainties to taste, fresh beauty for the use,
Herbs for their smell, and sappy plants to bear;
Things growing to themselves are growth's abuse: 166
  Seeds spring from seeds and beauty breedeth beauty;
  Thou wast begot; to get it is thy duty.

XXIX

'Upon the earth's increase why shouldst thou feed, 169
Unless the earth with thy increase be fed?
By law of nature thou art bound to breed,
That thine may live when thou thyself art dead; 172
  And so, in spite of death, thou dost survive,
  In that thy likeness still is left alive.'

XXX

By this the love-sick Queen began to sweat, 175
For where they lay, the shadow had forsook them,
And Titan, tiréd in the mid-day heat,
With burning eye did hotly overlook them; 178
  Wishing Adonis had his team to guide,
  So he were like him and by Venus' side.

XXXI

And now Adonis, with a lazy spright, 181
And with a heavy, dark, disliking eye,
His louring brows o'erwhelming his fair sight,

Like misty vapours when they blot the sky, 184
  Souring his cheeks, cries 'Fie, no more of love!
  The sun doth burn my face; I must remove.'

XXXII

'Ay me,' quoth Venus, 'young, and so unkind? 187
What bare excuses mak'st thou to be gone!
I'll sigh celestial breath, whose gentle wind
Shall cool the heat of this descending sun: 190
  I'll make a shadow for thee of my hairs;
  If they burn too, I'll quench them with my tears.

XXXIII

'The sun that shines from heaven, shines but warm, 193
And, lo, I lie between that sun and thee:
The heat I have from thence doth little harm,
Thine eye darts forth the fire that burneth me; 196
  And were I not immortal, life were done
  Between this heavenly and earthly sun.

XXXIV

'Art thou obdúrate, flinty, hard as steel? 199
Nay, more than flint, for stone at rain relenteth:
Art thou a woman's son, and canst not feel
What 'tis to love? how want of love tormenteth? 202
  O, had thy mother borne so hard a mind,
  She had not brought forth thee, but died unkinn'd.

XXXV

'What am I, that thou shouldst contemn me this? 205
Or what great danger dwells upon my suit?
What were thy lips the worse for one poor kiss?
Speak; fair; but speak fair words, or else be mute: 208
  Give me one kiss, I'll give it thee again,
  And one for interest, if thou wilt have twain.

XXXVI

'Fie, lifeless picture, cold and senseless stone,
Well-painted idol, image dull and dead,
Statue contenting but the eye alone,
Thing like a man, but of no woman bred!
  Thou art no man, though of a man's complexion,
  For men will kiss even by their own direction.'

XXXVII

This said, impatience chokes her pleading tongue,
And swelling passion doth provoke a pause;
Red cheeks and fiery eyes blaze forth her wrong;
Being judge in love, she cannot right her cause:
  And now she weeps, and now she fain would speak,
  And now her sobs do her intendments break.

XXXVIII

Sometime she shakes her head, and then his hand,
Now gazeth she on him, now on the ground;
Sometime her arms infold him like a band:
She would, he will not in her arms be bound;
  And when from thence he struggles to be gone,
  She locks her lily fingers one in one.

XXXIX

Fondling, she saith, 'Since I have hemm'd thee here
Within the circuit of this ivory pale,
I'll be a park, and thou shalt be my deer;
Feed where thou wilt, on mountain or in dale:
  Graze on my lips; and if those hills be dry,
  Stray lower, where the pleasant fountains lie.

XL

'Within this limit is relief enough,
Sweet bottom-grass and high delightful plain,
Round rising hillocks, brakes obscure and rough,

To shelter thee from tempest and from rain:
Then be my deer, since I am such a park:
No dog shall rouse thee, though a thousand bark.

XLI

At this Adonis smiles as in disdain,
That in each cheek appears a pretty dimple;
Love made those hollows, if himself were slain,
He might be buried in a tomb so simple;
Foreknowing well, if there he came to lie,
Why, there Love lived and there he could not die.

XLII

These lovely caves, these round enchanting pits,
Open'd their mouths to swallow Venus' liking:
Being mad before, how doth she now for wits?
Struck dead at first, what needs a second striking?
Poor Queen of love, in thine own law forlorn,
To love a cheek that smiles at thee in scorn!

XLIII

Now which way shall she turn? what shall she say?
Her words are done, her woes the more increasing;
The time is spent, her object will away,
And from her twining arms doth urge releasing:
'Pity,' she cries, 'some favour, some remorse!'
Away he springs and hasteth to his horse.

XLIV

But, lo, from forth a copse that neighbours by,
A breeding jennet, lusty, young and proud,
Adonis' trampling courser doth espy,
And forth she rushes, snorts and neighs aloud:
The strong-neck'd steed, being tied unto a tree,
Breaketh his rein, and to her straight goes he.

XLV

Imperiously he leaps, he neighs, he bounds, 265
And now his woven girths he breaks asunder;
The bearing earth with his hard hoof he wounds,
Whose hollow womb resounds like heaven's thunder; 268
 The iron bit he crusheth 'tween his teeth,
 Controlling what he was controllèd with.

XLVI

His ears up-prick'd; his braided hanging mane 271
Upon his compass'd crest now stand on end;
His nostrils drink the air, and forth again,
As from a furnace, vapours doth he send: 274
 His eye, which scornfully glisters like fire,
 Shows his hot courage and his high desire.

XLVII

Sometime he trots, as if he told the steps, 277
With gentle majesty and modest pride;
Anon he rears upright, curvets, and leaps,
As who should say 'Lo, thus my strength is tried; 280
 And this I do to captivate the eye
 Of the fair breeder that is standing by.'

XLVIII

What recketh he his rider's angry stir, 283
His flattering 'Holla,' or his 'Stand, I say'?
What cares he now for curb or pricking spur?
For rich caparisons or trappings gay? 286
 He sees his love, and nothing else he sees,
 For nothing else with his proud sight agrees.

XLIX

Look, when a Painter would surpass the life, 289
In limning out a well-proportion'd steed,
His Art with Nature's workmanship at strife,

As if the dead the living should exceed; 292
So did this horse excel a common one
In shape, in courage, colour, pace, and bone.

L

Round-hoof'd, short-jointed, fetlocks shag and long, 295
Broad breast, full eye, small head, and nostril wide,
High crest, short ears, straight legs, and passing strong,
Thin mane, thick tail, broad buttock, tender hide: 298
Look, what a horse should have he did not lack,
Save a proud rider on so proud a back.

LI

Sometime he scuds far off and there he stares; 301
Anon he starts at stirring of a feather;
To bid the wind a base he now prepares,
And whe'r he run or fly they know not whether; 304
For through his mane and tail the high wind sings,
Fanning the hairs, who wave like feath'red wings.

LII

He looks upon his love, and neighs unto her; 307
She answers him as if she knew his mind:
Being proud, as females are, to see him woo her,
She puts on outward strangeness, seems unkind, 310
Spurns at his love and scorns the heat he feels,
Beating his kind embracements with her heels.

LIII

Then, like a melancholy malcontent, 313
He vails his tail that, like a falling plume,
Cool shadow to his melting buttock lent:
He stamps, and bites the poor flies in his fume. 316
His love, perceiving how he is enraged,
Grew kinder, and his fury was assuaged.

LIV

His testy master goeth about to take him; 319
When, lo, the unback'd breeder, full of fear,
Jealous of catching, swiftly doth forsake him,
With her the horse, and left Adonis there: 322
  As they were mad, unto the wood they hie them,
  Out-stripping crows that strive to over-fly them.

LV

All swoln with chafing, down Adonis sits, 325
Banning his boist'rous and unruly beast:
And now the happy season once more fits,
That love-sick Love by pleading may be blest; 328
  For lovers say, the heart hath treble wrong
  When it is barr'd the aidance of the tongue.

LVI

An oven that is stopp'd, or river stay'd, 331
Burneth more hotly, swelleth with more rage:
So of concealéd sorrow may be said;
Free vent of words love's fire doth assuage; 334
  But when the heart's attorney once is mute,
  The client breaks, as desperate in his suit.

LVII

He sees her coming, and begins to glow:— 337
Even as a dying coal revives with wind—
And with his bonnet hides his angry brow,
Looks on the dull earth with disturbéd mind: 340
  Taking no notice that she is so nigh,
  For all askance he holds her in his eye.

LVIII

O, what a sight it was, wistly to view 343
How she came stealing to the wayward boy!
To note the fighting conflict of her hue,

How white and red each other did destroy!
  But now her cheek was pale, and by and by
  It flash'd forth fire, as lightning from the sky.

LIX

Now was she just before him as he sat,
And like a lowly lover down she kneels;
With one fair hand she heaveth up his hat,
Her other tender hand his fair cheek feels:
  His tenderer cheek receives her soft hand's print,
  As apt as new-fall'n snow takes any dint.

LX

O, what a war of looks was then between them!
Her eyes petitioners to his eyes suing;
His eyes saw her eyes as they had not seen them;
Her eyes woo'd still, his eyes disdain'd the wooing:
  And all this dumb play had his acts made plain
  With tears, which, Chorus-like, her eyes did rain.

LXI

Full gently now she takes him by the hand,
A lily prison'd in a gaol of snow,
Or ivory in an alabaster band;
So white a friend engirts so white a foe:
  This beauteous combat, wilful and unwilling,
  Show'd like two silver doves that sit a-billing.

LXII

Once more the engine of her thoughts began:
'O fairest mover on this mortal round,
Would thou wert as I am, and I a man,
My heart all whole as thine, thy heart my wound;
  For one sweet look thy help I would assure thee,
  Though nothing but my body's bane would cure thee.'

LXIII

'Give me my hand,' saith he, 'why dost thou feel it?'
'Give me my heart,' saith she, 'and thou shalt have it;
O, give it me, lest thy hard heart do steel it,
And being steel'd, soft sighs can never grave it:
  Then love's deep groans I never shall regard,
  Because Adonis' heart hath made mine hard.'

LXIV

'For shame,' he cries, 'let go, and let me go;
My day's delight is past, my horse is gone,
And 'tis your fault I am bereft him so:
I pray you hence, and leave me here alone;
  For all my mind, my thought, my busy care,
  Is how to get my palfrey from the mare.'

LXV

Thus she replies: 'Thy palfrey, as he should,
Welcomes the warm approach of sweet desire:
Affection is a coal that must be cool'd,
Else, suffer'd, it will set the heart on fire,
  The sea hath bounds, but deep desire hath none;
  Therefore no marvel though thy horse be gone.

LXVI

'How like a jade he stood, tied to the tree,
Servilely master'd with a leathern rein!
But when he saw his love, his youth's fair fee,
He held such petty bondage in disdain;
  Throwing the base thong from his bending crest,
  Enfranchising his mouth, his back, his breast.

LXVII

'Who sees his true-love in her naked bed,
Teaching the sheets a whiter hue than white,
But, when his glutton eyes so full hath fed,

His other agents aim at like delight? 400
Who is so faint, that dares not be so bold
To touch the fire, the weather being cold?

LXVIII

'Let me excuse thy courser, gentle boy; 403
And learn of him, I heartily beseech thee,
To take advantage on presented joy;
Though I were dumb, yet his proceedings teach thee: 406
O, learn to love; the lesson is but plain,
And once made perfect, never lost again.'

LXIX

'I know not love,' quoth he, 'nor will not know it, 409
Unless it be a boar, and then I chase it;
'Tis much to borrow, and I will not owe it;
My love to love is love but to disgrace it; 412
For I have heard it is a life in death,
That laughs and weeps, and all but with a breath.

LXX

'Who wears a garment shapeless and unfinish'd? 415
Who plucks the bud before one leaf put forth?
If springing things be any jot diminish'd,
They wither in their prime, prove nothing worth: 418
The colt that's back'd and burthen'd being young
Loseth his pride and never waxeth strong.

LXXI

'You hurt my hand with wringing; let us part, 421
And leave this idle theme, this bootless chat:
Remove your siege from my unyielding heart;
To love's alarms it will not open the gate: 424
Dismiss your vows, your feignéd tears, your flattery;
For where a heart is hard they make no battery.'

LXXII

'What! canst thou talk?' quoth she, 'hast thou a tongue?
O, would thou hadst not, or I had no hearing!
Thy mermaid's voice hath done me double wrong;
I had my load before; now press'd with bearing,
  Melodious discord, heavenly tune harsh-sounding,
  Ear's deep-sweet music, and heart's deep-sore wounding.

LXXIII

'Had I no eyes but ears, my ears would love
That inward beauty and invisible;
Or were I deaf, thy outward parts would move
Each part in me that were but sensible:
  Though neither eyes nor ears, to hear nor see,
  Yet should I be in love by touching thee.

LXXIV

'Say, that the sense of feeling were bereft me,
And that I could not see, nor hear, nor touch,
And nothing but the very smell were left me,
Yet would my love to thee be still as much;
  For from the stillitory of thy face excelling
  Comes breath perfumed that breedeth love by smelling.

LXXV

'But, O, what banquet wert thou to the taste,
Being nurse and feeder of the other four!
Would they not wish the feast might ever last,
And bid Suspicion double-lock the door,
  Lest Jealousy, that sour unwelcome guest,
  Should by his stealing in disturb the feast?'

LXXVI

Once more the ruby-colour'd portal open'd,
Which to his speech did honey passage yield;
Like a red morn, that ever yet betoken'd

Wrack to the seaman, tempest to the field, 454
  Sorrow to shepherds, woe unto the birds,
  Gusts and foul flaws to herdmen and to herds.

LXXVII

This ill presage advisedly she marketh: 457
Even as the wind is hush'd before it raineth,
Or as the wolf doth grin before he barketh,
Or as the berry breaks before it staineth, 460
  Or like the deadly bullet of a gun,
  His meaning struck her ere his words begun.

LXXVIII

And at his look she flatly falleth down, 463
For looks kill love, and love by looks reviveth:
A smile recures the wounding of a frown;
But blessed bankrupt, that by love so thriveth! 466
  The silly boy, believing she is dead,
  Claps her pale cheek, till clapping makes it red;

LXXIX

And all amazed brake off his late intent, 469
For sharply he did think to reprehend her,
Which cunning love did wittily prevent:
Fair fall the wit that can so well defend her! 472
  For on the grass she lies as she were slain,
  Till his breath breatheth life in her again.

LXXX

He wrings her nose, he strikes her on the cheeks, 475
He bends her fingers, holds her pulses hard,
He chafes her lips; a thousand ways he seeks
To mend the hurt that his unkindness marr'd: 478
  He kisses her; and she, by her good will,
  Will never rise, so he will kiss her still.

LXXXI

The night of sorrow now is turn'd to day:
Her two blue windows faintly she up-heaveth,
Like the fair sun, when in his fresh array
He cheers the morn and all the earth relieveth;
  And as the bright sun glorifies the sky,
  So is her face illumin'd with her eye;

LXXXII

Whose beams upon his hairless face are fix'd,
As if from thence they borrow'd all their shine,
Were never four such lamps together mix'd,
Had not his clouded with his brow's repine;
  But hers, which through the crystal tears gave light,
  Shone like the Moon in water seen by night.

LXXXIII

'O, where am I?' quoth she, 'in earth or heaven,
Or in the Ocean drench'd, or in the fire?
What hour is this? or morn, or weary even?
Do I delight to die, or life desire?
  But now I liv'd, and life was death's annoy;
  But now I died, and death was lively joy.

LXXXIV

'O, thou didst kill me: kill me once again:
Thy eyes' shrewd tutor, that hard heart of thine,
Hath taught them scornful tricks, and such disdain,
That they have murder'd this poor heart of mine;
  And these mine eyes, true leaders to their queen,
  But for thy piteous lips no more had seen.

LXXXV

'Long may they kiss each other, for this cure!
O, never let their crimson liveries wear!
And as they last, their verdure still endure,

To drive infection from the dangerous year! 508
That the star-gazers, having writ on death,
May say, the plague is banish'd by thy breath.

LXXXVI

'Pure lips, sweet seals in my soft lips imprinted, 511
What bargains may I make, still to be sealing?
To sell myself I can be well contented,
So thou wilt buy, and pay, and use good dealing; 514
Which purchase if thou make, for fear of slips,
Set thy seal-manual on my wax-red lips.

LXXXVII

'A thousand kisses buys my heart from me; 517
And pay them at thy leisure, one by one.
What is ten hundred touches unto thee?
Are they not quickly told and quickly gone? 520
Say, for non-payment that the debt should double,
Is twenty hundred kisses such a trouble?'

LXXXVIII

'Fair Queen,' quoth he, 'if any love you owe me, 523
Measure my strangeness with my unripe years:
Before I know myself, seek not to know me;
No fisher but the ungrown fry forbears: 526
The mellow plum doth fall, the green sticks fast,
Or being early pluck'd is sour to taste.

LXXXIX

'Look, the world's comforter, with weary gait, 529
His day's hot task hath ended in the west;
The owl, night's herald, shrieks; 'tis very late;
The sheep are gone to fold, birds to their nest, 532
And coal-black clouds that shadow heaven's light
Do summon us to part and bid good-night.

XC

'Now let me say "Good night," and so say you; 535
If you will say so, you shall have a kiss.'
'Good night,' quoth she, and, ere he says 'Adieu,'
The honey fee of parting tender'd is: 538
  Her arms do lend his neck a sweet embrace;
  Incorporate then they seem; face grows to face.

XCI

Till breathless he disjoin'd, and backward drew 541
The heavenly moisture, that sweet coral mouth,
Whose precious taste her thirsty lips well knew,
Whereon they surfeit, yet complain on drouth: 544
  He with her plenty press'd, she faint with dearth,
  Their lips together glued, fall to the earth.

XCII

Now quick desire hath caught the yielding prey, 547
And glutton-like she feeds, yet never filleth;
Her lips are conquerors, his lips obey,
Paying what ransom the insulter willeth; 550
  Whose vulture thought doth pitch the price so high,
  That she will draw his lips' rich treasure dry.

XCIII

And having felt the sweetness of the spoil, 553
With blindfold fury she begins to forage;
Her face doth reek and smoke, her blood doth boil,
And careless lust stirs up a desperate courage, 556
  Planting oblivion, beating reason back,
  Forgetting shame's pure blush and honour's wrack.

XCIV

Hot, faint, and weary, with her hard embracing, 559
Like a wild bird being tamed with too much handling,
Or as the fleet-foot roe that 's tired with chasing,

Or like the froward infant still'd with dandling, 562
He now obeys, and now no more resisteth,
While she takes all she can, not all she listeth.

XCV

What wax so frozen but dissolves with temp'ring, 565
And yields at last to every light impression?
Things out of hope are compass'd oft with vent'ring,
Chiefly in love, whose leave exceeds commission: 568
Affection faints not like a pale-faced coward,
But then woos best when most his choice is froward.

XCVI

When he did frown, O, had she then gave over, 571
Such nectar from his lips she had not suck'd.
Foul words and frowns must not repel a lover;
What though the rose have prickles, yet 'tis pluck'd! 574
Were beauty under twenty locks kept fast,
Yet love breaks through and picks them all at last.

XCVII

For pity now she can no more detain him; 577
The poor fool prays her that he may depart:
She is resolv'd no longer to restrain him;
Bids him farewell, and look well to her heart, 580
The which, by Cupid's bow she doth protest,
He carries thence incagéd in his breast.

XCVIII

'Sweet boy,' she says, 'this night I'll waste in sorrow, 583
For my sick heart commands mine eyes to watch.
Tell me, love's master, shall we meet to-morrow?
Say, shall we? shall we? wilt thou make the match?' 586
He tells her, no; to-morrow he intends
To hunt the boar with certain of his friends.

XCIX

'The boar!' quoth she; whereat a sudden pale, 589
Like lawn being spread upon the blushing rose,
Usurps her cheek; she trembles at his tale,
And on his neck her yoking arms she throws: 592
  She sinketh down, still hanging by his neck,
  He on her belly falls, she on her back.

C

Now is she in the very lists of love, 595
Her champion mounted for the hot encounter:
All is imaginary she doth prove,
He will not manege her, although he mount her; 598
  That worse than Tantalus' is her annoy,
  To clip Elysium and to lack her joy.

CI

Even so poor birds, deceiv'd with painted grapes, 601
Do surfeit by the eye and pine the maw:
Even so she languisheth in her mishaps,
As those poor birds that helpless berries saw, 604
  The warm effects which she in him finds missing,
  She seeks to kindle with continual kissing.

CII

But all in vain; good Queen, it will not be: 607
She hath assay'd as much as may be prov'd;
Her pleading hath deserv'd a greater fee;
She's Love, she loves, and yet she is not lov'd. 610
  'Fie, fie,' he says, 'you crush me; let me go;
  You have no reason to withhold me so.'

CIII

'Thou hadst been gone,' quoth she, 'sweet boy, ere this,
But that thou told'st me thou would'st hunt the boar. 614
O, be advised: thou know'st not what it is

With javelin's point a churlish swine to gore,
  Whose tushes never sheath'd he whetteth still,
  Like to a mortal butcher bent to kill.

CIV

'On his bow-back he hath a battel set
Of bristly pikes, that ever threat his foes;
His eyes, like glow-worms, shine when he doth fret;
His snout digs sepulchres where'er he goes;
  Being moved, he strikes whate'er is in his way,
  And whom he strikes his crooked tushes slay.

CV

'His brawny sides, with hairy bristles armèd,
Are better proof than thy spear 's point can enter:
His short thick neck cannot be easily harmèd;
Being ireful, on the lion he will venture:
  The thorny brambles and embracing bushes,
  As fearful of him, part; through whom he rushes.

CVI

'Alas, he nought esteems that face of thine,
To which Love's eyes pay tributary gazes;
Nor thy soft hands, sweet lips and crystal eyne,
Whose full perfection all the world amazes;
  But having thee at vantage,—wondrous dread!—
  Would root these beauties as he roots the mead.

CVII

'O, let him keep his loathsome cabin still;
Beauty hath nought to do with such foul fiends:
Come not within his danger by thy will;
They that thrive well take counsel of their friends.
  When thou didst name the boar, not to dissemble,
  I fear'd thy fortune, and my joints did tremble.

CVIII

'Didst thou not mark my face? was it not white? 643
Saw'st thou not signs of fear lurk in mine eye?
Grew I not faint? and fell I not downright?
Within my bosom, whereon thou dost lie, 646
  My boding heart pants, beats, and takes no rest,
  But, like an earthquake, shakes thee on my breast.

CIX

'For where Love reigns, disturbing Jealousy 649
Doth call himself affection's sentinel;
Gives false alarms, suggesteth mutiny,
And in a peaceful hour doth cry "Kill, kill!" 652
  Distemp'ring gentle Love in his desire,
  As air and water do abate the fire.

CX

'This sour informer, this bate-breeding spy, 655
This canker that eats up Love's tender spring,
This carry-tale, dissentious Jealousy,
That sometime true news, sometime false doth bring, 658
  Knocks at my heart and whispers in mine ear
  That if I love thee, I thy death should fear:

CXI

'And more than so, presenteth to mine eye 661
The picture of an angry, chafing boar,
Under whose sharp fangs on his back doth lie
An image like thyself, all stain'd with gore; 664
  Whose blood upon the fresh flowers being shed
  Doth make them droop with grief and hang the head.

CXII

'What should I do, seeing thee, so indeed, 667
That tremble at th' imagination?
The thought of it doth make my faint heart bleed,

And fear doth teach it divination: 670
I prophesy thy death, my living sorrow,
If thou encounter with the boar to-morrow.

CXIII

'But if thou needs wilt hunt, be ruled by me; 673
Uncouple at the timorous flying hare,
Or at the fox which lives by subtilty,
Or at the roe which no encounter dare: 676
Pursue these fearful creatures o'er the downs,
And on thy well-breath'd horse keep with thy hounds.

CXIV

'And when thou hast on foot the purblind hare, 679
Mark the poor wretch, to overshut his troubles,
How he outruns the wind, and with what care
He cranks and crosses with a thousand doubles: 682
The many musits through the which he goes
Are like a labyrinth to amaze his foes

CXV

'Sometime he runs among a flock of sheep, 685
To make the cunning hounds mistake their smell;
And sometime where earth-delving conies keep,
To stop the loud pursuers in their yell; 688
And sometime sorteth with a herd of deer:
Danger deviseth shifts; wit waits on fear:

CXVI

'For there his smell with others being mingled, 691
The hot scent-snuffing hounds are driven to doubt,
Ceasing their clamorous cry, till they have singled
With much ado the cold fault cleanly out; 694
Then do they spend their mouths: Echo replies,
As if another chase were in the skies.

CXVII

'By this, poor Wat, far off upon a hill,
Stands on his hinder legs with listening ear,
To hearken if his foes pursue him still:
Anon their loud alarums he doth hear;
  And now his grief may be comparéd well
  To one sore sick that hears the passing-bell.

CXVIII

'Then shalt thou see the dew-bedabbled wretch
Turn, and return, indenting with the way;
Each envious brier his weary legs doth scratch,
Each shadow makes him stop, each murmur stay:
  For misery is trodden on by many,
  And being low never relieved by any.

CXIX

'Lie quietly, and hear a little more;
Nay, do not struggle, for thou shalt not rise:
To make thee hate the hunting of the boar,
Unlike myself thou hear'st me moralize,
  Applying this to that, and so to so;
  For love can comment upon every woe.

CXX

'Where did I leave?' 'No matter where;' quoth he,
'Leave me, and then the story aptly ends:
The night is spent.' 'Why, what of that?' quoth she.
'I am,' quoth he, 'expected of my friends;
  And now 'tis dark, and going I shall fall.'
  'In night,' quoth she, 'desire sees best of all.

CXXI

'But if thou fall, O, then imagine this,
The earth, in love with thee, thy footing trips,
And all is but to rob thee of a kiss.

Rich preys make true men thieves; so do thy lips 724
  Make modest Dian cloudy and forlorn,
  Lest she should steal a kiss and die forsworn.

CXXII

'Now of this dark night I perceive the reason: 727
Cynthia for shame obscures her silver shine,
Till forging Nature be condemn'd of treason,
For stealing moulds from heaven that were divine; 730
  Wherein she framed thee in high heaven's despite,
  To shame the sun by day and her by night.

CXXIII

'And therefore hath she bribed the Destinies 733
To cross the curious workmanship of nature,
To mingle beauty with infirmities,
And pure perfection with impure defeature, 736
  Making it subject to the tyranny
  Of mad mischances and much misery;

CXXIV

'As burning fevers, agues pale and faint, 739
Life-poisoning pestilence and frenzies wood,
The marrow-eating sickness, whose attaint
Disorder breeds by heating of the blood: 742
  Surfeits, imposthumes, grief, and damn'd despair,
  Swear Nature's death for framing thee so fair.

CXXV

'And not the least of all these maladies 745
But in one minute's fight brings beauty under:
Both favour, savour, hue, and qualities,
Whereat th' impartial gazer late did wonder, 748
  Are on the sudden wasted, thaw'd, and done,
  As mountain snow melts with the midday sun.

CXXVI

'Therefore, despite of fruitless chastity, 751
Love-lacking vestals and self-loving nuns,
That on the earth would breed a scarcity
And barren dearth of daughters and of sons, 754
  Be prodigal: the lamp that burns by night
  Dries up his oil to lend the world his light.

CXXVII

'What is thy body but a swallowing grave, 757
Seeming to bury that posterity
Which by the rights of time thou needs must have,
If thou destroy them not in dark obscurity? 760
  If so, the world will hold thee in disdain,
  Sith in thy pride so fair a hope is slain.

CXXVIII

'So in thyself thyself art made away; 763
A mischief worse than civil home-bred strife,
Or theirs whose desperate hands themselves do slay,
Or butcher-sire that reaves his son of life. 766
  Foul-cankering rust the hidden treasure frets,
  But gold that 's put to use more gold begets.'

CXXIX

'Nay, then,' quoth Adon, 'you will fall again 769
Into your idle over-handled theme:
The kiss I gave you is bestow'd in vain,
And all in vain you strive against the stream; 772
  For, by this black-faced night, desire's foul nurse,
  Your treatise makes me like you worse and worse.

CXXX

'If love have lent you twenty thousand tongues, 775
And every tongue more moving than your own,
Bewitching like the wanton Mermaid's songs,

Yet from mine ear the tempting tune is blown; 778
For know, my heart stands armed in mine ear,
And will not let a false sound enter there;

CXXXI

'Lest the deceiving harmony should run 781
Into the quiet closure of my breast;
And then my little heart were quite undone,
In his bedchamber to be barr'd of rest. 784
No, Lady, no; my heart longs not to groan,
But soundly sleeps, while how it sleeps alone.

CXXXII

'What have you urged that I cannot reprove? 787
The path is smooth that leadeth on to danger:
I hate not love, but your device in love,
That lends embracements unto every stranger. 790
You do it for increase: O strange excuse,
When reason is the bawd to lust's abuse!

CXXXIII

'Call it not love, for Love to heaven is fled, 793
Since sweating Lust on earth usurp'd his name;
Under whose simple semblance he hath fed
Upon fresh beauty, blotting it with blame; 796
Which the hot tyrant stains and soon bereaves,
As caterpillars do the tender leaves.

CXXXIV

'Love comforteth like sunshine after rain, 799
But Lust's effect is tempest after sun;
Love's gentle spring doth always fresh remain,
Lust's winter comes ere summer half be done; 802
Love surfeits not, Lust like a glutton dies;
Love is all truth, Lust full of forgéd lies.

CXXXV

'More I could tell, but more I dare not say;
The text is old, the Orator too green.
Therefore, in sadness, now I will away;
My face is full of shame, my heart of teen:
  Mine ears, that to your wanton talk attended,
  Do burn themselves for having so offended.'

CXXXVI

With this, he breaketh from the sweet embrace
Of those fair arms which bound him to her breast,
And homeward through the dark lawnd runs apace;
Leaves Love upon her back, deeply distress'd:
  —Look, how a bright star shooteth from the sky,
  So glides he in the night from Venus' eye—

CXXXVII

Which after him she darts, as one on shore
Gazing upon a late-embarkéd friend,
Till the wild waves will have him seen no more,
Whose ridges with the meeting clouds contend:
  So did the merciless and pitchy night
  Fold in the object that did feed her sight.

CXXXVIII

Whereat amazed, as one that unaware
Hath dropp'd a precious jewel in the flood,
Or stonish'd as night-wand'rers often are,
Their light blown out in some mistrustful wood;
  Even so confounded in the dark she lay,
  Having lost the fair discovery of her way.

CXXXIX

And now she beats her heart, whereat it groans,
That all the neighbour caves, as seeming troubled,
Make verbal repetition of her moans;

Passion on passion deeply is redoubled: 832
'Ay me!' she cries, and twenty times 'Woe, woe!'
And twenty echoes twenty times cry so.

CXL

She marking them begins a wailing note, 835
And sings extemporally a woeful ditty;
How love makes young men thrall, and old men dote;
How love is wise in folly, foolish-witty: 838
Her heavy anthem still concludes in woe,
And still the choir of echoes answer so.

CXLI

Her song was tedious, and outwore the night, 841
For lovers' hours are long, though seeming short:
If pleas'd themselves, others, they think, delight
In such like circumstance, with such like sport: 844
Their copious stories, oftentimes begun,
End without audience, and are never done.

CXLII

For who hath she to spend the night withal 847
But idle sounds resembling parasites,
Like shrill-tongued tapsters answering every call,
Soothing the humour of fantastic wits? 850
She says ''Tis so:' they answer all ''Tis so;'
And would say after her, if she said 'No.'

CXLIII

Lo, here the gentle lark, weary of rest, 853
From his moist cabinet mounts up on high,
And wakes the morning, from whose silver breast
The sun ariseth in his majesty; 856
Who doth the world so gloriously behold
That Cedar-tops and hills seem burnish'd gold.

CXLIV

Venus salutes him with this fair good-morrow: 859
'O thou clear god, and patron of all light,
From whom each lamp and shining star doth borrow
The beauteous influence that makes him bright, 862
  There lives a son that suck'd an earthly mother,
  May lend thee light, as thou dost lend to other.'

CXLV

This said, she hasteth to a myrtle grove, 865
Musing the morning is so much o'erworn,
And yet she hears no tidings of her love:
She hearkens for his hounds, and for his horn: 868
  Anon she hears them chant it lustily,
  And all in haste she coasteth to the cry.

CXLVI

And, as she runs the bushes in the way, 871
Some catch her by the neck, some kiss her face,
Some twined about her thigh to make her stay:
She wildly breaketh from their strict embrace, 874
  Like a milch doe, whose swelling dugs do ache,
  Hasting to feed her fawn hid in some brake.

CXLVII

By this, she hears the hounds are at a bay; 877
Whereat she starts, like one that spies an adder
Wreath'd up in fatal folds just in his way,
The fear whereof doth make him shake and shudder; 880
  Even so the timorous yelping of the hounds
  Appals her senses and her spirit confounds.

CXLVIII

For now she knows it is no gentle chase, 883
But the blunt boar, rough bear, or lion proud,
Because the cry remaineth in one place,

Where fearfully the dogs exclaim aloud:
  Finding their enemy to be so curst,
  They all strain court'sy who shall cope him first.

CXLIX

This dismal cry rings sadly in her ear,
Through which it enters to surprise her heart;
Who, overcome by doubt and bloodless fear,
With cold-pale weakness numbs each feeling part:
  Like soldiers, when their captain once doth yield,
  They basely fly, and dare not stay the field.

CL

Thus stands she in a trembling ecstasy;
Till, cheering up her senses all dismay'd,
She tells them 'tis a causeless fantasy,
And childish error, that they are afraid;
  Bids them leave quaking, bids them fear no more:—
  And with that word she spied the hunted boar;

CLI

Whose frothy mouth, bepainted all with red,
Like milk and blood being mingled both together,
A second fear through all her sinews spread,
Which madly hurries her, she knows not whither:
  This way she runs, and now she will no further,
  But back retires to rate the boar for murther.

CLII

A thousand spleens bear her a thousand ways;
She treads the path that she untreads again;
Her more than haste is mated with delays,
Like the proceedings of a drunken brain,
  Full of respects, yet naught at all respecting;
  In hand with all things, nought at all effecting.

CLIII

Here kennell'd in a brake she finds a hound,
And asks the weary caitiff for his master,
And there another licking of his wound,
'Gainst venom'd sores the only sovereign plaster;
  And here she meets another sadly scowling,
  To whom she speaks, and he replies with howling.

CLIV

When he hath ceased his ill-resounding noise,
Another flap-mouth'd mourner, black and grim,
Against the welkin volleys out his voice;
Another and another answer him,
  Clapping their proud tails to the ground below,
  Shaking their scratch'd ears, bleeding as they go.

CLV

Look, how the world's poor people are amazéd
At apparitions, signs, and prodigies,
Whereon with fearful eyes they long have gazéd,
Infusing them with dreadful prophecies;
  So she at these sad signs draws up her breath
  And sighing it again, exclaims on Death.

CLVI

'Hard-favour'd tyrant, ugly, meagre, lean,
Hateful divorce of love,'—thus chides she Death,—
'Grim-grinning ghost, earth's worm, what dost thou mean
To stifle beauty and to steal his breath,
  Who when he lived, his breath and beauty set
  Gloss on the rose, smell to the violet?

CLVII

'If he be dead,—O no, it cannot be,
Seeing his beauty, thou shouldst strike at it:—
O yes, it may; thou hast no eyes to see,

But hatefully at random dost thou hit.
  Thy mark is feeble age, but thy false dart
  Mistakes that aim and cleaves an infant's heart.

CLVIII

'Hadst thou but bid beware, then he had spoke,
And, hearing him, thy power had lost his power.
The Destinies will curse thee for this stroke;
They bid thee crop a weed, thou pluck'st a flower:
  Love's golden arrow at him should have fled,
  And not Death's ebon dart, to strike him dead.

CLIX

'Dost thou drink tears, that thou provok'st such weeping?
What may a heavy groan advantage thee?
Why hast thou cast into eternal sleeping
Those eyes that taught all other eyes to see?
  Now Nature cares not for thy mortal vigour,
  Since her best work is ruin'd with thy rigour.'

CLX

Here overcome, as one full of despair,
She vail'd her eyelids, who, like sluices, stopt
The crystal tide that from her two cheeks fair
In the sweet channel of her bosom dropt;
  But through the flood-gates breaks the silver rain,
  And with his strong course opens them again.

CLXI

O, how her eyes and tears did lend and borrow!
Her eye seen in the tears, tears in her eye;
Both crystals, where they view'd each other's sorrow:
Sorrow that friendly sighs sought still to dry;
  But like a stormy day, now wind, now rain,
  Sighs dry her cheeks, tears make them wet again.

CLXII

Variable passions throng her constant woe, 967
As striving who should best become her grief;
All entertain'd, each passion labours so,
That every present sorrow seemeth chief, 970
  But none is best: then join they all together,
  Like many clouds consulting for foul weather.

CLXIII

By this, far off she hears some huntsman halloo; 973
A nurse's song ne'er pleased her babe so well:
The dire imagination she did follow
This sound of hope doth labour to expel; 976
  For now reviving joy bids her rejoice,
  And flatters her it is Adonis' voice.

CLXIV

Whereat her tears began to turn their tide, 979
Being prison'd in her eye, like pearls in glass;
Yet sometimes falls an orient drop beside,
Which her cheek melts, as scorning it should pass 982
  To wash the foul face of the sluttish ground,
  Who is but drunken when she seemeth drown'd.

CLXV

O hard-believing love, how strange it seems!— 985
Not to believe, and yet too credulous:
Thy weal and woe are both of them extremes;
Despair and hope makes thee ridiculous: 988
  The one doth flatter thee in thoughts unlikely,
  In likely thoughts the other kills thee quickly.

CLXVI

Now she unweaves the web that she hath wrought; 991
Adonis lives, and Death is not to blame;
It was not she that call'd him all to nought:

Now she adds honours to his hateful name;
She clepes him king of graves, and grave for kings,
Imperious, supreme of all mortal things.

CLXVII

'No, no,' quoth she, 'sweet Death, I did but jest;
Yet pardon me, I felt a kind of fear
When as I met the boar, that bloody beast,
Which knows no pity, but is still severe;
Then, gentle shadow,—truth I must confess,—
I rail'd on thee, fearing my love's decease.

CLXVIII

''Tis not my fault: the boar provok'd my tongue;
Be wreak'd on him, invisible commander;
'Tis he, foul creature, that hath done thee wrong;
I did but act, he 's author of thy slander:
Grief hath two tongues, and never woman yet
Could rule them both without ten women's wit.'

CLXIX

Thus hoping that Adonis is alive,
Her rash suspect she doth extenuate;
And that his beauty may the better thrive,
With Death she humbly doth insinuate;
Tells him of trophies, statues, tombs, and stories
His victories, his triumphs and his glories.

CLXX

'O Jove,' quoth she, 'how much a fool was I,
To be of such a weak and silly mind,
To wail his death who lives, and must not die
Till mutual overthrow of mortal kind!
For he being dead, with him is beauty slain,
And, beauty dead, black Chaos comes again.

CLXXI

'Fie, fie, fond love, thou art so full of fear 1021
As one with treasure laden, hemm'd with thieves;
Trifles unwitnesséd with eye, or ear,
Thy coward heart with false bethinking grieves.' 1024
  Even at this word she hears a merry horn,
  Whereat she leaps that was but late forlorn.

CLXXII

As falcons to the lure, away she flies; 1027
The grass stoops not, she treads on it so light;
And in her haste unfortunately spies
The foul boar's conquest on her fair delight; 1030
  Which seen, her eyes, as murder'd with the view,
  Like stars ashamed of day, themselves withdrew;

CLXXIII

Or, as the snail, whose tender horns being hit, 1033
Shrinks backward in his shelly cave with pain,
And there, all smother'd up, in shade doth sit,
Long after fearing to creep forth again; 1036
  So, at his bloody view, her eyes are fled
  Into the deep dark cabins of her head:

CLXXIV

Where they resign their office and their light 1039
To the disposing of her troubled brain;
Who bids them still consort with ugly night,
And never wound the heart with looks again; 1042
  Who, like a king perplexéd in his throne,
  By their suggestion gives a deadly groan.

CLXXV

Whereat each tributary subject quakes; 1045
As when the wind, imprison'd in the ground,
Struggling for passage, earth's foundation shakes,

Which with cold terror doth men's minds confound.
  This mutiny each part doth so surprise,
  That from their dark beds once more leap her eyes;

CLXXVI

And, being open'd, threw unwilling light
Upon the wide wound that the boar had trench'd
In his soft flank; whose wonted lily white
With purple tears, that his wound wept, was drench'd:
  No flower was nigh, no grass, herb, leaf, or weed,
  But stole his blood and seem'd with him to bleed.

CLXXVII

This solemn sympathy poor Venus noteth;
Over one shoulder doth she hang her head;
Dumbly she passions, franticly she doteth;
She thinks he could not die, he is not dead:
  Her voice is stopt, her joints forget to bow;
  Her eyes are mad that they have wept till now.

CLXXVIII

Upon his hurt she looks so steadfastly,
That her sight dazzling makes the wound seem three;
And then she reprehends her mangling eye,
That makes more gashes where no breach should be:
  His face seems twain, each several limb is doubled;
  For oft the eye mistakes, the brain being troubled.

CLXXIX

'My tongue cannot express my grief for one,
And yet,' quoth she, 'behold two Adons dead!
My sighs are blown away, my salt tears gone,
Mine eyes are turn'd to fire, my heart to lead:
  Heavy heart's lead, melt at mine eyes' red fire!
  So shall I die by drops of hot desire.

CLXXX

'Alas, poor world, what treasure hast thou lost!
What face remains alive that's worth the viewing?
Whose tongue is music now? what canst thou boast
Of things long since, or any thing ensuing?
  The flowers are sweet, their colours fresh and trim;
  But true, sweet beauty liv'd and died with him.

CLXXXI

'Bonnet nor veil henceforth no creature wear!
Nor sun nor wind will ever strive to kiss you:
Having no fair to lose, you need not fear;
The sun doth scorn you and the wind doth hiss you:
  But when Adonis liv'd, sun and sharp air
  Lurk'd like two thieves, to rob him of his fair:

CLXXXII

'And therefore would he put his bonnet on,
Under whose brim the gaudy sun would peep;
The wind would blow it off and, being gone,
Play with his locks : then would Adonis weep;
  And straight, in pity of his tender years,
  They both would strive who first should dry his tears.

CLXXXIII

'To see his face the lion walk'd along
Behind some hedge, because he would not fear him;
To recreate himself when he hath sung,
The tiger would be tame and gently hear him;
  If he had spoke, the wolf would leave his prey
  And never fright the silly lamb that day.

CLXXXIV

'When he beheld his shadow in the brook,
The fishes spread on it their golden gills;
When he was by, the birds such pleasure took,

That some would sing, some other in their bills
Would bring him mulberries and ripe-red cherries;
He fed them with his sight, they him with berries.

CLXXXV

'But this foul, grim, and urchin-snouted boar,
Whose downward eye still looketh for a grave,
Ne'er saw the beauteous livery that he wore;
Witness the entertainment that he gave:
If he did see his face, why then I know
He thought to kiss him, and hath killed him so.

CLXXXVI

''Tis true, 'tis true; thus was Adonis slain:
He ran upon the boar with his sharp spear,
Who did not whet his teeth at him again,
But by a kiss thought to persuade him there;
And nuzzling in his flank, the loving swine
Sheath'd unaware the tusk in his soft groin.

CLXXXVII

'Had I been tooth'd like him, I must confess,
With kissing him I should have kill'd him first;
But he is dead, and never did he bless
My youth with his; the more am I accurst.'
With this, she falleth in the place she stood,
And stains her face with his congealéd blood.

CLXXXVIII

She looks upon his lips, and they are pale;
She takes him by the hand, and that is cold;
She whispers in his ears a heavy tale,
As if they heard the woeful words she told;
She lifts the coffer-lids that close his eyes,
Where, lo, two lamps, burnt out, in darkness lies;

CLXXXIX

Two glasses, where herself herself beheld 1129
A thousand times, and now no more reflect;
Their virtue lost, wherein they late excell'd,
And every beauty robb'd of his effect: 1132
'Wonder of time,' quoth she, 'this is my spite,
That, thou being dead, the day should yet be light.

CXC

'Since thou art dead, lo, here I prophesy: 1135
Sorrow on love hereafter shall attend:
It shall be waited on with jealousy,
Find sweet beginning, but unsavoury end; 1138
Ne'er settled equally, but high or low,
That all love's pleasure shall not match his woe.

CXCI

'It shall be fickle, false and full of fraud, 1141
Bud, and be blasted, in a breathing-while;
The bottom poison, and the top o'erstraw'd
With sweets that shall the truest sight beguile: 1144
The strongest body shall it make most weak,
Strike the wise dumb and teach the fool to speak.

CXCII

'It shall be sparing and too full of riot, 1147
Teaching decrepit age to tread the measures;
The staring ruffian shall it keep in quiet,
Pluck down the rich, enrich the poor with treasures; 1150
It shall be raging-mad and silly-mild,
Make the young old, the old become a child.

CXCIII

'It shall suspect where is no cause of fear; 1153
It shall not fear where it should most mistrust;
It shall be merciful and too severe,

And most deceiving when it seems most just; 1156
  Perverse it shall be where it shows most toward,
  Put fear to valour, courage to the coward.

CXCIV

'It shall be cause of war and dire events, 1159
And set dissension 'twixt the son and sire;
Subject and servile to all discontents,
As dry combustious matter is to fire: 1162
  Sith in his prime Death doth my love destroy,
  They that love best their loves shall not enjoy.'

CXCV

By this, the boy that by her side lay kill'd 1165
Was melted like a vapour from her sight,
And in his blood that on the ground lay spill'd,
A purple flower sprung up, chequer'd with white, 1168
  Resembling well his pale cheeks and the blood
  Which in round drops upon their whiteness stood.

CXCVI

She bows her head, the new-sprung flower to smell, 1171
Comparing it to her Adonis' breath,
And says, within her bosom it shall dwell,
Since he himself is reft from her by death: 1174
  She crops the stalk, and in the breach appears
  Green dropping sap, which she compares to tears.

CXCVII

'Poor flower,' quoth she, 'this was thy father's guise— 1177
Sweet issue of a more sweet-smelling sire—
For every little grief to wet his eyes:
To grow unto himself was his desire, 1180
  And so 'tis thine; but know, it is as good
  To wither in my breast as in his blood.

CXCVIII

'Here was thy father's bed, here in my breast;
Thou art the next of blood, and 'tis thy right:
Lo, in this hollow cradle take thy rest,
My throbbing heart shall rock thee day and night:
  There shall not be one minute in an hour
  Wherein I will not kiss my sweet love's flower.'

CXCIX

Thus weary of the world, away she hies,
And yokes her silver doves; by whose swift aid,
Their mistress, mounted through the empty skies
In her light chariot, quickly is convey'd;
  Holding their course to Paphos, where their queen
  Means to immure herself and not be seen.

The Rape of Lucrece

TO THE

RIGHT HONOURABLE HENRY WRIOTHESLEY,

Earle of Southampton, and Baron of Titchfield.

The loue I dedicate to your Lordship is without end: whereof this Pamphlet without beginning is but a superfluous Moity. The warrant I haue of your Honourable disposition, not the worth of my untutord Lines makes it assured of acceptance. What I haue done is yours, what I haue to doe is yours, being part in all I haue, devoted yours. Were my worth greater, my duety would shew greater, meane time, as it is, it is bound to your Lordship; To whom I wish long life still lengthned with all happinesse.

Your Lordship's in all duety,

William Shakespeare.

THE ARGUMENT

Lucius Tarquinius, for his excessive pride surnamed Superbus, after he had caused his own father-in-law Servius Tullius to be cruelly murdered, and, contrary to the Roman laws and customs, not requiring or staying for the people's suffrages, had possessed himself of the kingdom, went, accompanied with his sons and other noblemen of Rome, to besiege Ardea. During which siege the principal men of the army meeting one evening at the tent of Sextus Tarquinius, the king's son, in their discourses after supper every one commended the virtues of his own wife: among whom Collatinus extolled the incomparable chastity of his wife Lueretia. In that pleasant humour they all posted to Rome; and intending, by their secret and sudden arrival, to make trial of that which every one had before avouched, only Collatinus finds his wife, though it were late in the night, spinning amongst her maids: the other ladies were all found dancing and revelling, or in several disports. Whereupon the noblemen yielded Collatinus the victory, and his wife the fame. At that time Sextus Tarquinius being inflamed with Lucrece' beauty, yet smothering his passions for the present, departed with the rest back to the camp; from whence he shortly after privily withdrew himself, and was, according to his estate, royally entertained and lodged by Lucrece at Collatium. The same night he treacherously stealeth into her chamber, violently ravished her, and early in the morning speedeth away. Lucrece, in this lamentable plight, hastily dispatcheth messengers, one to Rome for her father, another to the camp for Collatine. They came, the one accompanied with Junius Brutus, the other with Publius Valerius; and finding Lucrece attired in mourning habit, demanded the cause of her sorrow. She, first taking an oath of them for her revenge, revealed the actor, and whole manner of his dealing, and withal suddenly stabbed herself. Which done, with one consent they all vowed to root out the whole hated family of the Tarquins; and bearing the dead body to Rome, Brutus acquainted the people with the doer and manner of the vile deed, with a bitter invective against the tyranny of the king: wherewith the people were so moved, that with one consent and a general acclamation the Tarquins were all exiled, and the state government changed from kings to consuls.

The Rape of Lucrece

I

From the besieged Ardea all in post,
Borne by the trustless wings of false desire,
Lust-breathéd Tarquin leaves the Roman host,
And to Collatium bears the lightless fire
Which, in pale embers hid, lurks to aspire
  And girdle with embracing flames the waist
  Of Collatine's fair love, Lucrece the chaste.

II

Haply that name of 'chaste' unhaply set
This bateless edge on his keen appetite;
When Collatine unwisely did not let
To praise the clear unmatchéd red and white
Which triumph'd in that sky of his delight,
  Where mortal stars, as bright as heaven's Beauties,
  With pure aspects did him peculiar duties.

III

For he the night before, in Tarquin's tent,
Unlock'd the treasure of his happy state;
What priceless wealth the heavens had him lent
In the possession of his beauteous mate;
Reck'ning his fortune at such high-proud rate,
  That Kings might be espouséd to more fame,
  But King nor Peer to such a peerless dame.

IV

O happiness enjoy'd but of a few! 22
And, if possess'd, as soon decay'd and done
As is the morning's silver-melting dew
Against the golden splendour of the Sun!
An éxpired date, cancell'd ere well begun; 26
Honour and Beauty, in the owner's arms,
Are weakly fortress'd from a world of harms.

V

Beauty itself doth of itself persuade 29
The eyes of men without an Orator;
What needeth then apologies be made,
To set forth that which is so singular?
Or why is Collatine the publisher 33
Of that rich jewel he should keep unknown
From thievish ears, because it is his own?

VI

Perchance his boast of Lucrece' Sov'reignty 36
Suggested this proud issue of a King;
For by our ears our hearts oft tainted be:
Perchance that envy of so rich a thing,
Braving compare, disdainfully did sting 40
His high-pitch'd thoughts, that meaner men should vaunt
That golden hap which their superiors want.

VII

But some untimely thought did instigate 43
His all-too-timeless speed, if none of those:
His honour, his affairs, his friends, his state,
Neglected all, with swift intent he goes
To quench the coal which in his liver glows. 47
O rash false heat, wrapp'd in repentant cold,
Thy hasty spring still blasts, and ne'er grows old!

VIII

When at Collatium this false Lord arrivéd, 50
Well was he welcom'd by the Roman dame,
Within whose face Beauty and Virtue strivéd
Which of them both should underprop her fame:
When Virtue bragg'd, Beauty would blush for shame; 54
  When Beauty boasted blushes, in despite
  Virtue would stain that or with silver white.

IX

But Beauty, in that white intituléd 57
From Venus' doves, doth challenge that fair field:
Then Virtue claims from Beauty, Beauty's red,
Which Virtue gave the golden age, to gild
Their silver cheeks, and call'd it then their shield; 61
  Teaching them thus to use it in the fight,
  When shame assail'd, the red should fence the white.

X

This Heraldry in Lucrece' face was seen, 64
Argued by Beauty's red and Virtue's white:
Of either's colour was the other Queen,
Proving from world's minority their right:
Yet their ambition makes them still to fight; 68
  The sovereignty of either being so great,
  That oft they interchange each other's seat.

XI

This silent war of Lilies and of Roses, 71
Which Tarquin view'd in her fair face's field,
In their pure ranks his traitor eye encloses;
Where, lest between them both it should be kill'd,
The coward captive vanquishéd doth yield 75
  To those two armies that would let him go,
  Rather than triumph in so false a foe.

XII

Now thinks he that her husband's shallow tongue,— 78
The niggard prodigal that praised her so,—
In that high task hath done her beauty wrong,
Which far exceeds his barren skill to show:
Therefore that praise which Collatine doth owe, 82
  Enchanted Tarquin answers with surmise,
  In silent wonder of still gazing eyes.

XIII

This earthly saint, adoréd by this devil, 85
Little suspecteth the false worshipper;
For 'unstain'd thoughts do seldom dream on evil';
'Birds never limed no secret bushes fear';
So guiltless she securely gives good cheer 89
  And reverend welcome to her princely guest,
  Whose inward ill no outward harm express'd:

XIV

For that he colour'd with his high estate, 92
Hiding base sin in pleats of Majesty;
That nothing in him seem'd inordinate,
Save sometime too much wonder of his eye,
Which, having all, all could not satisfy; 96
  But, poorly rich, so wanteth in his store,
  That, cloy'd with much, he pineth still for more.

XV

But she, that never coped with stranger eyes, 99
Could pick no meaning from their parling looks,
Nor read the subtle-shining secrecies
Writ in the glassy margents of such books:
She touch'd no unknown baits, nor fear'd no hooks; 103
  Nor could she moralize his wanton sight,
  More than his eyes were open'd to the light

XVI

He stories to her ears her husband's fame,
Won in the fields of fruitful Italy;
And decks with praises Collatine's high name,
Made glorious by his manly chivalry
With bruiséd arms and wreaths of victory:
  Her joy with heaved-up hand she doth express,
  And, wordless, so greets heaven for his success.

XVII

Far from the purpose of his coming thither,
He makes excuses for his being there:
No cloudy show of stormy blust'ring weather
Doth yet in his fair welkin once appear;
Till sable Night, mother of dread and fear,
  Upon the world dim darkness doth display,
  And in her vaulty prison stows the day.

XVIII

For then is Tarquin brought unto his bed,
Intending weariness with heavy spright;
For, after supper, long he questionéd
With modest Lucrece, and wore out the night:
Now leaden slumber with life's strength doth fight;
  And every one to rest themselves betake,
  Save thieves, and cares, and troubled minds, that wake.

XIX

As one of which doth Tarquin lie revolving
The sundry dangers of his will's obtaining;
Yet ever to obtain his will resolving,
Though weak-built hopes persuade him to abstaining:
Despair to gain doth traffic oft for gaining,
  And when great treasure is the meed proposéd,
  Though death be adjunct, there 's no death supposéd.

XX

Those that much covet are with gain so fond 134
That what they have not, that which they possess,
They scatter and unloose it from their bond,
And so, by hoping more, they have but less;
Or, gaining more, the profit of excess 138
  Is but to surfeit, and such griefs sustain,
  That they prove bankrupt in this poor-rich gain.

XXI

The aim of all is but to nurse the life 141
With honour, wealth, and ease in waning age;
And in this aim there is such thwarting strife,
That one for all, or all for one we gage;
As life for honour in fell battle's rage; 145
  Honour for wealth; and oft that wealth doth cost
  The death of all, and all together lost.

XXII

So that in venturing ill we leave to be 148
The things we are for that which we expect;
And this ambitious, foul infirmity,
In having much, torments us with defect
Of that we have: so then we do neglect 152
  The thing we have, and, all for want of wit,
  Make something nothing by augmenting it.

XXIII

Such hazard now must doting Tarquin make, 155
Pawning his honour to obtain his lust;
And for himself himself he must forsake:
Then where is truth, if there be no self-trust?
When shall he think to find a stranger just, 159
  When he himself himself confounds, betrays
  To slanderous tongues and wretched hateful days?

XXIV

Now stole upon the time the dead of night, 162
When heavy sleep had closed up mortal eyes:
No comfortable star did lend his light,
No noise but owls' and wolves' death-boding cries;
Now serves the season that they may surprise 166
  The silly lambs: pure thoughts are dead and still,
  While Lust and Murder wakes to stain and kill.

XXV

And now this lustful Lord leap'd from his bed, 169
Throwing his mantle rudely o'er his arm;
Is madly toss'd between Desire and Dread;
Th' one sweetly flatters, th' other feareth harm;
But honest Fear, bewitch'd with Lust's foul charm, 173
  Doth too too oft betake him to retire,
  Beaten away by brain-sick rude desire.

XXVI

His falchion on a flint he softly smiteth, 176
That from the cold stone sparks of fire do fly;
Whereat a waxen torch forthwith he lighteth,
Which must be lode-star to his lustful eye;
And to the flame thus speaks advisedly, 180
  'As from this cold flint I enforced this fire,
  So Lucrece must I force to my desire.'

XXVII

Here pale with fear he doth premeditate 183
The dangers of his loathsome enterprise,
And in his inward mind he doth debate
What following sorrow may on this arise:
Then looking scornfully, he doth despise 187
  His naked armour of still, slaughter'd Lust,
  And justly thus controls his thoughts unjust:

XXVIII

'Fair torch, burn out thy light, and lend it not 190
To darken her whose light excelleth thine:
And die, unhallow'd thoughts, before you blot
With your uncleanness that which is divine;
Offer pure incense to so pure a shrine: 194
  Let fair humanity abhor the deed
  That spots and stains love's modest snow-white weed.

XXIX

'O, shame to knighthood and to shining Arms! 197
O foul dishonour to my household's grave!
O impious act, including all foul harms!
A martial man to be soft fancy's slave!
True valour still a true respect should have; 201
  Then my digression is so vile, so base,
  That it will live engraven in my face.

XXX

'Yea, though I die, the scandal will survive, 204
And be an eye-sore in my golden coat;
Some loathsome dash the Herald will contrive,
To cipher me how fondly I did dote;
That my posterity, shamed with the note, 208
  Shall curse my bones, and hold it for no sin
  To wish that I their father had not been.

XXXI

'What win I, if I gain the thing I seek? 211
A dream, a breath, a froth of fleeting joy.
Who buys a minute's mirth to wail a week?
Or sells eternity to get a toy?
For one sweet grape who will the vine destroy? 215
  Or what fond beggar, but to touch the crown,
  Would with the sceptre straight be strucken down?

XXXII

'If Collatinus dream of my intent, 218
Will he not wake, and in a desp'rate rage
Post hither, this vile purpose to prevent?
This siege that hath engirt his marriage,
This blur to youth, this sorrow to the sage, 222
  This dying virtue, this surviving shame,
  Whose crime will bear an ever-during blame?

XXXIII

'O, what excuse can my invention make, 225
When thou shalt charge me with so black a deed?
Will not my tongue be mute, my frail joints shake?
Mine eyes forego their light, my false heart bleed?
The guilt, being great, the fear doth still exceed; 229
  And éxtreme fear can neither fight nor fly,
  But coward-like with trembling terror die.

XXXIV

'Had Collatinus kill'd my son or sire, 232
Or lain in ambush to betray my life,
Or were he not my dear friend, this desire
Might have excuse to work upon his wife,
As in revenge or quittal of such strife: 236
  But as he is my kinsman, my dear friend,
  The shame and fault finds no excuse nor end.

XXXV

'Shameful it is; ay, if the fact be known: 239
Hateful it is; there is no hate in loving:
I'll beg her love; but she is not her own:
The worst is but denial and reproving:
My will is strong, past reason's weak removing. 243
  Who fears a sentence or an old man's saw
  Shall by a painted cloth be kept in awe.'

XXXVI

Thus graceless holds he disputation 246
'Tween frozen conscience and hot-burning will,
And with good thoughts makes dispensation,
Urging the worser sense for vantage still;
Which in a moment doth confound and kill 250
All pure effects, and doth so far proceed,
That what is vile shows like a virtuous deed.

XXXVII

Quoth he, 'She took me kindly by the hand, 253
And gazed for tidings in my eager eyes,
Fearing some hard news from the warlike band,
Where her belovéd Collatinus lies.
O, how her fear did make her colour rise! 257
First red as Roses that on lawn we lay,
Then white as lawn, the Roses took away.

XXXVIII

'And how her hand, in my hand being lock'd, 260
Forced it to tremble with her loyal fear!
Which struck her sad, and then it faster rock'd,
Until her husband's welfare she did hear;
Whereat she smiléd with so sweet a cheer, 264
That had Narcissus seen her as she stood,
Self-love had never drown'd him in the flood.

XXXIX

'Why hunt I then for colour or excuses? 267
All Orators are dumb when Beauty pleadeth;
Poor wretches have remorse in poor abuses;
Love thrives not in the heart that shadows dreadeth:
Affection is my Captain, and he leadeth; 271
And when his gaudy banner is display'd,
The coward fights and will not be dismay'd.

XL

'Then, childish fear, avaunt! debating, die! 274
Respect and reason wait on wrinkled age:
My heart shall never countermand mine eye;
Sad pause and deep regard beseems the sage;
My part is youth, and beats these from the stage. 278
  Desire my Pilot is, Beauty my prize;
  Then who fears sinking where such treasure lies?'

XLI

As corn o'ergrown by weeds, so heedful fear 281
Is almost choked by unresisted lust:
Away he steals with open list'ning ear,
Full of foul hope and full of fond mistrust;
Both which, as servitors to the unjust, 285
  So cross him with their opposite persuasion,
  That now he vows a league, and now invasion.

XLII

Within his thought her heavenly image sits, 288
And in the self-same seat sits Collatine:
That eye which looks on her confounds his wits;
That eye which him beholds, as more divine,
Unto a view so false will not incline; 292
  But with a pure appeal seeks to the heart,
  Which once corrupted takes the worser part;

XLIII

And therein heartens up his servile powers, 295
Who, flatter'd by their leader's jocund show,
Stuff up his lust, as minutes fill up hours;
And as their Captain, so their pride doth grow,
Paying more slavish tribute than they owe. 299
  By reprobate desire thus madly led,
  The Roman Lord marcheth to Lucrece' bed.

XLIV

The locks between her chamber and his will, 302
Each one by him enforced, retires his ward;
But, as they open, they all rate his ill,
Which drives the creeping thief to some regard:
The threshold grates the door to have him heard; 306
  Night-wand'ring weasels shriek to see him there;
  They fright him, yet he still pursues his fear.

XLV

As each unwilling portal yields him way, 309
Through little vents and crannies of the place
The wind wars with his torch to make him stay,
And blows the smoke of it into his face,
Extinguishing his conduct in this case; 313
  But his hot heart, which fond desire doth scorch,
  Puffs forth another wind that fires the torch:

XLVI

And being lighted, by the light he spies 316
Lucretia's glove, wherein her needle sticks:
He takes it from the rushes where it lies,
And griping it, the needle his finger pricks;
As who should say, 'This glove to wanton tricks 320
  Is not inured; return again in haste;
  Thou see'st our mistress' ornaments are chaste.'

XLVII

But all these poor forbiddings could not stay him; 323
He in the worst sense construes their denial:
The doors, the wind, the glove, that did delay him,
He takes for accidental things of trial;
Or as those bars which stop the hourly dial, 327
  Who with a lingering stay his course doth let,
  Till every minute pays the hour his debt.

XLVIII

'So, so,' quoth he, 'these lets attend the time,
Like little frosts that sometime threat the spring,
To add a more rejoicing to the prime,
And give the sneapéd birds more cause to sing.
Pain pays the income of each precious thing;
  Huge rocks, high winds, strong pirates, shelves and sands,
  The merchant fears, ere rich at home he lands.'

XLIX

Now is he come unto the chamber door,
That shuts him from the Heaven of his thought,
Which with a yielding latch, and with no more,
Hath barr'd him from the blesséd thing he sought.
So from himself impiety hath wrought,
  That for his prey to pray he doth begin,
  As if the Heavens should countenance his sin.

L

But in the midst of his unfruitful prayer,
Having solicited th' eternal power
That his foul thoughts might compass his fair fair,
And they would stand auspicious to the hour,
Even there he starts: quoth he, 'I must deflower:
  The powers to whom I pray abhor this fact,
  How can they then assist me in the act?

LI

'Then Love and Fortune be my Gods, my guide!
My will is back'd with resolution:
Thoughts are but dreams till their effects be tried:
The blackest sin is clear'd with absolution;
Against love's fire fear's frost hath dissolution.
  The eye of Heaven is out, and misty night
  Covers the shame that follows sweet delight.'

LII

This said, his guilty hand pluck'd up the latch, 358
And with his knee the door he opens wide.
The dove sleeps fast that this night-owl will catch:
Thus treason works ere traitors be espied.
Who sees the lurking serpent steps aside; 362
  But she, sound sleeping, fearing no such thing,
  Lies at the mercy of his mortal sting.

LIII

Into the chamber wickedly he stalks, 365
And gazeth on her yet unstainéd bed.
The curtains being close, about he walks,
Rolling his greedy eyeballs in his head:
By their high treason is his heart misled; 369
  Which gives the watch-word to his hand full soon
  To draw the cloud that hides the silver Moon.

LIV

Look, as the fair and fiery-pointed Sun, 372
Rushing from forth a cloud, bereaves our sight;
Even so, the curtain drawn, his eyes begun
To wink, being blinded by a greater light:
Whether it is that she reflects so bright, 376
  That dazzleth them, or else some shame supposéd;
  But blind they are, and keep themselves enclosèd.

LV

O, had they in that darksome prison died! 379
Then had they seen the period of their ill;
Then Collatine again, by Lucrece' side,
In his clear bed might have reposéd still:
But they must ope, this blesséd league to kill; 383
  And holy-thoughted Lucrece to their sight
  Must sell her joy, her life, her world's delight.

LVI

Her lily hand her rosy cheek lies under,
Coz'ning the pillow of a lawful kiss;
Who, therefore angry, seems to part in sunder,
Swelling on either side to want his bliss;
Between whose hills her head entombéd is:
  Where, like a virtuous monument, she lies,
  To be admired of lewd unhallowed eyes.

LVII

Without the bed her other fair hand was,
On the green coverlet; whose perfect white
Show'd like an April daisy on the grass,
With pearly sweat, resembling dew of night.
Her eyes, like Marigolds, had sheath'd their light,
  And canopied in darkness sweetly lay,
  Till they might open to adorn the day.

LVIII

Her hair, like golden threads, play'd with her breath;
O modest wantons! wanton modesty!
Showing life's triumph in the map of death,
And death's dim look in life's mortality:
Each in her sleep themselves so beautify,
  As if between them twain there were no strife,
  But that life liv'd in death, and death in life.

LIX

Her breasts, like ivory globes circled with blue,
A pair of maiden worlds unconqueréd,
Save of their Lord no bearing yoke they knew,
And him by oath they truly honouréd.
These worlds in Tarquin new ambition bred;
  Who, like a foul usurper, went about
  From this fair throne to heave the owner out.

LX

What could he see but mightily he noted?
What did he note but strongly he desiréd?
What he beheld, on that he firmly doted,
And in his will his wilful eye he tiréd.
With more than admiration he admiréd
  Her azure veins, her alabaster skin,
  Her coral lips, her snow-white dimpled chin.

LXI

As the grim lion fawneth o'er his prey,
Sharp hunger by the conquest satisfied:
So o'er this sleeping soul doth Tarquin stay,
His rage of lust by gazing qualified;
Slack'd, not suppress'd; for standing by her side,
  His eye, which late this mutiny restrains,
  Unto a greater uproar tempts his veins:

LXII

And they, like straggling slaves for pillage fighting,
Obdúrate vassals fell exploits effecting,
In bloody death and ravishment delighting,
Nor children's tears nor mother's groans respecting,
Swell in their pride, the onset still expecting:
  Anon his beating heart, alarum striking,
  Gives the hot charge and bids them do their liking.

LXIII

His drumming heart cheers up his burning eye,
His eye commends the leading to his hand;
His hand, as proud of such a dignity,
Smoking with pride, march'd on to make his stand
On her bare breast, the heart of all her land;
  Whose ranks of blue veins, as his hand did scale,
  Left their round turrets destitute and pale.

LXIV

They, mustering to the quiet cabinet 442
Where their dear governess and lady lies,
Do tell her she is dreadfully beset,
And fright her with confusion of their cries:
She, much amazed, breaks ope her lock'd-up eyes, 446
  Who, peeping forth this tumult to behold,
  Are by his flaming torch dimm'd and controll'd.

LXV

Imagine her as one in dead of night 449
From forth dull sleep by dreadful fancy waking,
That thinks she hath beheld some ghastly sprite,
Whose grim aspect sets every joint a-shaking;
What terror 'tis! but she, in worser taking, 453
  From sleep disturbéd, heedfully doth view
  The sight which makes supposéd terror true.

LXVI

Wrapp'd and confounded in a thousand fears, 456
Like to a new-kill'd bird she trembling lies;
She dares not look; yet, winking, there appears
Quick-shifting antics, ugly in her eyes:
Such shadows are the weak brain's forgeries; 460
  Who, angry that the eyes fly from their lights,
  In darkness daunts them with more dreadful sights.

LXVII

His hand, that yet remains upon her breast,— 463
Rude ram, to batter such an ivory wall!—
May feel her heart—poor citizen!—distress'd,
Wounding itself to death, rise up and fall,
Beating her bulk, that his hand shakes withal. 467
  This moves in him more rage and lesser pity,
  To make the breach and enter this sweet city.

LXVIII

First, like a trumpet, doth his tongue begin 470
To sound a parley to his heartless foe;
Who o'er the white sheet peers her whiter chin,
The reason of this rash alarm to know,
Which he by dumb demeanour seeks to show; 474
  But she with vehement prayers urgeth still
  Under what colour he commits this ill.

LXIX

Thus he replies: 'The colour in thy face, 477
That even for anger makes the Lily pale,
And the red rose blush at her own disgrace,
Shall plead for me and tell my loving tale:
Under that colour am I come to scale 481
  Thy never-conquer'd fort: the fault is thine,
  For those thine eyes betray thee unto mine.

LXX

'Thus I forestall thee, if thou mean to chide: 484
Thy beauty hath ensnared thee to this night,
Where thou with patience must my will abide;
My will that marks thee for my earth's delight,
Which I to conquer sought with all my might; 488
  But as reproof and reason beat it dead,
  By thy bright beauty was it newly bred.

LXXI

'I see what crosses my attempt will bring; 491
I know what thorns the growing rose defends;
I think the honey guarded with a sting;
All this beforehand counsel comprehends:
But Will is deaf and hears no heedful friends; 495
  Only he hath an eye to gaze on Beauty,
  And dotes on what he looks, 'gainst law or duty.

LXXII

'I have debated, even in my soul, 498
What wrong, what shame, what sorrow I shall breed;
But nothing can affection's course control,
Or stop the headlong fury of his speed.
I know repentant tears ensue the deed, 502
  Reproach, disdain, and deadly enmity;
  Yet strive I to embrace mine infamy.'

LXXIII

This said, he shakes aloft his Roman blade, 505
Which, like a falcon tow'ring in the skies,
Coucheth the fowl below with his wings' shade,
Whose crooked beak threats, if he mount, he dies:
So under his insulting falchion lies 509
  Harmless Lucretia, marking what he tells
  With trembling fear, as fowl hear falcon's bells.

LXXIV

'Lucrece,' quoth he, 'this night I must enjoy thee: 512
If thou deny, then force must work my way,
For in thy bed I purpose to destroy thee:
That done, some worthless slave of thine I'll slay,
To kill thine honour with thy life's decay; 516
  And in thy dead arms do I mean to place him,
  Swearing I slew him, seeing thee embrace him.

LXXV

'So thy surviving husband shall remain 519
The scornful mark of every open eye;
Thy kinsmen hang their heads at this disdain,
Thy issue blurr'd with nameless bastardy:
And thou, the author of their obloquy, 523
  Shalt have thy trespass cited up in rhymes,
  And sung by children in succeeding times.

LXXVI

'But if thou yield, I rest thy secret friend: 526
The fault unknown is as a thought unacted;
"A little harm done to a great good end"
For lawful policy remains enacted.
The poisonous simple sometimes is compacted 530
  In a pure compound; being so applied,
  His venom in effect is purified.

LXXVII

'Then, for thy husband and thy children's sake, 533
Tender my suit: bequeath not to their lot
The shame that from them no device can take,
The blemish that will never be forgot;
Worse than a slavish wipe or birth-hour's blot: 537
  For marks descried in men's nativity
  Are nature's faults, not their own infamy.'

LXXVIII

Here with a Cockatrice' dead-killing eye 540
He rouseth up himself and makes a pause;
While she, the picture of pure piety,
Like a white hind under the gripe's sharp claws,
Pleads, in a wilderness where are no laws, 544
  To the rough beast that knows no gentle right,
  Nor aught obeys but his foul appetite.

LXXIX

But when a black-faced cloud the world doth threat,
In his dim mist th' aspiring mountains hiding, 548
From earth's dark womb some gentle gust doth get,
Which blows these pitchy vapours from their biding,
Hindering their present fall by this dividing; 551
  So his unhallow'd haste her words delays,
  And moody Pluto winks while Orpheus plays.

LXXX

Yet, foul night-waking cat, he doth but dally, 554
While in his hold-fast foot the weak mouse panteth:
Her sad behaviour feeds his vulture folly,
A swallowing gulf that even in plenty wanteth:
His ear her prayers admits, but his heart granteth 558
No penetrable entrance to her plaining:
Tears harden lust, though marble wear with raining.

LXXXI

Her pity-pleading eyes are sadly fixéd 561
In the remorseless wrinkles of his face;
Her modest eloquence with sighs is mixéd,
Which to her oratory adds more grace.
She puts the period often from his place, 565
And midst the sentence so her accent breaks,
That twice she doth begin ere once she speaks.

LXXXII

She conjures him by high Almighty Jove, 568
By knighthood, gentry, and sweet friendship's oath,
By her untimely tears, her husband's love,
By holy human law, and common troth,
By Heaven and Earth, and all the power of both, 572
That to his borrow'd bed he make retire,
And stoop to honour, not to foul desire.

LXXXIII

Quoth she, 'Reward not hospitality 575
With such black payment as thou hast pretended;
Mud not the fountain that gave drink to thee;
Mar not the thing that cannot be amended;
End thy ill aim before thy shoot be ended; 579
He is no woodman that doth bend his bow
To strike a poor unseasonable doe.

LXXXIV

'My husband is thy friend; for his sake spare me:
Thyself art mighty; for thine own sake leave me:
Myself a weakling; do not then ensnare me:
Thou look'st not like deceit; do not deceive me.
My sighs, like whirlwinds, labour hence to heave thee:
  If ever man were moved with woman's moans,
  Be movéd with my tears, my sighs, my groans:

LXXXV

'All which together, like a troubled ocean,
Beat at thy rocky and wrack-threat'ning heart,
To soften it with their continual motion;
For stones dissolv'd to water do convert.
O, if no harder than a stone thou art,
  Melt at my tears, and be compassionate!
  Soft pity enters at an iron gate.

LXXXVI

'In Tarquin's likeness I did entertain thee:
Hast thou put on his shape to do him shame?
To all the Host of Heaven I complain me.
Thou wrong'st his honour, wound'st his princely name:
Thou art not what thou seem'st; and if the same,
  Thou seem'st not what thou art, a God, a King;
  For Kings like Gods should govern every thing.

LXXXVII

'How will thy shame be seeded in thine age,
When thus thy vices bud before thy spring!
If in thy hope thou dar'st do such outrage,
What dar'st thou not when once thou art a King?
O, be rememb'red, no outrageous thing
  From vassal actors can be wiped away;
  Then Kings' misdeeds cannot be hid in clay.

LXXXVIII

'This deed will make thee only lov'd for fear; 610
But happy Monarchs still are fear'd for love:
With foul offenders thou perforce must bear,
When they in thee the like offences prove:
If but for fear of this, thy will remove; 614
  For Princes are the glass, the school, the book,
  Where subjects' eyes do learn, do read, do look.

LXXXIX

'And wilt thou be the school where Lust shall learn? 617
Must he in thee read lectures of such shame?
Wilt thou be glass wherein it shall discern
Authority for sin, warrant for blame,
To privilege dishonour in thy name? 621
  Thou back'st reproach against long-living laud,
  And mak'st fair reputation but a bawd.

XC

'Hast thou command? by him that gave it thee, 624
From a pure heart command thy rebel will:
Draw not thy sword to guard iniquity,
For it was lent thee all that brood to kill.
Thy Princely office how canst thou fulfil, 628
  When, pattern'd by thy fault, foul sin may say,
  He learn'd to sin, and thou didst teach the way?

XCI

'Think but how vile a spectacle it were, 631
To view thy present trespass in another:
Men's faults do seldom to themselves appear;
Their own transgressions partially they smother:
This guilt would seem death-worthy in thy brother. 635
  O how are they wrapp'd in with infamies
  That from their own misdeeds askance their eyes!

XCII

'To thee, to thee, my heav'd-up hands appeal,
Not to seducing Lust, thy rash relier:
I sue for exiled majesty's repeal;
Let him return, and flatt'ring thoughts retire:
His true respect will prison false desire,
  And wipe the dim mist from thy doting eyne,
  That thou shalt see thy state and pity mine.'

XCIII

'Have done,' quoth he: 'my uncontrolléd tide
Turns not, but swells the higher by this let.
Small lights are soon blown out, huge fires abide,
And with the wind in greater fury fret:
The petty streams that pay a daily debt
  To their salt sovereign, with their fresh falls' haste
  Add to his flow, but alter not his taste.'

XCIV

'Thou art,' quoth she, 'a sea, a sovereign King;
And lo, there falls into thy boundless flood
Black lust, dishonour, shame, misgoverning,
Who seek to stain the Ocean of thy blood.
If all those petty ills shall change thy good,
  Thy sea within a puddle's womb is hearséd,
  And not the puddle in thy sea disperséd.

XCV

'So shall these slaves be King, and thou their slave;
Thou nobly base, they basely dignified;
Thou their fair life, and they thy fouler grave:
Thou loathéd in their shame, they in thy pride:
The lesser thing should not the greater hide;
  The cedar stoops not to the base shrub's foot,
  But low shrubs wither at the cedar's root.

XCVI

'So let thy thoughts, low vassals to thy state'— 666
'No more,' quoth he; 'by Heaven, I will not hear thee:
Yield to my love; if not, enforcéd hate,
Instead of love's coy touch, shall rudely tear thee;
That done, despitefully I mean to bear thee 670
  Unto the base bed of some rascal groom,
  To be thy partner in this shameful doom.'

XCVII

This said, he sets his foot upon the light, 673
For light and lust are deadly enemies:
Shame folded up in blind concealing night,
When most unseen, then most doth tyrannise.
The wolf hath seized his prey, the poor lamb cries; 677
  Till with her own white fleece her voice controll'd
  Entombs her outcry in her lips' sweet fold:

XCVIII

For with the nightly linen that she wears 680
He pens her piteous clamours in her head;
Cooling his hot face in the chastest tears
That ever modest eyes with sorrow shed.
O, that prone lust should stain so pure a bed! 684
  The spots whereof could weeping purify,
  Her tears should drop on them perpetually.

XCIX

But she hath lost a dearer thing than life, 687
And he hath won what he would lose again:
This forcéd league doth force a further strife;
This momentary joy breeds months of pain;
This hot desire converts to cold disdain: 691
  Pure Chastity is rifled of her store,
  And Lust, the thief, far poorer than before.

C

Look, as the full-fed hound, or gorgéd hawk, 694
Unapt for tender smell, or speedy flight,
Make slow pursuit, or altogether balk
The prey wherein by nature they delight;
So surfeit-taking Tarquin fares this night: 698
  His taste delicious, in digestion souring,
  Devours his will, that lived by foul devouring.

CI

O, deeper sin than bottomless conceit 701
Can comprehend in still imagination!
Drunken Desire must vomit his receipt,
Ere he can see his own abomination.
While Lust is in his pride, no exclamation 705
  Can curb his heat, or rein his rash desire,
  Till like a jade Self-will himself doth tire.

CII

And then with lank and lean discolour'd cheek, 708
With heavy eye, knit brow, and strengthless pace,
Feeble Desire, all recreant, poor, and meek,
Like to a bankrupt beggar wails his case:
The flesh being proud, Desire doth fight with Grace,
  For there it revels; and when that decays, 713
  The guilty rebel for remission prays.

CIII

So fares it with this faultful Lord of Rome, 715
Who this accomplishment so hotly chaséd;
For now against himself he sounds this doom,
That through the length of times he stands disgracéd:
Besides, his soul's fair temple is defacéd; 719
  To whose weak ruins muster troops of cares,
  To ask the spotted Princess how she fares.

CIV

She says, her subjects with foul insurrection 722
Have batter'd down her consecrated wall,
And by their mortal fault brought in subjection
Her immortality, and made her thrall
To living death and pain perpetual: 726
  Which in her prescience she controllèd still,
  But her foresight could not forestall their will.

CV

Ev'n in this thought through the dark night he stealeth,
A captive victor that hath lost in gain; 730
Bearing away the wound that nothing healeth,
The scar that will, despite of cure, remain;
Leaving his spoil perplex'd in greater pain. 733
  She bears the load of lust he left behind,
  And he the burthen of a guilty mind.

CVI

He like a thievish dog creeps sadly thence; 736
She like a wearied lamb lies panting there;
He scowls and hates himself for his offence;
She, desperate, with her nails her flesh doth tear;
He faintly flies, sweating with guilty fear; 740
  She stays, exclaiming on the direful night;
  He runs, and chides his vanish'd, loath'd delight.

CVII

He thence departs a heavy convertite; 743
She there remains a hopeless castaway;
He in his speed looks for the morning light;
She prays she never may behold the day,
'For day,' quoth she, 'night's scapes doth open lay, 747
  And my true eyes have never practis'd how
  To cloak offences with a cunning brow.

CVIII

'They think not but that every eye can see 750
The same disgrace which they themselves behold;
And therefore would they still in darkness be,
To have their unseen sin remain untold;
For they their guilt with weeping will unfold, 754
  And grave, like water that doth eat in steel,
  Upon my cheeks what helpless shame I feel.'

CIX

Here she exclaims against repose and rest, 757
And bids her eyes hereafter still be blind:
She wakes her heart by beating on her breast,
And bids it leap from thence, where it may find
Some purer chest to close so pure a mind. 761
  Frantic with grief thus breathes she forth her spite
  Against the unseen secrecy of night:

CX

'O comfort-killing Night, image of Hell! 764
Dim register and notary of shame!
Black stage for tragedies and murders fell!
Vast sin-concealing Chaos! nurse of blame!
Blind muffled bawd! dark harbour for defame! 768
  Grim cave of death! whisp'ring conspirator
  With close-tongu'd treason and the ravisher!

CXI

'O hateful, vaporous, and foggy Night! 771
Since thou art guilty of my cureless crime,
Muster thy mists to meet the Eastern light,
Make war against proportion'd course of time;
Or if thou wilt permit the Sun to climb 775
  His wonted height, yet ere he go to bed,
  Knit poisonous clouds about his golden head.

CXII

'With rotten damps ravish the morning air; 778
Let their exhaled unwholesome breaths make sick
The life of purity, the súpreme fair,
Ere he arrive his weary noon-tide prick;
And let thy musty vapours march so thick, 782
  That in their smoky ranks his smoth'red light
  May set at noon, and make perpetual night.

CXIII

'Were Tarquin Night, as he is but Night's child, 785
The silver-shining Queen he would distain;
Her twinkling handmaids too, by him defiled,
Through Night's black bosom should not peep again:
So should I have co-partners in my pain; 789
  And fellowship in woe doth woe assuage,
  As Palmers' chat makes short their pilgrimage.

CXIV

'Where now I have no one to blush with me, 792
To cross their arms and hang their heads with mine,
To mask their brows and hide their infamy;
But I alone, alone must sit and pine,
Seasoning the earth with showers of silver brine, 796
  Mingling my talk with tears, my grief with groans,
  Poor wasting monuments of lasting moans.

CXV

'O Night, thou furnace of foul-reeking smoke, 799
Let not the jealous Day behold that face
Which underneath thy black all-hiding cloak
Immodestly lies martyr'd with disgrace!
Keep still possession of thy gloomy place, 803
  That all the faults which in thy reign are made
  May likewise be sepúlchred in thy shade.

CXVI

'Make me not object to the tell-tale Day!
The light will show, character'd in ray brow,
The story of sweet chastity's decay,
The impious breach of holy wedlock vow:
Yea, the illiterate, that know not how
  To cipher what is writ in learned books,
  Will quote my loathsome trespass in my looks.

CXVII

'The nurse, to still her child, will tell my story,
And fright her crying babe with Tarquin's name:
The Orator, to deck his oratory,
Will couple my reproach to Tarquin's shame;
Feast-finding minstrels, tuning my defame,
  Will tie the hearers to attend each line,
  How Tarquin wrongéd me, I Collatine.

CXVIII

'Let my good name, that senseless reputation,
For Collatine's dear love be kept unspotted:
If that be made a theme for disputation,
The branches of another root are rotted,
And undeserv'd reproach to him allotted
  That is as clear from this attaint of mine
  As I, ere this, was pure to Collatine.

CXIX

'O unseen shame! invisible disgrace!
O unfelt sore! crest-wounding, private scar!
Reproach is stamp'd in Collatinus' face,
And Tarquin's eye may read the mot afar,
How "He in peace is wounded, not in war."
  Alas, how many bear such shameful blows,
  Which not themselves, but he that gives them knows!

CXX

'If, Collatine, thine honour lay in me, 834
From me by strong assault it is bereft.
My Honey lost, and I, a Drone-like Bee,
Have no perfection of my summer left,
But robb'd and ransack'd by injurious theft: 838
  In thy weak Hive a wandering wasp hath crept,
  And suck'd the Honey which thy chaste Bee kept.

CXXI

'Yet am I guilty of thy honour's wrack; 841
Yet for thy honour did I entertain him;
Coming from thee, I could not put him back,
For it had been dishonour to disdain him:
Besides, of weariness he did complain him, 845
  And talk'd of virtue: O unlook'd-for evil,
  When virtue is profaned in such a Devil!

CXXII

'Why should the worm intrude the maiden bud? 848
Or hateful Cuckoos hatch in Sparrows' nests?
Or Toads infect fair founts with venom mud?
Or tyrant folly lurk in gentle breasts?
Or Kings be breakers of their own behests? 852
  But no perfection is so absolute,
  That some impurity doth not pollute.

CXXIII

'The agéd man that coffers-up his gold 855
Is plagued with cramps and gouts and painful fits;
And scarce hath eyes his treasure to behold,
But like still-pining Tantalus he sits,
And useless barns the harvest of his wits; 859
  Having no other pleasure of his gain
  But torment that it cannot cure his pain.

CXXIV

'So then he hath it when he cannot use it, 862
And leaves it to be master'd by his young;
Who in their pride do presently abuse it:
Their father was too weak, and they too strong,
To hold their curséd-blesséd Fortune long. 866
  The sweets we wish for, turn to loathed sours
  Even in the moment that we call them ours.

CXXV

'Unruly blasts wait on the tender spring; 869
Unwholesome weeds take root with precious flowers;
The Adder hisses where the sweet Birds sing;
What Virtue breeds Iniquity devours:
We have no good that we can say is ours, 873
  But ill-annexéd Opportunity
  Or kills his life or else his quality.

CXXVI

'O Opportunity, thy guilt is great! 876
'Tis thou that execut'st the traitor's treason:
Thou set'st the wolf where he the lamb may get;
Whoever plots the sin, thou point'st the season;
'Tis thou that spurn'st at right, at law, at reason; 880
  And in thy shady cell, where none may spy him,
  Sits Sin, to seize the souls that wander by him.

CXXVII

'Thou makest the vestal violate her oath; 883
Thou blowest the fire when temperance is thaw'd;
Thou smother'st honesty, thou murder'st troth;
Thou foul abettor! thou notorious bawd!
Thou plantest scandal, and displacest laud: 887
  Thou ravisher, thou traitor, thou false thief,
  Thy honey turns to gall, thy joy to grief!

CXXVIII

'Thy secret pleasure turns to open shame,
Thy private feasting to a public fast,
Thy smoothing titles to a ragged name,
Thy sugar'd tongue to bitter wormwood taste:
Thy violent vanities can never last.
  How comes it then, vile Opportunity,
  Being so bad, such numbers seek for thee?

CXXIX

'When wilt thou be the humble suppliant's friend,
And bring him where his suit may be obtainéd?
When wilt thou sort an hour great strifes to end?
Or free that soul which wretchedness hath chainéd?
Give physic to the sick, ease to the painéd?
  The poor, lame, blind, halt, creep, cry out for thee;
  But they ne'er meet with Opportunity.

CXXX

'The Patient dies while the Physician sleeps;
The Orphan pines while the Oppressor feeds;
Justice is feasting while the Widow weeps;
Advice is sporting while Infection breeds:
Thou grant'st no time for charitable deeds:
  Wrath, Envy, Treason, Rape, and Murder's rages,
  Thy heinous hours wait on them as their Pages.

CXXXI

'When Truth and Virtue have to do with thee,
A thousand crosses keep them from thy aid:
They buy thy help; but Sin ne'er gives a fee,
He gratis comes; and thou art well appaid,
As well to hear as grant what he hath said.
  My Collatine would else have come to me,
  When Tarquin did, but he was stay'd by thee.

CXXXII

'Guilty thou art of murder, and of theft,
Guilty of perjury, and subornation,
Guilty of treason, forgery, and shift,
Guilty of incest, that abomination;
An accessáry by thine inclination
  To all sins past, and all that are to come,
  From the creation to the general doom.

CXXXIII

'Mis-shapen Time, copesmate of ugly Night,
Swift subtle post, carrier of grisly care,
Eater of youth, false slave of false delight,
Base watch of woes, sin's pack-horse, virtue's snare;
Thou nursest all and murd'rest all that are:
  O, hear me then, injurious, shifting Time!
  Be guilty of my death, since of my crime.

CXXXIV

'Why hath thy servant, Opportunity,
Betray'd the hours thou gav'st me to repose?
Cancell'd my fortunes, and enchainéd me
To endless date of never-ending woes?
Time's office is to fine the hate of foes;
  To eat up errors by opinion bred,
  Not spend the dowry of a lawful bed.

CXXXV

'Time's glory is to calm contending Kings,
To unmask falsehood and bring truth to light,
To stamp the seal of time in agéd things,
To wake the morn and sentinel the night,
To wrong the wronger till he render right,
  To ruinate proud buildings with thy hours,
  And smear with dust their glitt'ring golden towers;

CXXXVI

'To fill with worm-holes stately monuments, 946
To feed oblivion with decay of things,
To blot old books and alter their contents,
To pluck the quills from ancient ravens' wings,
To dry the old oak's sap, and cherish springs, 950
  To spoil Antiquities of hammer'd steel,
  And turn the giddy round of Fortune's wheel;

CXXXVII

'To show the beldam daughters of her daughter, 953
To make the child a man, the man a child,
To slay the tiger that doth live by slaughter,
To tame the unicorn and lion wild,
To mock the subtle in themselves beguiled, 957
  To cheer the ploughman with increaseful crops,
  And waste huge stones with little water-drops.

CXXXVIII

'Why work'st thou mischief in thy pilgrimage, 960
Unless thou couldst return to make amends?
One poor retiring minute in an age
Would purchase thee a thousand thousand friends,
Lending him wit that to bad debtors lends: 964
  O, this dread night, wouldst thou one hour come back,
  I could prevent this storm and shun thy wrack!

CXXXIX

'Thou ceaseless lackey to Eternity, 967
With some mischance cross Tarquin in his flight:
Devise extremes beyond extremity,
To make him curse this curséd crimeful night:
Let ghastly shadows his lewd eyes affright; 971
  And the dire thought of his committed evil
  Shape every bush a hideous shapeless devil.

CXL

'Disturb his hours of rest with restless trances,
Afflict him in his bed with bedrid groans;
Let there bechance him pitiful mischances,
To make him moan; but pity not his moans:
Stone him with harden'd hearts, harder than stones;
  And let mild women to him lose their mildness,
  Wilder to him than tigers in their wildness.

CXLI

'Let him have time to tear his curléd hair,
Let him have time against himself to rave,
Let him have time of Time's help to despair,
Let him have time to live a loathéd slave,
Let him have time a beggar's orts to crave,
  And time to see one that by alms doth live
  Disdain to him disdainéd scraps to give.

CXLII

'Let him have time to see his friends his foes,
And merry fools to mock at him resort;
Let him have time to mark how slow time goes
In time of sorrow, and how swift and short
His time of folly, and his time of sport;
  And ever let his unrecalling crime
  Have time to wail th' abusing of his time.

CXLIII

'O Time, thou tutor both to good and bad,
Teach me to curse him that thou taught'st this ill!
At his own shadow let the thief run mad,
Himself himself seek every hour to kill!
Such wretched hands such wretched blood should spill;
  For who so base would such an office have
  As slanderous deathsman to so base a slave?

CXLIV

'The baser is he, coming from a King, 1002
To shame his hope with deeds degenerate:
The mightier man, the mightier is the thing
That makes him honour'd, or begets him hate;
For greatest scandal waits on greatest state. 1006
  The Moon being clouded presently is miss'd,
  But little stars may hide them when they list.

CXLV

'The Crow may bathe his coal-black wings in mire,
And unperceiv'd fly with the filth away; 1010
But if the like the snow-white Swan desire,
The stain upon his silver down will stay.
Poor grooms are sightless night, kings glorious day:
  Gnats are unnoted wheresoe'er they fly, 1014
  But Eagles gazed upon with every eye.

CXLVI

'Out, idle words, servants to shallow fools! 1016
Unprofitable sounds, weak arbitrators!
Busy yourselves in skill-contending schools;
Debate where leisure serves with dull debaters;
To trembling clients be you mediators: 1020
  For me, I force not argument a straw,
  Since that my case is past the help of law.

CXLVII

'In vain I rail at Opportunity, 1023
At Time, at Tarquin, and uncheerful Night,
In vain I cavil with mine infamy,
In vain I spurn at my confirm'd despite:
This helpless smoke of words doth me no right. 1027
  The remedy indeed to do me good
  Is to let forth my foul defiléd blood.

CXLVIII

'Poor hand, why quiver'st thou at this decree? 1030
Honour thyself to rid me of this shame;
For if I die, my honour lives in thee;
But if I live, thou liv'st in my defame:
Since thou couldst not defend thy loyal Dame, 1034
And wast afeard to scratch her wicked foe,
Kill both thyself and her for yielding so.'

CXLIX

This said, from her be-tumbled couch she starteth, 1037
To find some desp'rate instrument of death:
But this no slaughter-house no tool imparteth
To make more vent for passage of her breath;
Which, thronging through her lips, so vanisheth 1041
As smoke from Ætna, that in air consumes,
Or that which from dischargéd cannon fumes.

CL

'In vain,' quoth die, 'I live, and seek in vain 1044
Some happy mean to end a hapless life.
I fear'd by Tarquin's falchion to be slain,
Yet for the self-same purpose seek a knife:
But when I fear'd I was a loyal wife: 1048
So am I now: O no, that cannot be;
Of that true type hath Tarquin rifled me.

CLI

'O, that is gone for which I sought to live, 1051
And therefore now I need not fear to die.
To clear this spot by death, at least I give
A badge of Fame to Slander's livery;
A dying life to living infamy: 1055
Poor helpless help, the treasure stol'n away,
To burn the guiltless casket where it lay!

CLII

'Well, well, dear Collatine, thou shalt not know 1058
The stainéd taste of violated troth;
I will not wrong thy true affection so,
To flatter thee with an infringéd oath;
This bastard graff shall never come to growth: 1062
He shall not boast who did thy stock pollute
That thou art doting father of his fruit.

CLIII

'Nor shall he smile at thee in secret thought, 1065
Nor laugh with his companions at thy state;
But thou shalt know thy int'rest was not bought
Basely with gold, but stol'n from forth thy gate.
For me, I am the mistress of my fate, 1069
And with my trespass never will dispense,
Till life to death acquit my forced offence.

CLIV

'I will not poison thee with my attaint, 1072
Nor fold my fault in cleanly-coin'd excuses;
My sable ground of sin I will not paint,
To hide the truth of this false night's abuses:
My tongue shall utter all; mine eyes, like sluices, 1076
As from a mountain-spring that feeds a dale,
Shall gush pure streams to purge my impure tale.'

CLV

By this, lamenting Philomel had ended 1079
The well-tuned warble of her nightly sorrow,
And solemn night with slow sad gait descended
To ugly Hell; when, lo, the blushing morrow
Lends light to all fair eyes that light will borrow: 1083
But cloudy Lucrece shames herself to see,
And therefore still in night would cloister'd be,

CLVI

Revealing day through every cranny spies, 1086
And seems to point her out where she sits weeping;
To whom she sobbing speaks: 'O eye of eyes,
Why pry'st thou through my window? leave thy peeping:
Mock with thy tickling beams eyes that are sleeping: 1090
  Brand not my forehead with thy piercing light,
  For day hath nought to do what 's done by night.'

CLVII

Thus cavils she with every thing she sees: 1093
True grief is fond and testy as a child,
Who wayward once, his mood with nought agrees:
Old woes, not infant sorrows, bear them mild;
Continuance tames the one; the other wild, 1097
  Like an unpractis'd swimmer plunging still,
  With too much labour drowns for want of skill.

CLVIII

So she, deep-drenchéd in a sea of care, 1100
Holds disputation with each thing she views,
And to herself all sorrow doth compare;
No object but her passion's strength renews;
And as one shifts, another straight ensues: 1104
  Sometime her grief is dumb and hath no words;
  Sometime 'tis mad and too much talk affords.

CLIX

The little birds that tune their morning's joy 1107
Make her moans mad with their sweet melody:
For "mirth doth search the bottom of annoy";
"Sad souls are slain in merry company";
"Grief best is pleas'd with grief's society": 1111
  "True sorrow then is feelingly sufficed
  When with like semblance it is sympathised."

CLX

"'Tis double death to drown in ken of shore"; 1114
"He ten times pines that pines beholding food";
"To see the salve doth make the wound ache more";
"Great grief grieves most at that would do it good";
"Deep woes roll forward like a gentle flood," 1118
  Who, being stopp'd, the bounding banks o'erflows;
  Grief dallied with nor law nor limit knows.

CLXI

'You mocking birds,' quoth she, 'your tunes entomb 1121
Within your hollow swelling feather'd breasts,
And in my hearing be you mute and dumb:
My restless discord loves no stops nor rests;
"A woeful Hostess brooks not mercy guests": 1125
  Relish your nimble notes to pleasing ears;
  "Distress likes dumps when time is kept with tears."

CLXII

'Come, Philomel, that sing'st of ravishment, 1128
Make thy sad grove in my dishevell'd hair:
As the dank earth weeps at thy languishment,
So I at each sad strain will strain a tear,
And with deep groans the diapason bear; 1132
  For burden-wise I'll hum on Tarquin still,
  While thou on Tereus descant'st better skill.

CLXIII

'And whiles against a thorn thou bear'st thy part, 1135
To keep thy sharp woes waking, wretched I,
To imitate thee well, against my heart
Will fix a sharp knife to affright mine eye;
Who, if it wink, shall thereon fall and die. 1139
  These means, as frets upon an instrument,
  Shall tune our heart-strings to true languishment.

CLXIV

'And for, poor bird, thou sing'st not in the day, 1142
As shaming any eye should thee behold,
Some dark deep desert, seated from the way,
That knows not parching heat nor freezing cold,
Will we find out; and there we will unfold 1146
  To creatures stern sad tunes, to change their kinds:
  Since men prove beasts, let beasts bear gentle minds.'

CLXV

As the poor frighted deer, that stands at gaze, 1149
Wildly determining which way to fly,
Or one encompass'd with a winding maze,
That cannot tread the way out readily;
So with herself is she in mutiny, 1153
  To live or die which of the twain were better,
  When life is shamed, and death reproach's debtor.

CLXVI

'To kill myself,' quoth she, 'alack, what were it, 1156
But with my body my poor soul's pollution?
They that lose half with greater patience bear it
Than they whose whole is swallow'd in confusion.
That mother tries a merciless conclusion 1160
  Who, having two sweet babes, when death takes one,
  Will slay the other and be nurse to none.

CLXVII

'My body or my soul, which was the dearer, 1163
When the one pure, the other made divine?
Whose love of either to myself was nearer,
When both were kept for Heaven and Collatine?
Ay me! the bark peel'd from the lofty pine, 1167
  His leaves will wither and his sap decay;
  So must my soul, her bark being peel'd away.

CLXVIII

'Her house is sack'd, her quiet interrupted, 1170
Her mansion batter'd by the enemy;
Her sacred temple spotted, spoil'd, corrupted,
Grossly engirt with daring infamy:
Then let it not be call'd impiety, 1174
  If in this blemish'd fort I make some hole
  Through which I may convey this troubled soul.

CLXIX

'Yet die I will not till my Collatine 1177
Have heard the cause of my untimely death;
That he may vow, in that sad hour of mine,
Revenge on him that made me stop my breath.
My stainéd blood to Tarquin I'll bequeath, 1181
  Which by him tainted shall for him be spent,
  And as his due writ in my testament.

CLXX

'My honour I'll bequeath unto the knife 1184
That wounds my body so dishonouréd.
'Tis honour to deprive dishonour'd life;
The one will live, the other being dead:
So of shame's ashes shall my fame be bred; 1188
  For in my death I murder shameful scorn:
  My shame so dead, mine honour is new-born.

CLXXI

'Dear Lord of that dear jewel I have lost, 1191
What legacy shall I bequeath to thee?
My resolution, love, shall be thy boast,
By whose example thou reveng'd mayst be.
How Tarquin must be used, read it in me: 1195
  Myself, thy friend, will kill myself, thy foe,
  And for my sake serve thou false Tarquin so.

CLXXII

'This brief abridgement of my will I make: 1198
My soul and body to the skies and ground;
My resolution, husband, do thou take;
Mine honour be the knife's that makes my wound;
My shame be his that did my fame confound; 1202
  And all my fame that lives disbursèd be
  To those that live, and think no shame of me.

CLXXIII

'Thou, Collatine, shalt oversee this will; 1205
How was I overseen that thou shalt see it!
My blood shall wash the slander of mine ill;
My life's foul deed, my life's fair end shall free it.
Faint not, faint heart, but stoutly say "So be it": 1209
  Yield to my hand; my hand shall conquer thee:
  Thou dead, both die, and both shall victors be.'

CLXXIV

This plot of death when sadly she had laid, 1212
And wiped the brinish pearl from her bright eyes,
With untuned tongue she hoarsely calls her maid,
Whose swift obedience to her mistress hies;
For "fleet-wing'd duty with thought's feathers flies."
  Poor Lucrece' cheeks unto her maid seem so 1217
  As winter meads when sun doth melt their snow.

CLXXV

Her mistress she doth give demure good-morrow, 1219
With soft slow tongue, true mark of modesty,
And sorts a sad look to her Lady's sorrow;
(For why? her face wore sorrow's livery)
But durst not ask of her audaciously 1223
  Why her two suns were cloud-eclipsèd so,
  Nor why her fair cheeks over-wash'd with woe.

CLXXVI

But as the earth doth weep, the Sun being set, 1226
Each flower moist'ned like a melting eye;
Even so the maid with swelling drops gan wet,
Her circled eyne, enforced by sympathy
Of those fair Suns set in her mistress' sky, 1230
Who in a salt-waved Ocean quench their light,
Which makes the maid weep like the dewy night.

CLXXVII

A pretty while these pretty creatures stand, 1233
Like ivory conduits coral cisterns filling:
One justly weeps; the other takes in hand
No cause, but company, of her drops spilling:
Their gentle sex to weep are often willing; 1237
Grieving themselves to guess at others' smarts,
And then they drown their eyes or break their hearts.

CLXXVIII

For men have marble, women waxen, minds, 1240
And therefore are they form'd as marble will;
The weak oppress'd, th' impression of strange kinds
Is form'd in them by force, by fraud, or skill:
Then call them not the authors of their ill, 1244
No more than wax shall be accounted evil
Wherein is stamp'd the semblance of a Devil.

CLXXIX

Their smoothness, like a goodly champaign plain, 1247
Lays open all the little worms that creep;
In men, as in a rough-grown grove, remain
Cave-keeping evils that obscurely sleep;
Through crystal walls each little mote will peep: 1251
Though men can cover crimes with bold stern looks,
Poor women's faces are their own faults' books.

CLXXX

No man inveigh against the witheréd flower, 1254
But chide rough winter that the flower hath kill'd;
Not that devour'd, but that which doth devour,
Is worthy blame. O, let it not be hild
Poor women's faults, that they are so fulfill'd 1258
With men's abuses: those proud Lords to blame
Make weak-made women tenants to their shame.

CLXXXI

The precedent whereof in Lucrece view; 1261
Assail'd by night with circumstances strong
Of present death, and shame that might ensue
By that her death, to do her husband wrong:
Such danger to resistance did belong, 1265
That dying fear through all her body spread:
And who cannot abuse a body dead?

CLXXXII

By this, mild patience bid fair Lucrece speak 1268
To the poor counterfeit of her complaining:
'My girl,' quoth she,'on what occasion break
Those tears from thee, that down thy cheeks are raining?
If thou dost weep for grief of my sustaining, 1272
Know, gentle wench, it small avails my mood:
If tears could help, mine own would do me good.

CLXXXIII

'But tell me, girl, when went'—and there she stay'd 1275
Till after a deep groan—'Tarquin from hence?'
'Madam, ere I was up,' replied the maid,
'The more to blame my sluggard negligence:
Yet with the fault I thus far can dispense; 1279
Myself was stirring ere the break of day,
And, ere I rose, was Tarquin gone away.

CLXXXIV

'But, Lady, if your maid may be so bold, 1282
She would request to know your heaviness.'
'O, peace!' quoth Lucrece: 'if it should be told,
The repetition cannot make it less;
For more it is than I can well express: 1286
  And that deep torture may be call'd a Hell
  When more is felt than one hath power to tell.

CLXXXV

'Go, get me hither paper, ink, and pen: 1289
Yet save that labour, for I have them here.
What should I say?—One of my husband's men
Bid thou be ready, by and by, to bear
A letter to my Lord, my Love, my Dear: 1293
  Bid him with speed prepare to carry it;
  The cause craves haste, and it will soon be writ.'

CLXXXVI

Her maid is gone, and she prepares to write, 1296
First hovering o'er the paper with her quill:
Conceit and grief an eager combat fight;
What wit sets down is blotted straight with will;
This is too-curious good, this blunt and ill: 1300
  Much like a press of people at a door,
  Throng her inventions, which shall go before.

CLXXXVII

At last she thus begins: 'Thou worthy Lord 1303
Of that unworthy wife that greeteth thee,
Health to thy person! next vouchsafe t' afford—
If ever, love, thy Lucrece thou wilt see—
Some present speed to come and visit me. 1307
  So, I commend me from our house in grief:
  My woes are tedious, though my words are brief.'

CLXXXVIII

Here folds she up the tenure of her woe, 1310
Hear certain sorrow writ uncertainly.
By this short schedule Collatine may know
Her grief, but not her grief's true quality:
She dares not thereof make discovery, 1314
  Lest he should hold it her own gross abuse,
  Ere she with blood had stain'd her stain'd excuse.

CLXXXIX

Besides, the life and feeling of her passion 1317
She hoards, to spend when he is by to hear her;
When sighs and groans and tears may grace the fashion
Of her disgrace, the better so to clear her
From that suspicion which the world might bear her. 1321
  To shun this blot, she would not blot the letter
  With words, till action might become them better.

CXC

To see sad sights moves more than hear them told; 1324
For then the eye interprets to the ear
The heavy motion that it doth behold,
When every part a part of woe doth bear.
'Tis but a part of sorrow that we hear: 1328
  Deep sounds make lesser noise than shallow fords,
  And sorrow ebbs, being blown with wind of words.

CXCI

Her letter now is seal'd, and on it writ 1331
'At Ardea to my lord with more than haste.'
The post attends, and she delivers it,
Charging the sour-faced groom to hie as fast
As lagging fowls before the Northern blast: 1335
  Speed more than speed but dull and slow she deems:
  Extremity still urgeth such extremes.

CXCII

The homely villain court'sies to her low; 1338
And, blushing on her with a steadfast eye,
Receives the scroll without or yea or no,
And forth with bashful innocence doth hie.
But they whose guilt within their bosoms lie 1342
  Imagine every eye beholds their blame;
  For Lucrece thought he blush'd to see her shame.

CXCIII

When, silly groom! God wot, it was defect 1345
Of spirit, life, and bold audacity.
Such harmless creatures have a true respect
To talk in deeds, while others saucily
Promise more speed, but do it leisurely: 1349
  Even so the pattern of this worn-out age
  Pawn'd honest looks, but laid no words to gage.

CXCIV

His kindled duty kindled her mistrust, 1352
That two red fires in both their faces blazéd;
She thought he blush'd, as knowing Tarquin's lust,
And, blushing with him, wistly on him gazéd;
Her earnest eye did make him more amazéd: 1356
  The more she saw the blood his cheeks replenish,
  The more she thought he spied in her some blemish.

CXCV

But long she thinks till he return again, 1359
And yet the duteous vassal scarce is gone.
The weary time she cannot entertain,
For now 'tis stale to sigh, to weep, and groan:
So woe hath wearied woe, moan tiréd moan, 1363
  That she her plaints a little while doth stay,
  Pausing for means to mourn some newer way.

CXCVI

At last she calls to mind where hangs a piece 1366
Of skilful painting, made for Priam's Troy:
Before the which is drawn the power of Greece,
For Helen's rape, the city to destroy,
Threat'ning cloud-kissing Ilion with annoy; 1370
  Which the conceited Painter drew so proud,
  As Heaven (it seem'd) to kiss the turrets bow'd.

CXCVII

A thousand lamentable objects there, 1373
In scorn of Nature, Art gave lifeless life:
Many a dry drop seem'd a weeping tear,
Shed for the slaughter'd husband by the wife:
The red blood reek'd, to show the Painter's strife; 1377
  And dying eyes gleam'd forth their ashy lights,
  Like dying coals burnt out in tedious nights.

CXCVIII

There might you see the labouring pioneer 1380
Begrimed with sweat, and smearéd all with dust;
And from the towers of Troy there would appear
The very eyes of men through loop-holes thrust,
Gazing upon the Greeks with little lust: 1384
  Such sweet observance in this work was had,
  That one might see those far-off eyes look sad.

CXCIX

In great commanders grace and majesty 1387
You might behold, triumphing in their faces;
In youth, quick bearing and dexterity;
And here and there the Painter interlaces
Pale cowards, marching on with trembling paces; 1391
  Which heartless peasants did so well resemble,
  That one would swear he saw them quake and tremble.

CC

In Ajax and Ulysses, O, what Art
Of Physiognomy might one behold!
The face of either cipher'd either's heart;
Their face their manners most expressly told:
In Ajax' eyes blunt rage and rigour roll'd;
  But the mild glance that sly Ulysses lent
  Show'd deep regard and smiling government.

CCI

There pleading might you see grave Nestor stand,
As 'twere encouraging the Greeks to fight;
Making such sober action with his hand,
That it beguiled attention, charm'd the sight:
In speech, it seem'd, his beard, all silver white,
  Wagg'd up and down, and from his lips did fly
  Thin winding breath, which purl'd up to the sky.

CCII

About him were a press of gaping faces,
Which seem'd to swallow up his sound advice;
All jointly list'ning, but with several graces,
As if some Mermaid did their ears entice,
Some high, some low, the Painter was so nice;
  The scalps of many, almost hid behind,
  To jump up higher seem'd, to mock the mind.

CCIII

Here one man's hand lean'd on another's head,
His nose being shadow'd by his neighbour's ear;
Here one being throng'd bears back, all boll'n and red;
Another smother'd seems to pelt and swear;
And in their rage such signs of rage they bear,
  As, but for loss of Nestor's golden words,
  It seem'd they would debate with angry swords.

CCIV

For much imaginary work was there; 1422
Conceit deceitful, so compact, so kind,
That for Achilles' image stood his spear,
Gripp'd in an armèd hand; himself behind,
Was left unseen, save to the eye of mind: 1426
  A hand, a foot, a face, a leg, a head,
  Stood for the whole to be imaginèd.

CCV

And from the walls of strong-besiegèd Troy 1429
When their brave hope, bold Hector march'd to field,
Stood many Trojan mothers, sharing joy
To see their youthful sons bright weapons wield;
And to their hope they such odd action yield, 1433
  That through their light joy seemèd to appear,
  Like bright things stain'd, a kind of heavy fear.

CCVI

And from the strand of Dardan, where they fought,
To Simois' reedy banks the red blood ran, 1437
Whose waves to imitate the battle sought
With swelling ridges; and their ranks began
To break upon the gallèd shore, and than 1440
  Retire again, till, meeting greater ranks,
  They join and shoot their foam at Simois' banks.

CCVII

To this well-painted piece is Lucrece come, 1443
To find a face where all distress is steel'd.
Many she sees where cares have carvèd some,
But none where all distress and dolour dwell'd,
Till she despairing Hecuba beheld, 1447
  Staring on Priam's wounds with her old eyes,
  Which bleeding under Pyrrhus' proud foot lies.

CCVIII

In her the Painter had anatomised 1450
Time's ruin, beauty's wrack, and grim care's reign:
Her cheeks with chops and wrinkles were disguised;
Of what she was, no semblance did remain:
Her blue blood changed to black in every vein, 1454
  Wanting the spring that those shrunk pipes had fed,
  Show'd life imprison'd in a body dead.

CCIX

On this sad shadow Lucrece spends her eyes, 1457
And shapes her sorrow to the beldame's woes,
Who nothing wants to answer her but cries,
And bitter words to ban her cruel foes:
The Painter was no God to lend her those; 1461
  And therefore Lucrece swears he did her wrong,
  To give her so much grief and not a tongue.

CCX

'Poor instrument,' quoth she, 'without a sound, 1464
I'll tune thy woes with my lamenting tongue;
And drop sweet balm in Priam's painted wound,
And rail on Pyrrhus that hath done him wrong;
And with my tears quench Troy that burns so long; 1468
  And with my knife scratch out the angry eyes
  Of all the Greeks that are thine enemies.

CCXI

'Show me the strumpet that began this stir, 1471
That with my nails her beauty I may tear.
Thy heat of lust, fond Paris, did incur
This load of wrath that burning Troy doth bear:
Thy eye kindled the fire that burneth here, 1475
  And here in Troy, for trespass of thine eye,
  The Sire, the son, the Dame, and daughter die.

CCXII

'Why should the private pleasure of some one 1478
Become the public plague of many moe?
Let sin, alone committed, light alone
Upon his head that hath transgresséd so;
Let guiltless souls be freed from guilty woe: 1482
For one's offence why should so many fall,
To plague a private sin in general?

CCXIII

'Lo, here weeps Hecuba, here Priam dies, 1485
Here manly Hector faints, here Troilus swounds,
Here friend by friend in bloody channel lies,
And friend to friend gives unadvisèd wounds,
And one man's lust these many lives confounds: 1489
Had doting Priam check'd his son's desire,
Troy had been bright with fame and not with fire,'

CCXIV

Here feelingly she weeps Troy's painted woes: 1492
For sorrow, like a heavy hanging bell,
Once set on ringing, with his own weight goes;
Then little strength rings out the doleful knell:
So Lucrece, set awork, sad tales doth tell 1496
To pencill'd pensiveness and colour'd sorrow;
She lends them words, and she their looks doth borrow.

CCXV

She throws her eyes about the painting round, 1499
And whom she finds forlorn she doth lament.
At last she sees a wretched image bound,
That piteous looks to Phrygian shepherds lent:
His face, though full of cares, yet show'd content; 1503
Onward to Troy with the blunt swains he goes,
So mild, that Patience seem'd to scorn his woes.

CCXVI

In him the Painter labour'd with his skill
To hide deceit, and give the harmless show
An humble gait, calm looks, eyes wailing still,
A brow unbent, that seem'd to welcome woe;
Cheeks neither red nor pale, but mingled so
  That blushing red no guilty instance gave,
  Nor ashy pale the fear that false hearts have.

CCXVII

But, like a constant and confirméd Devil,
He entertain'd a show so seeming just,
And therein so ensconced his secret evil,
That Jealousy itself could not mistrust
False-creeping Craft and Perjury should thrust
  Into so bright a day such black-faced storms,
  Or blot with Hell-born sin such Saint-like forms.

CCXVIII

The well-skill'd workman this mild image drew
For perjur'd Sinon, whose enchanting story
The credulous old Priam after slew;
Whose words like wildfire burnt the shining glory
Of rich-built Ilion, that the skies were sorry,
  And little stars shot from their fixéd places,
  When their glass fell wherein they view'd their faces.

CCXIX

This picture she advisedly perused,
And chid the Painter for his wondrous skill,
Saying, some shape in Sinon's was abused;
So fair a form lodged not a mind so ill:
And still on him she gazed; and gazing still,
  Such signs of truth in his plain face she spied,
  That she concludes the picture was belied.

CCXX

'It cannot be,' quoth she, 'that so much guile'— 1534
She would have said 'can lurk in such a look';
But Tarquin's shape came in her mind the while,
And from her tongue 'can lurk' from 'cannot' took:
'It cannot be,' she in that sense forsook, 1538
  And turn'd it thus, 'It cannot be, I find,
  But such a face should bear a wicked mind:

CCXXI

'For even as subtle Sinon here is painted, 1541
So sober-sad, so weary, and so mild,
(As if with grief or travail he had fainted),
To me came Tarquin, armèd to begild
With outward honesty, but yet defiled 1545
  With inward vice: as Priam him did cherish,
  So did I Tarquin; so my Troy did perish.

CCXXII

'Look, look, how list'ning Priam wets his eyes, 1548
To see those borrow'd tears that Sinon sheds!
Priam, why art thou old and yet not wise?
For every tear he falls a Trojan bleeds:
His eye drops fire, no water thence proceeds; 1552
  Those round clear pearls of his, that move thy pity,
  Are balls of quenchless fire to burn thy city.

CCXXIII

'Such Devils steal effects from lightless Hell; 1555
For Sinon in his fire doth quake with cold,
And in that cold hot burning fire doth dwell;
These contraries such unity do hold,
Only to flatter fools and make them bold: 1559
  So Priam's trust false Sinon's tears doth flatter,
  That he finds means to burn his Troy with water.'

CCXXIV

Here, all enraged, such passion her assails, 1562
That patience is quite beaten from her breast.
She tears the senseless Sinon with her nails,
Comparing him to that unhappy guest
Whose deed hath made herself herself detest: 1566
  At last she smilingly with this gives o'er;
  'Fool, fool!' quoth she, 'his wounds will not be sore.'

CCXXV

Thus ebbs and flows the current of her sorrow, 1569
And time doth weary time with her complaining.
She looks for night, and then she longs for morrow,
And both she thinks too long with her remaining:
Short time seems long in sorrow's sharp sustaining: 1573
  Though woe be heavy, yet it seldom sleeps;
  And they that watch, see time, how slow it creeps.

CCXXVI

Which all this time hath overslipp'd her thought, 1576
That she with painted images hath spent;
Being from the feeling of her own grief brought
By deep surmise of others' detriment;
Losing her woes in shows of discontent. 1580
  It easeth some, though none it ever curéd,
  To think their dolour others have enduréd.

CCXXVII

But now the mindful messenger, come back, 1583
Brings home his Lord and other company;
Who finds his Lucrece clad in mourning black:
And round about her tear-distainéd eye
Blue circles stream'd, like rainbows in the sky: 1587
  These water-galls in her dim element
  Foretell new storms to those already spent.

CCXXVIII

Which when her sad-beholding husband saw, 1590
Amazedly in her sad face he stares:
Her eyes, though sod in tears, look'd red and raw,
Her lively colour kill'd with deadly cares.
He hath no power to ask her how she fares: 1594
  Both stood, like old acquaintance in a trance,
  Met far from home, wond'ring each other's chance.

CCXXIX

At last he takes her by the bloodless hand, 1597
And thus begins: 'What uncouth ill event
Hath thee befall'n, that thou dost trembling stand?
Sweet love, what spite hath thy fair colour spent?
Why art thou thus attired in discontent? 1601
  Unmask, dear dear, this moody heaviness,
  And tell thy grief, that we may give redress.'

CCXXX

Three times with sighs she gives her sorrow fire, 1604
Ere once she can discharge one word of woe:
At length address'd to answer his desire,
She modestly prepares to let them know
Her honour is ta'en prisoner by the foe; 1608
  While Collatine and his consorted lords
  With sad attention long to hear her words.

CCXXXI

And now this pale Swan in her watery nest 1611
Begins the sad Dirge of her certain ending;
'Few words,' quoth she, 'shall fit the trespass best,
Where no excuse can give the fault amending:
In me moe woes than words are now depending; 1615
  And my laments would be drawn out too long,
  To tell them all with one poor tiréd tongue.

CCXXXII

'Then be this all the task it hath to say: 1618
Dear husband, in the interest of thy bed
A stranger came, and on that pillow lay
Where thou wast wont to rest thy weary head;
And what wrong else may be imaginéd 1622
By foul enforcement might be done to me,
From that, alas, thy Lucrece is not free.

CCXXXIII

'For in the dreadful dead of dark midnight, 1625
With shining falchion in my chamber came
A creeping creature, with a flaming light,
And softly cried, "Awake, thou Roman Dame,
And entertain my love; else lasting shame 1629
On thee and thine this night I will inflict,
If thou my love's desire do contradict.

CCXXXIV

'"For some hard-favour'd groom of thine," quoth he,
"Unless thou yoke thy liking to my will, 1633
I'll murder straight, and then I'll slaughter thee
And swear I found you where you did fulfil
The loathsome act of lust, and so did kill 1636
The lechers in their deed: this act will be
My fame and thy perpetual infamy."

CCXXXV

'With this, I did begin to start and cry; 1639
And then against my heart he sets his sword,
Swearing, unless I took all patiently,
I should not live to speak another word;
So should my shame still rest upon record, 1643
And never be forgot in mighty Rome
Th' adulterate death of Lucrece and her groom.

CCXXXVI

'Mine enemy was strong, my poor self weak,
And far the weaker with so strong a fear:
My bloody judge forbade my tongue to speak:
No rightful plea might plead for justice there:
His scarlet Lust came evidence to swear
  That my poor beauty had purloin'd his eyes;
  And when the judge is robb'd the prisoner dies.

CCXXXVII

'O, teach me how to make mine own excuse!
Or at the least this refuge let me find;
Though my gross blood be stain'd with this abuse,
Immaculate and spotless is my mind;
That was not forced; that never was inclined
  To accessary yieldings, but still pure
  Doth in her poison'd closet yet endure.'

CCXXXVIII

Lo, here, the hopeless merchant of this loss,
With head declined, and voice damm'd up with woe,
With sad set eyes, and wretched arms across,
From lips new-waxen pale begins to blow
The grief away that stops his answer so:
  But, wretched as he is, he strives in vain;
  What he breathes out his breath drinks up again.

CCXXXIX

As through an arch the violent roaring tide
Outruns the eye that doth behold his haste,
Yet in the eddy boundeth in his pride
Back to the strait that forced him on so fast;
In rage sent out, recall'd in rage, being past:
  Even so his sighs, his sorrows, make a saw,
  To push grief on, and back the same grief draw.

CCXL

Which speechless woe of his poor she attendeth, 1674
And his untimely frenzy thus awaketh:
'Dear Lord, thy sorrow to my sorrow lendeth
Another power; no flood by raining slaketh.
My woe too sensible thy passion maketh 1678
  More feeling-painful: let it then suffice
  To drown one woe, one pair of weeping eyes.

CCXLI

'And for my sake, when I might charm thee so, 1681
For she that was thy Lucrece,—now attend me:
Be suddenly revengéd on my foe,
Thine, mine, his own: suppose thou dost defend me
From what is past: the help that thou shalt lend me 1685
  Comes all too late, yet let the traitor die;
  For "sparing justice feeds iniquity."

CCXLII

'But ere I name him, you fair Lords,' quoth she, 1688
Speaking to those that came with Collatine,
'Shall plight your honourable faiths to me,
With swift pursuit to venge this wrong of mine;
For 'tis a meritorious fair design 1692
  To chase injustice with revengeful arms:
  Knights, by their oaths, should right poor Ladies' harms.'

CCXLIII

At this request, with noble disposition 1695
Each present Lord began to promise aid,
As bound in Knighthood to her imposition,
Longing to hear the hateful foe bewray'd.
But she, that yet her sad task hath not said, 1699
  The protestation stops. 'O, speak,' quoth she,
  'How may this forcéd stain be wiped from me?

CCXLIV

'What is the quality of my offence, 1702
Being constrain'd with dreadful circumstance?
May my pure mind with the foul act dispense,
My low-declinéd honour to advance?
May any terms acquit me from this chance? 1706
  The poisoned fountain clears itself again;
  And why not I from this compelléd stain?'

CCXLV

With this, they all at once began to say, 1709
Her body's stain her mind untainted clears;
While with a joyless smile she turns away
The face, that map which deep impression bears
Of hard misfortune, carv'd in it with tears, 1713
  'No, no,' quoth she, 'no Dame, hereafter living,
  By my excuse shall claim excuse's giving.'

CCXLVI

Here with a sigh, as if her heart would break, 1716
She throws forth Tarquin's name: 'He, he,' she says,
But more than 'he' her poor tongue could not speak;
Till after many accents and delays,
Untimely breathings, sick and short assays, 1720
  She utters this, 'He, he, fair Lords, 'tis he,
  That guides this hand to give this wound to me.'

CCXLVII

Even here she sheathéd in her harmless breast 1723
A harmful knife, that thence her soul unsheathéd:
That blow did bail it from the deep unrest
Of that polluted prison where it breathéd:
Her contrite sighs unto the clouds bequeathéd 1727
  Her wingéd sprite, and through her wounds doth fly
  Life's lasting date from cancell'd destiny.

CCXLVIII

Stone-still, astonish'd with this deadly deed,
Stood Collatine and all his Lordly crew;
Till Lucrece' father, that beholds her bleed,
Himself on her self-slaughter'd body threw;
And from the purple fountain Brutus drew
  The murderous knife, and, as it left the place,
  Her blood, in poor revenge, held it in chase;

CCXLIX

And bubbling from her breast, it doth divide
In two slow rivers, that the crimson blood
Circles her body in on every side,
Who, like a late-sack'd island, vastly stood
Bare and unpeopled in this fearful flood.
  Some of her blood still pure and red remain'd,
  And some look'd black, and that false Tarquin stain'd.

CCL

About the mourning and congealéd face
Of that black blood a wat'ry rigol goes,
Which seems to weep upon the tainted place:
And ever since, as pitying Lucrece' woes,
Corrupted blood some watery token shows;
  And blood untainted still doth red abide,
  Blushing at that which is so putrified.

CCLI

'Daughter, dear daughter,' old Lucretius cries,
'That life was mine which thou hast here deprivéd.
If in the child the father's image lies,
Where shall I live now Lucrece is unlivéd?
Thou wast not to this end from me derivéd.
  If children predecease progenitors,
  We are their offspring, and they none of ours.

CCLII

'Poor broken glass, I often did behold 1758
In thy sweet semblance my old age new born;
But now that fair fresh mirror, dim and old,
Shows me a bare-boned death by time outworn:
O, from thy cheeks my image thou hast torn, 1762
  And shiver'd all the beauty of my glass,
  That I no more can see what once I was!

CCLIII

'O time, cease thou thy course and last no longer 1765
If they surcease to be that should survive.
Shall rotten death make conquest of the stronger
And leave the falt'ring feeble souls alive?
The old Bees die, the young possess their hive: 1769
  Then live, sweet Lucrece, live again and see
  Thy father die, and not thy father thee!'

CCLIV

By this, starts Collatine as from a dream, 1772
And bids Lucretius give his sorrow place;
And then in key-cold Lucrece' bleeding stream
He falls, and bathes the pale fear in his face,
And counterfeits to die with her a space; 1776
  Till manly shame bids him possess his breath
  And live to be revengéd on her death.

CCLV

The deep vexation of his inward soul 1779
Hath serv'd a dumb arrest upon his tongue;
Who, mad that sorrow should his use control,
Or keep him from heart-easing words so long,
Begins to talk; but through his lips do throng 1783
  Weak words, so thick come in his poor heart's aid,
  That no man could distinguish what he said.

CCLVI

Yet sometime 'Tarquin' was pronouncéd plain, 1786
But through his teeth, as if the name he tore.
This windy tempest, till it blow up rain,
Held back his sorrow's tide, to make it more;
At last it rains, and busy winds give o'er: 1790
  Then son and father weep with equal strife
  Who should weep most, for daughter or for wife.

CCLVII

The one doth call her his, the other his, 1793
Yet neither may possess the claim they lay.
The father says 'She 's mine.' 'O, mine she is,'
Replies her husband: 'do not take away
My sorrow's interest; let no mourner say 1797
  He weeps for her, for she was only mine,
  And only must be wail'd by Collatine.'

CCLVIII

'O,' quoth Lucretius, 'I did give that life 1800
Which she too early and too late hath spill'd.'
'Woe, woe,' quoth Collatine, 'she was my wife,
I owed her, and 'tis mine that she hath kill'd.'
'My daughter' and 'my wife' with clamours fill'd 1804
  The dispers'd air, who, holding Lucrece' life,
  Answer'd their cries, 'my daughter' and 'my wife.'

CCLIX

Brutus, who pluck'd the knife from Lucrece' side, 1807
Seeing such emulation in their woe,
Began to clothe his wit in state and pride,
Burying in Lucrece' wound his folly's show.
He with the Romans was esteeméd so 1811
  As silly-jeering idiots are with Kings,
  For sportive words and utt'ring foolish things:

CCLX

But now he throws that shallow habit by, 1814
Wherein deep policy did him disguise;
And arm'd his long-hid wits advisedly,
To check the tears in Collatinus' eyes.
'Thou wrongéd Lord of Rome,' quoth he, 'arise: 1818
Let my unsounded self, suppos'd a fool,
Now set thy long-experienced wit to school.

CCLXI

'Why, Collatine, is woe the cure for woe? 1821
Do wounds help wounds, or grief help grievous deeds?
Is it revenge to give thyself a blow
For his foul act by whom thy fair wife bleeds?
Such childish humour from weak minds proceeds: 1825
  Thy wretched wife mistook the matter so,
  To slay herself, that should have slain her foe.

CCLXII

'Courageous Roman, do not steep thy heart 1828
In such relenting dew of lamentations;
But kneel with me and help to bear thy part,
To rouse our Roman Gods with invocations,
That they will suffer these abominations 1832
  (Since Rome herself in them doth stand disgracéd),
  By our strong arms from forth her fair streets chaséd.

CCLXIII

'Now, by the Capitol that we adore, 1835
And by this chaste blood so unjustly stainéd,
By heaven's fair sun that breeds the fat earth's store,
By all our country rights in Rome maintainéd,
And by chaste Lucrece' soul that late complainéd 1839
  Her wrongs to us, and by this bloody knife,
  We will revenge the death of this true wife.'

CCLXIV

This said, he struck his hand upon his breast, 1842
And kiss'd the fatal knife, to end his vow;
And to his protestation urged the rest,
Who, wond'ring at him, did his words allow:
Then jointly to the ground their knees they bow: 1846
  And that deep vow, which Brutus made before,
  He doth again repeat, and that they swore.

CCLXV

When they had sworn to this advisėd doom, 1849
They did conclude to bear dead Lucrece thence;
To show her bleeding body thorough Rome,
And so to publish Tarquin's foul offence:
Which being done with speedy diligence, 1853
  The Romans plausibly did give consent
  To Tarquin's everlasting banishment.

Sonnets

To . The . Onlie . Begetter . Of
These . Insving . Sonnets .
Mr. W. H. All . Happinesse .
And . That . Eternitie .
Promised .
By .
Our . Ever-Living . Poet
Wisheth .
The . Well-Wishing .
Adventurer . In .
Setting .
Forth

T. T.

Sonnets

I

From fairest creatures we desire increase,
That thereby beauty's *Rose* might never die,
But as the riper should by time decease,
His tender heir might bear his memory:
But thou, contracted to thine own bright eyes,
Feed'st thy light's flame with self-substantial fuel,
Making a famine where abundance lies,
Thyself thy foe, to thy sweet self too cruel.
Thou that art now the world's fresh ornament,
And only herald to the gaudy spring,
Within thine own bud buriest thy content,
And, tender churl, makest waste in niggarding:
  Pity the world, or else this glutton be,
  To eat the world's due, by the grave and thee.

II

When forty winters shall besiege thy brow,
And dig deep trenches in thy beauty's field,
Thy youth's proud livery, so gazed on now,
Will be a tatter'd weed of small worth held:
Then being ask'd, where all thy beauty lies,
Where all the treasure of thy lusty days;
To say, within thine own deep-sunken eyes,
Were an all-eating shame and thriftless praise.

How much more praise deserv'd thy beauty's use,
If thou couldst answer, 'This fair child of mine
Shall sum my count and make my old excuse,'
Proving his beauty by succession thine!
  This were to be new made when thou art old,
  And see thy blood warm when thou feel'st it cold.

III

Look in thy glass, and tell the face thou viewest,
Now is the time that face should form another;
Whose fresh repair if now thou not renewest,
Thou dost beguile the world, unbless some mother.
For where is she so fair whose unear'd womb
Disdains the tillage of thy husbandry?
Or who is he so fond will be the tomb
Of his self-love, to stop posterity?
Thou art thy mother's glass, and she in thee
Calls back the lovely April of her prime:
So thou through windows of thine age shalt see
Despite of wrinkles this thy golden time.
  But if thou live, rememb'red not to be,
  Die single, and thine image dies with thee.

IV

Unthrifty loveliness, why dost thou spend
Upon thyself thy beauty's legacy?
Nature's bequest gives nothing but doth lend,
And being frank she lends to those are free:
Then, beauteous niggard, why dost thou abuse
The bounteous largess given thee to give?
Profitless usurer, why dost thou use
So great a sum of sums, yet canst not live?
For having traffic with thyself alone,
Thou of thyself thy sweet self dost deceive:

Then how, when nature calls thee to begone,
What acceptable *Audit* canst thou leave?
  Thy unused beauty must be tomb'd with thee,
  Which, uséd, lives th' executor to be.

V

Those hours, that with gentle work did frame
The lovely gaze where every eye doth dwell,
Will play the tyrants to the very same,
And that unfair which fairly doth excel:
For never-resting time leads summer on
To hideous winter and confounds him there;
Sap check'd with frost and lusty leaves quite gone,
Beauty o'ersnow'd and bareness everywhere:
Then, were not summer's distillation left,
A liquid prisoner pent in walls of glass,
Beauty's effect with beauty were bereft,
Nor it nor no remembrance what it was:
  But flowers distill'd, though they with winter meet,
  Leese but their show; their substance still lives sweet.

VI

Then let not winter's ragged hand deface
In thee they summer, ere thou be distill'd:
Make sweet some vial; treasure thou some place
With beauty's treasure, ere it be self-kill'd.
That use is not forbidden usury
Which happies those that pay the willing loan;
That 's for thyself to breed another thee,
Or ten times happier, be it ten for one;
Ten times thyself were happier than thou art,
If ten of thine ten times refigured thee:
Then what could death do, if thou shouldst depart,
Leaving thee living in posterity?

Be not self-will'd, for thou art much too fair
To be death's conquest and make worms thine heir.

VII

Lo, in the Orient when the gracious light
Lifts up his burning head, each under eye
Doth homage to his new-appearing sight,
Serving with looks his sacred majesty;
And having climb'd the steep-up heavenly hill,
Resembling strong youth in his middle age,
Yet mortal looks adore his beauty still,
Attending on his golden pilgrimage;
But when from highmost pitch, with weary car,
Like feeble age, he reeleth from the day,
The eyes, 'fore duteous, now converted are
From his low tract and look another way:
So thou, thyself out-going in thy noon,
Unlook'd on diest, unless thou get a son.

VIII

Music to hear, why hear'st thou music sadly?
Sweets with sweets war not, joy delights in joy:
Why lov'st thou that which thou receiv'st not gladly,
Or else receiv'st with pleasure thine annoy?
If the true concord of well-tunéd sounds,
By unions married, do offend thine ear,
They do but sweetly chide thee, who confounds
In singleness the parts that thou shouldst bear.
Mark how one string, sweet husband to another,
Strikes each in each by mutual ordering;
Resembling sire, and child, and happy mother,
Who all in one, one pleasing note do sing:
Whose speechless song, being many, seeming one,
Sings this to thee: 'thou single wilt prove none.'

IX

Is it for fear to wet a widow's eye,
That thou consum'st thyself in single life?
Ah! if thou issueless shalt hap to die,
The world will wail thee, like a makeless wife;
The world will be thy widow and still weep,
That thou no form of thee hast left behind,
When every private widow well may keep,
By children's eyes, her husband's shape in mind.
Look, what an unthrift in the world doth spend,
Shifts but his place, for still the world enjoys it;
But beauty's waste hath in the world an end,
And kept unused, the user so destroys it.
  No love toward others in that bosom sits
  That on himself such murd'rous shame commits.

X

For shame deny that thou bear'st love to any,
Who for thyself art so unprovident.
Grant, if thou wilt, thou art belov'd of many,
But that thou none lov'st is most evident;
For thou art so possess'd with murd'rous hate
That 'gainst thyself thou stick'st not to conspire,
Seeking that beauteous roof to ruinate
Which to repair should be thy chief desire.
O, change thy thought, that I may change my mind!
Shall hate be fairer lodg'd than gentle love?
Be, as thy presence is, gracious and kind,
Or to thyself at least kind-hearted prove:
  Make thee another self, for love of me,
  That beauty still may live in thine or thee.

XI

As fast as thou shalt wane, so fast thou grow'st,
In one of thine from that which thou departest;

And that fresh blood which youngly thou bestow'st
Thou mayst call thine when thou from youth convertest.
Herein lives wisdom, beauty, and increase;
Without this, folly, age, and cold decay:
If all were minded so, the times should cease
And threescore year would make the world away.
Let those whom Nature hath not made for store,
Harsh featureless, and rude, barrenly perish:
Look, whom she best endow'd, she gave the more;
Which bounteous gift thou shouldst in bounty cherish:
  She carv'd thee for her seal, and meant thereby
  Thou shouldst print more, not let that copy die.

XII

When I do count the clock that tells the time,
And see the brave day sunk in hideous night;
When I behold the violet past prime,
And sable curls all silver'd o'er with white;
When lofty trees I see barren of leaves,
Which erst from heat did canopy the herd,
And Summer's green all girded up in sheaves,
Borne on the bier with white and bristly beard:
Then of thy beauty do I question make,
That thou among the wastes of time must go,
Since sweets and beauties do themselves forsake
And die as fast as they see others grow;
  And nothing 'gainst Time's scythe can make defence
  Save breed, to brave him when he takes thee hence.

XIII

O, that you were yourself! but, love, you are
No longer yours than you yourself here live:
Against this coming end you should prepare,
And your sweet semblance to some other give.

So should that beauty which you hold in lease
Find no determination; then you were
Yourself again after your self's decease,
When your sweet issue your sweet form should bear.
Who lets so fair a house fall to decay,
Which husbandry in honour might uphold
Against the stormy gusts of winter's day
And barren rage of death's eternal cold?
  O, none but unthrifts! Dear my love, you know
  You had a father; let your son say so.

XIV

Not from the stars do I my judgment pluck;
And yet methinks I have Astronomy,
But not to tell of good, or evil luck,
Of plagues, of dearths, or seasons' quality;
Nor can I fortune to brief minutes tell,
Pointing to each his thunder, rain and wind,
Or say with Princes if it shall go well,
By oft predict that I in heaven find:
But from thine eyes my knowledge I derive,
And, constant stars, in them I read such art
As truth and beauty shall together thrive,
If from thyself to store thou wouldst convert;
  Or else of thee this I prognosticate:
  Thy end is Truth's and Beauty's doom and date.

XV

When I consider everything that grows
Holds in perfection but a little moment,
That this huge stage presenteth nought but shows
Whereon the Stars in secret influence comment:
When I perceive that men as plants increase,
Cheeréd and check'd even by the self-same sky;

Vaunt in their youthful sap, at height decrease,
And wear their brave state out of memory:
Then the conceit of this inconstant stay
Sets you most rich in youth before my sight,
Where wasteful Time debateth with Decay,
To change your day of youth to sullied night;
  And all in war with Time for love of you,
  As he takes from you, I engraft you new.

XVI

But wherefore do not you a mightier way
Make war upon this bloody tyrant, Time?
And fortify yourself in your decay
With means more blessèd than my barren rhyme?
Now stand you on the top of happy hours,
And many maiden gardens, yet unset,
With virtuous wish would bear your living flowers,
Much liker than your painted counterfeit:
So should the lines of life that life repair,
Which this (Time's pencil or my pupil pen)
Neither in inward worth nor outward fair,
Can make you live your self in eyes of men.
  To give away your self keeps your self still,
  And you must live, drawn by your own sweet skill.

XVII

Who will believe my verse in time to come,
If it were fill'd with your most high deserts?
Though yet, heaven knows, it is but as a tomb
Which hides your life and shows not half your parts.
If I could write the beauty of your eyes
And in fresh numbers number all your graces,
The age to come would say 'This Poet lies;
Such heavenly touches ne'er touch'd earthly faces.'

So should my papers, yellowed with their age,
Be scorn'd like old men of less truth than tongue,
And your true rights be termed a Poet's rage,
And stretched metre of an antique song:
But were some child of yours alive that time,
You should live twice; in it and in my rhyme.

XVIII

Shall I compare thee to a Summer's day?
Thou art more lovely and more temperate:
Rough winds do shake the darling buds of May,
And Summer's lease hath all too short a date:
Sometime too hot the eye of heaven shines,
And often is his gold complexion dimm'd;
And every fair from fair sometime declines,
By chance, or nature's changing course untrimm'd:
But thy eternal Summer shall not fade,
Nor loose possession of that fair thou ow'st;
Nor shall Death brag thou wand'rest in his shade,
When in eternal lines to time thou grow'st:
So long as men can breathe or eyes can see,
So long lives this and this gives life to thee.

XIX

Devouring Time, blunt thou the Lion's paws,
And make the earth devour her own sweet brood;
Pluck the keen teeth from the fierce Tiger's jaws,
And burn the long-liv'd Phœnix in her blood;
Make glad and sorry seasons as thou fleet'st,
And do whate'er thou wilt, swift-footed Time,
To the wide world and all her fading sweets;
But I forbid thee one most heinous crime:
O, carve not with thy hours my love's fair brow,
Nor draw no lines there with thine antique pen;

Him in thy course untainted do allow
For beauty's pattern to succeeding men.
  Yet do thy worst, old Time: despite thy wrong,
  My love shall in my verse ever live young.

XX

A woman's face with Nature's own hand painted,
Hast thou, the Master Mistress of my passion;
A woman's gentle heart, but not acquainted
With shifting change, as is false women's fashion;
An eye more bright than theirs, less false in rolling,
Gilding the object whereupon it gazeth;
A man in hue, all *Hervs* in his controlling,
Which steals men's eyes and women's souls amazeth.
And for a woman wert thou first created;
Till Nature, as she wrought thee, fell a-doting,
And by addition me of thee defeated,
By adding one thing to my purpose nothing.
  But since she prick'd thee out for women's pleasure,
  Mine be thy love and thy love's use their treasure.

XXI

So is it not with me as with that Muse,
Stirr'd by a painted beauty to his verse,
Who heaven itself for ornament doth use.
And every fair with his fair doth rehearse;
Making a couplement of proud compare,
With Sun and Moon, with earth and sea's rich gems,
With April's first-born flowers, and all things rare
That heaven's air in this huge rendure hems.
O, let me, true in love, but truly write,
And then believe me, my love is as fair
As any mother's child, though not so bright
As those gold candles fix'd in heaven's air:

Let them say more that like of hearsay well;
I will not praise that purpose not to sell.

XXII

My glass shall not persuade me I am old,
So long as youth and thou are of one date;
But when in thee time's furrows I behold,
Then look I death my days should expiate.
For all that beauty that doth cover thee,
Is but the seemly raiment of my heart,
Which in thy breast doth live, as thine in me:
How can I then be elder than thou art?
O, therefore, love, be of thyself so wary
As I, not for myself, but for thee will;
Bearing thy heart, which I will keep so chary
As tender nurse her babe from faring ill.
Presume not on thy heart when mine is slain;
Thou gav'st me thine, not to give back again.

XXIII

As an unperfect actor on the stage,
Who with his fear is put besides his part,
Or some fierce thing replete with too much rage,
Whose strength's abundance weakens his own heart;
So I, for fear of trust, forget to say
The perfect ceremony of love's rite,
And in mine own love's strength seem to decay,
O'ercharged with burthen of mine own love's might.
O, let my books be then the eloquence
And dumb presagers of my speaking breast,
Who plead for love and look for recompense,
More than that tongue that more hath more express'd.
O, learn to read what silent love hath writ:
To hear with eyes belongs to love's fine wit.

XXIV

Mine eye hath play'd the painter and hath steel'd
Thy beauty's form in table of my heart;
My body is the frame wherein 'tis held,
And pérspective it is best Painter's art.
For through the Painter must you see his skill,
To find where your true image pictured lies,
Which in my bosom's shop is hanging still,
That hath his windows glazéd with thine eyes.
Now see what good-turns eyes for eyes have done:
Mine eyes have drawn thy shape, and thine for me
Are windows to my breast, where-through the Sun
Delights to peep, to gaze therein on thee;
  Yet eyes this cunning want to grace their art;
  They draw but what they see, know not the heart.

XXV

Let those who are in favour with their stars
Of public honour and proud titles boast,
Whilst I, whom fortune of such triumph bars,
Unlook'd for joy in that I honour most.
Great Princes' favourites their fair leaves spread
But as the Marygold at the sun's eye,
And in themselves their pride lies buriéd,
For at a frown they in their glory die.
The painful warrior famouséd for fight,
After a thousand victories once foil'd,
Is from the book of honour razéd quite,
And all the rest forgot for which he toil'd:
  Then happy I, that love and am belovéd
  Where I may not remove nor be removéd.

XXVI

Lord of my love, to whom in vassalage
Thy merit hath my duty strongly knit,

To thee I send this written ambassage,
To witness duty, not to show my wit:
Duty so great, which wit so poor as mine
May make seem bare, in wanting words to show it,
But that I hope some good conceit of thine
In thy soul's thought (all naked) will bestow it;
Till whatsoever star that guides my moving
Points on me graciously with fair aspéct
And puts apparel on my tatter'd loving,
To show me worthy of thy sweet respect:
  Then may I dare to boast how I do love thee;
  Till then, not show my head where thou mayst prove me.

XXVII

Weary with toil, I haste me to my bed,
The dear repose for limbs with travel tiréd;
But then begins a journey in my head,
To work my mind, when body's work's expired:
For then my thoughts, from far where I abide,
Intend a zealous pilgrimage to thee,
And keep my drooping eyelids open wide,
Looking on darkness which the blind do see:
Save that my soul's imaginary sight
Presents thy shadow to my sightless view,
Which, like a jewel, hung in ghastly night,
Makes black night beauteous and her old face new.
  Lo! thus, by day my limbs, by night my mind,
  For thee, and for myself, no quiet find.

XXVIII

How can I then return in happy plight,
That am debarr'd the benefit of rest?
When day's oppression is not eas'd by night,
But day by night, and night by day, oppress'd?

And each, though enemies to either's reign,
Do in consent shake hands to torture me,
The one by toil, the other to complain
How far I toil, still farther off from thee.
I tell the Day, to please him thou art bright,
And dost him grace when clouds do blot the heaven:
So flatter I the swart-complexion'd night,
When sparkling stars twire not thou gild'st the even.
  But day doth daily draw my sorrows longer
  And night doth nightly make grief's length seem stronger.

XXIX

When, in disgrace with Fortune and men's eyes,
I all alone beweep my outcast state,
And trouble deaf heaven with my bootless cries,
And look upon myself and curse my fate,
Wishing me like to one more rich in hope,
Featured like him, like him with friends possess'd,
Desiring this man's art and that man's scope,
With what I most enjoy contented least;
Yet in these thoughts myself almost despising.
Haply I think on thee, and then my state,
(Like to the Lark at break of day arising)
From sullen earth, sings hymns at Heaven's gate;
  For thy sweet love rememb'red such wealth brings
  That then I scorn to change my state with Kings.

XXX

When to the Sessions of sweet silent thought
I summon up remembrance of things past,
I sigh the lack of many a thing I sought,
And with old woes new wail my dear time's waste:
Then can I drown an eye, unused to flow,
For precious friends hid in death's dateless night,

And weep afresh love's long since cancell'd woe,
And moan th' expense of many a vanish'd sight:
Then can I grieve at grievances foregone,
And heavily from woe to woe tell o'er
The sad account of fore-bemoanéd moan,
Which I new pay as if not paid before.
  But if the while I think on thee, dear friend,
  All losses are restor'd, and sorrows end.

XXXI

Thy bosom is endearéd with all hearts,
Which I by lacking have supposéd dead,
And there reigns Love and all Love's loving parts,
And all those friends which I thought buriéd.
How many a holy and obsequious tear
Hath dear religious love stol'n from mine eye
As interest of the dead, which now appear
But things removed that hidden in there lie.
Thou art the grave where buried love doth live,
Hung with the trophies of my lovers gone,
Who all their parts of me to thee did give;
That due of many, now is thine alone:
  Their images I lov'd I view in thee,
  And thou, all they, hast all the all of me.

XXXII

If thou survive my well-contented day,
When that churl Death my bones with dust shall cover,
And shalt by fortune once more re-survey
These poor rude lines of thy deceaséd Lover:
Compare them with the bett'ring of the time,
And though they be outstripp'd by every pen,
Reserve them for my love, not for their rhyme,
Exceeded by the height of happier men.

O, then vouchsafe me but this loving thought:
'Had my friend's Muse grown with this growing age,
A dearer birth than this his love had brought,
To march in ranks of better equipage:
But since he died and Poets better prove,
Theirs for their style I'll read, his for his love.'

XXXIII

Full many a glorious morning have I seen
Flatter the mountain tops with sovereign eye,
Kissing with golden face the meadows green;
Gilding pale streams with heavenly alchemy:
Anon permit the basest clouds to ride
With ugly rack on his celestial face,
And from the forlorn world his visage hide,
Stealing unseen to west with this disgrace:
Even so my Sun one early morn did shine
With all-triumphant splendour on my brow;
But out, alack! he was but one hour mine;
The region cloud hath mask'd him from me now.
Yet him for this my love no whit disdaineth;
Suns of the world may stain, when heaven's sun staineth.

XXXIV

Why didst thou promise such a beauteous day,
And make me travel forth without my cloak,
To let base clouds o'ertake me in my way,
Hiding thy bravery in their rotten smoke?
'Tis not enough that through the cloud thou break,
To dry the rain on my storm-beaten face,
For no man well of such a salve can speak
That heals the wound and cures not the disgrace:
Nor can thy shame give physic to my grief;
Though thou repent, yet I have still the loss:

The offender's sorrow lends but weak relief
To him that bears the strong offence's cross.
  Ah! but those tears are pearl which thy love sheds,
  And they are rich, and ransom all ill deeds.

XXXV

No more be griev'd at that which thou hast done:
Roses have thorns, and silver fountains mud;
Clouds and eclipses stain both Moon and Sun,
And loathsome canker lives in sweetest bud.
All men make faults, and even I in this,
Authórising thy trespass with compare,
Myself corrupting, salving thy amiss,
Excusing thy sins, more than their sins are:
For to thy sensual fault I bring in sense—
Thy adverse party is thy Advocate—
And 'gainst myself a lawful plea commence:
Such civil war is in my love and hate,
  That I an accessory needs must be
  To that sweet thief which sourly robs from me.

XXXVI

Let me confess that we two must be twain,
Although out undivided loves are one:
So shall those blots that do with me remain,
Without thy help, by me be borne alone.
In our two loves there is but one respect,
Though in our lives a separable spite,
Which though it alter not love's sole effect,
Yet doth it steal sweet hours from love's delight.
I may not ever more acknowledge thee,
Lest my bewailéd guilt should do thee shame,
Nor thou with public kindness honour me,
Unless thou take that honour from thy name:

But do not so; I love thee in such sort
As, thou being mine, mine is thy good report.

XXXVII

As a decrepit father takes delight
To see his active child do deeds of youth,
So I, made lame by Fortune's dearest spite,
Take all my comfort of thy worth and truth.
For whether beauty, birth, or wealth, or wit,
Or any of these all, or all, or more,
Entituled in their parts, do crownéd sit,
I make my love engrafted to this store:
So then I am not lame, poor, nor despised,
Whilst that this shadow doth such substance give,
That I in thy abundance am sufficed
And by a part of all thy glory live.
Look, what is best, that best I wish in thee:
This wish I have; then ten times happy me!

XXXVIII

How can my Muse want subject to invent,
While thou dost breathe, that pour'st into my verse
Thine own sweet argument, too excellent
For every vulgar paper to rehearse?
O, give thyself the thanks, if aught in me
Worthy perusal stand against thy sight;
For who 's so dumb that cannot write to thee,
When thou thyself dost give invention light?
Be thou the tenth Muse, ten times more in worth
Than those old nine which rhymers invocate;
And he that calls on thee, let him bring forth
Eternal numbers to outlive long date.
If my slight Muse do please these curious days,
The pain be mine, but thine shall be the praise.

XXXIX

O, how thy worth with manners may I sing,
When thou art all the better part of me?
What can mine own praise to mine own self bring?
And what is 't but mine own when I praise thee?
Even for this let us divided live,
And our dear love lose name of single one,
That by this separation I may give
That due to thee which thou deserv'st alone.
O absence, what a torment wouldst thou prove,
Were it not thy sour leisure gave sweet leave
To entertain the time with thoughts of love,
Which time and thoughts so sweetly dost deceive!
  And that thou teachest how to make one twain,
  By praising him here who doth hence remain!

XL

Take all my loves, my love, yea, take them all;
What hast thou then more than thou hadst before?
No love, my love, that thou mayst true love call;
All mine was thine before thou hadst this more.
Then if for my love, thou my love receivést,
I cannot blame thee, for my love thou usést,
But yet be blamed, if thou this self deceivést
By wilful taste of what thy self refusést.
I do forgive thy robb'ry, gentle thief,
Although thou steal thee all my poverty;
And yet, love knows, it is a greater grief
To bear love's wrong than hate's known injury.
  Lascivious grace, in whom all ill well shows,
  Kill me with spites; yet we must not be foes.

XLI

Those pretty wrongs that liberty commits,
When I am sometime absent from thy heart,

Thy beauty and thy years full well befits,
For still temptation follows where thou art.
Gentle thou art, and therefore to be won,
Beauteous thou art, therefore to be assailéd;
And when a woman woos, what woman's son
Will sourly leave her till he have prevailéd?
Aye me! but yet thou mightst my seat forbear,
And chide thy beauty and thy straying youth,
Who lead thee in their riot even there
Where thou art forced to break a twofold truth;
  Hers, by thy beauty tempting her to thee,
  Thine, by thy beauty being false to me.

XLII

That thou hast her, it is not all my grief,
And yet it may be said I lov'd her dearly;
That she hath thee, is of my wailing chief,
A loss in love that touches me more nearly.
Loving offenders, thus I will excuse ye:
Thou dost love her, because thou know'st I love her;
And for my sake even so doth she abuse me,
Suff'ring my friend for my sake to approve her.
If I lose thee, my loss is my love's gain,
And losing her, my friend hath found that loss;
Both find each other, and I lose both twain,
And both for my sake lay on me this cross:
  But here's the joy; my friend and I are one;
  Sweet flattery! then she loves but me alone.

XLIII

When most I wink, then do mine eyes best see,
For all the day they view things unrespected;
But when I sleep, in dreams they look on thee,
And darkly bright, are bright in dark directed.

Then thou, whose shadow shadows doth make bright,
How would thy shadow's form form happy show
To the clear day with thy much clearer light,
When to unseeing eyes thy shade shines so!
How would, I say, mine eyes be blessėd made
By looking on thee in the living day!
When in dead night thy fair imperfect shade
Through heavy sleep on sightless eyes doth stay!
  All days are nights to see till I see thee,
  And nights bright days when dreams do show thee me.

XLIV

If the dull substance of my flesh were thought,
Injurious distance should not stop my way;
For then despite of space I would be brought,
From limits far remote, where thou dost stay.
No matter then although my foot did stand
Upon the farthest earth removed from thee;
For nimble thought can jump both sea and land
As soon as think the place where he would be.
But, ah! thought kills me that I am not thought,
To leap large lengths of miles when thou art gone,
But that, so much of earth and water wrought,
I must attend time's leisure with my moan,
  Receiving naught by Elements so slow
  But heavy tears, badges of either's woe.

XLV

The other two, slight air, and purging fire,
Are both with thee, wherever I abide;
The first my thought, the other my desire,
These present-absent with swift motion slide.
For when these quicker Elements are gone
In tender Embassy of love to thee,

My life, being made of four, with two alone
Sinks down to death, oppress'd with melancholy;
Until life's composition be recuréd
By those swift messengers return'd from thee,
Who, even but now come back again, assuréd
Of thy fair health, recounting it to me:
  This told, I joy; but then no longer glad,
  I send them back again and straight grow sad.

XLVI

Mine eye and heart are at a mortal war,
How to divide the conquest of thy sight;
Mine eye, my heart thy picture's sight would bar,
My heart, mine eye the freedom of that right.
My heart doth plead that thou in him dost lie,—
A closet never pierced with crystal eyes—
But the defendant doth that plea deny
And says in him thy fair appearance lies.
To side this title is impanneléd
A quest of thoughts, all tenants to the heart,
And by their verdict is determinéd
The clear eye's moiety and the dear heart's part:
  As thus; mine eye's due is thy outward part,
  And my heart's right thy inward love of heart.

XLVII

Betwixt mine eye and heart a league is took,
And each doth good turns now unto the other:
When that mine eye is famish'd for a look,
Or heart in love with sighs himself doth smother,
With my love's picture then my eye doth feast
And to the painted banquet bids my heart;
Another time mine eye is my heart's guest
And in his thoughts of love doth share a part:

So, either by thy picture or my love,
Thyself away art present still with me;
For thou not farther than my thoughts canst move,
And I am still with them and they with thee;
  Or, if they sleep, thy picture in my sight
  Awakes my heart to heart's and eye's delight.

XLVIII

How careful was I, when I took my way,
Each trifle under truest bars to thrust,
That to my use it might unuséd stay
From hands of falsehood, in sure wards of trust!
But thou, to whom my jewels trifles are,
Most worthy comfort, now my greatest grief,
Thou, best of dearest and mine only care,
Art left the prey of every vulgar thief.
Thee have I not lock'd up in any chest,
Save where thou art not, though I feel thou art,
Within the gentle closure of my breast,
From whence at pleasure thou mayst come and part;
  And even thence thou wilt be stol'n, I fear,
  For truth proves thievish for a prize so dear.

XLIX

Against that time, if ever that time come,
When I shall see thee frown on my defects,
When as thy love hath cast his utmost sum,
Call'd to that audit by advised respects;
Against that time when thou shalt strangely pass
And scarcely greet me with that sun, thine eye,
When love, converted from the thing it was,
Shall reasons find of settled gravity;
Against that time do I ensconce me here
Within the knowledge of mine own desert,

And this my hand against myself uprear,
To guard the lawful reasons on thy part:
  To leave poor me thou hast the strength of laws,
  Since why to love I can allege no cause.

L

How heavy do I journey on the way,
When what I seek, my weary travel's end,
Doth teach that ease and that repose to say
'Thus far the miles are measur'd from thy friend!'
The beast that bears me, tiréd with my woe,
Plods dully on, to bear that weight in me,
As if by some instinct the wretch did know
His rider lov'd not speed, being made from thee:
The bloody spur cannot provoke him on
That sometimes anger thrusts into his hide;
Which heavily he answers with a groan,
More sharp to me than spurring to his side:
  For that same groan doth put this in my mind;
  My grief lies onward and my joy behind.

LI

Thus can my love excuse the slow offence
Of my dull bearer when from thee I speed:
From where thou art, why should I haste me thence?
Till I return, of posting is no need.
O, what excuse will my poor beast then find,
When swift extremity can seem but slow?
Then should I spur, though mounted on the wind;
In wingéd speed no motion shall I know:
Then can no horse with my desire keep pace;
Therefore desire, of perfect'st love being made,
Shall neigh, no dull flesh in his fiery race;
But love, for love, thus shall excuse my jade;

Since from thee going he went wilful-slow,
Towards thee I'll run, and give him leave to go.

LII

So am I as the rich, whose blesséd key
Can bring him to his sweet up-lockéd treasure,
The which he will not every hour survey,
For blunting the fine point of seldom pleasure.
Therefore are feasts so solemn and so rare,
Since, seldom coming, in the long year set,
Like stones of worth they thinly placéd are,
Or captain jewels in the carcanet.
So is the time that keeps you as my chest,
Or as the wardrobe which the robe doth hide,
To make some special instant special blest,
By new unfolding his imprison'd pride.
Blesséd are you, whose worthiness gives scope,
Being had, to triumph, being lack'd to hope.

LIII

What is your substance, whereof are you made,
That millions of strange shadows on you tend?
Since every one hath, every one, one shade,
And you, but one, can every shadow lend.
Describe *Adonis*, and the counterfeit
Is poorly imitated after you;
On *Helen's* cheek all art of beauty set,
And you in *Grecian* tires are painted new:
Speak of the spring and foison of the year,
The one doth shadow of your beauty show,
The other as your bounty doth appear;
And you in every blesséd shape we know.
In all external grace you have some part,
But you like none, none you, for constant heart.

LIV

O, how much more doth beauty beauteous seem
By that sweet ornament which truth doth give!
The Rose looks fair, but fairer we it deem
For that sweet odour which doth in it live.
The Canker-blooms have full as deep a dye
As the perfuméd tincture of the Roses,
Hang on such thorns, and play as wantonly
When summer's breath their maskéd buds discloses:
But, for their virtue only is their show,
They live unwoo'd and unrespected fade,
Die to themselves. Sweet Roses do not so;
Of their sweet deaths are sweetest odours made:
  And so of you, beauteous and lovely youth,
  When that shall vade, my verse distils your truth.

LV

Not marble, nor the gilded monuments
Of Princes, shall outlive this powerful rhyme;
But you shall shine more bright in these contents
Than unswept stone besmear'd with sluttish time.
When wasteful war shall *Statues* overturn,
And broils root out the work of masonry,
Nor *Mars* his sword nor war's quick fire shall burn
The living record of your memory.
'Gainst death and all-oblivious enmity
Shall you pace forth; your praise shall still find room,
Even in the eyes of all posterity
That wear this world out to the ending doom.
  So, till the judgment that yourself arise,
  You live in this, and dwell in lovers' eyes.

LVI

Sweet love, renew thy force; be it not said
Thy edge should blunter be than appetite.

Which but to-day by feeding is allay'd,
To-morrow sharpen'd in his former might:
So, love, be thou; although to-day thou fill
Thy hungry eyes even till they wink with fulness,
To-morrow see again, and do not kill
The spirit of Love with a perpetual dulness.
Let this sad *Int'rim* like the Ocean be
Which parts the shore, where two contracted new
Come daily to the banks, that, when they see
Return of love, more blest may be the view;
  Or call it Winter, which being full of care
  Makes Summer's welcome thrice more wish'd, more rare.

LVII

Being your slave, what should I do but tend
Upon the hours and times of your desire?
I have no precious time at all to spend,
Nor services to do, till you require.
Nor dare I chide the world-without-end hour
Whilst I, my sovereign, watch the clock for you,
Nor think the bitterness of absence sour
When you have bid your servant once adieu;
Nor dare I question with my jealous thought
Where you may be, or your affairs suppose,
But, like a sad slave, stay and think of nought,
Save, where you are, how happy you make those.
  So true a fool is love that in your Will,
  Though you do any thing, he thinks no ill.

LVIII

That God forbid, that made me first your slave,
I should in thought control your times of pleasure,
Or at your hand th' account of hours to crave,
Being your vassal, bound to stay your leisure!

O, let me suffer, being at your beck,
Th' imprison'd absence of your liberty;
And patience, tame to sufferance, bide each check,
Without accusing you of injury.
Be where you list, your charter is so strong,
That you yourself may privilege your time
To what you will; to you it doth belong
Yourself to pardon of self-doing crime.
  I am to wait, though waiting so be hell;
  Not blame your pleasure, be it ill or well.

LIX

If there be nothing new, but that which is
Hath been before, how are our brains beguiled,
Which, labouring for invention, bear amiss
The second burthen of a former child!
O, that record could with a backward look,
Even of five hundred courses of the sun,
Show me your image in some antique book,
Since mind at first in character was done!
That I might see what the old world could say
To this composéd wonder of your frame;
Whether we are mended, or whe'r better they,
Or whether revolution be the same.
  O, sure I am, the wits of former days
  To subjects worse have given admiring praise.

LX

Like as the waves make towards the pebbled shore,
So do our minutes hasten to their end;
Each changing place with that which goes before,
In sequent toil all forwards do contend.
Nativity, once in the main of light,
Crawls to maturity, wherewith being crown'd,

Crooked eclipses 'gainst his glory fight,
And Time that gave doth now his gift confound.
Time doth transfix the flourish set on youth,
And delves the parallels in beauty's brow,
Feeds on the rarities of nature's truth,
And nothing stands but for his scythe to mow:
And yet to times in hope my verse shall stand,
Praising thy worth, despite his cruel hand.

LXI

Is it thy will thy image should keep open
My heavy eyelids to the weary night?
Dost thou desire my slumbers should be broken.
While shadows like to thee do mock my sight?
Is it thy spirit that thou send'st from thee
So far from home into my deeds to pry,
To find out shames and idle hours in me,
The scope and tenure of thy jealousy?
O, no! thy love, though much, is not so great:
It is my love that keeps mine eye awake;
Mine own true love that doth my rest defeat,
To play the watchman ever for thy sake:
For thee watch I whilst thou dost wake elsewhere,
From me far off, with others all too near.

LXII

Sin of self-love possesseth all mine eye,
And all my soul, and all my every part;
And for this sin there is no remedy,
It is so grounded inward in my heart.
Methinks no face so gracious is as mine,
No shape so true, no truth of such account;
And for myself mine own worth do define,
As I all other in all worths surmount.

But when my glass shows me myself indeed,
Beated and chopp'd with tann'd antiquity,
Mine own self-love quite contrary I read;
Self so self-loving were iniquity.
'Tis thee, my self, that for myself I praise,
Painting my age with beauty of thy days.

LXIII

Against my love shall be, as I am now,
With Time's injurious hand crush'd and o'erworn;
When hours have drain'd his blood and fill'd his brow
With lines and wrinkles; when his youthful morn
Hath travell'd on to Age's steepy night,
And all those beauties whereof now he 's King
Are vanishing or vanish'd out of sight,
Stealing away the treasure of his Spring;
For such a time do I now fortify
Against confounding Age's cruel knife,
That he shall never cut from memory
My sweet love's beauty, though my lover's life:
His beauty shall in these black lines be seen,
And they shall live, and he in them still green.

LXIV

When I have seen by Time's fell hand defacéd
The rich proud cost of outworn buried age;
When sometime lofty towers I see down-razéd
And brass eternal slave to mortal rage;
When I have seen the hungry Ocean gain
Advantage on the Kingdom of the shore,
And the firm soil win of the watery main,
Increasing store with loss, and loss with store;
When I have seen such interchange of state,
Or state itself confounded to decay;

Ruin hath taught me thus to ruminate,
That Time will come and take my love away.
  This thought is as a death, which cannot choose
  But weep to have that which it fears to lose.

LXV

Since brass, nor stone, nor earth, nor boundless sea,
But sad mortality o'er-sways their power,
How with this rage shall beauty hold a plea,
Whose action is no stronger than a flower?
O, how shall summer's honey breath hold out
Against the wrackful siege of battering days,
When rocks impregnable are not so stout,
Nor gates of steel so strong, but Time decays?
O fearful meditation! where, alack,
Shall Time's best jewel from Time's chest lie hid?
Or what strong hand can hold his swift foot back?
Or who his spoil of beauty can forbid?
  O, none, unless this miracle have might,
  That in black ink my love may still shine bright.

LXVI

Tired with all these, for restful death I cry,
As, to behold Desert a beggar born,
And needy Nothing trimm'd in jollity,
And purest Faith unhappily forsworn,
And gilded Honour shamefully misplaced,
And maiden Virtue rudely strumpeted,
And right Perfection wrongfully disgraced,
And Strength by limping Sway disabled,
And Art made tongue-tied by Authority,
And Folly, Doctor-like, controlling skill,
And simple Truth miscall'd Simplicity,
And captive Good attending captain Ill:

Tired with all these, from these would I be gone,
Save that, to die, I leave my love alone.

LXVII

Ah! wherefore with infection should he live,
And with his presence grace impiety,
That sin by him advantage should achieve
And lace itself with his society?
Why should false, painting imitate his cheek
And steal dead seeing of his living hue?
Why should poor Beauty indirectly seek
Roses of shadow, since his Rose is true?
Why should he live, now Nature bankrupt is,
Beggar'd of blood to blush through lively veins;
For she hath no exchequer how but his,
And, proud of many, lives upon his gains?
O, him she stores, to show what wealth she had
In days long since, before these last so bad.

LXVIII

Thus is his cheek the map of days outworn,
When beauty liv'd and died as flowers do now,
Before these bastard signs of fair were borne,
Or durst inhabit on a living brow;
Before the golden tresses of the dead,
The right of sepulchres, were shorn away,
To live a second life on second head;
Ere beauty's dead fleece made another gay:
In him those holy antique hours are seen,
Without all ornament, itself and true,
Making no summer of another's green,
Robbing no old to dress his beauty new;
And him as for a map doth Nature store,
To show false Art what beauty was of yore.

LXIX

Those parts of thee that the world's eye doth view,
Want nothing that the thought of hearts can mend;
All tongues, the voice of souls, give thee that due,
Uttering bare truth, even so as foes commend.
Thy outward thus with outward praise is crown'd;
But those same tongues that give thee so thine own,
In other accents do this praise confound
By seeing farther than the eye hath shown.
They look into the beauty of thy mind,
And that, in guess, they measure by thy deeds;
Then, churls, their thoughts, although their eyes were kind,
To thy fair flower add the rank smell of weeds:
  But why thy odour matcheth not thy show,
  The soil is this, that thou dost common grow.

LXX

That thou art blamed shall not be thy defect,
For slander's mark was ever yet the fair;
The ornament of beauty is suspect,
A Crow that flies in heaven's sweetest air.
So thou he good, slander doth but approve
Thy worth the greater, being woo'd of Time;
For Canker-Vice the sweetest buds doth love,
And thou present'st a pure unstained prime.
Thou hast pass'd by the ambush of young days,
Either not assail'd, or victor being charged;
Yet this thy praise cannot be so thy praise,
To tie up envy evermore enlarged:
  If some suspect of ill mask'd not thy show,
  Then thou alone kingdoms of hearts shouldst owe.

LXXI

No longer mourn for me when I am dead,
Than you shall hear the surly sullen bell

Give warning to the world that I am fled
From this vile world, with vilest worms to dwell:
Nay, if you read this line, remember not
The hand that writ it; for I love you so,
That I in your sweet thoughts would be forgot,
If thinking on me then should make you woe.
O, if, I say, you look upon this verse,
When I, perhaps, compounded am with clay,
Do not so much as my poor name rehearse;
But let your love even with my life decay:
  Lest the wise world should look into your moan,
  And mock you with me after I am gone.

LXXII

O, lest the world should task you to recite
What merit liv'd in me, that you should love
After my death, dear love, forget me quite,
For you in me can nothing worthy prove;
Unless you would devise some virtuous lie,
To do more for me than mine own desert,
And hang more praise upon deceaséd I
Than niggard truth would willingly impart:
O, lest your true love may seem false in this,
That you for love speak well of me untrue,
My name be buried where my body is,
And live no more to shame nor me nor you.
  For I am shamed by that which I bring forth,
  And so should you, to love things nothing worth.

LXXIII

That time of year thou mayst in me behold,
When yellow leaves, or none, or few, do hang
Upon those boughs which shake against the cold,
Bare ruin'd choirs, where late the sweet birds sang.

In me thou see'st the twilight of such day
As after Sunset fadeth in the West,
Which by and by black night doth take away,
Death's second self, that seals up all in rest.
In me thou see'st the glowing of such fire,
That on the ashes of his youth doth lie,
As the death-bed whereon it must expire,
Consumed with that which it was nourish'd by.
  This thou perceiv'st, which makes thy love more strong,
  To love that well which thou must leave ere long.

LXXIV

But be contented: when that fell arrest
Without all bail shall carry me away,
My life hath in this line some interest,
Which for memorial still with thee shall stay.
When thou reviewest this, thou dost review
The very part was consecrate to thee:
The earth can have but earth, which is his due;
My spirit is thine, the better part of me:
So then thou hast but lost the dregs of life,
The prey of worms, my body being dead,
The coward conquest of a wretch's knife,
To base of thee to be rememberéd.
  The worth of that is that which it contains,
  And that is this, and this with three remains.

LXXV

So are you to my thoughts as food to life,
Or as sweet-season'd showers are to the ground;
And for the peace of you I hold such strife
As 'twixt a miser and his wealth is found;
Now proud as an enjoyer, and anon
Doubting the filching age will steal his treasure,

Now counting best to be with you alone,
Then better'd that the world may see my pleasure;
Sometime all full with feasting on your sight,
And by and by clean starvéd for a look;
Possessing or pursuing no delight,
Save what is had or must from you be took.
  Thus do I pine and surfeit day by day,
  Or gluttoning on all, or all away.

LXXVI

Why is my verse so barren of new pride?
So far from variation or quick change?
Why with the time do I not glance aside
To new-found methods and to compounds strange?
Why write I still all one, ever the same,
And keep invention in a noted weed,
That every word doth almost tell my name,
Showing their birth and where they did proceed?
O, know, sweet love, I always write of you,
And you and love are still my argument;
So all my best is dressing old words new,
Spending again what is already spent:
  For as the Sun is daily new and old,
  So is my love still telling what is told.

LXXVII

Thy glass will show thee how thy beauties wear,
Thy dial how thy precious minutes waste;
The vacant leaves thy mind's imprint will bear,
And of this book this learning mayst thou taste.
The wrinkles, which thy glass will truly show
Of mouthéd graves will give thee memory;
Thou by thy dial's shady stealth mayst know
Time's thievish progress to eternity.

Look, what thy memory cannot contain
Commit to these waste blanks, and thou shalt find
Those children nurs'd, deliver'd from thy brain,
To take a new acquaintance of thy mind.
These offices, so oft as thou wilt look,
Shall profit thee and much enrich thy book.

LXXVIII

So oft have I invoked thee for my Muse,
And found such fair assistance in my verse,
As every *Alien* pen hath got my use,
And under thee their poesy disperse.
Thine eyes, that taught the dumb am high to sing,
And heavy ignorance aloft to fly,
Have added feathers to the learned's wing,
And given grace a double Majesty.
Yet be most proud of that which I compile,
Whose influence is thine, and born of thee:
In others' works thou dost but mend the style,
And Arts with thy sweet graces gracéd be;
But thou art all my art, and dost advance
As high as learning my rude ignorance.

LXXIX

Whilst I alone did call upon thy aid,
My verse alone had all thy gentle grace,
But now my gracious numbers are decay'd,
And my sick Muse doth give another place.
I grant, sweet love, thy lovely argument
Deserves the travail of a worthier pen,
Yet what of thee thy Poet doth invent
He robs thee of and pays it thee again.
He lends thee virtue, and he stole that word
From thy behaviour; beauty doth he give

And found it in thy cheek: he can afford
No praise to thee; but what in thee doth live.
  Then thank him not for that which he doth say,
  Since what he owes thee thou thyself dost pay.

LXXX

O, how I faint when I of you do write,
Knowing a better spirit doth use your name,
And in the praise thereof spends all his might,
To make me tongue-tied, speaking of your fame!
But since your worth, wide as the Ocean is,
The humble as the proudest sail doth bear,
My saucy bark, inferior far to his,
On your broad main doth wilfully appear.
Your shallowest help will hold me up afloat,
Whilst he upon your soundless deep doth ride;
Or, being wreck'd, I am a worthless boat,
He of tall building and of goodly pride;
  Then if he thrive and I be cast away,
  The worst was this; my love was my decay.

LXXXI

Or I shall live your epitaph to make,
Or you survive when I in earth am rotten;
From hence your memory death cannot take,
Although in me each part will be forgotten.
Your name from hence immortal life shall have,
Though I, once gone, to all the world must die:
The earth can yield me but a common grave,
When you entombéd in men's eyes shall lie.
Your monument shall be my gentle verse,
Which eyes not yet created shall o'er-read,
And tongues to be your being shall rehearse
When all the breathers of this world are dead;

You still shall live—such virtue hath my pen—
Where breath most breathes, even in the mouths of men.

LXXXII

I grant thou wert not married to my Muse,
And therefore mayst without attaint o'erlook
The dedicated words which writers use
Of their fair subject, blessing every book.
Thou art as fair in knowledge as in hue,
Finding thy worth a limit past my praise,
And therefore art enforced to seek anew
Some fresher stamp of the time-bettering days.
And do so, love; yet when they have devised
What strainéd touches Rhetoric can lend,
Thou truly fair wert truly sympathized
In true plain words by thy true-telling friend;
And their gross painting might be better used
Where cheeks need blood; in thee it is abused.

LXXXIII

I never saw that you did painting need,
And therefore to your fair no painting set;
I found; or thought I found, you did exceed
The barren tender of a Poet's debt:
And therefore have I slept in your report,
That you yourself being extant well might show
How far a modern quill doth come too short,
Speaking of worth, what worth in you doth grow.
This silence for my sin you did impute,
Which shall be most my glory, being dumb;
For I impair not beauty being mute,
When others would give life and bring a tomb.
There lives more life in one of your fair eyes
Than both your Poets can in praise devise.

LXXXIV

Who is it that says most? which can say more
Than this rich praise, that you alone are you?
In whose confine immuréd is the store
Which should example where your equal grew.
Lean penury within that pen doth dwell,
That to his subject lends not some small glory;
But he that writes of you, if he can tell
That you are you, so dignifies his story.
Let him but copy what in you is writ,
Not making worse what nature made so clear,
And such a counterpart shall fame his wit,
Making his style admiréd every where.
  You to your beauteous blessings add a curse,
  Being fond on praise, which makes your praises worse

LXXXV

My tongue-tied Muse in manners holds her still,
While comments of your praise, richly compiled,
Reserve their character with golden quill
And precious phrase by all the Muses filed.
I think good thoughts whilst other write good words,
And like unletter'd clerk still cry 'Amen'
To every Hymn that able spirit affords
In polish'd form of well-refinéd pen.
Hearing you praised, I say ''Tis so, 'tis true,'
And to the most of praise add something more;
But that is in my thought, whose love to you,
Though words come hindmost, holds his rank before.
  Then others for the breath of words respect,
  Me for my dumb thoughts, speaking in effect.

LXXXVI

Was it the proud full sail of his great verse,
Bound for the prize of (all-too-precious) you,

That did my ripe thoughts in my brain inhearse,
Making their tomb the womb wherein they grew?
Was it his spirit, by spirits taught to write
Above a mortal pitch, that struck me dead?
No, neither he, nor his compeers by night
Giving him aid, my verse astonishéd.
He, nor that affable familiar ghost
Which nightly gulls him with intelligence,
As victors of my silence cannot boast;
I was not sick of any fear from thence:
  But when your countenance fill'd up his line,
  Then lack'd I matter; that enfeebled mine.

LXXXVII

Farewell! thou art too dear for my possessing,
And like enough thou know'st thy estimate:
The charter of thy worth gives thee releasing;
My bonds in thee are all determinate.
For how do I hold thee but by thy granting?
And for that riches where is my deserving?
The cause of this fair gift in me is wanting,
And so my patent back again is swerving.
Thyself thou gav'st, thy own worth then not knowing,
Or me, to whom thou gav'st it, else mistaking;
So thy great gift, upon misprision growing,
Comes home again, on better judgment making.
  Thus have I had thee, as a dream doth flatter,
  In sleep a King, but waking no such matter.

LXXXVIII

When thou shalt be disposed to set me light,
And place my merit in the eye of scorn,
Upon thy side against myself I'll fight,
And prove thee virtuous, though thou art forsworn.

With mine own weakness being best acquainted,
Upon thy part I can set down a story
Of faults conceal'd, wherein I am attainted;
That thou in losing me shalt win much glory:
And I by this will be a gainer too;
For bending all my loving thoughts on thee,
The injuries that to myself I do,
Doing thee vantage, double-vantage me.
  Such is my love, to thee I so belong,
  That for thy right, myself will bear all wrong.

LXXXIX

Say that thou didst forsake me for some fault,
And I will comment upon that offence:
Speak of my lameness, and I straight will halt;
Against thy reasons making no defence.
Thou canst not, love, disgrace me half so ill,
To set a form upon desiréd change,
As I'll myself disgrace: knowing thy will,
I will acquaintance strangle and look strange;
Be absent from thy walks; and in my tongue
Thy sweet belovéd name no more shall dwell,
Lest I, too much profane, should do it wrong,
And haply of our old acquaintance tell.
  For thee against myself I'll vow debate,
  For I must ne'er love him whom thou dost hate.

XC

Then hate me when thou wilt; if ever, now;
Now, while the world is bent my deeds to cross,
Join with the spite of fortune, make me bow,
And do not drop in for an after-loss:
Ah, do not, when my heart hath 'scaped this sorrow,
Come in the rearward of a conquer'd woe,

Give not a windy night a rainy morrow,
To linger out a purpos'd overthrow.
If thou wilt leave me, do not leave me last,
When other petty griefs have done their spite,
But in the onset come; so shall I taste
At first the very worst of fortune's might;
  And other strains of woe, which now seem woe,
  Compared with loss of thee will not seem so.

XCI

Some glory in their birth, some in their skill,
Some in their wealth, some in their bodies' force,
Some in their garments, though new-fangled ill,
Some in their hawks and hounds, some in their horse;
And every humour hath his adjunct pleasure,
Wherein it finds a joy above the rest:
But these particulars are not my measure;
All these I better in one general best.
Thy love is better than high birth to me,
Richer than wealth, prouder than garments' cost,
Of more delight than hawks or horses be;
And having thee, of all men's pride I boast:
  Wretched in this alone, that thou mayst take
  All this away, and me most wretched make.

XCII

But do thy worst to steal thyself away,
For term of life thou art assuréd mine,
And life no longer than thy love will stay,
For it depends upon that love of thine.
Then need I not to fear the worst of wrongs,
When in the least of them my life hath end;
I see a better state to me belongs
Than that which on thy humour doth depend.

Thou canst not vex me with inconstant mind,
Since that my life on thy revolt doth lie;—
O, what a happy title do I find,
Happy to have thy love, happy to die!
  But what's so blessed-fair that fears no blot?
  Thou mayst be false, and yet I know it not.

XCIII

So shall I live, supposing thou art true,
Like a deceivéd husband; so love's face
May still seem love to me, though alter'd new:
Thy looks with me, thy heart in other place.
For there can live no hatred in thine eye,
Therefore in that I cannot know thy change—
In many's looks the false heart's history
Is writ in moods and frowns and wrinkles strange.
But heaven in thy creation did decree
That in thy face sweet love should ever dwell;
Whate'er thy thoughts or thy heart's workings be,
Thy looks should nothing thence but sweetness tell.
  How like *Eve's* apple doth thy beauty grow,
  If thy sweet virtue answer not thy show!

XCIV

They that have power to hurt, and will do none,
That do not do the thing they most do show,
Who, moving others, are themselves as stone,
Unmovéd, cold, and to temptation slow:
They rightly do inherit heaven's graces
And husband nature's riches from expense;
They are the Lords and owners of their faces,
Others, but stewards of their excellence.
The summer's flower is to the summer sweet,
Though to itself it only live and die,

But if that flower with base infection meet,
The basest weed outbraves his dignity:
For sweetest things turn sourest by their deeds;
Lilies that fester smell far worse than weeds.

XCV

How sweet and lovely dost thou make the shame
Which, like a canker in the fragrant Rose,
Doth spot the beauty of thy budding name!
O, in what sweets dost thou thy sins enclose!
That tongue that tells the story of thy days,
Making lascivious comments on thy sport,
Cannot dispraise but in a kind of praise;
Naming thy name, blesses an ill report.
O, what a mansion have those vices got,
Which for their habitation chose out thee,
Where beauty's veil doth cover every blot,
And all things turn to fair that eyes can see!
Take heed, dear heart, of this large privilege;
The hardest knife ill-used doth lose his edge.

XCVI

Some say thy fault is youth, some wantonness;
Some say thy grace is youth and gentle sport;
Both grace and faults are lov'd of more and less:
Thou mak'st faults graces, that to thee resort.
As on the finger of a thronéd Queen
The basest jewel will be well esteem'd;
So are those errors that in thee are seen
To truths translated and for true things deem'd.
How many Lambs might the stern Wolf betray,
If like a Lamb he could his looks translate!
How many gazers mightst thou lead away,
If thou wouldst use the strength of all thy state!

But do not so; I love thee in such sort,
As, thou being mine, mine is thy good report.

XCVII

How like a Winter hath my absence been
From thee, the pleasure of the fleeting year!
What freezings have I felt, what dark days seen!
What old December's bareness every where!
And yet this time removed was summer's time,
The teeming Autumn, big with rich increase,
Bearing the wanton burthen of the prime,
Like widowed wombs after their Lord's decease:
Yet this abundant issue seem'd to me
But hope of orphans and unfather'd fruit;
For Summer and his pleasures wait on thee,
And, thou away, the very birds are mute;
Or, if they sing, 'tis with so dull a cheer,
That leaves look pale, dreading the Winter 's near,

XCVIII

From you have I been absent in the spring,
When proud-pied April, dress'd in all his trim,
Hath put a spirit of youth in every thing,
That heavy *Saturn* laugh'd and leap'd with him.
Yet nor the lays of birds nor the sweet smell
Of different flowers in odour and in hue
Could make me any summer's story tell,
Or from their proud lap pluck them where they grew;
Nor did I wonder at the Lily's white,
Nor praise the deep vermilion in the Rose;
They were but sweet, but figures of delight,
Drawn after you, you pattern of all those.
Yet seem'd it Winter still, and, you away,
As with your shadow I with these did play.

XCIX

The forward violet thus did I chide:
Sweet thief, whence didst thou steal thy sweet that smells,
If not from my love's breath? The purple pride
Which on thy soft cheek for complexion dwells
In my love's veins thou hast too grossly dyed.
The Lily I condemnéd for thy hand,
And buds of marjoram had stol'n thy hair;
The Roses fearfully on thorns did stand,
One blushing shame, another white despair;
A third, nor red nor white, had stol'n of both,
And to his robb'ry had annex'd thy breath;
But, for his theft, in pride of all his growth
A vengeful canker eat him up to death.
  More flowers I noted, yet I none could see
  But sweet or colour it had stol'n from thee.

C

Where art thou, Muse, that thou forget'st so long
To speak of that which gives thee all thy might?
Spend'st thou thy fury on some worthless song,
Dark'ning thy power to lend base subjects light?
Return, forgetful Muse, and straight redeem
In gentle numbers time so idly spent;
Sing to the ear that doth thy lays esteem
And gives thy pen both skill and argument.
Rise, resty Muse, my love's sweet face survey,
If Time have any wrinkle graven there;
If any, be a *Satire* to decay,
And make Time's spoils despiséd every where.
  Give my love fame faster than Time wastes life;
  So thou prevent'st his scythe and crooked knife.

CI

O truant Muse, what shall be thy amends
For thy neglect of truth in beauty dyed?
Both truth and beauty on my love depends;
So dost thou too, and therein dignified.
Make answer, Muse: wilt thou not haply say
'Truth needs no colour with his colour fix'd;
Beauty no pencil, beauty's truth to lay;
But best is best, if never intermix'd?'
Because he needs no praise, wilt thou be dumb?
Excuse not silence so; for 't lies in thee
To make him much outlive a gilded tomb,
And to be praised of ages yet to be.
  Then do thy office, Muse; I teach thee how
  To make him seem long hence as he shows now.

CII

My love is strengthen'd, though more weak in seeming;
I love not less, though less the show appear:
That love is merchandised whose rich esteeming
The owner's tongue doth publish every where.
Our love was new, and then but in the spring,
When I was wont to greet it with my lays,
As *Philomel* in summer's front doth sing,
And stops his pipe in growth of riper days:
Not that the summer is less pleasant now
Than when her mournful hymns did hush the night,
But that wild music burthens every bough,
And sweets grown common lose their dear delight.
  Therefore, like her, I sometime hold my tongue,
  Because I would not dull you with my song.

CIII

Alack, 'what poverty my Muse brings forth,
That having such a scope to show her pride,

The argument all bare is of more worth
Than when it hath my added praise beside!
O, blame me not, if I no more can write!
Look in your glass, and there appears a face
That over-goes my blunt invention quite,
Dulling my lines, and doing me disgrace.
Were it not sinful then, striving to mend,
To mar the subject that before was well?
For to no other pass my verses tend,
Than of your graces and your gifts to tell;
  And more, much more, than in my verse can sit
  Your own glass shows you when you look in it.

CIV

To me, fair friend, you never can be old,
For as you were when first your eye I eyed,
Such seems your beauty still. Three Winters cold
Have from the forests shook three Summers' pride;
Three beauteous springs to yellow *Autumn* turn'd,
In process of the seasons have I seen;
Three April perfumes in three hot Junes bum'd,
Since first I saw you fresh, which yet are green.
Ah! yet doth beauty, like a dial-hand,
Steal from his figure and no pace perceived;
So your sweet hue, which methinks still doth stand,
Hath motion, and mine eye may be deceived:
  For fear of which, hear this, thou age unbred;
  Ere you were born was beauty's summer dead.

CV

Let not my love be call'd idolatry,
Nor my belovéd as an idol show,
Since all alike my songs and praises be
To one, of one, still such, and ever so.

Kind is my love to-day, to-morrow kind,
Still constant in a wondrous excellence;
Therefore my verse to constancy confined,
One thing expressing, leaves out difference.
'Fair, kind, and true' is all my argument,
'Fair, kind, and true' varying to other words;
And in this change is my invention spent,
Three themes in one, which wondrous scope affords.
'Fair, kind, and true,' have often liv'd alone,
Which three, till now, never kept seat in one.

CVI

When in the chronicle of wasted time
I see descriptions of the fairest wights,
And beauty making beautiful old rhyme
In praise of Ladies dead and lovely Knights,
Then, in the blazon of sweet beauty's best,
Of hand, of foot, of lip, of eye, of brow,
I see their antique pen would have express'd
Even such a beauty as you master now.
So all their praises are but prophecies
Of this our time, all you prefiguring;
And, for they look'd but with divining eyes,
They had not still enough your worth to sing:
For we, which now behold these present days,
Have eyes to wonder, but lack tongues to praise.

CVII

Not mine own fears, nor the prophetic soul
Of the wide world dreaming on things to come,
Can yet the lease of my true love control,
Supposed as forfeit to a confined doom.
The mortal Moon hath her eclipse endured,
And the sad Augurs mock their own presage;

Incertainties now crown themselves assured,
And peace proclaims olives of endless age.
Now with the drops of this most balmy time
My love looks fresh, and Death to me subscribes,
Since, spite of him, I'll live in this poor rhyme,
While he insults o'er dull and speechless tribes:
And thou in this shalt find thy monument,
When tyrants' crests and tombs of brass are spent.

CVIII

What 's in the brain that ink may character,
Which hath not figured to thee my true spirit?
What 's new to speak, what now to register,
That may express my love or thy dear merit?
Nothing, sweet boy; but yet, like prayers divine,
I must each day say o'er the very same,
Counting no old thing old, thou mine, I thine,
Even as when first I hallow'd thy fair name.
So that eternal love in love's fresh case
Weighs not the dust and injury of age,
Nor gives to necessary wrinkles place,
But makes antiquity for aye his page,
Finding the first conceit of love there bred
Where time and outward form would show it dead.

CIX

O, never say that I was false of heart,
Though absence seem'd my flame to qualify!
As easy might I from myself depart,
As from my soul, which in thy breast doth lie:
That is my home of love: if I have ranged,
Like him that travels I return again,
Just to the time, not with the time exchanged,
So that myself bring water for my stain.

Never believe, though in my nature reign'd
All frailties that besiege all kinds of blood,
That it could so preposterously be stain'd,
To leave for nothing all thy sum of good;
For nothing this wide Universe I call,
Save thou, my Rose; in it thou art my all.

CX

Alas, 'tis true, I have gone here and there,
And made myself a motley to the view,
Gor'd mine own thoughts, sold cheap what is most dear,
Made old offences of affections new;
Most true it is that I have look'd on truth
Askance and strangely: but, by all above,
These blenches gave my heart another youth,
And worse essays proved thee my best of love.
Now all is done, have what shall have no end:
Mine appetite I never more will grind
On newer proof, to try an older friend,
A God in love, to whom I am confined.
Then give me welcome, next my heaven the best,
Even to thy pure and most most loving breast.

CXI

O, for my sake do you with Fortune chide,
The guilty goddess of my harmful deeds,
That did not better for my life provide,
Than public means which public manners breeds.
Thence comes it that my name receives a brand,
And almost thence my nature is subdued
To what it works in, like the Dyer's hand:
Pity me then and wish I were renew'd;
Whilst, like a willing patient, I will drink
Potions of eisel 'gainst my strong infection;

No bitterness that I will bitter think,
Nor double penance, to correct correction.
  Pity me then, dear friend, and I assure ye
  Even that your pity is enough to cure me.

CXII

Your love and pity doth th' impression fill
Which vulgar scandal stamp'd upon my brow;
For what care I who calls me well or ill,
So you o'er-green my bad, my good allow?
You are my All the world, and I must strive
To know my shames and praises from your tongue;
None else to me, nor I to none alive,
That my steel'd sense or changes right or wrong:
In so profound *Abysm* I throw all care
Of others' voices, that my Adder's sense
To critic and to flatterer stoppéd are:—
Mark how with my neglect I do dispense—
  You are so strongly in my purpose bred
  That all the world besides me thinks y' are dead.

CXIII

Since I left you, mine eye is in my mind;
And that which governs me to go about
Doth part his function, and is partly blind,
Seems seeing, but effectually is out;
For it no form delivers to the heart
Of bird, of flower, or shape, which it doth latch;
Of his quick objects hath the mind no part,
Nor his own vision holds what it doth catch;
For if it see the rud'st or gentlest sight,
The most sweet favour or deformed'st creature,
The mountain or the sea, the day or night,
The crow or dove, it shapes them to your feature:

Incapable of more, replete with you,
My most true mind thus maketh mine untrue.

CXIV

Or whether doth my mind, being crown'd with you,
Drink up the monarch's plague, this flattery?
Or whether shall I say, mine eye saith true,
And that your love taught it this *Alchemy*,
To make of monsters and things indigest
Such cherubins as your sweet self resemble,
Creating every bad a perfect best,
As fast as objects to his beams assemble?
O, 'tis the first; 'tis flatt'ry in my seeing,
And my great mind most kingly drinks it up:
Mine eye well knows what with his gust is 'greeing,
And to his palate doth prepare the cup:
If it be poison'd, 'tis the lesser sin,
That mine eye loves it and doth first begin.

CXV

Those lines that I before have writ do lie,
Even those that said I could not love you dearer:
Yet then my judgment knew no reason why
My most full flame should afterwards burn clearer.
But reckoning time, whose million'd accidents
Creep in 'twixt vows, and change decrees of Kings,
Tan sacred beauty, blunt the sharp'st intents,
Divert strong minds to th' course of alt'ring things:
Alas, why, fearing of Time's tyranny,
Might I not then say 'Now I love you best,'
When I was certain o'er incertainty,
Crowning the present, doubting of the rest?
Love is a Babe; then might I not say so,
To give full growth to that which still doth grow.

CXVI

Let me not to the marriage of true minds
Admit impediments. Love is not love
Which alters when it alteration finds,
Or bends with the remover to remove:
O, no! it is an ever-fixéd mark
That looks on tempests and is never shaken;
It is the star to every wand'ring bark,
Whose worth 's unknown, although his height be taken.
Love 's not Time's fool, though rosy lips and cheeks
Within his bending sickle's compass come;
Love alters not with his brief hours and weeks,
But bears it out even to the edge of doom.
  If this be error and upon me provéd,
  I never writ, nor no man ever lovéd.

CXVII

Accuse me thus: that I have scanted all
Wherein I should your great deserts repay,
Forgot upon your dearest love to call,
Whereto all bonds do tie me day by day;
That I have frequent been with unknown minds,
And given to Time your own dear-purchas'd right;
That I have hoisted sail to all the winds
Which should transport me farthest from your sight.
Book both my wilfulness and errors down,
And on just proof surmise accumulate;
Bring me within the level of your frown,
But shoot not at me in your waken'd hate;
  Since my appeal says I did strive to prove
  The constancy and virtue of your love.

CXVIII

Like as, to make our appetites more keen,
With eager compounds we our palate urge;

As, to prevent our maladies unseen,
We sicken to shun sickness when we purge;
Even so, being full of your ne'er-cloying sweetness,
To bitter sauces did I frame my feeding;
And, sick of welfare, found a kind of meetness
To be diseas'd, ere that there was true needing.
Thus policy in love, t' anticipate
The ills that were not, grew to faults assuréd
And brought to medicine a healthful state
Which, rank of goodness, would by ill be curéd:
  But thence I learn, and find the lesson true,
  Drugs poison him that so fell sick of you.

CXIX

What potions have I drunk of *Siren* tears,
Distill'd from limbecks foul as hell within,
Applying fears to hopes, and hopes to fears,
Still losing when I saw myself to win!
What wretched errors hath my heart committed,
Whilst it hath thought itself so blesséd never!
How have mine eyes out of their spheres been fitted
In the distraction of this madding fever!
O benefit of ill! now I find true
That better is by evil still made better;
And ruin'd love, when it is built anew,
Grows fairer than at first, more strong, far greater.
  So I return rebuked to my content
  And gain by ill thrice more than I have spent.

CXX

That you were once unkind befriends me now,
And for that sorrow, which I then did feel,
Needs must I under my transgression bow,
Unless my nerves were brass or hammer'd steel.

For if you were by my unkindness shaken
As I by yours, y' have pass'd a hell of time,
And I, a tyrant, have no leisure taken
To weigh how once I suffer'd in your crime.
O, that our night of woe might have remembr'red
My deepest sense, how hard true sorrow hits,
And soon to you, as you to me, then tend'red
The humble salve which wounded bosoms fits!
  But that, your trespass, now becomes a fee;
  Mine ransoms yours, and yours must ransom me.

CXXI

'Tis better to be vile than vile esteemèd,
When not to be, receives reproach of being;
And the just pleasure lost, which is so deemèd,
Not by our feeling, but by others' seeing:
For why should others' false adulterate eyes
Give salutation to my sportive blood?
Or on my frailties why are frailer spies,
Which in their wills count bad what I think good?
No, I am that I am, and they that level
At my abuses, reckon up their own:
I may be straight, though they themselves be bevel;
By their rank thoughts my deeds must not be shown;
  Unless this general evil they maintain,
  All men are bad, and in their badness reign.

CXXII

Thy gift, thy tables, are within my brain
Full character'd with lasting memory,
Which shall above that idle rank remain
Beyond all date, even to eternity;
Or at the least, so long as brain and heart
Have faculty by nature to subsist;

Till each to razed oblivion yield his part
Of thee, thy record never can be miss'd.
That poor retention could not so much hold,
Nor need I tallies thy dear love to score;
Therefore to give them from me was I bold,
To trust those tables that receive thee more:
  To keep an adjunct to remember thee
  Were to import forgetfulness in me.

CXXIII

No! Time, thou shalt not boast that I do change:
Thy pyramids built up with newer might
To me are nothing novel, nothing strange;
They are but dressings of a former sight:
Our dates are brief, and therefore we admire
What thou dost foist upon us that is old,
And rather make them borne to our desire
Than think that we before have heard them told:
Thy registers and thee I both defy,
Not wond'ring at the present nor the past,
For thy records, and what we see doth lie,
Made more or less by thy continual haste:
  This I do vow and this shall ever be;
  I will be true, despite thy scythe and thee.

CXXIV

If my dear love were but the child of state,
It might for Fortune's bastard be unfather'd,
As subject to Time's love or to Time's hate,
Weeds among weeds, or flowers with flowers gather'd.
No, it was builded far from accident;
It suffers not in smiling pomp, nor falls
Under the blow of thralléd discontent,
Whereto th' inviting time our fashion calls:

It fears not policy, that *Heretic*,
Which works on leases of short-numb'red hours,
But all alone stands hugely politic,
That it nor grows with heat nor drowns with showers.
  To this I witness call the fools of Time,
  Which die for goodness, who have liv'd for crime.

CXXV

Were 't aught to me I bore the canopy,
With my extern the outward honouring,
Or laid great bases for eternity,
Which proves more short than waste or ruining?
Have I not seen dwellers on form and favour
Lose all, and more, by paying too much rent
For compound sweet; foregoing simple savour,
Pitiful thrivers, in their gazing spent?
No, let me be obsequious in thy heart,
And take thou my oblation, poor but free,
Which is not mix'd with seconds, knows no art,
But mutual render, only me for thee.
  Hence, thou suborn'd *Informer*! a true soul
  When most impeach'd stands least in thy control.

CXXVI

O thou, my lovely Boy, who in thy power
Dost hold Time's fickle glass, his sickle, hour;
Who hast by waning grown, and therein show'st
Thy lovers withering, as thy sweet self grow'st!
If Nature, sovereign mistress over wrack,
As thou goest onwards, still will pluck thee back,
She keeps thee to this purpose, that her skill
May Time disgrace and wretched minutes kill.
Yet fear her, O thou minion of her pleasure!
She may detain, but not still keep, her treasure:

Her *Audit*, though delay'd, answer'd must be,
And her *Quietus* is to render thee.

CXXVII

In the old age black was not counted fair,
Or if it were, it bore not beauty's name;
But now is black beauty's successive heir,
And Beauty slander'd with a bastard shame:
For since each hand hath put on Nature's power,
Fairing the foul with Art's false borrow'd face,
Sweet Beauty hath no name, no holy bower,
But is profaned, if not lives in disgrace.
Therefore my Mistress' eyes are raven black,
Her eyes so suited, and they mourners seem
At such who, not born fair, no beauty lack,
Sland'ring Creation with a false esteem:
Yet so they mourn, becoming of their woe,
That every tongue says beauty should look so.

CXXVIII

How oft, when thou, my music, music play'st,
Upon that blesséd wood whose motion sounds
With thy sweet fingers, when thou gently sway'st
The wiry concord that mine ear confounds,
Do I envý those jacks that nimble leap
To kiss the tender inward of thy hand,
Whilst my poor lips, which should that harvest reap,
At the wood's boldness by thee blushing stand!
To be so tickled, they would change their state
And situation with those dancing chips,
O'er whom thy fingers walk with gentle gait
Making dead wood more bless'd than living lips:
Since saucy jacks so happy are in this,
Give them thy fingers, me thy lips to kiss

CXXIX

Th' expense of Spirit in a waste of shame
Is lust in action; and till action, lust
Is perjur'd, murd'rous, bloody, full of blame,
Savage, extreme, rude, cruel, not to trust;
Enjoy'd ho sooner, but despiséd straight,
Past reason hunted; and no sooner had,
Past reason hated, as a swallowed bait,
On purpose laid to make the taker mad:
Mad in pursuit, and in possession so;
Had, having, and in quest to have, extreme;
A bliss in proof, and proved, a very woe;
Before, a joy proposed; behind, a dream.
  All this die world well knows; yet none knows well
  To shun the heaven that leads men to this hell.

CXXX

My Mistress' eyes are nothing like the Sun;
Coral is far more red than her lips' red;
If snow be white, why then her breasts are dun;
If hairs be wires, black wires grow on her head.
I have seen Roses damask'd, red and white,
But no such Roses see I in her cheeks;
And in some perfumes is there more delight
Than in the breath that from my Mistress reeks.
I love to hear her speak, yet well I know
That Music hath a far more pleasing sound;
I grant I never saw a goddess go;
My Mistress, when she walks, treads on the ground:
  And yet, by heaven, I think my love as rare
  As any she belied with false compare.

CXXXI

Thou art as tyrannous, so as thou art,
As those whose beauties proudly make them cruel;

For well thou know'st to my dear doting heart
Thou art the fairest and most precious jewel.
Yet in good faith some say that thee behold,
Thy face hath not the power to make love groan:
To say they err, I dare not be so bold,
Although I swear it to myself alone.
And, to be sure that is not false I swear,
A thousand groans, but thinking on thy face,
One on another's neck, do witness bear
Thy black is fairest in my judgment's place.
  In nothing art thou black save in thy deeds,
  And thence this slander, as I think, proceeds.

CXXXII

Thine eyes I love, and they, as pitying me,
Knowing thy heart torments me with disdain,
Have put on black and loving mourners be,
Looking with pretty ruth upon my pain.
And truly not the morning Sun of Heaven
Better becomes the grey cheeks of the East,
Nor that full Star that ushers in the Even
Doth half that glory to the sober West,
As those two mourning eyes become thy face:
O, let it then as well beseem thy heart
To mourn for me, since mourning doth thee grace,
And suit thy pity like in every part.
  Then will I swear beauty herself is black
  And all they foul that thy complexion lack.

CXXXIII

Beshrew that heart that makes my heart to groan
For that deep wound it gives my friend and me!
Is 't not enough to torture me alone,
But slave to slavery my sweet'st friend must be?

Me from myself thy cruel eye hath taken,
And my next self thou harder hast engrosséd:
Of him, myself, and thee, I am forsaken;
A torment thrice threefold thus to be crosséd.
Prison my heart in thy steel bosom's ward,
But then my friend's heart let my poor heart bail;
Whoe'er keeps me, let my heart be his guard;
Thou canst not then use rigour in my gaol:
  And yet thou wilt; for I, being pent in thee,
  Perforce am thine, and all that is in me.

CXXXIV

So, now I have confess'd that he is thine,
And I myself am mortgaged to thy will,
Myself I'll forfeit, so that other mine
Thou wilt restore, to be my comfort still:
But thou wilt not, nor he will not be free,
For thou art covetous and he is kind;
He learn'd but surety-like to write for me
Under that bond that him as fast doth bind.
The statute of thy beauty thou wilt take,
Thou usurer, that put'st forth all to use,
And sue a friend came debtor for my sake;
So him I lose through my unkind abuse.
  Him have I lost; thou hast both him and me:
  He pays the whole, and yet am I not free.

CXXXV

Whoever hath her wish, thou hast thy *Will*,
And *Will* to boot, and *Will* in overplus;
More than enough am I that vex thee still,
To thy sweet will making addition thus.
Wilt thou, whose will is large and spacious,
Not once vouchsafe to hide my will in thine?

Shall will in others seem right gracious,
And in my will no fair acceptance shine?
The sea, all water, yet receives rain still
And in abundance addeth to his store;
So thou, being rich in *Will*, add to thy *Will*
One will of mine, to make thy large *Will* more.
  Let no unkind, no fair beseechers kill;
  Think all but one, and me in that one *Will*.

CXXXVI

If thy soul check thee that I come so near,
Swear to thy blind soul that I was thy *Will*,
And will, thy soul knows, is admitted there;
Thus far for love, my love-suit, sweet, fulfil.
Will will fulfil the treasure of thy love,
Ay, fill it full with wills, and my will one.
In things of great receipt with ease we prove
Among a number one is reckon'd none:
Then in the number let me pass untold,
Though in thy stores' account I one must be;
For nothing hold me, so it please thee hold
That nothing me, a something sweet to thee:
  Make but my name thy love, and love that still,
  And then thou lovest me, for my name is *Will*.

CXXXVII

Thou blind fool, Love, what dost thou to mine eyes,
That they behold, and see not what they see?
They know what beauty is, see where it lies,
Yet what the best is, take the worst to be.
If eyes corrupt by over-partial looks,
Be anchor'd in the bay where all men ride,
Why of eyes' falsehood hast thou forgéd hooks,
Whereto the judgment of my heart is tied?

Why should my heart think that a several plot
Which my heart knows the wide world's common place?
Or mine eyes seeing this, say this is not,
To put fair truth upon so foul a face?
  In things right true my heart and eyes have erréd,
  And to this false plague are they now transferréd.

CXXXVIII

When my love swears that she is made of truth,
I do believe her, though I know she lies,
That she might think me some untutor'd youth,
Unlearnéd in the world's false subtleties.
Thus vainly thinking that she thinks me young,
Although she knows my days are past the best,
Simply I credit her false-speaking tongue:
On both sides thus is simple truth suppress'd.
But wherefore says she not she is unjust?
And wherefore say not I that I am old?
O, love's best habit is in seeming trust,
And age in love loves not to have years told:
  Therefore I lie with her, and she with me,
  And in our faults by lies we flattered be.

CXXXIX

O, call not me to justify the wrong,
That thy unkindness lays upon my heart;
Wound me not with thine eye but with thy tongue;
Use power with power, and slay me not by Art.
Tell me thou lov'st elsewhere; but in my sight,
Dear heart, forbear to glance thine eye aside:
What need'st thou wound with cunning, when thy might
Is more than my o'er-press'd defence can bide?
Let me excuse thee: ah! my love well knows
Her pretty looks have been mine enemies,

And therefore from my face she turns my foes,
That they elsewhere might dart their injuries:
  Yet do not so; but since I am near slain,
  Kill me outright with looks, and rid my pain.

CXL

Be wise as thou art cruel; do not press
My tongue-tied patience with too much disdain;
Lest sorrow lend me words and words express
The manner of my pity-wanting pain.
If I might teach thee wit, better it were,
Though not to love, yet, love, to tell me so;
As testy sick-men, when their deaths be near,
No news but health from their Physicians know;
For if I should despair, I should grow mad,
And in my madness might speak ill of thee:
Now this ill-wresting world is grown so bad,
Mad slanderers by mad ears believéd be.
  That I may not be so, nor thou belied,
  Bear thine eyes straight, though thy proud heart go wide.

CXLI

In faith, I do not love thee with mine eyes,
For they in thee a thousand errors note;
But 'tis my heart that loves what they despise,
Who in despite of view is pleas'd to dote;
Nor are mine ears with thy tongue's tune delighted,
Nor tender feeling, to base touches prone,
Nor taste, nor smell, desire to be invited
To any sensual feast with thee alone:
But my five wits nor my five senses can
Dissuade one foolish heart from serving thee,
Who leaves unsway'd the likeness of a man,
Thy proud heart's slave and vassal wretch to be:

Only my plague thus far I count my gain,
That she that makes me sin awards me pain.

CXLII

Love is my sin, and thy dear virtue hate,
Hate of my sin, grounded on sinful loving:
O, but with mine compare thou thine own state,
And thou shalt find it merits not reproving;
Or, if it do, not from those lips of thine,
That have profaned their scarlet ornaments,
And seal'd false bonds of love as oft as mine,
Robb'd others' beds' revénues of their rents.
Be it lawful I love thee, as thou lov'st those
Whom thine eyes woo as mine importune thee:
Root pity in thy heart, that when it grows
Thy pity may deserve to pitied be.
If thou dost seek to have what thou dost hide,
By self-example mayst thou be denied!

CXLIII

Lo! as a careful housewife runs to catch
One of her feathered creatures broke away,
Sets down her babe and makes all swift dispatch
In púrsuit of the thing she would have stay;
Whilst her neglected child holds her in chase,
Cries to catch her whose busy care is bent
To follow that which flies before her face,
Not prizing her poor infant's discontent;
So runn'st thou after that which flies from thee,
Whilst I thy babe chase thee afar behind;
But if thou catch thy hope, turn back to me,
And play the mother's part, kiss me, be kind:
So will I pray that thou mayst have thy *Will*,
If thou turn back, and my loud crying still.

CXLIV

Two loves I have of comfort and despair,
Which like two spirits do suggest me still:
The better angel is a man right fair,
The worser spirit a woman colour'd ill.
To win me soon to hell, my female evil
Tempteth my better angel from my side,
And would corrupt my saint to be a devil,
Wooing his purity with her foul pride.
And whether that my angel be turn'd fiend
Suspect I may, yet not directly tell;
But being both from me, both to each friend,
I guess one angel in another's hell:
  Yet this shall I ne'er know, but live in doubt,
  Till my bad angel fire my good one out.

CXLV

Those lips that Love's own hand did make
Breath'd forth the sound that said 'I hate'
To me that languish'd for her sake;
But when she saw my woeful state,
Straight in her heart did mercy come,
Chiding that tongue that ever sweet
Was used in giving gentle doom,
And taught it thus anew to greet;
'I hate' she alter'd with an end,
That follow'd it as gentle day
Doth follow night, who like a fiend
From heaven to hell is flown away;
  'I hate' from hate away she threw,
  And saved my life, saying 'not you.'

CXLVI

Poor soul, the centre of my sinful earth—
My sinful earth these rebel powers array—

Why dost thou pine within and suffer dearth,
Painting thy outward walls so costly gay?
Why so large cost, having so short a lease,
Dost thou upon thy fading mansion spend?
Shall worms, inheritors of this excess,
Eat up thy charge? is this thy body's end?
Then, soul, live thou upon thy servant's loss,
And let that pine to aggravate thy store;
Buy terms divine in selling hours of dross;
Within be fed, without be rich no more:
So shalt thou feed on Death, that feeds on men,
And Death once dead, there's no more dying then.

CXLVII

My love is as a fever, longing still
For that which longer nurseth the disease,
Feeding on that which doth preserve the ill,
Th' uncertain sickly appetite to please.
My reason, the Physician to my love,
Angry that his prescriptions are not kept,
Hath left me, and I desperate now approve
Desire is death, which Physic did except.
Past cure I am, now Reason is past care,
And frantic-mad with evermore unrest;
My thoughts and my discourse as mad men's are,
At random from the truth vainly express'd;
For I have sworn thee fair and thought thee bright,
Who art as black as hell, as dark as night.

CXLVIII

O me! what eyes hath Love put in my head,
Which have no correspondence with true sight!
Or, if they have, where is my judgment fled,
That censures falsely what they see aright?

If that be fair whereon my false eyes dote,
What means the world to say it is not so?
If it be not, then love doth well denote
Love's eye is not so true as all men's: no,
How can it? O, how can Love's eye be true,
That is so vex'd with watching and with tears?
No marvel then, though I mistake my view;
The sun itself sees not till heaven clears.
  O cunning Love! with tears thou keep'st me blind,
  Lest eyes well-seeing thy foul faults should find.

CXLIX

Canst thou, O cruel! say I love thee not,
When I against myself with thee partake?
Do I not think on thee, when I forgot
Am of myself, all tyrant for thy sake?
Who hateth thee that I do call my friend?
On whom frown'st thou that I do fawn upon?
Nay, if thou lour'st on me, do I not spend
Revenge upon myself with present moan?
What merit do I in myself respect,
That is so proud thy service to despise,
When all my best doth worship thy defect,
Commanded by the motion of thine eyes?
  But, love, hate on, for now I know thy mind;
  Those that can see thou lov'st, and I am blind.

CL

O, from what power hast thou this powerful might,
With insufficiency my heart to sway?
To make me give the lie to my true sight,
And swear that brightness doth not grace the day?
Whence hast thou this becoming of things ill,
That in the very refuse of thy deeds

There is such strength and warrantise of skill
That, in my mind, thy worst all best exceeds?
Who taught thee how to make me love thee more,
The more I hear and see just cause of hate?
O, though I love what others do abhor,
With others thou shouldst not abhor my state:
  If thy unworthiness rais'd love in me,
  More worthy I to be belov'd of thee.

CLI

Love is too young to know what conscience is;
Yet who knows not conscience is born of love?
Then, gentle cheater, urge not my amiss,
Lest guilty of my faults thy sweet self prove.
For, thou betraying me, I do betray
My nobler part to my gross body's treason;
My soul doth tell my body that he may
Triumph in love; flesh stays no farther reason;
But, rising at thy name, doth point out thee,
As his triumphant prize: proud of this pride,
He is contented thy poor drudge to be,
To stand in thy affairs, fall by thy side,
  No want of conscience hold it that I call
  Her 'love' for whose dear love I rise and fall.

CLII

In loving thee thou know'st I am forsworn,
But thou art twice forsworn, to me love swearing;
In act thy bed-vow broke and new faith torn
In vowing new hate after new love bearing.
But why of two oaths' breach do I accuse thee,
When I break twenty? I am perjur'd most;
For all my vows are oaths but to misuse thee,
And all my honest faith in thee is lost:

For I have sworn deep oaths of thy deep kindness,
Oaths of thy love, thy truth, thy constancy,
And, to enlighten thee, gave eyes to blindness,
Or made them swear against the thing they see;
For I have sworn thee fair; more perjured I,
To swear against the truth so foul a lie!

CLIII

Cupid laid by his brand, and fell asleep:
A maid of *Dian's* this advantage found,
And his love-kindling fire did quickly steep
In a cold valley-fountain of that ground;
Which borrow'd from this holy fire of love
A dateless lively heat, still to endure,
And grew a seething bath, which yet men prove
Against strange maladies a sovereign cure.
But at my mistress' eye Love's brand new-firéd,
The boy for trial needs would touch my breast;
I, sick withal, the help of bath desired,
And thither hied, a sad distemper'd guest,
But found no cure: the bath for my help lies
Where *Cupid* got new fire—my mistress' eyes.

CLIV

The little Love-God lying once asleep,
Laid by his side his heart-inflaming brand,
Whilst many Nymphs that vow'd chaste life to keep,
Came tripping by; but in her maiden hand
The fairest votary took up that fire
Which many legions of true hearts had warm'd;
And so the General of hot desire
Was sleeping by a Virgin hand disarm'd.
This brand she quenchéd in a cool well by,
Which from Love's fire took heat perpetual,

Growing a bath and healthful remedy
For men diseas'd; but I, my Mistress' thrall,
  Came there for cure, and this by that I prove,
  Love's fire heats water, water cools not love.

A Lover's Complaint

A Lover's Complaint

I

From off a hill whose concave womb re-worded
A plaintful story from a sist'ring vale,
My spirits t' attend this double voice accorded,
And down I laid to list the sad-tuned tale;
Ere long espied a fickle maid full pale, 5
Tearing of papers, breaking rings a-twain,
Storming her world with sorrow's wind and rain.

II

Upon her head a platted hive of straw, 8
Which fortified her visage from the Sun,
Whereon the thought might think sometime it saw
The carcass of a beauty spent and done:
Time had not scythéd all that youth begun, 12
Nor youth all quit; but, spite of heaven's fell rage,
Some beauty peep'd through lattice of sear'd age.

III

Oft did she heave her napkin to her eyne, 15
Which on it had conceited characters,
Laund'ring the silken figures in the brine
That season'd woe had pelleted in tears,
And often reading what contents it bears; 19
As often shrieking undistinguish'd woe,
In clamours of all size, both high and low.

IV

Sometimes her levell'd eyes their carriage ride, 22
As they did batt'ry to the spheres intend;
Sometime diverted their poor balls are tied
To th' orbéd earth; sometimes they do extend
Their view right on; anon their gazes lend 26
To every place at once, and, nowhere fix'd,
The mind and sight distractedly commix'd.

V

Her hair, nor loose nor tied in formal plat, 29
Proclaim'd in her a careless hand of pride;
For some, untuck'd, descended her sheav'd hat,
Hanging her pale and pinéd cheek beside;
Some in her threaden fillet still did bide, 33
And true to bondage would not break from thence,
Though slackly braided in loose negligence.

VI

A thousand favours from a maund she drew 36
Of amber, crystal, and of bedded jet,
Which one by one she in a river threw,
Upon whose weeping margent she was set;
Like usury, applying wet to wet, 40
Or Monarchs' hands that let not bounty fall
Where want cries some, but where excess begs all.

VII

Of folded schedules had she many a one, 43
Which she perused, sigh'd, tore, and gave the flood;
Crack'd many a ring of posied gold and bone,
Bidding them find their sepulchres in mud;
Found yet moe letters sadly penn'd in blood, 47
With sleided silk feat and affectedly
Enswath'd, and seal'd to curious secrecy.

VIII

These often bath'd she in her fluxive eyes,
And often kiss'd, and often gave to tear;
Cried 'O false blood, thou register of lies,
What unapprovéd witness dost thou bear!
Ink would have seem'd more black and damnéd here!'
This said, in top of rage the lines she rents,
Big discontent so breaking their contents.

IX

A reverend man that grazed his cattle nigh—
Sometime a blusterer, that the ruffle knew
Of Court, of City, and had let go by
The swiftest hours observéd as they flew—
Towards this afflicted fancy fastly drew:
And, privileged by age, desires to know
In brief the grounds and motives of her woe.

X

So slides he down upon his grainéd bat,
And comely-distant sits he by her side;
When he again desires her, being sat,
Her grievance with his hearing to divide:
If that from him there may be aught applied
Which may her suffering ecstasy assuage,
'Tis promised in the charity of age.

XI

'Father,' she says, 'though in me you behold
The injury of many a blasting hour,
Let it not tell your judgment I am old;
Not age, but sorrow, over me hath power:
I might as yet have been a spreading flower,
Fresh to myself, if I had self-applied
Love to myself and to no Love beside.

XII

'But, woe is me! too early I attended
A youthful suit—it was to gain my grace—
Of one by nature's outwards so commended,
That maidens' eyes stuck over all his face:
Love lack'd a dwelling, and made him her place;
And when in his fair parts she did abide,
She was new lodg'd and newly Deified.

XIII

'His browny locks did hang in crooked curls;
And every light occasion of the wind
Upon his lips their silken parcels hurls.
What's sweet to do, to do will aptly find:
Each eye that saw him did enchant the mind,
For on his visage was in little drawn
What largeness thinks in Paradise was sawn.

XIV

'Small show of man was yet upon his chin;
His phœnix down began but to appear
Like unshorn velvet on that termless skin
Whose bare out-bragg'd the web it seem'd to wear:
Yet show'd his visage by that cost more dear:
And nice affections wavering stood in doubt
If best were as it was, or best without.

XV

'His qualities were beauteous as his form,
For maiden-tongued he was, and thereof free;
Yet, if men moved him, was he such a storm
As oft 'twixt May and April is to see,
When winds breathe sweet, unruly though they be.
His rudeness so with his authórised youth
Did livery falseness in a pride of truth.

XVI

'Well could he ride, and often men would say 106
"That horse his mettle from his rider takes:
Proud of subjection, noble by the sway,
What rounds, what bounds, what course, what stop he makes!"
And controversy hence a question takes, 110
Whether the horse by him became his deed,
Or he his manege by th' well-doing steed.

XVII

'But quickly on this side the verdict went: 113
His real habitude gave life and grace
To appertainings and to ornament,
Accomplish'd in himself, not in his case:
All aids, themselves made fairer by their place, 117
Can for additions; yet their purposed trim
Pieced not his grace, but were all graced by him.

XVIII

'So on the tip of his subduing tongue 120
All kind of arguments and question deep,
All replication prompt, and reason strong,
For his advantage still did wake and sleep:
To make the weeper laugh, the laugher weep, 124
He had the dialect and different skill,
Catching all passions in his craft of will:

XIX

'That he did in the general bosom reign 127
Of young, of old, and sexes both enchanted
To dwell with him in thoughts, or to remain
In personal duty, following where he haunted:
Consents bewitch'd, ere he desire, have granted, 131
And, dialogu'd for him what he would say,
Ask'd their own wills and made their wills obey.

XX

'Many there were that did his picture get,
To serve their eyes, and in it put their mind;
Like fools that in th' imagination set
The goodly objects which abroad they find
Of lands and mansions, theirs in thought assign'd;
And labouring in moe pleasures to bestow them
Than the true gouty landlord which doth owe them:

XXI

'So many have, that never touch'd his hand,
Sweetly supposed them mistress of his heart:
My woeful self, that did in freedom stand,
And was my own fee-simple, not in part,
What with his art in youth, and youth in art,
Threw my affections in his charméd power,
Reserv'd the stalk and gave him all my flower.

XXII

'Yet did I not, as some my equals did,
Demand of him, nor being desiréd yielded;
Finding myself in honour so forbid,
With safest distance I mine honour shielded:
Experience for me many bulwarks builded
Of proofs new-bleeding, which remain'd the foil
Of this false jewel, and his amorous spoil.

XXIII

'But, ah, who ever shunn'd by precedent
The destin'd ill she must herself assay?
Or forced examples 'gainst her own content,
To put the by-past perils in her way?
Counsel may stop awhile what will not stay;
For when we rage, advice is often seen
By blunting us to make our wits more keen.

XXIV

'Nor gives it satisfaction to our blood,
That we must curb it upon others' proof:
To be forbid the sweets that seem so good,
For fear of harms that preach in our behoof.
O appetite, from judgment stand aloof!
The one a palate hath that needs will taste,
Though Reason weep, and cry "It is thy last."

XXV

'For further I could say "This man's untrue,"
And knew the patterns of his foul beguiling;
Heard where his plants in others' orchards grew,
Saw how deceits were gilded in his smiling;
Knew vows were ever brokers to defiling;
Thought characters and words merely but art,
And bastards of his foul adulterate heart.

XXVI

'And long upon these terms I held my city,
Till thus he gan besiege me: "Gentle maid,
Have of my suffering youth some feeling pity,
And be not of my holy vows afraid:
That's to ye sworn to none was ever said;
For feasts of love I have been call'd unto,
Till now did ne'er invite, nor never vow.

XXVII

'"All my offences that abroad you see
Are errors of the blood, none of the mind;
Love made them not: with acture they may be,
Where neither party is nor true nor kind:
They sought their shame that so their shame did find;
And so much less of shame in me remains,
By how much of me their reproach contains.

XXVIII

'"Among the many that mine eyes have seen, 190
Not one whose flame my heart so much as warméd,
Or my affection put to th' smallest teen,
Or any of my leisures ever charméd:
Harm have I done to them, but ne'er was harméd; 194
Kept hearts in liveries, but mine own was free,
And reign'd, commanding in his monarchy.

XXIX

'"Look here, what tributes wounded fancies sent me,
Of palid pearls and rubies red as blood; 198
Figuring that they their passions likewise lent me
Of grief and blushes, aptly understood
In bloodless white and the encrimson'd mood; 201
Effects of terror and dear modesty,
Encamp'd in hearts, but fighting outwardly.

XXX

'"And, lo, behold these talents of their hair, 204
With twisted metal amorously impleach'd,
I have receiv'd from many a several fair,
Their kind acceptance weepingly beseech'd,
With the annexions of fair gems enrich'd, 208
And deep-brain'd sonnets that did amplify
Each stone's dear nature, worth, and quality:

XXXI

'"The Diamond,—why, 'twas beautiful and hard, 211
Whereto his invised properties did tend;
The deep-green Em'rald, in whose fresh regard
Weak sights their sickly radiance do amend;
The heaven-hued Sapphire and the Opal blend 215
With objects manifold: each several stone,
With wit well blazon'd, smiled or made some moan.

XXXII

'"Lo, all these trophies of affections hot, 218
Of pensiv'd and subdued desires the tender,
Nature hath charged me that I hoard them not,
But yield them up where I myself must render;—
That is, to you, my origin and ender: 222
For these, of force, must your oblations be,
Since I their altar, you enpatron me.

XXXIII

'"O, then, advance of yours that phraseless hand, 225
Whose white weighs down the airy scale of praise;
Take all these similes to your own command,
Hollow'd with sighs that burning lungs did raise;
What me your minister, for you obeys, 229
Works under you; and to your audit comes
Their distract parcels in combinéd sums.

XXXIV

'"Lo, this device was sent me from a Nun, 232
Or Sister sanctified, of holiest note;
Which late her noble suit in court did shun,
Whose rarest havings made the blossoms dote;
For she was sought by spirits of richest coat, 236
But kept cold distance, and did thence remove,
To spend her living in eternal love.

XXXV

'"But, O my sweet, what labour is 't to leave 239
The thing we have not, mast'ring what not strives,
Playing the place which did no form receive,
Playing patient sports in unconstrained gyves?
She that her fame so to herself contrives, 243
The scars of battle 'scapeth by the flight,
And makes her absence valiant, not her might.

XXXVI

'"O, pardon me, in that my boast is true:
The accident which brought me to her eye
Upon the moment did her force subdue,
And now she would the cagéd cloister fly:
Religious love put out Religion's eye:
Not to be tempted, would she be immured,
And now, to tempt all, liberty procured.

XXXVII

'"How mighty then you are, O, hear me tell!
The broken bosoms that to me belong
Have emptied all their fountains in my well,
And mine I pour your Ocean all among:
I strong o'er them, and you o'er me being strong,
Must for your victory us all congest,
As compound love to physic your cold breast.

XXXVIII

'"My parts had power to charm a sacred Sun,
Who, disciplin'd, ay, dieted in grace,
Believ'd her eyes when they t' assail begun,
All vows and consecrations giving place:
O most potential love! vow, bond, nor space,
In thee hath neither sting, knot, nor confine,
For thou art all, and all things else are thine.

XXXIX

'"When thou impressest, what are precepts worth
Of stale example? When thou wilt inflame,
How coldly those impediments stand forth
Of wealth, of filial fear, law, kindred, fame!
Love's arms are peace, 'gainst rule, 'gainst sense, 'gainst shame,
And sweetens, in the suffering pangs it bears,
The aloes of all forces, shocks, and fears.

XL

'"Now all these hearts that do on mine depend, 274
Feeling it break, with bleeding groans they pine;
And supplicant their sighs to you extend,
To leave the batt'ry that you make 'gainst mine,
Lending soft audience to my sweet design, 278
And credent soul to that strong-bonded oath
That shall prefer and undertake my troth."

XLI

'This said, his wat'ry eyes he did dismount, 281
Whose sights till then were levell'd on my face;
Each cheek a river running from a fount
With brinish current downward flow'd apace:
O, how the channel to the stream gave grace! 285
Who glazed with Crystal gate the glowing Roses
That flame through water which their hue encloses.

XLII

'O father, what a hell of witchcraft lies 288
In the small orb of one particular tear!
But with the inundation of the eyes
What rocky heart to water will not wear?
What breast so cold that is not warméd here? 292
O cleft effect! cold modesty; hot wrath:
Both fire, from hence, and chill extincture, hath.

XLIII

'For, lo, his passion, but an art of craft, 295
Even there resolv'd my reason into tears;
There my white stole of chastity I daff'd,
Shook off my sober guards and civil fears;
Appear to him; as he to me appears, 299
All melting; though our drops this diff'rence bore,
His poison'd me, and mine did him restore.

XLIV

'In him a plenitude of subtle matter, 302
Applied to cautels, all strange forms receives,
Of burning blushes, or of weeping water,
Or swounding paleness; and he takes and leaves,
In either's aptness, as it best deceives, 306
To blush at speeches rank, to weep at woes,
Or to turn white and swound at tragic shows:

XLV

'That not a heart which in his level came 309
Could 'scape the hail of his all-hurting aim,
Showing fair Nature is both kind and tame;
And, veil'd in them, did win whom he would maim:
Against the thing he sought, he would exclaim; 313
When he most burn'd in heart-wish'd luxury,
He preach'd pure maid, and prais'd cold chastity.

XLVI

'Thus merely with the garment of a Grace 316
The naked and concealéd fiend he cover'd;
That th' unexperient gave the tempter place,
Which like a Cherubin above them hover'd.
Who, young and simple, would not be so lover'd? 320
Ay me! I fell; and yet do question make
What I should do again for such a sake.

XLVII

'O, that infected moisture of his eye, 323
O, that false fire which in his cheek so glow'd,
O, that forced thunder from his heart did fly,
O, that sad breath his spongy lungs bestow'd,
O, all that borrow'd motion seeming ow'd, 327
Would yet again betray the fore-betray'd,
And new pervert a reconciléd maid!'

Notes

Notes

VENUS AND ADONIS

I. *The Text.*—The Text is taken from the First Quarto, 1593, as reproduced in facsimile by William Griggs from the unique original in the Bodleian Library, Oxford (Shakespeare—Quarto Facsimiles, No. 12). Spelling and punctuation have been modernised generally, but not invariably, in accordance with the use of *The Cambridge Shakespeare*. In every other case of a departure from the Quarto text the fact is noted. This Quarto, according to the Editors of *The Cambridge Shakespeare*, 'is printed with remarkable accuracy, doubtless from the author's own MS.' *The Variorum Shakespeare* of 1821, *Shakespeare's Poems* (Kelmscott), and *The Poems of William Shakespeare* (Robert Bell) have also been used for the Text and Notes. Throughout the Notes the First Quarto is referred to as Q.

II. *The Use of the Apostrophe as a Guide to the Metrical Pronunciation.*—In this the practice of *The Cambridge Shakespeare* has not been followed. In the First Quartos of *Venus*, *Lucrece*, and *The Sonnets* a mute 'e' is omitted, and an apostrophe substituted, so uniformly as to reveal the practice of the author, which, indeed, was the practice of his age. When, therefore, in the Quartos the 'e' is not omitted from the word which furnishes the rhyme, that word must be pronounced as a disyllable, e.g. 'His brawny sides with hairy bristles armèd' (*Venus*, 625). 'To retain the "e" when it is an essential part of the verb and to substitute an apostrophe where the "e" is a part of the inflection,' in accordance with the use of the *Cambridge* Editors, does not obviate all ambiguity. Such words as 'lovest' and 'owest' are not always monosyllabic, even in modern poetry. Thus Shelley:—

'I love all that thou *lovest*,
Spirit of Delight!
The fresh Earth in new leaves *drest*':—

and, in Shakespeare's day, the legitimate 'auricular figures of *adding* and *rabbating*' (*The Arte of English Poesie*, 1589) gave a wider licence. The Elizabethans added and suppressed syllables, shifted the accent, and varied the spelling of words with a freedom accorded by contemporary critics 'sometimes... for pleasure to give a better sound, sometimes upon necessitie' (*Ibid.*). But they were ever careful to indicate what they had done, and to ensure the correct delivery of their lines. It would be awkward to omit the mute 'e' where such omission must suggest an unpleasing mispronunciation; for example, to write, as they did, 'plac'd' for 'placed,' when that word scans as a monosyllable. In order, therefore, to avoid such phonetic suggestions, and at the same time to retain that certainty of correct delivery which their method ensured, the practice adoped in this Edition is: (1) to accent ambiguous 'e's that are to be sounded; (2) to print without an accent mute 'e's, the omission of which would suggest a mispronunciation; (3) to omit all other mute 'e's, substituting an apostrophe. 'The wrong ranging the accent of a sillable...as to say *gratious* for *grátious*' (*Arte of English Poesie*) has also been indicated by an accent; and 'your swallowing or eating up of one letter by another' (*Ibid.*), by its omission and an apostrophe, e.g. *Venus and Adonis*, l. 668:—

'That tremble at th' imaginatíon':—

and Sonnet CXXXV. 7:—

'Shall will in others seem right gracious.'

III. *The Use of Capitals.*— See Note III. on *Lucrece*, and Note V. on the Sonnets. The practice therein described has been followed in *Venus and Adonis*.

IV. *Date of the Composition of Venus and Adonis.*— See Notes on ll. 397, 507-10.

V. *Notes on the Text.*

3. '*Rose cheek'd* Adonis'; cf. Marlowe's *Hero and Leander*:—

'The men of wealthy Sestos every yeare,
For his sake whom their goddess held so deare,
Rose-cheek'd Adonis, kept a solemne fast.'

9. *Stain,* injury. Cf. Sonnet CIX.:—

'So that myself bring water for thy stain.'

14. *rein*, raine Q. here and *passim.*

19. *satiety*, sacietie Q.

26. *The precedent* (president Q.) *of pith and livelihood.* Cf. *Antony and Cleopatra*, I. ii. 53; *Othello*, III. iv. 36. The idea occurs in Bandello's novel of *Romeo and Juliet.*

51. *hairs*, heares Q. rhyming with 'teares.'

53. *miss*, misse Q. Malone suggests *'miss for amiss.* Cf. Sonnet xxxv.:—

'Myself corrupting, salving thy amiss.'

In tracing the meaning of obsolete words I have availed myself of an interesting work, 'ΗΓΕΜῺΝ ΕΙΣ ΤᾺΣ ΓΛΩ̃ ΣΣΑΣ | id est | Ductor in Linguas | *The Guide Into Tongues* | an etymological dictionary in eleven languages,' published 'By the Industry and Labor of John Minshæus, and dedicated to James I., anno 1617.' Among the subscribers were Sir Francis Bacon, the Earls of Pembroke and Southampton, the Duke of Lennox, etc. I am indebted to Dr. Gatty for the loan of his copy, which once belonged to James I. In it two meanings are given for the verb to misse:—to MISSE, *or erre*...vide to ERRE, *or* WANDER, b. *to* MISSE, *or want*...vide to WANT. The noun in this passage is from the first meaning of the verb = error.

56. *Tires*, from French *tirer*, a term of falconry used of a hawk tearing its food. Cf. Jonson's *Poetaster*, iv. 1:—

'*Horace.* What, and be tired on by yond vulture!'

63. *prey*, pray Q.

68. *fast'ned*, fastned Q.

78. *best*, brest in Q. 11, Q. 12, Q. 13. Lintott and Gildon, 'Her breast.'

84. *comptless*, comptlesse Q. = inestimable.

86. *dive-dapper*, didapper, dabchick, from its habit of diving: the little grebe (*Podiceps minor.*)

90. *winks*, here akin to *wince*, formerly also *winch*, from O. Fr. *guinchir, guenchir*, to start aside, no doubt sometimes written *winchir*: from O.G. *wenken*, to start aside. *Imp. Dic.*, cf. *blink, blench*.

110. *Leading him prisoner in a red-rose chain.* Malone refers to Ronsard:—

> 'Les muses lièrent un jour
> De chaines de Roses Amour.'
>
> *Odes*, bk. iv. 23 (ed. 1623).

Richelet points out that the Ode is taken from *Anacreon*, published in France, 1554. Sidney, Daniel, and Drayton, later Wither and Herrick, discover unmistakable traces of Ronsard's influence. Ronsard travelled in England. Queen Elizabeth gave him a diamond, comparing its water to the purity of his verse. Puttenham, *Arte of English Poesie*, 1589, denounces plagiarisms from Ronsard:—'Another of reasonable good facilitie in translation finding certaine of the hymnes of *Pyndarus* and of *Anacreon's* Odes...very well translated by *Ronsard*, the French Poet...comes our minion and translates the same out of French into English...but doth so impudently robbe the French Poet both of his prayse and also of his French Termes, that I cannot so much pittie him as be angry with him for his injurious dealing.'

114. *mast'ring*, maistring Q.

131-2. *Fair flowers that are not gather'd in their prime*
Rot, and consume themselves in little time:—

an echo of Ronsard's reiterated maxim:—

> 'Je vous envoye un bouquet que ma main
> Vient de trier de ces fleurs épanies;
> Qui ne les eust à ce vespre cueillies,
> Cheutes à terre elles fussent demain.
> Cela vous soit un exemple certain
> Que vos beautez, bien qu'elles soient fleuries,
> En peu de temps seront toutes flaitries,
> Et comme fleurs, periront tout soudain.'—1560.

Ronsard made this theme his own, but it has ever appealed to poets. Before Ronsard, Wyatt had written:—

'What vaileth the flower
To stand still and wither,
If no man it savour
It serves only for sight,
And fadeth towards night'—

and, long before Wyatt, Ovid:—

'Nec violæ semper, nec hiantia lilia florent,
Et riget amissa spina relicta rosa.'

137-38. *for thee...abhor me*. The rhyme is imperfect.

151. *Primrose*, Primrose Q. See Note III. (5), *Lucrece*.

177. *tiréd* = attired. Boswell.

184-85. *Like...Souring*, Likd...So wring, Q.

191. *hairs*, heares Q. rhyming with 'teares,' as above, l. 51.

204. *unkinn'd*, unkind Q. 'That is, unnatural. *Kind* and *nature* were formerly synonymous'—MALONE. But *unkind*, l. 187, is spelt *unkinde*, Q., whilst here we have *unkind* although rhyming to *minde*. I am persuaded by the sense of the couplet, and specially by the *but*:—

'O had thy mother borne so hard a minde,
She had not brought forth thee, but died unkind':—

that the word is not the adjective but a past participle, which would now be spelt *unkinned*, without offspring, cf.:—

'*Unfathered* heirs and loathly births of nature.'
2 *Henry IV*., IV. iv. 122.

'But hope of orphans and *unfathered* fruit.'
Sonnet XCVII.

The poet, probably, played on the double meaning. Cf. *Hamlet*:—

'A little more than kin and less than kind.'

205. *What am I that thou shouldst contemn me this?* Steevens:—'I suppose, without regard to the exactness of the rhyme, it should read—*thus*.' Malone interprets:—'That thou shouldst contemptuously refuse this favour that I ask.'

213. *Statue*, statüe Q. Cf. Sonnet LV. 5, where the word is printed in italics. It was but newly accepted and occurs four times in the *Plays as statua*. See Note III. (8), *Lucrece*.

220. *judge*, Iudge Q. See Note III. (1), *Lucrece*.

222. *intendments* = intentions. Cf. *As You Like It*, I. i.:— 'Either you shall stay him from his intendment or brook such disgrace well as he shall run into.'

> 'But fear the main intendment of the Scot.'—*Henry V*., I. ii.
>
> 'Ay, and said nothing but what I protest intendment of doing.'—*Othello*, IV. ii.
>
> 'But I spying his intendment, discharged my petronel in his bosom.'—Jonson, *Every Man in his Humour*.

229. *Fondling, she saith*, '*Since*.... The Cambridge has:— 'Fondling,' she saith, 'since.... But the word is descriptive of Venus' action, not a term of endearment applied to Adonis.

231 and 239. *deer*, deare Q. A play upon words.

240. *rouse*, a term of art in venery. Guillim in *A Display of Heraldrie*, 2nd Ed., 1632;—*Enlarged by the Author himselfe in his lifetime: Together with his owne Addition of explaining the Termes of Hawking and Hunting*, lays down in detail 'apt termes of *Hunting* pertaining both to *Beasts of Venery* and of Chase':—

<table>
<tr><td rowspan="5">'You shall say</td><td>Dislodge</td><td rowspan="5">the</td><td>Bucke</td></tr>
<tr><td>Start</td><td>Hare</td></tr>
<tr><td>un-Kennell</td><td>Foxe</td></tr>
<tr><td>Rowse</td><td>Hart</td></tr>
<tr><td>Bowlt</td><td>Conie.'</td></tr>
</table>

257. *remorse* = compunction, tenderness, pity.

> 'If so your heart were touched with that remorse
> As mine to him.' *Measure for Measure*, II. ii.
>
> 'Curse on th' unpard'ning prince, whom tears can draw
> To no remorse.' Dryden.

260-61. *jennet...courser*, Iennet...Courser, Q. See Note III. (4), *Lucrece*.

272. *compass'd* = arch'd. 'A compass'd ceiling' is a phrase yet in use.—Malone. *Troilus and Cressida*, i. 2:—'She came to him the other day in the compass'd window,' i.e. the *bow* window.—Steevens.

272. *stand*. This verb is governed by *mane*, which, as composed of many hairs, is used in the plural.

279. *curvets*, a term of the manege, 'the ground of all high airs,' is generally derived from French *courbette*, but more properly, according to ancient manuals on horsemanship, from Italian *corvetta* = a curvet; *corvo* = a raven. The horse was made to rear and prance forward with his hind legs together, and this action was likened to the hopping of a raven. *The Guide into Tongues*, 1617 (see note on l., 53), gives:—to curvet, *or praunce*. Italian, *corvéttare*.

The manege seems to have originated in Italy, the French word being derived from the Italian *maneggio*, a riding-school.

279. *leaps*, rhyming with *steps*. The word is still pronounced 'leps' in Ireland.

284. *holla*. 'This seems to have been formerly a term of the manege. So, in *As You Like It*, "Cry *holla* to thy tongue, I pr'ythee: it curvets unseasonably." See Cotgrave's *French Dictionary*, "Hola, interjection. Enough, soft, soft; no more of that if you love me."'—Thus Malone. But the term seems, before it entered the manege, to have hailed from the Champ Clos. Littré quotes 'la pluie fit le holla' [entre des combattants], D'Aub., *Hist.*, i. 289. Charles D'Orleans, bidding his heart be still, wrote:—'Si, lui dis je: mon cueur hola!'—*Chanson*, li. Owing to modern pronunciation, and a lax use resulting from it in literature, 'Holla' is often confounded with 'Halloo,' from the French *Haler* = to halloo on hounds. Its sense is exactly the opposite, and survives, I am told, in a street cry:—'Stop-thief. Stop-thief. Holla! Holla! Holla!' Holla = stop, as in the pleasant Elizabethan ditty, 'Holla, my Fancy, whither wilt thou stray?' Sir Walter Scott places the two expressions, accurately, in the mouth of the Earl of Huntinglen:—'"Ho la," said the Earl of Huntinglen, "halt there"' and, in the same passage:—'I should love well to make the oaks of my old forest of Dalgarno ring once more with halloo, and horn, and hound.'—*The Fortunes of Nigel.*

299. *horse*, Horse Q. See Note III. (4), *Lucrece*.

303. *'To bid the wind a base'* = to challenge the wind for speed. Cf. *Two Gentlemen of Verona*, I. ii. 97:—

'Indeed I bid the base for Proteus.'

And Marlowe:—

'We will find comfort, money, men, and friends,
Ere long to bid the English King a base.'

From the game *base, prisoner's base, or county base* as it was originally called. Cf. *Cymbeline*, V. 3:—

'Lads more like to run
The county base, than to commit such slaughter.'
'So ran they all as they had been at bace.'
Spenser, *Faery Queen*, V. viii.

304.*whe'r, where* Q = whether. Cf. Sonnet LIX. 11, Q:—

'Whether we are mended, or where better they.'

So, in *King John* (II. i. 166):—

'Now shame upon thee whe'r he does or no':—

and in a poem by G. Turberville, 1567:—

'I doubt *where* Paris would have chose
Dame Venus for the best.'—Malone.

314. *vails* = lowers. French *avaler*, from Latin *ad; vallis*. Cf. *Merchant of Venice*, I. i.:—

'Vailing her high top lower than her ribs.'

322. *horse*, Horse Q.

331. *oven*, Oven Q.

335. *the heart's attorney* = the tongue. Cf. *Richard III.*, IV. iv.:—

'Why should calamity be full of words?
Windy attorneys to their client woes.'

343. *wistly* = wistfully.

345. *hue*, hew Q: the usual spelling. Cf. Sonnet XX.:—'A man in hew.'

354. *new-fall'n*, new falne Q.

359-60. *dumb play...Chorus-like*. An illustration from the Dumb-Show which preceded and the Chorus which commented on a Play.

363. *ivory*, Iuorie Q. *alabaster*, allablaster Q.

376. *steel'd*, steeld Q. Cf. Sonnet XXIV. 1, Q.:—

'Mine eye hath play'd the painter and hath steeld
Thy beauties forme in table of my heart.'

397. *'Who sees his true-love in her naked bed.'* The phrase 'naked bed' is of interest. It occurs in the *Mirror for Magistrates*:—'When in my *naked bed* my limbs I lay,' but its frequency in the works of Shakespeare's play-writing contemporaries is due to their derision of a line, *Jeronimo* or *Hieronymo*, II. v.:—

'What outcry calls me from my naked bed.'

which was constantly ridiculed by Jonson and others on account of this phrase. The first *Jeronymo* 'was acted by Lord Strange's men' [Shakespeare's Company] 'at the Rose twenty-two times in the year 1592' (Fleay). This echo may therefore suggest that Shakespeare wrote *Venus and Adonis* not long before its publication (1593). We know from Dekker's *Satiromastix* that Jonson 'took mad Ieronimo's part,' when he 'ambled by a play-waggon.' But he did not admire the play. In *Cynthia's Revels* he hits at the 'civet-wit' in the audience, who 'prunes his mustaccio, lisps, and, with some score of affected oaths, swears down all that sit about him:—"that the old Hieronymo, as it was first acted, was the only best, and judiciously penn'd play of Europe."'

416. *Who plucks the bud before one leaf put forth.* Cf. Henry Constable's *Sheepheard's Song of Venus and Adonis*:—

'I am now too young
To be wonne by beauty;
Tender are my yeeres,
I am yet a bud.'

421. *You hurt my hand with wringing.* Cf. *ibid.*:—

'Thou wringest mee too hard,
Pre-thee, let me goe.'

429. *Mermaid's*, Marmaides Q.

430. *before;...bearing,* before,...bearing, Q.; before,... bearing: Malone and modern editions. The sense seems to be 'I had my load before; (but I am) now press'd (down) with bearing, melodious discord,' etc. etc.

433-50. Cf. Chapman's *Ovid's Banquet of Sense* (1595), in which Ovid discourses to Corinna (Julia) of '*Auditus, Olfactus, Visus, Gustus, Tactus.*'—*The Argument.*

456. *flaws* = sudden gusts. Cf. *Hamlet*, V. i.:—'Should patch a wall to expel the winter's flaw.'

> 'The flaw-blown sleet.'—Keats.
> 'What flaws and whirles of weather.'
> Beaumont and Fletcher, *Pilgrim*, III. vi.

466. *bankrupt*, bankrout Q.

494. *Ocean*, Ocean Q. See Note III. (6), *Lucrece*.

500. *shrewd*, shrowd Q.; shrewd Q. 3.

507. *verdure*, verdour Q:—'The poet evidently alludes to a practice of his own age, when it was customary, in time of the plague, to strew the rooms of every house with rue and other strong-smelling herbs, to prevent infection'—Malone.

508-10. *To drive infection from the dangerous year!*
That the star-gazers, having writ on death,
May say, the plague is banish'd by thy breath.

This vivid allusion to the Plague may give a clue to the date of the poem's composition. It is more than improbable that Shakespeare should have written thus at Stratford of the Plague and of the excitement it caused. He refers to the Plague in London, where it nearly affected him as an actor, affording the City authorities their stock pretext for prohibiting plays, to which they objected in deed on puritanical grounds. Fleay quotes one of their arguments in 1575:—'To play in plague-time increases the plague by infection: to play out of plague-time calls down the plague from God.' Now in 1586 there seems to have been a visitation, but too slight to call forth such a comment from the poet, even supposing he had then reached London, which is doubtful. In 1592, however, the theatres were closed on account of the Plague from July to December, and the Michaelmas term was kept at Hertford (*Stow*, p. 765, cited by Fleay, *History of the Stage*, p. 94). It is probable, therefore, that Shakespeare wrote the poem during the enforced idleness of the second half of the year 1592; and this falls in with the suggestion (*supra*) that the phrase *naked bed* echoes a line in the play acted by his company twenty-two times in that year.

515. *slips* = counterfeit coin. Cf. *Borneo and Juliet*:—

'What counterfeit did I give you?
Mercutio. The *slip*, sir, the *slip*.'

521. *Say, for non-payment that the debt should double*:— 'The poet was thinking of a conditional bond's becoming forfeited for non-payment; in which case the entire penalty (usually the double of the principal sum lent by the obligee) was formerly recoverable at law.'—Malone.

545. *He*, Ho Q.

561. *roe*, Roe Q. See Note III. (4), *Lucrece*.

565-67. *temp'ring...vent'ring*, tempring...ventring Q.—an imperfect rhyme.

589-90. *whereat a sudden pale,*
Like lawn being spread upon the blushing rose.

Cf. *Sheepheard's Song of Venus and Adonis*:—

'At the name of boare
Venus seemed dying:
Deadly-colour'd pale
Roses overcast.'

and *Rape of Lucrece*:—

'First red as roses that on lawn we lay,
Then white as lawn, the roses took away.'

598. *manege*, mannage Q.; the context shows that 'manege,' not 'manage,' was intended. Cf. *A Lover's Complaint*, 111-12:—

'Whether the horse by him became his deed,
Or he his *manege*, by th' well-doing steed.'

(Manege is printed *mannad'g* in Q. 1609.)

600. *clip* = embrace.

601. *Even so*, thus in Q. Modern editions put 'even as,' with a comma after 'maw' in l. 602 instead of a colon. But the first alteration from Q. breaks the rhythm, and the second makes the construction awkward in l. 604. The poet alludes to the picture by Zeuxis.

619. *Battel*, battell Q. I retain the obsolete spelling as better befitting the almost obsolete sense, viz. a division of an army arrayed. Cf. Ovid, *Metam.*, Bk. viii.:—

> 'Sanguine *et igne micant oculi*, riget ardua cervix:
> *Et setæ densis similes hastilibus horrent.*'

628. *venture*, venter Q. rhyming with 'enter.'

632. *eyes pay* Malone (1790), eyes paies Q.

639. *within his danger*:—a phrase which occurs frequently in North's *Plutarch* (1579).

652. *kill, kill!* the cry of soldiers entering a town to sack it, cf.—'To the Sack, to the Sack, Kill! Kill!'—North's *Plutarch—Life of Sylla.*

655. *bate-breeding*, 'bate' = contention. *The Guide into Tongues*, (1617), gives 'Debatemaker, or make-bate...vide Contentions.'

> 'Shall ever civil bate
>
> Gnaw and devour our taste?'
>
> Countess of Pembroke's *Antonius.*

657. *carry-tale*. Cf. 'No tell-tale nor no bread-bate.'—*Merry Wives*, I. iv. 12.

674. *Uncouple at the timorous flying hare*. Cf. *The Sheepheard's Song*, 'Course the fearful hare.'

676. *roe*, Roe Q.

680. *overshut his troubles*. Steevens suggested '*overshoot*, i.e. fly beyond.' Malone adds:—'To *shut up*, in Shakespeare's age, signified to *conclude*. I believe therefore the text is right.'

682. *cranks* = turns.

683. *musits*. '*Musits* are said by the lexicographers to be the places through which the hare goes for relief.'—Malone. The lexicographers make out their ignorance of sport with this display of humour. A hare's muse (French *musse*) is still the common and only term for the round hole made in a fence through which a hare traces her run. *Musit* is from the Fr. diminutive *mussette*.

687. *conies*, Conies Q. See Note III. (4), *Lucrece*.

695. *spend their mouths*, a term of venery. Cf.:—'He will spend his mouth, and promise, like Brabbler the hound.'—*Troilus and Cressida*, V. i. 99.

705. *doth*, do Q.

712. *moralize*:—'The practice of moralising works—that is, of drawing moral applications from treatises, fables, and romances—prevailed extensively in the Middle Ages, and was, at first, chiefly cultivated by religious writers.... It is to this custom Venus alludes when she says it is unlike herself to moralize.'—Bell.

736. *defeature*. Cf. *Comedy of Errors*, V. i. 299:—

> 'Careful hours with time's deformed hand
> Have written strange defeatures in my face.'

740. *wood* = mad. (*The Guide into Tongues*, 1617.)

748. *th' impartial*, the th' impartiall Q.

777. *Mermaids*, Marmaids Q.

787. *reprove* = disprove, refute. Cf. 2 *Henry VI.*, III. i. 40:—

> 'My lords
> Reprove my allegation if you can.'

798. *caterpillers*, Caterpillers Q. See Note III. (4), *Lucrece*.

808. *teen* = vexation.

813. *lawnd*, or laund = an open space of untilled ground in a wood. Cf. 3 *Henry VI.*, III. i. 2:—

> 'Under this thick-grown brake we'll shrowd ourselves
> For through this lawnd anon the deer will come.'

848. *parasites*, parasits in Q. rhyming with 'wits.'

849. Cf. the 'Anon, anon, Sir' scene, 1 *Henry IV.*, II. iv.

849. *tapsters*, Tapsters Q. See Note III. (1), *Lucrece*.

858. *cedar-tops*, Ceader tops Q. See Note III. (5), *Lucrece*.

870. *Coasteth* = approaches; Q. 9 has 'posteth.'

871-72. *And, as she runs the bushes in the way,*
Some catch her by the neck, some kiss her face,

In Q.

> And as she runnes, the bushes in the way,
> Some catch her by the necke, some kisse her face,

Modern Editions omit the comma after 'way,' but this makes the next phrase awkward. I omit the comma after 'runs,' believing that verb to be transitive, as in the phrase 'the fox ran the meadows,' or, possibly, as in 'he ran the blockade,' or 'ran the gauntlet.' The comma which I omit is rhythmical, not grammatical. See Note II. on *The Sonnets*.

873. *twined*, twin'd Q.

875. *doe*, Doe Q. See Note III. (4), *Lucrece*.

877. *at a bay*, a term of venery for the action of hounds baying in a circle round the exhausted stag or boar. It seems to reflect the old French *abai, abbai*, more closely than does the modern English *at bay* (French *aux abois*), which is used of the quarry in its extremity rather than of the hounds that surround it. *The Guide into Tongues* (1617) has 'an Abbay or Barking q. (= as it were) at a Bay, vi. Bay or Barke,' and, under Bay, 'barke, or hold at a Bay.'

888. *who shall cope him first* = encounter him. Cf. *As You Like It*, II. i. 67:—

> 'I love to cope him in these sudden fits.'

Cope, v. t. = to encounter, perhaps from Ice. *kapp*, contention; *kappi*, a champion—derivatives from Latin *campus*, a field (of battle). Thus the *Imperial Dictionary, The Guide into Tongues* (1617), derives the word from Low German 'Kop, the head, as it were to come head to head, or face to face.'

889. *This dismal cry*, viz. the strange intonation of the hounds' 'cry' when baying. 'Cry' is a term of venery. Cf. *A Midsummer Night's Dream*, IV. i.:—

> 'A cry more tuneable
> Was never halloo'd to, nor cheer'd with horn':—

and 'full cry.'

902. *together*, togither Q. rhyming with 'whither.'

909. *mated* = confounded: from French *mater*, to fatigue, Old French *mat*, worn out: all from the chess term, Persian *shâh mât*, English *check mate*, literally 'the king is dead.'

920. *Another flap-mouth'd mourner*. The whole passage attests the Poet's intimate knowledge of the chase, and it reflects

the use of such themes in courtly mediaeval poetry. Cf. the death of Begon in *Garin le Loherain*. He, too, is ineffectually dissuaded from hunting a boar, and, when dead, is mourned by his hounds.

> 'Seul ont Begon en la forest laissie;
> Et jouste lui reviendrent si trois chien,
> Hulent et braient com fuissent enragie...
> Gentis hons fu, moult l'amoient si chien.'
>
> Ker, *Epic and Romance*.

940. *random*, randon Q. The old form from Old French *randon*, French *randonnée*. 'Terme de chasse. Tour, circuit fait sur un même lieu par une bête qu'on a lancée.'—Littré.

956. *vail'd* = let fall.

963. *Both crystals, where they view'd each other's sorrow*:—Magic crystals, as Dr. Dee's, in which one in sympathy with another could see the scene of his distress.

973. *halloo*, hallow Q. This spelling is given by *The Guide into Tongues*, 1617.

995. *clepes* = calls.

1002. *decease*, decesse Q. rhyming with 'confesse.' (Fr. *décès*, Lat. *decessus*.)

1003. *boar*, Bore Q. See Note III. (4), *Lucrece*.

1028. *The grass stoops not, she treads on it so light*. Cf. Virgil, *Æneid*, viii. 808:—

> 'Illa vel, intactæ segetis per summa volaret
> Gramina.'

1031. *as murder'd* Q. 3, are murder'd Q. 1.

1046-47. *As when the wind, imprison'd in the ground,*
Struggling for passage, earth's foundation shakes.

This was the received explanation of an earthquake. Cf. 1 *Henry*, III. i. 32:—

> 'Oft the teeming earth
> Is with a kind of colic pinch'd and vex'd
> By the imprisoning of unruly wind
> Within her womb; which, for enlargement striving,
> Shakes the old beldame earth and topples down
> Steeples.'

1048. *Which with cold terror doth men's minds confound.* 'When Shakespeare was sixteen years old (1580) there was an earthquake in England.'—Malone.

1054. *was drench'd*, had drēcht Q.

1083. *Having no fair to lose*, fair = beauty.

1093. *lion*, Lion Q. See Note III. (4), *Lucrece.*

1096. *tiger*, Tygre Q. (*Ibid.*)

1105. *Urchin-snouted*; urchin = hedgehog (*The Guide into Tongues*).

1105. *boar*, Boare Q. See Note III. (4), *Lucrece.*

1112. *boar* (*Ibid.*).

1128. *two lamps...in darkness lies*:—'It is obvious from this example, as from numerous others, that the Elizabethan violations of time and form cannot always be referred to haste or accident, but that they were sometimes adopted designedly to suit the metre or the rhyme. In such cases as the present, it is possible that the final came into use as a substitute for the Saxon termination *th*.'—Bell.

1149. *staring*, perhaps = bristly and unkempt, as in the 'staring coat' of an ungroomed horse.

THE RAPE OF LUCRECE

I. *The Text.*—The Text is taken from the First Quarto of 1594, as reproduced in facsimile from the copy in the British Museum by Mr. Charles Praetorius. Spelling and punctuation have been modernised generally, but not invariably, in accordance with the use of *The Cambridge Shakespeare*. In every other case of a departure from the Quarto, the fact is noted. *The Variorum Shakespeare* of 1821, *Shakespeare's Poems* (Kelmscott), and *The Poems of William Shakespeare* (Robert Bell), have also been used for the text and notes. Throughout the Notes the First Quarto (B.M.) is referred to as Q.

II. *The Use of the Apostrophe as a Guide to the Metrical Pronunciation.* See Note II. on *Venus and Adonis.*

III. *The Use of Capitals.*—Cf. Note V. on *The Sonnets*. The use of capitals in the First Quartos of *Venus*, *Lucrece*, and *The Sonnets* is not arbitrary, and much, both of the author's intention and of the manner of his age, is lost by a hard and fast conformation to modern practice. In the First Quarto of *Lucrece* capitals are used to denote:—

(1) Professions and Occupations, viz.:—Orator, where the capital is retained in this Edition by analogy with the occasional modern practice in the cases of Poet, Painter, Musician. You find also, Iudge l. 220, Authors l. 1244, Clients l. 1020, Plowman l. 958, Messenger l. 1583, Merchant l. 1660, Citizen l. 464, Groom ll. 1345, 1632-45; and, somewhat similarly, Father l. 1731: in which cases the modern practice has been followed.

(2) Technical Terms, especially of War, viz.:—Tent l. 15, Armies l. 76, Trumpet l. 470, Falchion ll. 509, 1046, 1626, Fort l. 482, Sentinel l. 942, (Battering-) Ram l. 464, Cannon l. 1043, Foe l. 1696; and similarly, in the case of other buildings and appliances, City ll. 464-5, 1544, Monument l. 391, Cabinet l. 442, Curtain l. 374, Cell l. 881, Schedule (Cedule) l. 1312, Bell l. 1492. In the last instance 'Bell' is used as an image, or emblem.

(3) This use is very frequent in the case of Animals, introduced as in Fables, e.g. l. 836, 'My Honey lost, and I a Drone-like Bee'; l. 849, 'Or hateful Cuckoos hatch in Sparrows'

nests?' ll. 1009-1015, where 'the Crow' is contrasted with 'the Swan,' and Gnats with Eagles. In such cases the capital has been retained to emphasise the antithetical illustration.

(4) It is also employed in the Quarto, but not retained in this Edition; in the case of Animals, apart from any such fabular intention, e.g. Owls ll. 164, 360, Lambs ll. 166, 737, Hound, Hawk, l. 694, Faulcon ll. 505-9, Hind l. 543, Doe l. 581, Deer l. 1144, Cat l. 554, Tigers l. 980, Lion l. 421, Lion and Unicorn l. 956, Birds l. 1121.

(5) In the case of Flowers, where it is retained in this Edition, e.g. ll. 258-59, 'Roses.... Lawn' (the capital given to lawn, for antithetical effect, has not, however, been retained); and of Trees, Cedar ll. 664-65, Bark...Pine l. 1167.

(6) For the Sun, Moon, and Ocean, where it is retained, though not for Sea, l. 1100.

(7) For Honour, almost invariably, Virtue l. 846, Fame ll. 1188, 1202-03, where it is not retained unless these qualities are personified, as in the case of Beauty, almost constantly. In beauty, l. 80, it is omitted.

(8) The use of capitals in words newly introduced may best be illustrated from a passage in *The Arte of English Poesie* (1589):—After warning the 'maker' to avoid antiquated, provincial, 'inkhorne terms brought in by men of learning,' and 'strange terms of other languages by secretaries and marchaunts and trauailours,' the author allows certain exceptions:—'Ye have also this word *conduict*, a French word, but well allowed...also this word *idiome*, taken from the Greekes, yet serving aptly... this word *significative* borrowed of the Latine and French, but to us brought in first by some Noble-mans Secretarie... and many more like usurped Latine and French words: as, *methode, methodicall, placation, function, assubtiling, refining, compendious, prolixe, figurative, inveigle...numerous, metrical... penetrate, indignitie...savage* for wilde: *obscure* for darke... *audacious* for bold.' In the First Quartos this same theory is exemplified by the same practice, viz. of printing such words with capitals and sometimes (in *The Sonnets*) in italics, e.g. in *Lucrece*, Oratorie l. 564, Apologies l. 31, Hospitalitie l. 75,

Cure l. 732, Diapason l. 1132, Pilgrimage l. 960, Sou'raigntie l. 36, Lamentations l. 1829, Ivory l. 407, Antiques l. 459; and, more doubtfully, Arch l. 1667, Act l. 1824, Edie (Eddy) l. 1669, Down l. 1012. In these cases the capital has not been retained, but they are not necessarily errors. The Swan's *Down* has a capital in Guillim's *Display of Heraldrie* (1610), and the word is derived in *The Guide into Tongues* (1617), from Low German *dunne veders*: a *dun* = tenuis, exilis; *veder* = pluma.

IV. *Notes on the Text.*

1. *all in post.* Cf. *The Palace of Pleasure*, William Painter:—'Whervpon thei rode to Rome in poste.'

8-9. *Haply that name of 'chaste' unhaply set*

This bateless edge on his keen appetite. Cf. Ovid, *Fasti*, ii.:—

'Verba placent, et vox, *et quod corrumpere non est*:
Quoque minor spes est, hoc magis ille cupit';

bateless = not to be 'bated,' i.e. blunted. Cf. *Love's Labour Lost*, I. i. 6:—

'That honour, which shall *bate* his scythe's keen edge.'

10. *Let* = forbear. Cf. Chaucer:—

'That man is bounden to his observance
For Goddes sake to *leten* of his will.'

13. *heaven's Beauties* = the stars.

19. *high-proud,* hyphened by Malone.

24. *silver-melting,* hyphened by Malone.

36. *Sov'reignty,* Sou'raingtie Q.

37. *Suggested* = tempted. Cf. *King Richard II.*, III. iv. 75:—

'What Eve, what serpent, hath suggested thee,
To make a second fall of cursèd man.'

50. *Collatium.* Thus in the Bodleian version of the First Quarto; Colatia in all the other early Quartos.

56. *Virtue would stain that or with silver white*:—*Or* (*ore* Q., *o'er* Modern Editions) may involve a play on the two words *ore* = or = gold in heraldry; and *ore* = o'er, over. But the first is here the primary sense. Malone conjectured this, instancing the use of *ore* = or = gold, in *Hamlet*; and adding, 'The terms of heraldry in the next stanza seem to favour this supposition:

and the opposition between *or* and the *silver* white of Virtue is entirely in Shakespeare's manner. So afterwards:—

> "Which virtue gave the *golden* age, to gild
> Their silver cheeks...."

But Malone did not push his conjecture far enough. The conceits of this whole passage (ll. 54-72), based as it is on heraldic terms throughout, can only be understood in the light of contemporary heraldic lore as expounded, for example, by Guillim in his *Display of Heraldrie* (1610). Guillim gives a long account of the composition and significance of the several colours used in blazon, much of which bears directly on this passage. E.g.:—'This colour (white) is most commonly taken in *Blazon* for the metal *silver*, and is termed *Argent*, wheresoever the same is found in Field or Charge. In the Second Edition (1632) there follows:—To this metall is given the second place next to *gold*.... For in Blazon it betokeneth innocency, cleannesse of life and chastity.' Coming (First Edition) to *yellow*, he writes:—'This *colour* is bright *yellow*, which is compounded of much *white*, and a little *red*, as if you should take two parts of *white*, and but one of *red*. This *colour* in *Armes* is blazed by the name of *Or*, which is as much as to say *aurum*, which is gold.' It is possible to interpret this line by assuming that Shakespeare uses 'or' = *gold*, for the *red* of Beauty's blush—Beauty's 'red' of line 59 (he uses 'gold' for 'red' in *Macbeth*: 'His silver skin laced with his golden blood'). But, on this assumption, the remainder of the passage becomes unintelligible. And whenever Shakespeare, in an age of technical conceits, indulges in one ostentatiously, it will always be found that his apparent obscurity arises from our not crediting him with a technical knowledge which he undoubtedly possessed, be it of heraldry, of law, or of philosophic disputation. When he says:—'Virtue would stain *that* or with silver white,' he means that Virtue, by an admixture of 'silver white':—the blazon of chastity (*supra*) with 'that' = Beauty's blushes = 'Beauty's red' of l. 59:—obtained, in accordance with Heraldry, the 'mixed colour,' *gold*, which is 'blazed by the name of *Or*.' Virtue's *white*, mixed with Beauty's *red*, has now produced heraldic *or*.

57-58. *But Beauty in that white intituléd*
From Venus' doves, doth challenge that fair field.

In Q. there is a comma after 'intituléd.' But Shakespeare constantly places a comma, without grammatical signification, at the end of a line (see Note V. on *The Sonnets*). These lines do not, even when taken alone, give any clear sense, unless so punctuated as to yield this meaning:—'But Beauty, also intituled = formally blazoned in *white* (which is virtue's colour) by derivation from Venus' doves, doth challenge that fair *field* = disputes Virtue's exclusive right to a *field*, again the proper heraldic term, of white.' And, unless this interpretation be accepted, it will be found that 67:—*Of either's colour was the other Queen* and 70:—*That oft they interchange their seat*—yield no sense at all.

59. *Then Virtue claims from Beauty, Beauty's red*:—Beauty having claimed Virtue's white, by instancing 'Venus' doves,' Virtue retorts with a counter-claim on Beauty's red, which she founds, ll, 60-64:—

'Which Virtue gave the golden age, to gild
Their silver cheeks, and call'd it then their shield
Teaching them thus to use it in the fight,
When shame assailed, that red should fence the white':—

on the fact that she, Virtue, gave *red* to the *Golden Age*, so that, again by admixture in accordance with heraldry, they (the people of the world's innocent prime) might 'gild their silver cheeks'—in fact, turn their *white*, the symbol of 'innocency,' into *gold*. Virtue calls this their *shield*; teaching them, when the *white* innocency is assailed, to 'fence' = defend it with *red* blushes. Thus the Poet brings his conceit round to the point of departure from Lucrece' blush. The ensuing lines:—

'This heraldry in Lucrece' face was seen,
Argued by Beauty's red and Virtue's white:
Of either's colour was the other Queen':—

are now intelligible; for Beauty, starting with *red*, has claimed *white*, and Virtue, starting with *white*, has claimed *red*.

67. *Proving from world's minority their right*:—This also is now intelligible. It refers back to the 'golden age' of

the world's infancy, when Virtue had *red* in *her* gift, and it refers also, as I hold, to the priority of *white* among heraldic colours, according to the science of Shakespeare's day. Cf. Guillim:—'*White* challengeth the precedency of *black* (according to Upton) in respect of priority of time, for that it was in nature before black'—and, *à fortiori*, before *red*, which is 'exactly compounded of *white* and *black*.'

69. *The sovereignty of either being so great*:—'Sovereignty' is also used by Guillim and his predecessors for the dignity attaching to certain dispositions of heraldic bearings:—'Moreover (as Leigh sheweth) they are also called, *most worthy partitions*, in respect that albeit the *Field* be *charged* in divers parts thereof, whether with things of one or of divers kinds, yet is every one of them as effectual as if it were only one by the *soveraigntie* of these *partitions*.'

Heraldry was the one science of the nobility before whom minstrels sang in the Middle Ages, and a knowledge of it, as expounded by ancient writers, may throw light on many dark passages of mediæval song. 'The eyes of vair' of Aucassin and Nicolete ('les iex vairs') which have remained inscrutable to Mr. Lang, Mr. Bourdillon, and M. Roquefort, may shine again with recovered brilliancy. Guillim writes, summing up the wisdom of his forbears, 'If your *vaire* doth consist of *Argent* and *Azure*, you must in *blazon* thereof, say onely, hee beareth *vaire*, and it sufficeth: but if it be composed of any other *colours*, then you must say, he beareth *vaire* of these or those *colours*.' So Nicolete's eyes shone like a shield of blue and silver.

87-88. These lines are marked as quotations in Q.

93. *pleats*:—thus in all the Quartos. Ewing substituted 'plaits,' and Boswell adduces:—

> 'Time shall unfold what *plaited* cunning hides.'—*Lear*, I. i. 279.

But this 'plaited' is due to Pope. The first two Quartos have 'pleated,' and the sense in both passages suggests the pleats or folds of an ample robe, not a covering of 'plaited' or 'platted' interweaving. Cf. *Lear*, IV. vi. 162:—

> 'Through tatter'd clothes small vices do appear;
> Robes and furr'd gowns hide all....'

100. *parling* = speaking.

102. *Writ in the glassey margents of such books.* Cf. *Romeo and Juliet*, I. iii. 86:—

> 'And what obscured in this fair volume lies,
> Find written in the margent of his eyes.
> This precious book of love, this unbound lover,
> To beautify him only lacks a cover.'

Margent = margin. 'In all our ancient English books, the comment is printed in the margin.'—Malone.

113. *thither*, thither Q. Hither Cambridge, with an erroneous attribution of 'thither' to Q. 7 alone.

121. *Intending* = pretending. *spright*, sprite Q.

135. *That what they have not, that which they possess.*— Thus in the first four Quartos. In later Editions:—

> 'That oft they have not...'

But the earlier reading, though a little involved, conveys a subtiler sense:—'Those that covet much are rendered so foolish by their rapacity that what they have not, viz. that which they (apparently) possess but cannot truly be said to have, they scatter and unloose, and so have less by hoping to get more; or, if they do gain more, the profit of this excess is but to surfeit and to suffer such griefs that they prove bankrupt by this poor-rich gain.' Malone cites Daniel's *Cleopatra* (1594):—'For what thou hast, thou still dost lacke,' and a sentence of *Publius Syrus*:—'Tam avaro deest quod habet, quam quod non habet.'

147. *all together*, the seventh and eighth Quartos; altogether in the rest.

148. *venturing*, ventring Q.

168. *wakes*, Qq; wake, Malone (Capell MS.).

188. *His naked armour of still, slaughter'd lust*:—'Still slaughtered' Q.; 'still-slaughter'd,' Malone; 'i.e. still-slaughtering; unless the poet means to describe it as a passion that is always a killing, but never dies.'—Steevens. But the line continues the sense of the preceding passage: (171) he is toss'd between Desire and Dread; (172) Desire flatters his enterprise; Dread fears harm from it; (173) Honest Fear, bewitched by Lust, too often

retires; (183) but Fear again gets the upper hand, and Tarquin debates the sorrow that must arise from his contemplated crime; till (187) he despises (188) his naked or defenceless protection from Lust, now still and slaughtered by Fear.

198. *O foul dishonour to my household's grave*. This opens another passage based on Shakespeare's knowledge of heraldry. Cf.:—'household's grave' with *Titus Andronicus*, V. iii. 194:—

> 'Lavinia shall forthwith
> Be closéd in our household's monument.'

The escutcheons of ancestors were displayed on the mortuary chapels of noble families. But, possibly, 'grave' is here a noun, from the verb 'to grave.' Cf. *Merchant of Venice*, II. vii. 36:—

> 'Let's see once more this saying *graved* in gold.'

The epithet 'household' is twice applied by Shakespeare to armorial bearings:—

> '*Clifford*. Might I but know thee by thy *household* badge.
> *Warwick*. Now, by my father's badge, old Nevil's crest,
> The rampant bear chain'd to the ragged staff.'
> 2 *Henry VI*., V. i. 202.

> '*Bolingbroke*. From my own windows torn my *household* coat,
> Razed out my imprese, leaving me no sign,
> Save men's opinions and my living blood,
> To show the world I am a gentleman.'
> *Richard II*., III. i. 24.

This use of 'household coat,' in juxtaposition with 'imprese,' a term of heraldic science, gives some slight colour to my suggestion that by 'household's grave' Shakespeare meant the same thing; and the suggestion is further strengthened by his play on the word in the couplet of this same stanza:—

> 'Then my digression is so vile, so base
> That it will live *engraven* in my face':—

leading up, as it does, to the next stanza (204-10), in which he deals explicitly with 'abatements,' which are 'accidentall markes annexed to Coate-Armour, denoting some ungentleman-like, dishonorable, or disloyall demeanour, quality, or staine in the Bearer, whereby the dignity of the Coate-Armour is greatly abased.'—*A Display of Heraldrie.* Among such abatements. Guillim goes on to give one 'unto him that discourteously intreateth either *Maid* or *Widdow against their will.*'

217. *strucken*, strokē Q.

239. *ay*, I Q., is frequently so spelt by contemporary writers.

245. *Shall by a painted cloth be kept in awe*:—'In the old tapestries or *painted cloths*, many moral sentences were wrought. So, in *If This Be not a Good Play, the Devil is in't*, by Dekker,

> "What says the prodigal child in the painted cloth?"'—Malone.

313. *conduct* = conductor.

333. *sneaped* = nipped, pinched. Cf. Ray:—

> 'Herbs and fruits sneaped with cold weather.'

The first sense is to reprimand or chide, as in 2 *Henry IV.*, II. i. 133:—

> 'My lord, I will not undergo this sneap without reply.'

335. *Shelves and sands.* Cf. Milton:—'On the tawny sands and shelves.'

342. *prey to pray*, 'pray to pray' Q.

400. *Her hair, like golden threads*:—Cf. *flavique capilli* in Ovid's version of the story.

408. '*A pair of maiden worlds unconqueréd*':—Mr. Grant White and Mr. Bell take exception to the epithet 'maiden.' 'Is not this line contradicted in the two lines following?' Mr. Furnivall justly replies:—'Shakespeare used "maiden" here as we do of a castle, which admits its own lord but not a foe.'

417. *tiréd*, tyred Q., a term of falconry. See Note on *Venus and Adonis*, l. 56.

419. *alabaster*, alablaster Q.

428-43. A sustained conceit taken from the assault of a fortress. It is resumed 464-83.

459. *antics*, antiques Q.

460. This line is marked as a quotation in Q.

471. *heartless* = spiritless.

476. *Under what colour*:—a play on the double sense of the word :—(1) pretext; (2) standard, in pursuit of the conceit.

495. *Will*, Will Q.:—It is but fair to note this in view of the controversy arising out the word when so printed in *The Sonnets*. See Note V. on *The Sonnets*.

534. *tender* = hold dear, regard.

Bequeath not to their lot
The shame that from them no device can take,
The blemish that will never be forgot:
Worse than a slavish wipe:—

Here the Poet, again, follows the science of heraldry. Cf. *A Display of Heraldrie*:—'This (a batune, baston) is the *proper* and most *usuall note* of *illegitimation* (perhaps for the affinitive betwixt *Baston* and *Bastards*; or else for that *bastards* lost the priviledge of *freemen*, and so were subject to the *servile stroke*:)...which *Marke* (as some doe hold) neither they nor their children shall ever remove or lay aside.'

543. *grype* = griffin, from Latin *gryps*. 'All the modern editions read:—

"*Beneath the gripe's* sharp claws."

The gryphin was meant, which in our author's time was usually written grype or gripe.'—Malone. Steevens cites Cotgrave to the same effect, but sets against him Mr. Reed's edition of *Dodsley's Old Plays*, i. 124, 'where *gripe* seems to be used for vulture:—

"Ixion's wheele
Or cruel *gripe* to gnaw my growing harte."
Ferrex and Porrex.'

Bell writes:—'It is here evidently intended for a real bird, and not for an imaginary griffin.' But was the griffin imaginary to Shakespeare? His frequent use in *Lucrece* of the lore subsequently collected in Guillim's *Display of Heraldrie* makes it not improbable that the Cockatrice of l. 540 suggested the Grype or Griffon of l. 543, for in that work they are described, with but the Wiverne between them. Now none of these creatures is presented by Guillim as imaginary. They are, it is true, '*exorbitant Animals*, much more prodigious than all the former,' and not to be 'reckoned amongst those good *Creatures* that God created before the transgression of Adam.' But they exist, although, 'If *Man* had not transgressed the Law of his *Maker*, this dreadfull deformity (in likelihood) had not happened in the procreation of *Animals*.' Guillim is no sceptic, and 'an Unicorne sejant' is for him not even exorbitant:—'Some have made doubt whether there be any such *Beast*, as this, or no. But the great esteeme of his *Horne* (in many places to be seene) may take away that needelesse scruple.' *The Guide into Tongues* (1617) gives a minute description of the Grype, instancing its hostility to horses:—'est animal pennatum et quadrupes: ideoque per terram currunt ut Leones, per aëra volant ut Aquilæ. Omni parte corporis Leones sunt, Alis, et facie, et pedibus, Acquilis similes. Multum equos infestant, adeoque equitem armatum cum equo in sublime rapiunt.'

550. *blows*, Malone; 'blow' in all the Quartos.

555. *panteth*, pateth Q:—Probably for 'pāteth,' then having been let drop by the printer on to 'fōllie,' at the end of the next line.

639. *rash relier* Q:—Sewell without authority suggested 'not to seducing lust's outrageous fire.' The Edition of 1616 has 'rash reply.' But to 'rely' originally transitive, was formerly but another form of to 'rally,' both, at the furthest source, from *re-ad-ligare*.

640. *repeal* = recall. Cf. *Richard II.*, II. ii. 49:—

> 'The banished Bolingbroke *repeals* himself':—

and 2 *Henry VI.*, III. ii. 349:—

> 'I will repeal thee, or, be well assured
> Adventure to be banishéd myself.'

643. *Eyne*, eien Q.

669-672. Cf. Ovid, *Fasti*, II.:—

> 'Nil agis; eripiam, dixit, pro crimine vitam:
> Falsus adulterii testis adulter erit:
> Interimam famulum, cum quo deprensa fereris.'

677. Cf. Ovid, *Fasti*, II.:—

> 'Ut quondam stabulis deprensa relictis
> Parva sub infesto quum jacet agna lupo':—

and Chaucer:—

> 'Right as a wolf that fynt a lomb aloon,
> To whom shal she compleyne, or makë moon?'
>
> *Legende*, ll. 1798-99.

680. *nightly linen*:—'Grant White identifies the "linnen" with the night-rail of the nightgownless Elizabethan time.'—Furnivall. Night-gowns were not worn in bed in Shakespeare's day, and the word, when he uses it, stands for a dressing-gown:—

> 'I have seen her rise from her bed, throw her night-gown upon her.'
>
> *Macbeth*, V. i. 3.

But night-rail seems to have the same meaning, viz. 'a loose robe worn over the dress at night.'—Imperial Dictionary. 'Nightly linen' probably = linen sheets.

684. *prone* = headstrong, Malone. The 1600 edition has 'proud.'

688. Cf. Ovid, *Fasti*, II.:—

> 'Quid victor, gaudes? haec te victoria perdet.'

696. *balk*, bauk Q. = to turn aside from, as when a horse refuses.

722. Cf. Sonnet CXLVI. 1, 2.

743. *convertite* = convert. Cf. *As You Like It*, V. iv. 190:—

> 'Out of these convertites
> There is much matter to be heard and learned.'

747. *scapes*; 'any loose or wanton acts, or misdemeanours. Cf. *Winter's Tale*, III. iii.:—

> "A very pretty barne! sure some *scape*; though I am not very bookish, I can read waiting-gentlewoman in the *scape*."
> "Thou lay'st thy scapes on names adored."—Milton, *Paradise Regained*, ii.' Bell.

812. *quote*, cote Q. Cf. French *coter*, to quote. The sense is here to mark, observe. Cf. *Hamlet*, II. i. 112:—

> 'I am sorry that with better heed and judgment
> I had not quoted him.'

828. *crest-wounding* = dishonouring to the crest or cognisance.

830. *the mot* = the motto on the scroll. That Shakespeare wrote *Lucrece* with an intimate knowledge of heraldry, as it was afterwards anatomized in Guillim's *Display*, is again apparent from this passage. Guillim has a paragraph described—'Crest upon an Escroll' (6, v.), in which he argues that the proper place for a crest, though the fashion be now 'inveterate and overworn' was 'upon an Escroll' and adds:—'You may yet observe that our most noble Prince of *Wales* himself to this day thus beareth his *badge*'—and the Poet here puts the two together. His 'crest-wounding' is reminiscent of a feature in the most drastic abatement—'his crest divided' (Guillim); his 'mot' or motto, 'How he in peace is wounded, not in war,' is reminiscent of a passage in the same section:—'And therefore because the dastard dares not come so neere the *enemy*, to beare his strokes on his shield, hee must be content to take this piercing of some of his owne side in *Armes*.'

Shakespeare, who loved terms of art, in *Lucrece* borrows from Heraldry as freely as, in *The Sonnets*, he borrows from Law. Some have argued that he was a lawyer. Others might argue, with equal probability, that he was a Herald, or a Platonist. He was none of these essentially. But he was the greatest exploiter of technical terms in an age which, following the precepts of the Pleïade, set itself to illustrate language by impressing the vocabulary of every science and every craft. Cf. Joachim Du Bellay's *Deffençe et Illustration de la langue Françoise* (1549).

831. *How, 'He in peace is wounded, not in war'*:—In Q. 'How, etc. The line is marked as a quotation, also the next line, apparently by a printer's error.

836-39-40-49-50. Roman capitals are used in Q wherever the Poet cites from an adage or a fable.

853. *absolute* = perfect. Cf. *Hamlet*, V. ii:—

'Believe me an absolute gentleman':—

and *passim* in the Plays. The line is marked as a quotation in Q.

859. *barns* = garners up.

867-68. These lines are marked as a quotation or adage in Q.

899. *Sort an hour* = allot an hour.

914. *appaid*:—'From the old verb *apayen*, to please, to satisfy:—

"Therewith was Perkyn appayéd
And preised hem faste." *Piers Ploughman*.'—Bell.

925. *copesmate* = companion. So, in *Hubbard's Tale*:—

'Till that the foe his *copesmate* he had found.'—Steevens.

936. *fine* = to finish.

985. *orts* = fragments, refuse.

1021. *force* = esteem.

1054. *A badge of Fame to Slander's livery*:—The badge was the device, crest, or arms of the master, on a separate piece of cloth, or silver, worn in the form of a shield on the left sleeve. The colour of the livery was generally blue. Cf. Bishop Hall:—

'Some badgeless blue upon his back.'

1092. *nought to do* = nought to do with.

1109-10-11-12-13-14-15-16-17-18-25-27 are printed Q. with 'at the beginning of each line, as being antithetical adages; cf. l. 528. That they are rhymed versions of existing adages, I do not doubt. Compare l. 1110, 'Sad souls are slain in merry company,' and 'But it is an old proverb, that it is a little comfort to the miserable, to have companions.'—Kemp's *Nine Days' Wonder*, 1600.

1127. *dumps* = melancholy tunes. Cf. *Two Gentlemen of Verona*, III. ii. 85:—

'To their instruments
Tune a deploring *dump*.'

In this passage the Poet lays the terminology of Music under contribution:—discord, stops, rests (1124); notes (1126); dumps, time is kept (1127).

1132. *diapason*:—The Poet resumes his conceit founded on musical terms, drawing, in this and the two ensuing lines, on the part-song of his day. Diapason originally meant the interval of an octave.

1133. *burder-wise*, burthen-wise Q:—Burden or burthen is a word of complex origin. It came to mean the refrain of a song. *Burden*, the drone of a bag-pipe, is derived from French

Bourdon, low-Latin *Burdo*, a bumble-bee; but in the case of the organ-pipe and the actual part of the bagpipe, as distinguished from the rude bass played on it, it picked up an association with the other French *Bourdon*, low-Latin *Bordo* or *Burdo*, a pilgrim's staff (properly an ass or mule, for which the staff was a substitute), from the similarity in shape of these instruments to a staff. *Burden* here, as did diapason in the preceeding line, means a simple form of bass.

1134. *descant'st*, descants Q. = Discant (*dis-cantus*, a double song). This was originally the melody or 'counterpoint' sung with a plainsong; thence, the upper voice or leading melody in a piece of part-music. Cf. Sonnet IX. ll. 9-12 of Drayton's *Idea*, 1599:—

> 'My hollow sighs the deepest base doe beare,
> True diapason in distincted sound:
> My panting hart the treble makes the ayre,
> And descants finely on the musiques ground.'

This Sonnet does not appear in the Edition of 1594, and was not republished in the edition of 1619. It therefore has an interesting bearing on the charge of plagiarism, preferred now against Shakespeare and now against Drayton. If there be borrowing here, it was done by Drayton. *The Guide into Tongues* (1617) shows that 'Descant, or discant, to sing descant' had come from the first sense of the noun (= a contrapuntal melody in the treble) to = to sing 'notes which are sung with celeritie,' and 'to sing with a small, yet pleasant and shrill voice as birds doe.'

better skill:—Malone, followed by Bell, put a comma after 'descant'st' and suggested that 'better skill' stands elliptically for 'with better skill.' But that is not so. Shakespeare here, as ever, exhibits a complete grasp of technical terms. He makes *Lucrece* contrast her sad, monotonous accompaniment of groans—humming on Tarquin still—with the treble descant of the nightingale, complaining in a higher register and with more frequent modulations of the wrong wrought her by Tereus, according to Ovid's tale. The one he compares to a single droning base, chiefly in the diapason or lower octave; the other to the 'better skill' or more ingenious artifice of a contrapuntal melody scored above it. The three lines also convey, still more subtily, a compliment from Shakespeare the singer of *Lucrece* to Ovid the singer of *Philomela*. As in the conceits founded on heraldry (*supra*) and on law in *The Sonnets*, Shakespeare contrives an ingenious piece of artistry, whether of sense, of imagery, or of sound. The defined and constant interpretation of technical terms adds point to his meaning. The suggestion which they carry of other things, in themselves pleasing, accords, as it were, an accompaniment of fainter imagery: the shock of surprise occasioned by their melodious introduction endows his music with novelty and charm. And from their successful adaptation to these several uses a special appreciation is born, intellectual, it may be, rather than æsthetic; comparable to, but keener than, the enjoyment which Voltaire found in the 'difficulté surmontée' of French Alexandrine couplets.

1139. *Who, if it wink, shall thereon fall and die*:—The construction is, 'which *heart*, if the *eye* wink, shall fall thereon,' viz. on the *knife*.

1143. *shaming* is here intransitive. Cf. *As You Like It*, IV. iii. 136:—

> 'I do *shame*
> To tell you what I was':—

and Raleigh:—

> 'To its trunk authors give such a magnitude as I *shame* to repeat.'

1157. *pollution*, pollusion Q., rhyming with '*confusion*.'

1167 and 1169. *peel'd* (Lintott), pild Q. = *pill'd*. There were two verbs, *pille* (French *piller*, Latin *pilo*), 'to plunder,' and *pill* (French *peler*, from Latin *pellis*, a skin or bark) = to peel. *The Guide into Tongues* gives both:—to Pille = 'to take by extortion,' and to Pill = 'corticem detrahere, to Barke or pill trees.' Cf. Marston's Prologue to *2 Antonio and Mellida*:—

> 'Whilst snarling gusts nibble the juiceless leaves
> From the nak'd shudd'ring branch; and pills the skin
> From off the soft and delicate aspects.'

The two words came to be confused. E.g.:—

'Commons are always bare, *pilled*, and shorn, as the sheep that feed upon them.'—South; and

'To *peel* the chiefs, the people to devour.'—Dryden.

1182. *by him tainted*:—Malone notes—'The first copy has, by an apparent error of the press, "which *for* him tainted." The correction was made in the octavo 1598.' The error only exists in the two Bodleian copies of Q. The B.M. copy gives 'by him.'

1205. *oversee*. 'Overseers were frequently added in Wills from the superabundant caution of our ancestors.... In some old wills the term *overseer* is used instead of *executor*.'—Malone.

1208. *life's...life's*, lives...lifes Q.

1216. *For 'fleet-winged*, etc. "For in Q, i.e. cited as an adage.

1218. *sun*, sun Q. without a capital = sunshine. There is but one other example (l. 1837) of this word being printed without a capital.

1220. *slow tongue*, slow-tongue Q.

1222. (*For why?*...livery), (For why...liverie) Q.

1226. *Sun*, Sun Q., with a Roman capital. See Note III. (6). But here it, also, leads up to the metaphorical Suns and Ocean of 1230-31, where the conceit is pointed by this use of capitals.

1227. *each flower moist'ned*, Each flowre moistned with a melting eye, Q:—The melody of the line suffers from the abandonment of the ancient pronunciation—flowré moistnéd.

1229. *eyne*, eien Q.

1241. *will* = may will.

1254. *witheréd flower*, withered Q. = witheréd. See Note II., *Venus and Adonis*.

1257. *hild*, the old form of held. In Sonnet II. 4 *held* rhymes to *field*, l. 2.

1258. *fulfill'd* = completely filled.

1261. *Precedent* (Gildon), president Q.

1264. *counterfeit*, counterfaite Q. = counterpart or likeness, i.e. her maid also weeping. Cf. *Merchant of Venice*, III. ii. 116:—

'What find here? Fair Portia's counterfeit.'

1272. *of my sustaining* = that I sustain.

1298. *conceit*, conceipt Q; the conceiving of what she shall write.

1310. *tenure*, tenour Malone; tenure Q., tenor, according to *Imp. Dict.*, in law = a transcript or copy which implies that a correct copy is set out, and therefore that the instrument must have been set out correctly, even though the pleader need not have set out more than the substance or purport of the instrument. This technical term exactly illustrates the nature of Lucrece' letter and of the circumstances under which it was sent.

1329. *sounds* = narrow seas. Malone objects that *sounds* are 'shallow seas, such as may and can be sounded.' But the suggested derivation is false. *Sound* is from Anglo-Saxon *sund*, akin to *sunder*. Malone and Steevens both hold that the poet wrote *floods* and not *sounds*. But Shakespeare's choice is characteristic, both in respect of the word and of the thing intended. (1) *Sounds*, on which a heavy accent falls, echoes by alliteration the 'sorrow' of the preceding, and leads up to the ' sorrow ' of the succeeding line; while the slight paronomasia of *sounds* and *noise* is also in his manner. (2) Shakespeare's imagery is so acutely visualised that in seeking a contrast to a *ford*, or wide shallow in a river, he took a *sound*, or narrow and deep strait of the sea. The substitution of *floods* would injure the melody, the imagery, and the literary antithesis of a fine passage.

1331. The whole episode of the letter is reminiscent of the letters signed 'le vostre T' and 'la vostre C' in Chaucer's *Troilus and Criseyde*, Book v.

1350. *the pattern* = the groom. Later editions transpose 'the' and 'this.'

1358. *blemish*, an imperfect rhyme to 'replenish.'

1366-67. *a piece Of skilful painting* = a painted hanging in lieu of arras.

1368. *drawn* = drawn up, not delineated. Cf. 1 *Henry IV.*, IV. i. 126:—

'He cannot draw his power these fourteen days.'

1380. *pioneer*, Pyoner Q. Originally a 'foot-soldier,' but here a worker in sap and mine.

1407. *purl'd*. Pope suggested *curl'd*; but Malone cites:—

'Whose stream an easie breath doth seem to blow,
Which on the sparkling gravel runs in *purles*
As though the waves had been of silver *curles*.'

Drayton, *Mortimeriados*, 1596.

Two words seem to have fused, *purl* from the sound; cf. *purr*, and *purl*, a stitch in embroidery. The *Imperial Dictionary* gives *purl*, 'a circle made by the motion of a fluid'; perhaps akin to *purl*, a fall from a horse, according to Skeat from old *pirle*, a whirligig, from *pirr*, to whirl. But *The Guide into Tongues* (1617) gives a Purle = a Purfle from French Pourfilé = intertextus. A stitch is still so called, although now spelt, as it seems, erroneously, 'pearlstitch.' The reticulated ripples described by Drayton and the linked spirals of ascending breath described here by our poet are as like this stitch as they are unlike circles.

1417. *boll'n* = swollen. Golding uses the word in his *Ovid*, Phaer in his *Virgil*. Cf. Ben Jonson:—

'Thin, and boln out like a snail.'

Akin to *bulge*.

1418. *to pelt* = to rage. Cf. E. Filmer:—

'Put her ladyship in a horrid *pelt*
And made her rail at me.'

1425. *gripp'd*, grip't Q.

1440. *galléd*. Cf. *Henry V*., III. i. 12:—

'As doth a galléd rock
O'erhang and jutty his confounded base.'

1444. *steel'd*, steld Q., i.e. engraved. Cf. Sonnet XXIV. 1, 2 (1609):—

'Mine eye hath play'd the painter and hath steeld
Thy beauties forme in table of my heart.'

Stell'd was substituted in this passage (*Lucrece*, 1444) for *steld* (*stêl'd*, Malone; *spell'd*, Malone conj.) by Gildon; and *stell'd* was also substituted for *steeld* by Dyce (Capell MS.) in Sonnet

XXIV. Dowden accepts *stell'd* in the Sonnet, and cites *Lucrece*. But *stell'd*, fixed, akin to *stalled* (*stell* is an enclosure for cattle in northern English), makes worse sense in both passages than *steel'd*, engraved. And it has less authority in the Quartos.

Steld (*Lucrece*, 1444), it is true, rhymes with 'dweld': but it does not follow that the two words were pronounced then as we pronounce *dwell'd* now. For *steeld* (Sonnet XXIV. 1) rhymes with 'held,' and 'held' rhymes with 'field' (Sonnet II.), and—printed 'hild'—with 'fulfild' (*Lucrece*, 1257).

Shakespeare certainly uses a verb to 'steel' in *Venus and Adonis*, 377:—

> 'O give it me, lest thy hard heart do steele it,
> And being *steeld*, soft sighes can never grave it.'

'Soft sighs,' naturally, cannot 'grave' a substance that has been 'steel'd.' But the Poet's eye, in Sonnet XXIV., could, like a painter, steel or engrave the Friend's 'beauty's form' on 'the table of his heart,' and the sorrows of Hecuba may well be said (*Lucrece*, 1444) to have steel'd or *engraven all* distress in her *face*. That *steel'd* (= engraved) was intended is confirmed by the next line:—

> '*Many* (faces) she sees where cares have *carvéd some*.'

1452. *chops*:—Later editions read *chaps*. Both forms of the word were used in Shakespeare's time, and there is no reason for abandoning the stronger for the weaker. Cf.:—

> 'Beated and chopp'd with tann'd antiquity.'—Sonnet LXII, 10.

1486. *swounds*, sounds Q.

1525. *'stars shot from their fixéd places'*:—Perhaps a reminiscence of:—

> 'De cœlo lapsa per umbras
> Stella facem ducens multa cum luce cucurrit.
> Illam, summa super labentem culmina tecti,
> Cernimus.' Virgil, *Æneid*, II.

The whole preceding passage seems 'clearly derived from the second book of the *Æneid*.'—Baynes.

1526. *When their glass fell wherein they viewed their faces* = the burnished roof of Priam's palace in which the stars erstwhile had been reflected. Boswell cites Lydgate's description:—

'That verely when so the sonne shone,
Upon the golde meynt amonge the stone,
They gave a light withouten any were,
As doth Apollo in his mid-day sphere.'

1544. *To me came Tarquin arméd to begild*
With outward honesty:—Thus in Q., with 'beguild' for *begild.*

The line goes on, 'but yet defild.' Malone substituted:—

'To me came Tarquin armed; so beguiled
With outward honesty, but yet defiled
With inward vice: as Priam him did cherish,' etc.:—

and the emendation has been generally accepted. But (1) an error so great as of 'armed to beguild' for 'armed; so beguild' (= beguiled) would be without a parallel in the carefully printed Quarto (1594); (2) the (;) would be unusual, also, I think, unparalleled, at this point in the stanza; (3) the (;) would deprive the epithet 'armed' of meaning, reducing it to padding; (4) the emendation demands that *beguil'd* = beguiling; and (5) it makes the grammatical construction of the whole stanza most awkward. On the other hand, 'gild' is frequently spelt 'guild'; cf. (*supra*) l. 60:—

'Which Vertue gave the golden age, to *guild*
Their silver cheeks':—

and in the *Sonnets* (1609) 'guilded, LV.; 'guil'st' for 'gildest,' XXVIII.; 'guilding,' XXXIII.; in *A Lover's Complaint* (1609), 'guilded,' l. 172.

Steevens, confirming Malone, cites *The Merchant of Venice*, III. ii. 97:—

'Thus ornament is but a guiléd shore
To a most dangerous sea':—

and 'guiled' is given by the Quartos and First Folio. The second and third Folios have 'guilded' = 'gilded.'—Rowe. As the whole of Bassanio's speech before the caskets is an attack on gold—('golden locks'—'gaudy gold'), 'guilded' may be the correct reading.

1549. *sheds*, sheeds Q., rhyming with 'bleeds.'

1551. *falls* = lets fall. Cf. *Othello*, IV. i.:—

> 'Every tear she *falls* would prove a crocodile.'

1588. *water-galls*, an appearance in the sky known for a presage of rain; a rainbow-coloured spot, a weather-gall. Cf. H. Walpole:—

> 'False good news are always produced by true good, like the water-gall by the rainbow.'

1590. *sad-beholding*, hyphened by Sewell.

1650. *scarlet lust*:—Lust, the Judge (1652), gives evidence that he has been robbed (*ibid.*) Scarlet is, therefore, a conceit drawn from a judge's scarlet robe.

1679. *feeling-painful*, hyphened by Sewell.

1687. *for 'sparing...*; 'For sparing.... Q., an adage indicated by the inverted comma.

1714-15. *'No, no,' quoth she, 'no Dame, hereafter living,*
By my excuse shall claim excuse's giving':—

This touch, which is omitted by Ovid, comes from Painter's *Palace of Pleasure* (1566):—'No unchast or ill woman shall hereafter take example of *Lucrece*.' I quote from Mr. Furnivall's transcript. Malone quotes an Edition of 1567, and gives:—'No unchaste or ill woman shall hereafter impute no dishonest act to Lucrece.' He also cites Livy: 'nec ulla deinde impudica exemplo *Lucretiæ* vivet.' Shakespeare, who in most of the poem borrows his facts from Ovid, doubtless followed Painter or Livy here, since the reason put into Lucrece' mouth by Livy renders her act more intelligible than Ovid's 'veniam vos datis, ipsa nego.'

1745. *rigol* = circle, a ring (Italian *rigolo*, German *ringel*). Cf. 2 *Henry IV*., IV. v. 36:—

> 'This sleep is sound indeed; this is a sleep
> That from this golden *rigol* (the crown) hath divorced
> So many English Kings.'

1768. *faltering*, foultring Q.

1774. *key-cold.* Cf. *Richard III.*, I. ii.:—

> 'Poor key-cold figure of a holy king.'

1797. *my sorrow's interest* = tears. Cf. Sonnet XXXI.:—

> 'How many a holy and obsequious tear
> Hath dear religious love stol'n from mine eye
> As interest of the dead.'

1801. *too late,* 'means too recently.'—Malone. It may mean too late to save her from Tarquin's crime.

1803. *owed* = owned.

1838. *country rights* = rights of our country. Cf. *Maccabees:*—

> 'He spoke in his country language.'

1854. *plausibly* = with applause, by acclamation.

SONNETS

I. *The Text.*—The text adopted in this edition has been the facsimile in photo-lithography by Charles Praetorius, from the Museum copy of the First Quarto, 1609. Spelling and punctuation have been modernised, generally, but not invariably, in accordance with the use of *The Cambridge Shakespeare*. Every other departure from the text of the First Quarto has been noted. In order to determine on the acceptance of necessary emendations, the Text and Notes of *The Cambridge Shakespeare*, *The Third Variorum of* 1821, Dowden's *Shakespeare's Sonnets*, 1881, Tyler's *Shakespeare's Sonnets*, 1890, *Shakespeare's Poems*, Kelmscott edition, by F.S. Ellis, 1893, and Robert Bell's *The Poems of William Shakespeare*, have been collated throughout, but with an earnest effort to restore the text of the First Quarto, wherever such a course seemed defensible.

II. *Early Editions of the Sonnets.*—The symbols of reference to early editions employed in these Notes have been adopted from *The Cambridge Shakespeare*. It will, therefore, prove convenient to quote, first, the account of Early Editions given by the editors of the *Cambridge* in their preface to Vol. ix.:—

'The *Sonnets* appeared for the first time in 1609. The title of some copies is as follows:—

> Shake-speares | Sonnets. | Never before Imprinted | At London | By *G. Eld* for *T.T.* and are | to be solde by *William Aspley*. | 1609. |

'In others the imprint is:—

> At London | By *G. Eld* for *T.T.* and are | to be solde by *Iohn Wright*, dwelling | at Christ Church gate. | 1609. |

'At the end of the Sonnets was printed in the same edition A Lovers Complaint.

'In 1640 a number of the Sonnets, together with some of the Poems from *The Passionate Pilgrim* and *A Lover's Complaint*, were collected into a volume, with some translations from Ovid and other pieces evidently not by Shakespeare, and published with the following title:—

> Poems: | Written | By | Wil. Shake-speare. | Gent. | Printed at *London* by *Tho. Cotes*, and are | to be sold by *Iohn Benson*, dwelling in | St. *Dunstans* church-yard. 1640. |

'The order of the poems in this volume is very arbitrary, but it is followed in the editions by Gildon (1710) and Sewell (1725 and 1728), as well as those published by Ewing (1771), and by Evans (1775). In all these editions, Sonnets 18, 19, 43, 56, 75, 76, 96, and 126 are omitted, and Sonnets 138 and 144 are given in the form in which they appear in the *Passionate Pilgrim*.

'It was in 1709 (according to Lowndes, *Bibliographer's Manual*, ed. Bohn) that the whole of Shakespeare's minor poems were issued in a small 8vo form, under the title:—

A collection of Poems, in Two Volumes; Being all the Miscellanies of Mr. *William Shakespeare*, which were Publish'd by himself in the Year 1609, and now correctly Printed from those Editions. The First Volume contains. I. Venus and Adonis. II. The Rape of Lucrece. III. The Passionate Pilgrim. IV. Some Sonnets set to sundry Notes of Musick. The Second Volume contains One Hundred and Fifty Four Sonnets, all of them in Praise of his Mistress. II. A Lover's Complaint of his Angry Mistress. *London*: Printed for *Bernard Lintott*, at the *Cross-Keys*, between the Two Temple-Gates, in *Fleet-street*.

'No editor's name is given, and in Bohn's edition of Lowndes it is wrongly assigned to Gildon, who, as appears by Sewell's Preface, edited the Poems in 1710, with an introduction containing remarks upon the plays. The readings from this edition are therefore quoted by us as those of Lintott. In Capell's copy, with which he evidently intended to go to press, there are many corrections and emendations, which we have referred to as "Capell MS." This volume appears afterwards to have passed through Farmer's hands, as there is a note in his handwriting at the end of the "Advertisement." Possibly, therefore, it may have been seen by Malone, and as many of the alterations proposed by Capell were adopted by Malone or subsequent editors, we have indicated this coincidence by quoting them as "Malone (Capell MS.)" or the like.'

It will be seen from this lucid exposition by the Cambridge Editors that *The Sonnets* were not republished, as they appeared during their author's lifetime in 1609, until 1709(?) in the second volume of Lintott's edition; and that, when so published, they were erroneously put forward as having all been written to the poet's mistress. A like carelessness marks the description of *A Lover's Complaint*, which is not the complaint of a man against his 'angry mistress,' but of a woman forsaken by a man. The cause of this error is not far to seek; nor the reason for its persistence. John Benson's medley of 1640 had been followed by Gildon, Sewell, Ewing, and Evans, and was incorporated, also, into Rowe's editions of *Shakespeare*, in six vols., of 1709 and 1714. It lingered on at Boston, U.S.A., in editions of 1807, 1810 (cited by Dowden), but in this country it was scotched, if not killed, when, as Mr. Dowden points out, Malone in 1780 published his supplement to the edition of *Shakespeare's Plays* of 1778, and avowed, as the opinion of himself, Dr. Farmer, Mr. Tyrwhitt, and Mr. Steevens, that more than one hundred of the sonnets were addressed to a 'male object.' These gentlemen were probably guided to this conclusion by the republication of the *Sonnets*, in their original order, in Vol. iv. of Steevens's *Twenty Plays*, 1766. (Dowden.)

The only early editions of the *Sonnets*, as they originally appeared, are therefore (1) Lintott's second volume, undated, but attributed to 1709, according to Lowndes, and 'advertised in the *Post Boy* of 24th-27th February 1710-11' (Dowden); and (2) in Vol. iv. of Steevens's *Twenty Plays*, 1766.

III. *The Date of the Sonnets' Composition.*—A clue, so far as I am aware, unnoted, which may assist in dating the *Sonnets*, occurs in Sonnet xcviii. 1-4 (I retain the spelling and type of the Quarto 1609):—

'From you have I been absent in the spring
When proud pide Aprill (drest in all his trim)
Hath put a spirit of youth in everything:
That heauie *Saturne* laught and leapt with him.'

Our Poet, describing an absence in the spring, here associates Saturn with the burst of new life in April. A visual apprehension of Nature, at once accurate and sensuous, is a marked feature of his style, and, specially, in the case of the luminaries and of all effects of light in the heavens. The sun, the moon, 'that full star that ushers in the even,' 'the grey cheeks of the East' before dawn, 'the twilight...after sunset fadeth in the West,' are noted with a vivid appreciation in *Venus, Lucrece*, and the *Sonnets*. And, again, in accordance with the prevailing belief of his age, he attributes occult power to the stars. Indeed, he derives the ascription of 'heaviness' to Saturn in this passage from books on Astrology: a science which seems to have engaged his interest no less than the other sciences of his day. Knowing the astrological characteristics of Saturn, he finds it effective to contrast that 'leaden' planet with the exhilarating outburst of April. But he would not, I am convinced, have done so had not Saturn been a visible feature in the sky during the month of April to which he refers. To have dragged Saturn, without reason or rhyme, into a description of a particular month of April would have been a freak without a parallel in his poems. I am indebted to my friend, Dr. Dobie, for the information, derived by him from competent authorities, that, taking the years 1592-1609, Saturn was in opposition, and, therefore, a somewhat conspicuous feature in the sky during the month of April in the years 1600-01. This is confirmed by Mr. Heath, of the Royal Observatory, Edinburgh, with whom Mr. W. Blaikie has kindly conferred on this question. Mr. Heath informs me that Leovitius in his Ephemeris (*Ephemeridum Novum atque insigne opus ab Anno Domini* 1556 *usque* 1606) gives the dates of the opposition of Saturn as follow:—1599, March 24; 1600, April 4; 1601, April 17; 1602, April 29; 1603, May 11. The planet would have been bright for some nights both before and after opposition, but, since it rose, according to Mr. Blaikie, about sunset in April 1600 and gradually later in the Aprils of succeeding years, my suggestion that Shakespeare had the real planet in his mind would still fit in with the years 1602 and 1603, when opposition fell respectively on April 29 and May 11, while it would hardly fit in with an earlier date than 1600. Saturn would have been a conspicuous figure in the evening sky, rising in the heavens to much the same height as Sirius. In confirmation of my theory, it should be remembered that Saturn goes through a series of changes according as his rings are tilted towards us or presented edge on. During the early years of the century, the apparent opening of the rings would be steadily increasing until April 1st, 1605, which Mr. Heath has calculated as the date of maximum opening, when the planet at opposition must have shown a very large bright disc. This calculation tallies with Galileo's historical mystification at the disappearance of Saturn's accessories (the rings were not then known) in 1612 (Grant's *History of Physical Astronomy*, 255). To sum up: if, as I hold, Shakespeare wrote Sonnet xcviii. with the real Saturn in his mind, then he cannot have written it before 1600 and may, with greater probability, have written it in 1601 or 1602, when Saturn was more conspicuous and gradually presenting a larger disc. Now Sonnet xcviii. comes in at a point where the First Series (i.-cxxvi.) is most obviously broken; xcvi. closes Group F (lxxxvii.-xcvi.); xcvii. refers to an absence in late summer and autumn; xcviii., as I have said, to an absence in April; xcix. is a variant of xcviii.; c. opens the 'satire to decay,' which is a continuous poem of retrospect (c.-cxxvi.). And we learn from civ. that this poem was written three years after the Poet first made acquaintance with the Friend. Assuming, therefore, that the explanation of this reference to Saturn, which I submit as the most plausible, be accepted as the correct explanation, we may infer that the latest group (c.-cxxvi.) was not written *before* May 1600, possibly not *before* May 1602; and that the earlier groups, which are fairly continuous, were not written *before* 1597, possibly not before 1599.

In cvii. l. 5:—

> 'The mortall Moone hath her eclipse indur'de,'

many have found an allusion to some contemporary crisis in politics—the revolt of Essex or the death of the Queen. I am disposed to think it more probable that the line refers to an actual eclipse of the moon, which had been made the ground for gloomy prognostications. When contemporary poets allude to political crises they make their reference explicit. Drayton, e.g. in *Idea*, li. (1619)—first published in that year, but written apparently in 1604—has:—

> 'Lastly, mine eyes amazédly have seen
> Essex's great fall! Tyrone his peace to gain!

The quiet end of that long living Queen!
This King's fair Entrace! and our peace with Spain!'

Shakespeare in the *Sonnets* has no such explicit references, and his phrase, 'the mortall moone,' if it mean 'the moon in deadly case,' is quite in his manner of describing a natural phenomenon such as an eclipse. There were twenty-one eclipses of the moon, total or partial, visible at Greenwich during the years 1592-1609. So that the champions of an early date for the *Sonnets* may find their affair in this matter as readily as the champions of a late date. But if we accept Tyler's suggestion that the reference to 'this most balmy time' in cvii. proves that the sonnet was written in late spring, summer, or early autumn, and if my suggestion for the dating of xcviii. be also accepted, then, of such eclipses, three remain available. Taking the Greenwich mean time of central conjunction you have:—

June 4th, 1602. 6.18 p.m. Duration ... 3 hours 42 min.
Total, seen only as partial at Greenwich.

May 24th, 1603. 11.30 p.m. Duration ... 2 hours 46 min.
Partial, but seen for the full duration at Greenwich.

April 3rd, 1605. 8.24 p.m. Duration ... 0 hours 20 min.
Total and entirely seen at Greenwich.

These three, also, occurred at hours which ensured the excitement of greater comment than in the case of eclipses in the small hours of the morning. The eclipse of May 24, 1603—since it lasted much longer than the eclipse of April 3, 1605, and since, owing to its hour and the time of the year, it must have been more noticeable than the eclipse of June 4, 1602—may, perhaps, be given the pride of place. Its acceptance also admits of one of those secondary allusions—in this case to the death of Elizabeth, March 23, 1603—which are so common in Shakespeare's verse. I ought to add that Mr. Heath and Mr. Blaikie agree in thinking that I have not given sufficient weight to the eclipse of 1605.

The article on Shakespeare was published in the *Dictionary of National Biography* since the Introduction to this volume was in type. In it Mr. Sidney Lee throws over the theory put forward in his earlier article on William Herbert:—viz. that most of the

Sonnets were written after 1597 and addressed to Herbert:—for the theory that 'the bulk of them were composed within a brief period of the publication of his (Shakespeare's) narrative poems in 1594,' and that they were addressed to Southampton. No better illustration of the Personal Problem's perplexity could be found than in a change of front so sudden on the part of so earnest a scholar. But, since Mr. Lee argues at length against the date which I have ventured to ascribe to the Sonnets, it is due to him that I should examine his argument. I do so with reluctance, for Mr. Lee rests his argument in favour of a date prior to 1595, in part on the assumption that Southampton was the youth addressed in the First Series of Sonnets, and any such attempt at identification, of necessity speculative and laborious, must, as I have said, prove detrimental to an æsthetic appreciation of their lyrical excellence. I shall, therefore, endeavour to restrict myself, in so far as I may, to the simple question of date. In support of the assumed identification, Mr. Lee puts in no new piece of evidence, but insists, somewhat unduly, on one already familiar, viz.: that 'some of the phrases in the dedication to *Lucrece* closely resemble expressions that were addressed to the young friend.' This cannot, as he urges, be said 'to identify the latter with Southampton.' At most it raises a presumption, to be discounted in view of the warmly affectionate language common in contemporary dedications. On the other hand, if anything may safely be asserted, it is that the Youth's Christian name was 'Will.' Mr. Lee attributes this 'misinterpretation' to the 'misprinting in the early editions of the second "will" as "*Will*" in cxxxv. l. 1'—an error for l. 2? I have argued (Note V., on the Typography of the Quarto 1609) that such words are so printed by design throughout the Sonnets. In any case it is impossible to *prove* the identity of the youth, and, therefore, illegitimate to found an argument for this or that date on any assumed identification. The proof of an early date would disprove the Herbert theory, of a late date, the Southampton theory. But even on the question of date more than probability cannot be hoped for. Let me, however, assay Mr. Lee's arguments for a date prior to 1595.

(1) 'Shakespeare's early proficiency as a sonneteer and his enthusiasm for the sonnet form are both attested by his introduction of two admirably turned sonnets into the dramatic dialogue of *Love's Labour's Lost.*' But one sonnet in the play—*If Love make me forsworn, how shall I swear to love*—like many of Sidney's and of Drayton's in his first edition (1594), is written in Alexandrines. Another—*So sweet a kiss the golden sun gives not*—is a caudated sonnet with two couplets instead of one after the third quatrain. Mr. Lee may have omitted this sonnet from his reference on that account, but on that very account does it militate against his argument, since it leaves but one out of the three—*Did not the heavenly rhetoric of thine eye*—in the form which Shakespeare sustained, excepting cxlv., throughout *The Sonnets*. These three, then, show that he handled the sonnet form at the date (?) of their composition with a hesitancy still common among sonneteers—Sidney, Drayton, Daniel—in 1594, but of which he shows no trace in *The Sonnets* (1609). (2) 'Meres, writing in 1598, mentions Shakespeare's "sugred sonnets among his private friends." But are the majority of *The Sonnets* "sugred"'? (3) 'That all the Sonnets were in existence before Meres wrote is rendered probable by the fact that William Jaggard piratically inserted in 1599 two of the most mature of the series (Nos. cxxxviii. and cxliv.) in his *Passionate Pilgrim.*' In what sense are these two 'mature'? That they came late in the whole collection proves nothing. They were placed in the Second Series (*vide* Introduction, p. cxv) because they were not addressed to the youth to whom all the numbers (i.-cxxvi.) of the First Series were addressed. But they were obviously written at the same time and on the same theme as the sonnets of Group C (xxxiii.-xlii.). Certainly they are not 'mature,' if compared with lvi.-cxxv., either in thought or expression:—

'Therefore I lie with her, and she with me,
And in our faults by lies we flattered be.'—cxxxviii.

'I guess one angel in another's hell.
Yet this shall I ne'er know, but live in doubt
Till my bad angel fire my good one out.'—cxliv.

These are a 'wanton burden of the prime' by far removed from the solemnity of the later groups 'big with rich increase.'

Indeed the presumption raised by Jaggard's *Passionate Pilgrim* is all the other way. It is largely made up of numbers pirated from publications which shortly preceded it:—e.g. 8 and 20 from Barnefield, 1598; 11 from Griffin, 1596; 17 from Weelkes, 1597.[1] If all *The Sonnets* had been in existence for more than four years, it is improbable that Jaggard would have failed to secure more than two, anxious as he was to palm off the whole of his precious collection for Shakespeare's; on the other hand it is probable that he took the two which he did secure, even as he took the new numbers by other poets, and the two sonnets and a song from *Love's Labour's Lost*, published in 1598—viz., because they were new and accessible. *Love's Labour's Lost* may well have been written earlier, as many have argued from internal evidence (Dowden conjectures in 1590). But, if that be so, and, again, if the first acting version contained these sonnets, which cannot be proved, we must consider the well-known jealousy with which players guarded their property in unpublished MS. plays. That two of the *Sonnets* (cxxxviii., cxliv.) were printed by Jaggard with variations from the text of 1609—proves that they and their analogues in the Second Series and in the First (xxxiii.-xlii.) existed early in 1599; that no more were printed makes it probable that the later groups did not exist. And this probability is increased by the fact that Group C (xxxiii.-xlii.) is followed by occasional and unconnected numbers, and that the next Group, D (lvi.-lxxiv.), opens after a silence:—'Sweet love renew thy force.'

(4) 'A line from a fully accredited sonnet (xciv.) was quoted in *Edward III.*, which was probably written before 1595.' Here, against Mr. Lee, I set Dowden (*Shakespeare's Sonnets*, 1881). 'The last line of xciv.,

Lilies that fester smell far worse than weeds,

occurs also in the play, *King Edward III.* (printed 1596), in a part of the play ascribed by some critics to Shakespeare. We cannot say for certain whether the play borrows from the

1. Halliwell-Phillipps.

sonnet, or the sonnet from the play. The latter seems to me the more likely supposition of the two.' Dowden also cites Tyler's 'ingenious argument' (republished, *Shakespeare's Sonnets*, 1890, pp. 18-21) that lv. is a paraphrase of a passage in Meres' *Palladis Tamiœ* (1598). The argument is more than ingenious; it is convincing. For Shakespeare echoes Meres not only in his quotation from Horace—*Exegi monimentum*, etc.—but in the quotation from Ovid—*Jamque opus exegi*, etc.—which Meres set beside it, and, for a clincher, in the comment which Meres added in his own English and Latin:—'So say I severally of Sir Philip Sidneys, Spencers, Daniels, Draytons, Shakespeares and Warners workes—

Non jovis ira, imbres, Mars, ferrum, flamma, senectus,
Hoc opus unda, lues, turbo, venena ruit.'

If Tyler's argument be accepted, it follows that lv. was written after 1598.

(5) Mr. Lee cites 'Willobie his Avisa' (1594), and, again, I set Dowden against him:—'Assuming that W.S. is William Shakespeare'—a large assumption—'we learn that he had loved and recovered from the infection of his passion before the end of 1594. The chaste Avisa is unlike as possible the dark woman of the Sonnets; nor does anything appear which can connect Henry Willobie with Shakespeare's young friend of the Sonnets, except the fact that the initials of the only begetter's name were W.H.—those of Henry Willobie reversed—and that Henry Willobie assails the chastity of a married woman. He is, however, repulsed by the chaste Avisa. Except in the reference to W.S.'s love and his recovery from passion, I see no possible point of connection between Willobie's Avisa and Shakespeare's Sonnets.' Mr. Lee's citation is beside the mark, unless his assumptions be accepted:—(1) that W.S. = Shakespeare; (2) that Henry Willobie = Southampton. But there was a real Henry Willobie who matriculated in St. John's, Oxford, 1591, whereas Southampton graduated in St. John's, Cambridge, 1589; (3) that Southampton = the Friend of the Sonnets. And these assumptions can hardly be called plausible.

If I may hazard my own opinion, I would say that the balance of external evidence suggests for the earliest groups only (A, B, C, i-xlii., and the Second Series, cxxvii.-cliv.) a date before, but not long before, 1599: that the internal evidence of civ. proves the latest groups (c.-cxxv.) to have been written three years later: that the melancholy languor, the metaphysical speculation, the poetical perfection, of the later groups (D, E, F, G, lvi.-cxxv.) disclose a near affinity to *Hamlet*, entered in the Stationers' Register, July 26, 1602. I would, further, submit that, in the events of the year 1601:—the execution of Essex; the imprisonment of Shakespeare's early patron Southampton in consequence of the Rising; the arrest of his colleague Phillips in connection with it; the exile of his company in Scotland while the 'Children of the Chapel' enjoyed the favour it had lost; the jar and fret of the Poetomachia; the imprisonment of Mary Fytton, who affected masquerade and had befriended his colleague Kempe; the imprisonment of William Herbert, who had 'prosecuted him with favour'—there is enough to account for the mood in which much of *Hamlet* and many of the later Sonnets are conceived. I am not therefore bound to accept Tyler's identification of the youth with William Herbert and of the Dark Lady with Mary Fytton. But neither am I precluded from doing so. And Tyler at least has proved that, in the last years of Elizabeth's reign, some such a drama as that which we guess behind certain of the Sonnets, was possible among the most highly placed of her play-loving courtiers and court-ladies. Lady Newdegate-Newdigate (*Gossip from a Muniment Room*, 1897) shows further that Mary Fytton's actual experience was at least as complicated as the love-drama suggested by Group C. and the Second Series of the *Sonnets*. For we find Sir William Knollys, into whose charge the young maid of honour had been confided by her father, courting her during the lifetime of his own wife, and both before, and after, she became Will Herbert's mistress.

IV. *The Rival Poets.*—(1) There were more rival Poets than one. This is evident from Sonnet lxxviii. 1-4:—

> 'So oft have I invoked thee for my Muse,
> And found such fair assistance in my verse
> As *every* alien pen hath got my use,
> And under thee their poetry disperse';

and from lxxxiii. 11-14:—

> 'For I impair not beauty being *mute*,
> When *others* would give life and bring a tomb,
> There lives more life in one of your fair eyes
> Than both your poets can in praise devise.'

Here, when the Poet is 'mute' and *hors concours*, 'others' would give life, and two among them fail to add anything to the mere beauty of the Friend; and from lxxxii. 1-4:—

> 'I grant thou wert not married to my Muse
> And therefore may'st without attaint o'erlook
> The dedicated words which *writers* use
> Of their fair subject, blessing every book.'

But in xxi. one Poet is singled out:—

> 'So is it not with me as with that Muse,
> Stirr'd by a painted beauty to his verse,
> Who heaven itself for ornament doth use,
> And every fair with his fair doth rehearse.'

And the same, or another, is singled out in lxxix. 4:—

> 'And my sick Muse doth give another place';

and in lxxx.:—

> 'O How I faint when I of you do write
> Knowing a better spirit doth use your name.'

(2) These others, including the one singled out, affect learning, which our poet rejects as unsuited to a beauty best praised by simple statement; cf. xxi. 1-4 (*supra*), and 9:—

> 'O let me, true in love, but truly write....'

lxxviii. 5-8.

> 'Thine eyes that taught the dumb on high to sing
> And heavy ignorance aloft to fly,
> Have added feathers to the learned's wing
> And given grace a double majesty.'

lxxx. 11-12.

> 'I am a worthless boat,
> He of tall building and of goodly pride.

lxxxii. 5-8.

> 'Thou art as fair in knowledge as in hue,
> Finding thy worth a limit past my praise;

And, therefore, art enforced to seek anew
Some fresher stamp of the time-bettering days.

lxxxv. 1-8.

'My tongue-tied Muse in manners holds her still,
While comments of your praise richly-compiled,
Reserve their character with golden quill
And precious phrase by all the Muses filed.
I think good thoughts, whilst others write good words,
And, like unletter'd clerk, still crie, Amen,
To every hymn that able spirit affords
In polished form of well refinéd pen.'

(3) The one Poet singled out cannot, I submit, be confidently identified. We know from Sidney's *Apology* (see Introduction, p. cvi.) that the practice of 'eternizing' was common; but much of this verse has perished. We know from Shakespeare's Sonnets that other Poets 'eternized' his Friend in a style which was learned, novel, and florid; but their 'couplements of proud compare' and 'precious phrase' are no longer extant, or, if extant, have been so dissembled as to disguise all evidence of dedication to the same person. Any guess, however ingenious, must therefore be qualified by the acknowledgment that masses of material, vital to the issue, which once existed are no longer accessible, and that, in the sonnet-sequences of Daniel and, particularly, of Drayton, who do 'eternize' after Shakespeare's manner, there is some impenetrable mystification. It is clear that of Daniel's sonnets only a minority were truly addressed to 'Delia,' and among Drayton's one at least (x. of ed. 1619) is addressed to a man:—

'To nothing fitter can I thee compare
Than to the *son* of some rich penny-father';

while another (xxii., 1619) is even more startling. The feminine was substituted for the masculine gender in several of Shakespeare's Sonnets by the Editors of 1640. To sum up: we have but little out of much evidence which once existed, and, of that little, some is suspect.

(4) But the quest for *the* Rival Poet is not barren. It reveals a certain amount of verse, Drayton's in particular, which is akin to Shakespeare's, insomuch as that it deals with metaphysical

conceits with Platonic speculation, and with attacks on Time. It reveals also a *coterie* of poets who did affect learning, who praised each other, and who ignored Shakespeare or damned him with faint praise. Let me pass these arrogant ones in review:—

Ben Jonson.—Jonson praised Shakespeare (with a fair admixture of criticism) after his death; but not before it (see Introduction, pp. lvii., lviii.). He collaborated with Chapman and with Marston. He praises Drayton effusively, comparing him to Theocritus, Virgil, Ovid, Orpheus, and Lucan:—

> 'It hath been question'd, Michael, if I be
> A friend at all; or, if at all, to thee.'

Thus he opens *The Vision of Ben Johnson on the Muses of his Friend, M. Drayton,* and thus he closes it:—

> 'I call the world, that envies me, to see
> If I can be a friend, and friend to thee.'

Drayton returns the compliment to

> 'Learned Johnson...
> Who had drunk deep of the Pierian spring
> Where knowledge did him worthily prefer,
> And long was lord here of the theatre.'
>
> *Epistle to Henry Reynolds.*

Chapman also praises Jonson, and so does Marston. Jonson was the leader of this learned fraternity of log-rollers. He told Drummond that 'he loved Chapman.' But he did not, so far as we know, 'eternize.' He did, however, dedicate his works to young noblemen: *Sejanus* to Lord Aubigny (see Introduction, p. xxix.), *Catiline* to William Herbert, Earl of Pembroke, in 1611, and also his Epigrams, with a dedication at which many have paused:—'My lord, while you cannot change your merit, I dare not *change your title*: it was that made it, and not I. *Under which name*, I here offer to your lordship the ripest of my studies, my Epigrams; which though they carry danger in the sound, do not therefore seek your shelter; for, when I made them, I had nothing in my conscience, to expressing of which I did need a *cypher*.' One Epigram is addressed to Herbert:—

> 'I do but name thee, Pembroke, and I find
> It is an epigram on all mankind.'

Sometimes his 'dedications' seem to have led him further than he cared to go. He addresses his Muse (Epigram lxv.):—

> 'Away, and leave me, thou thing most abhorred,
> That hast betray'd me to a worthless lord;
> Made me commit most fierce idolatry
> To a great image through thy luxury.'

Marston.—Marston was one of the learned fraternity. He collaborated with Jonson and Chapman, complimented Jonson, and burlesqued Shakespeare (see Introduction, pp. lxii., lxiii.). His sixth satire (*Scourge of Villainy*, 1598) declares his 'nasty' Pygmalion—the epithet is his own—which is imitated from Shakespeare's *Venus and Adonis*, to be a parody, written to note

> 'The odious spot
> And blemish that deforms the lineaments
> Of modern poesy's habiliments.'

And he goes on, in abominable verse, but with the very trick of Jonson and the other pedants, when appraising Shakespeare's art:—

> 'O that the beauties of invention,
> For want of judgment's disposition,
> Should all be spoil'd! O that such treasury,
> Such strain of well-conceited poesy,
> Should moulded be in such a shapeless form,
> That want of art should make such wit a scorn.'

In view of Shakespeare's Sonnet lxxxvi.—'his spirit, by spirits taught to write...he, nor that affable familiar ghost'—we may note Marston's pretensions here:—

> 'Think'st thou *that genius that attends my soul*,
> And guides my fist to scourge magnificos,
> Will deign my mind be ranked in Paphian shows';

and in his contribution to Robert Chester's *Love's Martyr* (1601):—

> 'Tell me, genuine Muse!
> Now yield your aids, *you spirits that infuse*
> *A sacred rapture*, light my weaker eye.'

George Chapman.—Chapman was the most arrogant of the 'Grecian' camp (see Introduction, pp. lxv., lxvi.). Jonson and

Drayton prefixed commendatory verses to his *Hesiod* (1618). Minto discovers him for *the* Rival Poet. Minto quotes from the Dedication of his *Shadow of Night* (1594):—'Now what a supererogation in wit this is, to think Skill so mightily pierced with their loves that she should prostitutely show them her secrets, when she will scarcely be looked upon by others but with invocation, fasting, watching; yea, not without having drops of their souls like a heavenly familiar.' This reproof of the unlearned is quite in his manner, and in the manner of his log-rolling friends, but it makes no such claim as Marston's to supernatural guidance. Dowden is disposed to corroborate Minto, but Chapman did not 'eternize.' His sonnets to Pembroke and Southampton are but two out of sixteen addressed to peers and peeresses, all appended, as an acknowledgment of Patronage, to his *Homer's Iliads*. He styles Pembroke 'the learned,' and harps, as ever, on 'god-like learning.' His reference to his 'adventurous bark' in verses appended to the *Odyssey* would fit in with Shakespeare's allusion to the 'proud full sail' of the Rival's 'great verse.' But these verses were written after the Sonnets were published, viz. in 1614. One of Chapman's many diatribes against the unlearned has, however, an alluring aspect. In the preface to the reader prefixed to *Homer's Iliads* he writes:—'But there is a certain envious windsucker (= kestrel) that hovers up and down, laboriously engrossing all the air with his luxurious ambition, and buzzing into every ear my detraction, affirming I turn Homer out of Latin only, etc., that sets all his associates, and the whole rabbel of my maligners on their wings with him, to bear about my impair, and poison my reputation. One that, as he thinks, whatsoever he gives to others, he takes from himself.... For so this castrill (= kestrel) with too hot a liver, and lust after his own glory, and to devour all himself, discourageth all appetites to fame of another. I have stricken, single him as you can.' This is but Greene's attack on Shakespeare in other terms—'the upstart crow, beautified with other men's feathers'—and, since on this quest to avoid the far-fetched is to return empty-handed, we may remember that Shakespeare's new-gotten crest was a falcon. This would scarce be worth noting, but for a certain passage in Drayton.

Michael Drayton.—Jonson refers to Drayton's *Owl*:—

'I saw Minerva's fowl
Perched over head, the wise Athenian owl.'

The Owl is an allegory on the convention of Chaucer's *Parliament of Fowls.* In it the poet who has fallen asleep dreams of an Owl, evidently himself, who is attacked by birds of prey, 'the envious Crow, the hateful Buzzard,' and others, 'that only live upon the poorer's spoil.' The Eagle arrives and the Owl pleads his cause:—'Though now thus poor' he hails from 'Athens, the Muses' nursery, the source of science and philosophy.' In fact the Owl talks for all the world like the learned log-rollers:—'I seek not fame, knowledge I love, and glory in the same.' And the chief object of his complaint is the Buzzard, who tricks himself out as a Falcon:—

'I saw a Buzzard, scorning of the black,
That but of late did clothe his *needy back*,
With Ostrich feathers *had trickt up his crest*,
As he were bred a Falcon at the least.
Thus struts he daily in his borrow'd plume,
And but for shame he boldly durst presume
With princely Eaglets to compare his sight.'

Drayton *did* 'eternize'; and with an accent so unmistakably akin to Shakespeare's that the charge of plagiarism has been preferred, now against one and now against the other. I have instanced (Note on *Lucrece*, 1128-1134) a more than suspicious likeness between those lines, published by Shakespeare in 1594, and a sonnet of Drayton's which appears for the first time in the *Idea* of 1599. Fleay, who argues on the other side—'that these sonnets were the immediate model of Shakespeare's, I cannot doubt'—omitted to collate the *Idea* of 1619 with the previous versions of 1594 and 1599. Tyler has pointed this out, and the case against Fleay is overwhelming. He instances (*Chronicle of the English Drama*, ii. 226) Drayton iii. and xvii.:—both are in the edition of 1594, but both have been completely rewritten (iii., numbered x. in 1594, has there two quatrains written, excepting line 5, in Alexandrines):—with xi., xx., xxix., xxxi., xliv.:—but those which appear, mostly under other numbers in 1599, are not in the *Amours* of 1594:—and xliii., xlvii., lxi.:—but these are not to be found in either of the early Editions, and appear for the first time in 1619, ten years after Shakespeare's Sonnets were published. Drayton was condemned for a plagiary even in 1598 in Guilpin's *Skialetheia*:—

> 'Drayton's condemned of some for imitation
> But others say 'twas the best Poets fashion.'

Drayton in the *Epistle to Henry Reynolds*, whilst lavishing warm, but orthodox, praise on 'learn'd Jonson' and 'reverend Chapman,' gives to Shakespeare the cool, but orthodox, tribute of the 'learned' for his 'smoothe comick vein' and 'natural brain.' He had praised him (in the *Matilda*) more frankly, together with Daniel and Elstred. But the stanza in which he applauds *Lucrece* in the Edition of 1594 was omitted from the Edition of 1596, and never reprinted. For Drayton, too, was one of the 'learned'—hailed as such by Barnefield in his *Encomium of the Lady Pecunia* in 1598. And, finally, Drayton was part author of *The True and Honorable History of Sir John Oldcastle* (1600), which (see Introduction, pp. l., li., lii.) was a retort on Shakespeare's *Henry IV*.

Such were the relations between Drayton, one of the learned fraternity, and Shakespeare, in so far as we may divine them. In *Idea*, where many sonnets resemble Shakespeare's, let me instance the one which is obviously addressed to a man:—

> 'To nothing fitter can I thee compare,
> Than to the son of some rich penny-father...
> Thy Gifts, thou in obscurity dost waste!
> False friends, thy Kindness! born but to deceive thee.
> Thy Love that is on the unworthy placed!
> Time hath thy Beauty, which with age will leave thee!
> Only that little, which to me was lent,
> I give thee back! when all the rest is spent.'

This Sonnet x. in Edition 1619 appears for the first time, as xii., in 1599. It is followed in both Editions by one on Shakespeare's theme of *Identity*:—

> 'Since You one were, I never since was one;
> Since You in Me, my self since out of Me...

> Give me my self! and take your self again!...
> O that I could fly
> From my self You, or from your own self I!'

xliii. (only in Edition 1619) attacks the unlearned, who are favoured by the object of Drayton's verse:—

> 'Why should your fair eyes, with such sovereign grace,
> Disperse their rays on every vulgar spirit,
> Whilst I in darkness, in the self-same place,
> Get not one glance to recompense my merit?'

The second quatrain seems suggested by Shakespeare's cxvi. (see Note). The third goes on:—

> 'O why should Beauty (custom to obey)
> To their gross sense apply herself so ill!
> Would God ! I were as ignorant as they!
> When I am made unhappy by my skill!'

This modest expression of regret is the symmetrical opposite at every point to Shakespeare's references to the Rival. He is the 'unletter'd clerk' who 'cries, Amen,' to the 'precious phrase by all the Muses filed.'

In xliv. (only in Edition 1619) Drayton 'eternizes' in Shakespeare's very accent:—

> 'Whilst thus my pen strives to eternize thee,
> Age rules my lines with wrinkles in my face;
> Where, in the Map of all my misery
> Is modelled out the World of my disgrace:
> Whilst in despite of tyrannizing times,
> Medea like, I make thee young again!
> Proudly thou scorn'st my world-outwearing rhymes,
> And murder'st Virtue with thy coy disdain!
> And though in youth, my youth untimely perish,
> To keep Thee from oblivion and the grave;
> Ensuing Ages yet my Rhymes shall cherish,
> Where I entombed, my better part shall save;
> And though this earthly body fade and die,
> My Name shall mount upon eternity!'

In xlvii. (only in Edition 1619) Drayton explains that he despised the applause of the 'thronged theatres':—

'When the proud Round on every side hath rung...
No public glory vainly I pursue:
All that I seek is to eternize you!'

Shakespeare twice (lxxx., lxxxvi.) compares the Rival's verse to a ship 'of proud full sail' that rides the 'soundless deep': and Drayton in i. (only in Edition 1619) introduces himself—'Like an adventurous seafarer am I...called to tell of his discovery, how far he sailed, what countries he had seen.' Shakespeare dwells on the simplicity of his verse; on the 'false art,' 'strainèd touches,' 'false painting,' and 'precious phrase,' of the Rival; and Drayton boasts, 'fantasticly I sing' (1599), and asks (xx. 1619):—

'Why in this sort I wrest Invention so?
And why these giddy metaphors I use....'

If compelled to select one of Shakespeare's contemporaries for the Rival Poet, I should select Drayton; although his sonnets, twice recast, were ostensibly addressed to Idea, and although in some numbers he addresses Idea, the Type of Heavenly Beauty, in the feminine gender. But there is no compulsion, nor possibility, of certitude, and this much of knowledge must be the sole certain reward of a wild-goose-chase:—that Jonson, Chapman, Marston, and Drayton constituted a society for mutual admiration, whose members applauded each other's efforts, whilst they ignored, burlesqued, or patronised Shakespeare's. Three of the four seem to have opposed Shakespeare in the Poetomachia (see Introduction, chap. viii.), and the fourth, Drayton, was similarly employed in *The True and Honorable History of Sir John Oldcastle*. Curiously enough, the three all wrote obscure poems on the Phœnix and the Turtle, appended, with one by Shakespeare, to Robert Chester's *Love's Martyr*. And Drayton, also, had a sonnet on the same theme. It is impossible to understand exactly what these poems are about. But it is interesting to note that they all contain attacks on Time and that they all draw on the catch-words of Platonism:—

'Nought lasts that doth to outward worth contend
All love in smooth brows born is tomb'd in wrinkles...

And Time and Change (that all things else devours,
But truth eternized in a constant heart)....'—Chapman.

'Now, true love
No such effects doth prove;
That is an essence, far more gentle, fine,
Pure, perfect, nay divine;
It is a golden chain let down from Heaven....'—Jonson.

'Now yield your aids, you spirits that infuse
A sacred rapture, light my weaker eye...
That whilst of this same Metaphysical,
God, man, nor woman, but elix'd of all,
My laboring thoughts with strainéd ardour sing,
My muse may mount with an uncommon wing.'

Dares then thy too audacious sense
Presume define that boundless Ens
That amplest thought transcendeth....
By it all beings deck'd and strainèd,
Ideas that are idly feignèd
Only here subsist invested...'—Marston.

'*Property* was thus appalléd
That the self was not the same
Single nature's double name
Neither two nor one was calléd....

Truth may seem, but cannot be;
Beauty brag, but 'tis not she;
Truth and beauty buried be.'—Shakespeare.

These four poems were thus announced:—'*Divers Poeticall Essaies on the Turtle and Phœnix*. Done by the best and chiefest of our moderne writers, with their names subscribed to their particular workes; never before extant. And now first consecrated by them all generally to the love and merit of the true noble Knight, Sir John Salisburie. Dignum laude virum musa vetat mori. MDC.I. (Printed at the end of *Love's Martyr*, etc., by Robert Chester) London: Imprinted for E.B. 1601. page 176.'

Drayton's sonnet to the Phœnix—one of the many numbers of *Idea* (xvi. in Edition 1619, rewritten from *Amour*, vi., Edition 1594)—evidently *not* addressed to a living lady, ends:—

> 'As you are consuming,
> Only by dying born the very same,
> And winged by Fame, you to the stars ascend!
> So you, of time shall live beyond the end.'

V. *The Typography of the Quarto* (1609), *considered in its bearing on the authority of that text, with an analysis of the system of Punctuation observed therein* (see Note III. on *Lucrece*).—In Sonnet i. 2, *Rose* stands thus in Q. I retain the initial capital and italics, because I am satisfied that the words in this type were printed so designedly throughout the Sonnets. Controversy has centred round two of them:—*Hews*, xx. 7, and *Will*, cxxxv. 1, 2, 11, 12, 14; cxxxvi. 2, 5, 14; cxliii. 13. Mr. Sidney Lee writes (*Dictionary of National Biography*, vol. li. p. 365):—'There is nothing in the wording of these punning Sonnets to warrant the assumption that his friend bore the same appellation (this misinterpretation is attributable to the misprinting in the early editions of the second "will" as "*Will*" in cxxxv. 1)'—an error for 2. Mr. Dowden, in discussing l. 7 of xx. as printed in the Quarto:—

> 'A man in hew all *Hews* in his controwling':—

discounts the possible significance of 'hews' (hues) having been printed '*Hews*,' by pointing out that other words in the *Sonnets* 'have also capital letters and are in italics.' That is true. But Mr. Dowden does not give a complete list. Had he done so he might have been struck, as I have been struck, by the fact that, excepting *Rose*, i. 2; *Hews*, xx. 7; *Informer*, cxxv. 13; and the Wills, cxxxv., cxxxvi., cxliii., *every word so printed, is either a proper name, or else, of Greek or Latin extraction*. Viz.:—*Audit*, iv. 12; *Adonis, Hellens, Grecian*, liii. 5, 7, 8; *Statues*, lv. 5 (and note that this word is printed Statüe—*Venus and Adonis*, 213—and Statua four times in the Plays); *Mars*, lv. 7; *Intrim*, lvi. 9; *Alien*, lxxviii. 3; *Eaves* (Eve's), apple, xciii. 13; *Saturne*, xcviii. 4; *Satire*, c. 11; *Philomell*, cii. 7; *Autumne*, civ. 5; *Abisme*, cxii. 9; *Alcumie*, cxiv. 4; *Syren*, cxix. 1; *Heriticke*, cxxiv. 9; *Audite, Quietus*, cxxvi. 11, 12; *Cupid, Dyans, Cupid*, cliii. 1, 2, 14. These words, if other than proper names, were so printed then, as French words are so printed now, viz.:—because they were but partially incorporated into the

English language (see Note III. on *Lucrece*). This destroys the presumption of accident and creates a presumption of design, leaving the commentator still free to draw such conclusions as he can from the selection of capitals and italics for *Rose, Hews, Informer, and Will.*

The last two present no difficulty, except to those who would abstract every personal element out of the *Sonnets*. '*Informer*' is clearly a personal apostrophe; 'Will,' as clearly embodies a play on the poet's name, and occasionally, as I hold with Dowden, but against Mr. Lee, on the name of his Friend also. 'Will,' although not in italics, has a capital in lvii. 13:—

> 'So true a foole is love, that in your Will,
> (Though you doe any thing) he thinks no ill':—

and it is, obviously, so printed there with a like reference to the poet's name. It is only fair to note, once more, in this connection the 'Will' in *Lucrece*, 495:—

> 'But Will is deafe, and hears no heedfull friends,
> Onely he hath an eye to gaze on Beautie,
> And dotes on what he looks, 'gainst law or duty.'

For if it be a misprint, it may be urged in support of Mr. Lee's contention in respect of the second *Will* (cxxxv. 2), and, if it be not a misprint, it may serve the turn of those who, holding the 'personal theory,' differ from my conclusion on the date of the *Sonnets* (*supra*, Note III.), and accept Mr. Sidney Lee's, viz. that the *Sonnets* were written immediately after *Lucrece*.

Returning to the two which do present a difficulty—*Rose* and *Hews*—I believe, as I have stated in the Introduction, that 'Beauty's *Rose*' stands here poetically for the *Idea* or Eternal Type of Beauty, or, at least, for the emblem of that idea. It stands, indeed, for one of the many things which, according to Sir Philip Sidney (*Apologie for Poetrie*, 1595), 'lye darke before the imaginatione and judging power, if they bee not illuminated or figured foorth by the speaking picture of Poesie.' It is used to this end with a capital, lxvii. 8:—

> 'Why should poore beautie indirectly seeke
> Roses of shaddow, since his Rose is true?'—

and, again with a capital, as the emblem of the Friend, cix. 14:—

'For nothing this wide Universe I call,
Save thou my Rose, in it thou art my all.'

Of *Hews* it is enough to say here that, if its capital and italics be a freak of the printer, they constitute the only freak of that kind in the whole edition of 1609. This goes far to show that the Quarto was not carelessly issued, and to defeat many conclusions drawn from the opposite assumption, e.g. that it was a pirated edition published without Shakespeare's knowledge or against his wishes, and that the present order of the *Sonnets* may therefore be treated as haphazard. To press this home, another feature of the Quarto's typography must now be considered. The number of capitals employed, apart from italics where we employ them no longer, has been urged in support of the view that the Quarto was unauthorised. It is therefore necessary, in order to confirm my argument, that I should trace design in the use of capitals throughout the edition, even when given to words in ordinary type.

If all such words be collected, it will be found that they fall, with scarce an exception, into well-defined classes; that the employment of capitals for such classes, though now obsolete, is rational and not arbitrary; and that it was of a kind sanctioned by contemporary usage. Some words, with a double justification for their capitals, might be placed with almost equal propriety under either of two headings; but, in order to avoid confusion, I shall content myself with accounting for every word so printed under some one heading. Proceeding from the more to the less obvious classes, all these words may be grouped thus:—

(1) They are *Personal Appellations*.—'Will.' lvii.; 'deceased Lover,' xxxii.; 'thou the Master Mistris,' xx.; 'my lovely Boy,' cxxvi.; 'Mistersse,' = mistresse, cxxvii.; 'Mistres,' cxxx.; 'Mistrisse,' cliv.; 'little Love-God,' cliv.

(2) *Of foreign extraction borrowed, often from Greek or Latin, as terms of art*—'Antique,' xvii.; 'Image,' xxiv., lxi; 'Nymphes,' cliv.; 'Chronicle,' cvi.; 'Elements,' xlv.; 'Lymbecks,' cxix.; 'Augurs,' cvii.; 'Epitaph,' lxxxi.; 'Idolatrie,' 'Idoll,' cv.; 'Character,' 'Himne,' 'Amen,' lxxxv.; and three, which are also

legal—'Sessions,' xxx.; 'Advocate,' xxxv.; 'Charter,' lxxxvii. The empressment of legal terms into the service of poetry is noticed in the *Arte of English Poesie*, 1589, viz.:—'A terme borrowed of our common Lawyers *impression*, also a new terme, but well expressing the matter and more than our English word.' And, in *The Guide into Tongues*, 1617, a special feature is made of legal terms.

(3) *Titles of Dignity*.—'God,' lviii., cx.; 'King(s),' xxix., lxiii., lxxxvii., cxv.; 'Queene,' xcvi.; 'Princes,' xiv., xxv.; 'Lords,' xciv., xcvii.; 'Ladies,' 'Knights,' cvi.; 'Generall,' cliv.; used of the Love-God in a conceit with Legions (*Ibid.*):—

> 'Which many Legions of true hearts had warm'd
> And so the Generall of hot desire.'

'Legions' might have been placed under (2), but, apart from that and its use in this conceit, it is akin to what may be termed words of *magnitude*, though not *titles*, e.g. 'Kingdome,' lxiv.; 'Maiestie,' lxxviii.; 'Embassie,' xlv. Of a kindred character are:—

(4) *The Names of the Greater Divisions of Time, of Cosmical Processes, the Luminaries, and the Larger Features of the Universe*.—'Winter(s),' ii., lvi., xcvii., xcviii., civ.; 'Sommer(s),' xii., xviii. (3), lvi., xcvii.; 'Spring,' lxiii.; 'Autumne,' xcvii.; 'Aprill', iii., xxi., xcviii., civ.; 'Maie,' xviii.; 'December,' xcvii.; 'Creation,' cxxvii.; 'Universe,' cix.; 'Ocean,' lvi., lxiv., lxxx.; 'Heaven,' xxix., cxxxii.; 'Sunne,' xxi., xxxiii., xxxv., lix., cxxx., cxxxii.; 'Moone,' xxi., xxxv., cvii.; 'Stars,' 'Starre,' xv., cxxxii.; 'Eaven,' cxxxii.; 'Sunset fadeth in the West,' lxxiii.; 'West,' cxxxii.; 'East,' cxxxii.; 'Orient,' vii.

(5) *Personifications*.—'Beautie,' cxxvii.; 'Time,' xv., xix., lxiv., cxxiii.; 'Times fool,' cxvi.; 'Love,' 'Love's,' xxxi., lvi, cxlv.; 'Fortune,' xxix., xxxvii.; 'Muse,' xxi., xxxii., xxxviii., lxxix., lxxxii., lxxxv., c., ci., ciii.; 'Age's,' lxiii.; 'Day,' xxviii.; 'Reason,' cxlvii.; 'Phisick,' cxlvii.; 'Nothing', 'Folly,' 'Truth,' 'Simplicity,' 'Captaine,' 'Ill,' lxvi.; 'Nature,' 'Art,' lxviii., cxxvii.; 'Nature,' cxxvi.; 'Art,' cxxxix. Here Art is not, properly, personified, and might be classed under the next heading:—

(6) *Names of Arts and Sciences*.—'Astronomy,' xiv.; 'Musicke,' cxxx.; 'Rhetorick,' lxxxii.; and those who practise

them: 'Poet,' 'Poets,' xvii., xxxii., lxxix., lxxxiii.; 'Painter('s),' xxiv.; 'Phisition('s),' cxl., cxlvii.; 'Doctor-like,' lxvi.; 'the Dyers hand,' cxi.; and the instrument of an art, used as its emblem—'such vertue hath my Pen,' lxxxi., 'Leane penurie within that Pen doth dwell,' lxxxiv.; 'their antique Pen would have exprest,' cvi. The last example may serve for a transition to the last class, which is harder to define, viz.:—

(7) *Names of Animals and Plants used Emblematically, Proverbially, or Typically.*—'How many Lambs might the sterne Wolfe betray,' xcvi.; 'Croe or Dove,' cxiii.; 'A Crow that flies in heavens sweetest ayre' = a clue to carrion, lxx.; 'my Adders sense,' cxii.; 'Raven-black,' cxxvii.; 'The Lyons pawes,' 'the fierce Tygers yawes,' 'the long liv'd Phænix, xix.; 'the Larke at breake of daye,' xxix.; 'Some (glory) in their Hawkes and Hounds, some in their Horse,' xci.:—where Hawkes, Hounds, Horse stand for the establishments and pursuits of Hawking, Hunting, and the Manege.

'Roses,' 'Rose,' liv., lxvii., cxxx.; 'Rose,' xcv., cix.; 'Rose(s)' compared with 'Lillie(s),' xcviii., xcix.; 'Canker bloomes' contrasted with 'Roses,' liv.; 'For Canker vice the sweetest buds doth love,' lxx.; 'But as the Marygold at the Suns eye,' xxv.; 'And peace proclaimes Olives of endless age,' cvii.; 'Potions of Eysell gainst my strong infection,' cxi.

Also emblematical are—'Dyall hand,' civ.; 'Virgin hand,' cliv.; 'But hope of Orphans and unfathered fruite,' xcvii.; 'Love is a Babe,' cxv.; 'Captaine Iewells,' lii.; 'Iewell,', xcvi. The 'sausie Iackes' (cxxviii.) are quasi-personified. But, in the last examples, I believe that the awkwardness of the letter *i* as a consonant before a vowel had something to do with determining the type.

There remain some few instances, too complex for any simple scheme of classification, but which, most certainly, are not misprinted:—

> 'Thy end is Truthes and Beauties doome and date.'—xiv.
> 'Unless my Nerves were brasse or hammered steele.'—cxx.
> 'Th'expence of Spirit in a waste of shame.'—cxxix.
> 'As I by yours, y'have past a hell of Time.'—cxx.

Every word in the Quarto printed with a capital, which does not depend on punctuation, is thus susceptible of rational explanation, except two. These may or may not be misprints:—

> 'Uttring bare truth, even so as foes Commend.'—lxix.
> 'This brand she quenchéd in a cool Well by.'—cliv.

The Quarto may therefore be accepted on this count as an edition carefully revised and corrected. Further evidence is forthcoming from the fact that, whereas the thirteen remaining lines of each sonnet begin with a roman capital, according to the usual practice of printing verse, the first line begins with a large initial for which space is invariably allowed by setting the second line somewhat to the right. And this large initial is followed, invariably, by a Roman capital for the second letter of line 1, immediately above the Roman capital for the first letter of line 2; thus:—

> 'From fairest creatures we desire increase,
> That thereby beauties *Rose* might never die,
> But as the riper should by time decease...'
> 'O Least the world should taske you to recite,
> What merit liv'd in me that you should loue.
> After my death (deare love) for get me quite....'[1]

Four words remain printed with capitals which do depend on punctuation:—

> 'They live unwoo'd, and unrespected fade,
> Die to themselves. Sweet Roses doe not so.'—liv. 11.

A capital is still retained after a period in modern printing. But in the Quarto a capital is also placed, twice, after a colon—a use which survives in our *Book of Common Prayer*—

> 'To me faire friend you never can be old,
> For as you were when first your eye I eyde,
> Such seemes your beautie still: Three Winters colde,
> Have from the forests shooke....'—civ.
> 'Most true it is, that I have lookt on truth
> Asconce and strangely: But by all above.'—cx.:—

1. I find that I have overlooked one other exception:—
'Noe Longer mourne.'—lxxi.

and once after a semi-colon:—

'Lose all and more by paying too much rent
For compound sweet; Forgoing simple savor.'—cxxv.

The capital in the last example may be accidentally repeated from the beginning of the line, and modern editors remove the semi-colon, acting on the assumption that the Quarto was carelessly printed in respect of punctuation. This I doubt. It is therefore necessary to examine next, the system, or absence of system, in the punctuation of the Quarto.

Punctuation.—In the Quarto—let it be said at once—stops are not used, as now they are, exclusively to point the syntax of each sentence. They are also used, frequently, to point rhythmical or rhetorical pauses. Thus a comma is placed often at the end, occasionally at some other point in a line, to emphasise such a pause. This practice may pertain to the poet's idiosyncrasy as much as to the fashion of printing in his day: it has been observed in the poetry of Shelley and of others engrossed in the music of their verse. But, if this constant feature be excepted and a moderate allowance be made for the transposition of stops at the ends of two consecutive lines, the remainder of error to be accounted for by careless editing is by no means abnormal. On the other hand, in many instances the punctuation is so exquisitely adapted to the sense, rhetoric, and rhythm of the phrase as to confirm my plea for the authority of the text. The examples quoted to illustrate the use of capitals from civ. and cx. serve also to illustrate the rhetorical use of punctuation. In them a capital followed the colon, as I hold, to emphasise the rhetorical pause; whereas in the examples which I am about to quote the effect is produced by punctuation alone:—

'But why of two othes breach doe I accuse thee,
When I break twenty: I am perjured most,
For all my vowes are othes but to misuse thee:
And all my honest faith in thee is lost.'—clii. 6.

'Then let not winters wragged hand deface,
In thee thy summer ere thou be distil'd:
Make sweet some viall; treasure thou some place,
With beauties treasure ere it be selfe kil'd':—vi. 3.

'He lends thee vertue, and he stole that word,
From thy behaviour, beautie doth he give
And found it in thy cheeke: he can affoord
No praise to thee, but what in thee doth live.'—lxxix. 11.

'Tell me thou lov'st elde-where; but in my sight,
Dear heart forbeare to glance thine eye aside,
What needst thou wound with cunning when thy might
Is more than my ore-prest defence can bide!'—cxxxix. 5.

The pause in the first line of this quatrain is heavily pointed to prepare for the unpausing outburst of the last two. And, in the only remaining example of a colon set elsewhere than at the end of a line, there is revealed a piece of punctuation so exquisite as to affirm an author's hand[1]:—

'If it be not, then love doth well denote,
Loves('s) eye is not so true as all mean('s): no,
How can it? O how can loves('s) eye be true,
That is so vext with watching and with teares?'—cxlviii. 7-10.

No journeyman-printer, no pirate-publisher, achieved that effect. It leads up, with the prescience of consummate art, to the rhythmical stress on the second 'can' in line 9, and, in its own way, it is as subtle.

A like intention may be traced in the handling of the comma. Its frequency may suggest accident, rather than design. But this frequency arises from a use which has now been abandoned, in addition to the grammatical use which is still retained. Commas in the Quarto serve a double purpose: they point the syntax, but they also, and often, mark the end of a line or the major pause after the fourth or the sixth syllable, and this even when the sense demands no stop. That they were not peppered over the page at random is apparent from their unvarying coincidence with pauses, whether of grammar, rhythm, or rhetoric, e.g.:—

'Take all my loves, my love, yea take them all.
What hast thou then more than thou hadst before?
No love, my love, that thou maist true love call,
All mine was thine, before thou hadst this more':—xl. 1-4.

1. ix. 3, the Quarto has 'Ah; if thou issulesse,' for 'Ah!'

'Nay if you read this line, remember not,
The hand that writ it, for I love you so,
That I in your sweet thoughts would be forgot,
If thinking on me then should make you woe.'—lxxi. 5-8.

'And do so love, yet when they have devisde,
What strained touches Rhethorick can lend,
Thou truly faire, wert truly simpathizde,
In true plaine words, by thy true telling friend.'—lxxxii. 9-12.

'So shall I live, supposing thou art true,
Like a deceived husband, so loves face,
May still seeme love to me, though alter'd new:
Thy lookes with me, thy heart in other place.'—xciii. 1-4.

These stops are rhythmical: for Shakespeare's quatrains and the Psalms were 'printed as they are to be sung or said.' Like Shelley, he preferred rhythmical effect to 'syntactical standing.'

Incidentally, the punctuation of the *Sonnets* exhibits their structure; showing that they were built up of three quatrains, each of which is a separate measure, with a couplet at the close. The *Sonnets* proper number one hundred and fifty-three in all, for cxxvi. is not a sonnet but an envoy in six couplets to the first series, and out of this possible maximum the Quarto has a comma or no stop but twenty-three times at the end of the first quatrain, but eighteen times at the end of the second, and but thirty-two times at the end of the third. By adopting the modern system of punctuation even these numbers are by much reduced. The *Cambridge Shakespeare* has a heavier stop than a comma after the first quatrain in all but nine cases; after the second, in all but seven; after the third, in all but five. The significance of this proportion of heavy stops to commas at the end of the quatrains is apparent if contrasted with the single instance in the Quarto of a period, and the eight instances of a colon or semi-colon, being placed in the body of a line. But the alterations made in the *Cambridge Shakespeare* in the direction of heavier stops at the end of the quatrains do not prove that the Quarto was carelessly printed. For, taking the most important pause, viz. after the second quatrain, in only two instances (v. 8 and xxi. 8) can it be said with confidence that the comma in the Quarto is due to a misprint, and in one instance (cxii.) the *Cambridge* seems to err in substituting a period. But the reduction, effected by modern grammatical use in the number of commas at this break, does confirm the theory of structure in quatrains. Accepting these alterations in all but cxii., you have a heavy stop after the second quatrain in all the sonnets but eight. And this figure can be reduced still further, for in three sonnets (xii., lxxxiv., xciii.) I hope to show, when I reach them, that the *Cambridge Shakespeare* errs in substituting commas for a colon and two periods. Out of one hundred and fifty-three sonnets, therefore, only five have but commas after line 8, viz. lxvi., but it proceeds by continuous enumeration from l. 2 to l. 12; xcix., but the explanation is apparent, for the sonnet is irregular with a fifth line added to the first quatrain; and cxii., cxxxii., cxlviii., in each of which an exceptional effect is produced by departing, intentionally, from the normal practice. By the insignificance of their number, these five exceptions confirm the consistency of Shakespeare's practice; by the fact that each can be explained they confirm the authority of the Quarto text. Additional confirmation may be found in the unerring, though obsolete, use of parentheses, e.g.:—

> 'O if (I say) you looke upon this verse,
> When I (perhaps) compounded am with clay.'

Against this argument must be set three undoubted corruptions of the text:—

1\.

> 'Poore soule the center of my sinfull earth,
> My sinfull earth these rebbell powres that thee array.'
>
> cxlvi. 1, 2;

2\.

> 'Though thou repent, yet I have still the losse,
>
> . . . . . .
>
> To him that beares the strong offences losse.'—xxxiv. 10-12:—

where the second 'losse' may fairly be set down to the compositor in view of xlii. 10 and 12:—

> 'And loosing her, my friend hath found that losse,
>
> . . . . . .
>
> And both for my sake lay on me this crosse';

3. The occasional confusion of *their* with *thy*; cf. Malone: 'The same mistake has several times happened in these Sonnets, owing probably to abbreviations having been formerly used for the words *their* and *thy*, so nearly resembling each other as not to be easily distinguished. I have observed the same error in some of the old English plays';

and three suspicious features:—

1. Line 11. xxv., ending 'quite' does not rhyme with line 9, ending 'worth.'
2. The couplet of xcvi. is repeated from xxxvi.
3. Empty parentheses are placed after cxxvi., which is not a sonnet (*supra*), as if to indicate the compositor's expectation of a couplet.

There are also some half-dozen of trifling misprints, but these, both in number and character, can be paralleled from the Quarto of *Venus and Adonis* (1593), a text the authority of which has never been challenged.

To sum up:—The use of italics, capitals, and stops in the Quarto of 1609, though often obsolete, is most rarely irrational; the number of undoubted corruptions is so small as to be negligible; the weight, therefore, of the argument inclines irresistibly towards maintaining the text wherever it will yield a meaning. Acting on this conclusion, I have more than once reinstated the Quarto text in preference to a modern emendation.

VI. *The Use of the Apostrophe as a Guide to the Metrical Pronunciation.* See Note II. on *Venus and Adonis*. The scrupulous employment of the Apostrophe throughout the Quarto (1609), whenever a syllable is not to be sounded, gives further support to the authority of that text. Having considered every case in which a word imports an extra syllable into a line, I can find but two in which the Quarto can be said with any certainty to err:—civ. 10-12...perceiu'd...deceaued; cxxiv. 2-4...unfathered...gatherd. No question arises out of certain lightly sounded words which then, as now, were printed with their full number of syllables, e.g.:—euery 11-times, euen 12-times, spirit 4-times, heauen 3-times. With these may be classed:—Soueraine, xxxiii. 2, lvii. 6; generall, cxxi. 13; several, cxxxvii. 9; Being, li. 10; We are, lix. 11; Be it, cxlii. 9. And no question arises where the extra syllable adds an obviously intended charm to the rhythm as in:—livery, ii. 3; flattery, xlii. 14; melancholie, xlv. 8; sufferance, lviii. 7; laboring, lix. 3; shallowest, lxxx. 9; varrying = varying, cv. 10; preposterously, cix. 11; reckening, cxv. 5; adulterat, cxxi. 5; slanderers, cxl. 12; desperate, cxlvii. 7.

There remain eight cases of ambiguous e's in Q.:—yellowed, xvii. 9; widdowed, xcvii. 8; swollowed = swallowed, cxxix. 7; louest, cxxxvi. 14; in which the *e* has been printed but not accented, and:—unlettered, lxxxv. 6; unfathered, xcvii. 10; suffered, cxx. 8; fethered, cxliii. 2—in which the *e* has been omitted in accordance with the usage of modern editions.

VII. *Notes on the Text.*

Group A, i.-xix. See Introduction, p. cx.

I. 2. *Rose*:—Printed thus with a capital and italics in Q. See Note V. on the Typography of the Quarto (1609), and Introduction, p. cxxii.

5. *contracted*:—not the adjective = *narrowed*, but the participle = *betrothed*. Cf. *Measure for Measure*, V. i. 380:—

> 'Say, wast thou e'er *contracted* to this woman?'

Twelfth Night, V. i. 268:—

> 'You would have been *contracted* to a maid';

and 1 *Henry IV*., IV. ii. 17:—

> 'Inquire me out *contracted* bachelors, such as had been asked twice on the banns.'

6. *self-substantial fuel*, hyphened by Sewell = fuel of the same substance as thy 'light's flame,' viz. thine eye-sight:—Bound by vow to your own eyes you feed your sight on the sight of your-self.

13-14. *Pity the world, or else this glutton be, To eat the world's due, by the grave and thee*:—*Pity the world*, of which you are the present ornament and only earnest of future increase in beauty (9-10), *or else* prevent the confirmation of that earnest, which is due to the world, *by the grave* (= your death) *and thee* (= your refusal to propagate your beauty before dying).

II. 4. *tatter'd*, Gildon; totter'd Q.

7. *deep-sunken*, hyphened by Sewell. Cf. i. 5, contracted to thine own bright eyes.

8. *thriftless* = profitless. Cf. *Winter's Tale*, I. ii. 109:—

'Their profits
Their own particular thrifts';

and *Twelfth Night*, II. ii. 40:—

'What thriftless sighs shall poor Olivia breathe!'

10-11. *This...excuse*:—first marked as a quotation by Malone (Capell MS.).

11. *shall sum my count* = shall complete and balance my account, i.e. with the world, since (l. 12) the child's beauty is, being inherited, the father's: '*and make my old excuse*.' This is obscure. *Old* may be a noun for 'eld,' as in lxviii. 12:—

'Robbing no old to dress his beauty new.'

Cf. 'to rob him of his fair,' *Venus and Adonis*, 1086. In that case *excuse* is a participle for 'excused'. *Old*, sometimes = 'more than enough, copious, abundant' (*Imp. Dict*), e.g.:—

'If a man were porter of hell-gate, he should have *old* turning the key.'

Macbeth, II. iii. 2;

'Here will be an *old* abusing of God's patience and the king's English.'

Merry Wives of Windsor, I. iv. 5;

'There was *old* to do about ransoming the Bridegroim.'

Walter Scott:—

but not, to my knowledge, outside humorous application.

12. *thine!* Knight, thine. Q.

13-14. *ould...could*:—The first word is thus spelt five times as against thirteen of 'old,' the second four times thus against two of 'cold.'

III. 5. *unear'd*, to ear is to plough or till.

V. 1. *hours*, howers Q., a dissyllable.

4. '*unfair*' = deprive of beauty. Cf. 'to rob him of his fair,' *Venus and Adonis*, 1086, and 'Fairing the foul with art's false

borrow'd face,' cxxvii. 6. Shakespeare has 'unfather'd,' xcvii. 10, 2 *Henry IV.*, IV. iv. 122; and 'I'll unhair thy head.'—*Antony and Cleopatra*, II. v. 64.

7, 8. *gone,...everywhere*: gon...everywhere, Q., a misprint; the stops have been transposed.

14. *Leese* = lose, a form used constantly by Chaucer.

VI. 1. *ragged*, wragged Q.

4. *beauty's*, beautits Q. The *t* is very like an *e*.

8. *one*; one, Q. A slight pause only is indicated because of the rhetorical run on the repetitions of 'ten.'

VII. 5. *steep-up*, steepe up Q., hyphened by Gildon.

9. *pitch*, pich Q.

VIII. 5-14:—Cf. this conceit drawn from harmony with *Lucrece*, 1132-1154.

8. *the parts that,* a parte, wch:—thus in a copy of this Sonnet MS. (B.M. Add., 15226), which Dowden assigns to James I.'s reign.

14. '*thou single wilt prove none*,' marked as a quotation by Malone. Tyler compares cxxxvi. 8, 'Among a number one is reckoned none.' This is *not* 'according to Cocker,' who states this view:—'Most Authors maintain that Unit is the Beginning of Numbers and it self no Number,' but argues learnedly against it (Cocker's *Arithmetick*). Cf. Marlowe, *Hero and Leander*:—

> 'One is no number; maids are nothing, then,
> Without the sweet society of men.'

IX. 3. *Ah!* Ah; Q.

4. *makeless* = mateless, from Anglo-Saxon *maca*, a mate; match is another form, as in Kirk and Church. Cf. *The Faërie Queene*:—

> 'And of faire Britomart ensample take
> That was as true in love, as turtle to her make;'
>
> 'Th' Elfe, therewith astownd,
> Upstarted lightly from his looser Make':—

and Surrey (The Second Number in *Tottel's Miscellany*, 1557):—

> 'The turtle to her make hath tolde her tale.

10. *his* = its.

X. 1. *For shame* = for very shame, for shame's sake. Modern Editions have 'For shame!' (Sewell). But this destroys the rhythm.

9. *mind!*, mind, Q.

12. *kind-hearted*, kind harted Q.

XI. 2. *departest*, transitive. Cf. 2 *Henry IV.*, IV. v. 91:—

'Depart the chamber, leave us here alone':—

and 3 *Henry VI.*, II. ii. 73:—

'I would your highness would depart the field.'

3. *youngly* = in youth.

4. *convertest* = tarnest from youth to age. Cf. xiv. 13:—

'If from thyself to store thou wouldst convert.'

The quatrain is obscure. Tyler explains 1, 2, 'As fast as the father declines, so fast in his child, his second self, does he grow towards, or in, that youthful beauty which he is leaving behind—"from that which thou departest."' This, no doubt, is the meaning, but it is hard to see how the construction bears it out. It would be easy if the line ran:—'In one of thine, tow'rds that which thou departest': but it does not. I retain the comma after 'grow'st,' as in Q., and remove the comma after 'thine,' to make clearer the only meaning which I can extract:—*So fast thou grow'st, in one of thine from that* (= in one of thy children deriving from that = the period of youth) *which thou departest* (= leavest behind). The next two lines would, then, develop the idea naturally:—and the fresh blood which you bestow in your youth on your child, you may still call yours when you yourself turn from youth to age.

9. *store* = multiplication, reproduction, from the meaning, multitude, as in *Two Gentlemen of Verona,* III. i. 205:—

'Here's too small a pasture for such store of muttons.'

XII. 4. *all silver'd o'er* Malone, or silver'd ore Q. Malone's emendation is rendered probable by 'all girded up,' in l. 7.

8. *beard*: Q. and Kelmscott; beard:—Bell; beard, Cambridge.

14. *Save breed, to brave him when he takes thee hence.*

Save breed to brave him, when he takes thee hence,

Q., where the comma marks the delivery and not the grammar of the line.

XIII. 1. *but, love, you* Gildon, but love you Q.

6. *determination,* the proper legal term.

7. *Yourself...your self's,* You selfe...your selfes Q.

13. *unthrifts! Dear my love* Kelmscott, Bell, Dowden; unthrifts, deare my love Q.; unthrifts: dear Cambridge.

14. *You had a father; let your son say so.* You had a Father, let your Son say so. Q. This is simply another poetical turn for the advice:—'beget a son.' It does not mean that the Friend's father was dead. Tyler cites *Merry Wives of Windsor*, III. iv. 36, 'where Shallow, urging Slender to woo Ann Page in manly fashion—to do as his father did—says:—"She's coming, to her, coz, O boy, *thou had'st a father*," a hint which, however, Slender misunderstands.'

XIV. 2. *Astronomy* = astrology.

4, 5. In Q...quality,...tell; the stops have been transposed.

5. *minutes*, mynuits Q.

9, 10. *But from thine eyes my knowledge I derive,*
And, constant stars, in them I read such art.

Cf. Sidney, *Astrophel and Stella* (1591):—

'Though dusty Wits dare scorn astrology....
Proof makes me sure
Who oft fore-judge my after-following race,
By only those two stars in Stella's face.'

12. *to store*, *supra*, xi. 9.

XV. 6. *Cheeréd and check'd*, Cheared and checkt Q. I have accented cheeréd, for the *e* if mute is invariably cut out in Q. The music of the line depends on its being sounded.

7. *Vaunt* = exult, display themselves. Cf. *Richard III.*, V. iii. 288:—

'The foe vaunts in the field.'

9. *conceit* = conception, apprehension.

XVI. 9-12. This quatrain is obscure at the first reading, owing to the complicated play on the word 'lines,' in 'lines of life,' l. 9. Tyler and Dowden agree, substantially, that it connotes (1) children, referring back to 'living flowers' in 7; (2) delineation in a portrait, echoing 'painted counterfeit' in 8; (3) lines of the poet's verse. I believe that the conceit, while including those meanings which are subsequently developed, starts from a fourth drawn from Palmistry, and that this determined its unusual cast;—*lines of life*. The line of life in Palmistry exhibits the principal events in life, particularly marriage and the birth of children. Cf. *Merchant of Venice*, II. ii 146:—

'Here's a simple *line of life*: here's a small trifle of wives: alas, fifteen wives is nothing! a'leven widows and nine maids is a simple coming in for a man...'

Thus the sense is:—Many a maid, l. 6, if you should *marry*, would bear you 'living flowers' = *children*, l. 7, much liker than any *portrait* of yourself, l. 8; so should *the lines of life* = *marriage* and *procreation*, with a play on the meaning, (2) = *delineation*, repair that life of yours, l. 9, which this = my record, with a play on the meaning lines of verse—and then in parentheses, Q.—('Times pensel' = history, record at large, 'or my pupill pen' = my humbler art); 'neither in inward worth nor outward fair' = beauty, l. 11, can (do, for it cannot) make you live your self (i.e., very self) in eyes of men, l. 12. The use of the relative 'which,' l. 10, is irregular.

The play on the double sense line = delineation, and line = a verse is developed in xvii. 1, 2:—

'My verse...if it were fill'd with your most high deserts?'

Cf. lxiii. 13:—

'His beauty shall in these black *lines* be seen';

and lxxxvi. 13, of the Rival Poet:—

'But when your countenance fill'd up his *line*.'

In xvii. 13, 14, there is a transition from this double sense, line = lineage and verse, to xviii. in l. 12:—

'When in eternal *lines* to time thou grow'st'.

where the poet attributes the gift of immortality to his verse alone. Many parallels for these several uses of 'line' may be found in the Plays, e.g. *lineage*. Cf. *Henry V.*, I. ii. 71:—

'Of the true line and stock of Charles the Great.'

A child's reproduction of his father's image. Cf. *Winter's Tate*, I. ii, 153:—

'Looking on the lines
Of my boy's face methought I did recoil
Twenty-three years, and saw myself unbreech'd.'

XVII. 12. *metre* Gildon, miter Q.

XVIII. 10-12. *...ow'st...grow'st*: thus in Q.; owest...growest Malone, for which there is no authority. Owest...grow'st Cambridge, which exhibits the inconvenience of forsaking the strictly phonetic practice observed in Q.

XIX. 5. *fleet'st.* An imperfect rhyme to 'sweets.' Dyce puts 'fleets.'

This Sonnet closes Group A.

XX. 2. *Master Mistress*, Master Mistris Q., master-mistress Malone. I omit Malone's hyphen, as it is risky to tamper with enigmas.

7. *Hews*:—I retain the Q. type and spelling, being persuaded that the word was so printed intentionally. (See Note V.) The line in Q. is:—

'A man in hew all *Hews* in his controwling.'

Hew is the usual spelling for 'hue,' and here means shape, figure, and not tint. Dowden cites Nash's *Pierce Pennilesse*, pp. 82-83 (Shakespeare Society's Reprint):—'The spirits of the water have slow bodies, resembling birds and women, of which kinde the Naiades and Nereides are much celebrated amongst poets. Nevertheless, however they are restrayned to their severall similitudes, it is certain that all of them desire no forme or figure so much as the likenesse of a man, and doo thinke themselves in heaven when they are infeoft in that *hue*.' Spenser uses 'hew' twice for shape, embodiment. The line, then, means 'a man in shape all shapes in his controlling.' Cf. liii. 5-8, 12:—

'Describe *Adonis*, and the counterfeit
Is poorly imitated after you;
On *Hellen's* cheek all art of beauty set,

And you in *Grecian* tires are painted new...
And you in every blesséd shape we know.'

It states that the Friend was the eternal pattern of Beauty. But the type selected for 'hues,' thanks to contemporary spelling, *Hews*, enabled the poet to convey something more which was apparent to the person addressed and is not apparent now. Of this I am convinced. But beyond this all is guess-work. Some hold that Mr. W.H. of the dedication was the Friend, and that his name was William Hughes; others seek an anagram in the letters. Fortunately they serve the turn of both the two chief camps which identify the Friend, the one with William Herbert, the other with Southampton. Anagrams were fashionable:—

'Henry Wriothesley Earle of Southampton
Anagram:
Vertue is thy Honour; O the praise of all men':—

and *Hews* contains the initials of his name and title. Others may riddle it: He = Herbert, W.S. = Shakespeare, or they may find in H.W.S. the initials of the two with an E added to sound them. Many identify the Rival Poet with Chapman, and, viewing the ardour with which this riddle-maree is prosecuted, it is strange that a passage in Chapman's Preface to the Reader (*Homer's Iliads*) has so far escaped their attention: 'another right learned, honest, and entirely loved friend of mine, M. Robert Hews.' It is improbable that we shall ever know the hidden suggestion of this word. It remains *cos ingeniorum.*

XXI. *So is it not with me,* etc.:—This sonnet offers the first attack on the false art of a Rival Poet. It is intimately connected with the preceding sonnet, and is obviously personal. Yet it does not follow that the events which suggested it were to the poet more than an occasion for writing in a strain of contemporary fashion. Cf. Du Bellay (*Contre les Petrarquides*), who, deriding the false art of Petrarch's imitators, writes:—

'De voz beautez, ce n'est que tout fin or,
Perles, crystal, marbre, et ivoyre encor,
Et tout l'honneur de l'Indique thresor,
Fleurs, lis, œillets, et roses.'

The whole poem, of several pages, offers a close parallel to the similar attacks in the *Sonnets*. A poet was expected to disclaim the practice of Petrarch's imitators and to trounce his rivals for observing it. Drayton does both.

13, 14. *Let them say more that like of hearsay well;*
I will not praise that purpose not to sell.

Cf. *Love's Labour's Lost*, IV. iii. 234:—

'Lend me the flourish of all gentle tongues,—
Fie painted rhetoric! O, she needs it not:
To things of sale a seller's praise belongs,
She passes praise....'

and Daniel, to Delia, 1594:—

'None other fame, mine unambitious Muse
Affected ever, but t' eternize Thee!
All other honours do my hopes refuse,
Which meaner prized and momentary be.
For, God forbid! I should my papers blot
With mercenary lines, with servile pen;
Praising virtues in them that have them not,
Basely attending on the hopes of men.'—Sonnet liii.

XXII. 3. *furrows*, forrwes Q., sorrows Gildon, sorrowes Kelmscott. Cf. *Richard II.*, I. iii. 229:—

'Thou canst help time to furrow me with age,
But stop no wrinkle.'

4. *expiate*. Expiate = to atone for a crime and thus to close the last chapter of its history. Here the sense of completing is kept and the sense of atoning dropped; Malone paraphrases 'should fill up the measure of my days,' and cites *Richard III.*, III. iii. 23:—

'Make haste; the hour of death is expiate.'

XXIII. 6. *rite* Malone, right Q.

9. *books*, looks Sewell.

14. *with...wit*, wit...wiht Q.

XXIV. (connected with the preceding sonnet) 1. *steel'd*, steeld Q. See notes on *Lucrece*, 1444, and *Venus and Adonis*, 376.

4. *And perspective it is* best *Painter's art*, viz. the art of depicting objects on the plane of a canvas, but so that they appear, as in nature, to be in many planes, one behind the

other, seen through the *frame* as if through a square aperture. The conceit begins, l. 1, with the Poet's 'eye' as a Painter, who has drawn the Friend's beauty on the Poet's heart. It goes on to a play on the word 'frame,' l. 3; the body is the physiological *frame* which holds the heart and other organs, but, taking the other sense of frame, perspective, l. 4, is the best of a painter's art; and, l. 5, taking the etymological derivation of perspective with a reversion to the conceit that the Friend's beauty is engraved on the Poet's physical heart, to see the skill of the Picture you must look through the Painter = the Poet's eye. The Poet's bosom, l. 7, being the shop wherein the picture hangs, has, l. 8, borrowed the Friend's eyes: making, l. 9, a good exchange of 'eyes for eyes.' The Poet's eyes, l. 10, have been engaged in drawing the Friend's shape; the Friend's eyes, l. 11, meanwhile have been windows, in their place, to the Poet's breast, through which, l. 12, the sun delights to peep, to gaze at the image of the Friend. This is a conceit with a vengeance, but it does work out! Cf. Henry Constable's *Diana*, Sonnet v. (1594):—

> 'Thine eyes, the glass where I behold my heart.
> Mine eye, the window through the which thine eye
> May see my heart; and there thyself espy
> In bloudy colours, how thou painted art!'

9. *Good-turns*, good-turnes Q. I retain the hyphen because it ensures the correct delivery of the line. The locution is used for a service rendered no less than nine times in the Plays.

XXV. 4. *Unlook'd for* = not sought out, not 'distinguished,' as a favourite was said to be 'distinguished' by a look or word from his sovereign. It is not possible to *prove* the date of the *Sonnets* from internal evidence; but if, as to me seems probable, the earlier Sonnets were written in 1599, no lines could have been penned more apposite than the next eight (5-12) to the fall and disgrace of Essex after his military failure in Ireland. They breathe the very spirit of Rowland White's regret for that dazzling favourite and famous Captain, foiled at last (*supra* Introduction):—

> 'Great Princes' favourites their fair leaves spread
> But as the Marygold at the sun's eye,

And in themselves their pride lies buriéd,
For at a frown they in their glory die.
The painful warrior famouséd for fight
After a thousand victories once foil'd,
Is from the book of honour razéd quite,
And all the rest forgot for which he toil'd':—

They might, indeed, have been written by a follower of Essex after the fatal eve of Michaelmas, 1599, for the epitaph of his reputation.

6. *Marygold*:—Cf. *The Interpreter*, 1622, a Puritan satire reprinted by Arber, *An English Garner*, vi. p. 235:—

'He's as bold
And confident as the bright marigold!
That flatterer, that favourite of the sun':—

where Buckingham is evidently intended. Dowden describes the flower:—'The garden marigold, or Ruddes (*calendula officinalis*); it turns its flowers to the sun, and follows his guidance in their opening and shutting. The old name is goldes; it was the Heliotrope, Solsequium, or Turnesol of our forefathers. (Condensed from "Marigold" in Ellacombe's *Plant Lore and Garden Craft of Shakespeare*.)' *The Guide into Tongues* (1617) gives:—(1) Marigolde = Orange Flower. *French*, Soulsi, quasi solem sequens. *German*, Ringel-blum; and adds, 'officin: vocant calthulam, solis sponsam, caltham poëticam seu Virgilii Calendulam. (2) Marigold of Peru = sun-flower, or golden flower of Peru.

9. *fight*, worth Q. Malone accepted this emendation from Theobald, 'who likewise proposed, if worth were retained, to read: razéd *forth*,' in l. 11. This neglect of the rhyme may be due to an oversight of the author, but the emendation by the 'Porson of Shakespeare' has passed into the language.

13, 14. *belovéd...removéd*. I have accented the final syllables, in accordance with the principle explained in Note II on *Venus and Adonis*, of which the use observed by the Quartos in respect of the two words—loved, beloved—affords a good example. The words occur in all fourteen times; nine times, where the metre demands that the *e* should be mute, it is omitted; three times, where the metre demands that the *e* should be sounded, it is printed: there remain two cases in the final couplets of this sonnet and of cxvi. In both Q. prints the *e* with, I cannot doubt, the intention that it should be sounded.

Group B, xxvi.-xxxii.

XXVI. 3. *ambassage* Q. embassage, Ewing.

8. *In thy soul's thought (all naked) will bestow it*:—Bestow = 'lodge' (Dowden), also 'equip'; 'clothe' (Tyler); 'put him up,' as we say, colloquially. 'It,' which is to be so entertained = 'Duty' of l. 5, made to seem 'bare,' l. 6, and (all naked) refers to this 'bare Duty.' I retain the parenthesis of Q. as it makes the reference back to 'Duty' clearer.

11. *tatter'd*, tottered Q.; cf. ii. 4.

12. *thy*, 'their' Q. Malone's emendation. See (*supra*) Note V. He has made a like change, xxvii. 10, xxxv. 8, xxxvii. 7, xliii. 11, xlv. 12, xlvi. 3, 8, 13, 14, etc., and not always with adequate warrant from the sense. Even in this case it ill possible that 'their,' Q., may be the right reading, referring to the stars, suggested by 'whatsoever star' in l. 9; for this, in turn, refers back to 'their *stars*' of the preceding sonnet.

XXVII. 10. *thy* Malone, their Q. It is just conceivable that 'their' should stand, referring to 'my thoughts' in l. 5.

11. *hung in ghastly night,* (hunge in gastly night) Q.

XXVIII. 1, 2. The marked query in these two lines suggests that they are a rejoinder to some kindly expression of good wishes for the poet's happy return in a letter from the Friend.

9. *I tell the Day, to please him thou art bright,* Cambridge, Kelmscott; I tell the Day to please him thou art bright, Q.; I tell the day, to please him, thou art bright, Malone, Dowden, Tyler, Bell.

12. *twire*, 'peep. Cf. Ben Jonson, *Sad Shepherd*, Act II. SC. i.:—

> "Which maids will *twire* at, tween their fingers, thus";

Beaumont and Fletcher, *Woman Pleas'd*, Act IV., Sc. i.:—

> "I saw the wench that twir'd and twinkled at thee
> The other day";

Marston, *Antonio and Mellida*, Act IV. (*Works*, vol. i. p. 32, ed. Halliwell):—

> "I sawe a thing stirre under a hedge, and I peep't, and a spyed a thing, and I peer'd and *tweerd* underneath."'—Dowden

Scott, whose *Fortunes of Nigel* proves that he had steeped himself in Elizabethan Drama, has there:—'all of them are twiring and peeping betwixt their fingers when you pass.'

12. *gild'st the even,* guil'st th' eauen Q.

13, 14. Printed in Q.:—

> 'But day doth daily draw my sorrowes longer, [stronger
> And night doth nightly make greefes length seeme

The Cambridge, following Dyce 1857 (Capell MS. and Collier, conj.), has 'longer...*strength* seem stronger.' Malone, Dowden, Tyler, Bell, Kelmscott, retain *length*. The sense is:—'Day daily draws out my sorrows to a greater length, but they are not attenuated or weakened for all their length: night nightly makes that length seem stronger.'

XXIX. 2. *outcast*, out-cast Q.

4. *fate*, fate. Q.

11. (Like to the Larke at breake of daye arising), Q. Modern editions omit the parentheses and put no comma after 'arising.' But it is his 'state' which sings at heaven's gate from the sullen earth—like to the lark.

XXX. 1. *Sessions* Q., i.e. the Court, as it were, Assizes. Cf. *Othello*, III. iii. 140:—

> 'Who has a breast so pure,
> But some uncleanly apprehensions
> Keep leets and law-days, and in session sit
> With meditations lawful.'

6. *dateless* = endless.

8. *moan the expense.* Dowden:—'pay my account of moans for. The words are explained by what follows:—

> "Tell o'er
> The sad account of fore-bemoaned moan."'

sight. Malone would understand 'sigh.' 'sight' might stand for 'sighed'—it is so used by Chaucer—but not for the noun. The change is not needed:—'sight' = sight of persons beloved. Cf. 2 *Henry VI.*, I. i. 32:—

'Her sight did ravish; but her grace in speech.'

XXXI. 5. *obsequious* = 'dutiful,' Tyler; = 'funereal,' Dowden. I agree. Cf. *Titus Andronicus*, V. iii. 152:—

'Draw you near
To shed *obsequious tears* upon this trunk.'

7. *interest.* Cf. *Lucrece*, 1796-99:—

'Do not take away
My sorrow's interest, let no mourner say
He weeps for her, for she was only mine
And only must be wail'd by Colatine.'

8. *there* Q., thee Gildon. I retain the Q. reading:—'there' refers back to 'thy bosom,' l. 1; 'And there,' l. 3. Thus:—'hidden in there' = hidden in thy bosom, the subject of all the first eight lines with which the sonnet opens. The third quatrain, after a period, opens with a second idea, developed from the first:—'Thou art the grave.'

XXXII. *If thou survive*, etc.:—Closes Group B.

7. *Reserve them* = keep them carefully. Cf. *Othello*, III. iii. 295:—

'But she so loves the token,
For he conjured her she should ever keep it,
That she *reserves* it evermore about her
To kiss and talk to.'

XXXIII. *Full many a glorious*, etc.:—Opens Group C, xxxiii.-xlii.

2. *Flatter...with sovereign eye*:—That is, as a sovereign flatters a courtier with a look. Cf. xxv. 4-8.

6. *rack* = thin flying broken clouds or any portion of floating vapour in the sky. Cf. *Antony and Cleopatra*, IV. xiv. 10:—

'Sometime we see a cloud that's dragonish;
A vapour sometime like a bear or lion,
A tower'd citadel, a pendent rock,
A forked mountain, or blue promontory

With trees upon't, that nod unto the world,
And mock our eyes with air....
That which is now a horse, even with a thought
The *rack* dislimns, and makes it indistinct
As water is in water.'

12. *region*:—Dowden cites *Clarendon Press Hamlet*:—'Originally a division of the sky marked out by the Roman augurs. In later times the atmosphere was divided into three regions—upper, middle, and lower. By Shakespeare the word is used to denote the air generally.' Cf. Bacon:—

'The winds in the upper *region*, which move the clouds above, which we call the *rack*...pass without noise.'

'But as we often see, against some storm,
A silence in the heavens, the *rack* stand still,
The bold wind speechless and the orb below
As hush as death, anon the dreadful thunder
Doth rend the *region*.'—*Hamlet*, II. ii. 506.
'Region kites.'—*Hamlet*, II. ii. 606.
'Through the airy region.'—*Romeo and Juliet*, II. ii. 21.

14. *stain...staineth*, intransitive. Cf. *Love's Labour's Lost*, II. i. 48:—

'If virtue's gloss will *stain* with any soil.'

The meaning, when transitive, is to dim. Cf. *Titus Andronicus*, III. i. 213:—

'With our sighs we'll breathe the welkin dim,
And *stain* the sun with fog....'

XXXIV. 4. *rotten*. Cf. *Timon of Athens*, IV. iii. 2:—

'O blessed breeding sun, draw from the earth
Rotten humidity.'

12. *cross* Malone (Capell MS.), losse Q. Cf. xlii. 12:—

'And both for my sake lay on me this crosse':—

which confirms Malone's conjecture.

13. *sheds*, 'sheeds' Q., rhyming with 'deeds.'

XXXV. 4. *And loathsome canker lives in sweetest bud*:—

lxx. 7. 'For Canker vice the sweetest buds doth love.'
xcv. 2. 'Which like a canker in the fragrant Rose.'

7. *amiss*:—

> 'Each toy seems prologue to some great amiss.'
>
> *Hamlet*, IV. v. 18.

8. *Excusing thy sins, more than their sins are.*
Excusing their sins more than their sins are.—Q.
Excusing thy sins more than thy sins are.
Malone (Capell MS.)

Malone's emendation is generally accepted, but, as he adds himself, 'The latter words of this line, whichever reading we adopt, are not very intelligible.' Steevens explains:—'Excusing thy sins more than thy sins are' = 'making the excuse more than proportioned to the offence.' I retain the second 'their,' and put a comma after the first 'sins,' believing that 'than their sins are' refers back to:—'All men make faults,' the sentence which opens the quatrain. The sense is:—'All men make faults, and even I in saying so, giving authority for thy trespass by thus comparing it to the faults of all men; I myself am guilty of corrupting in so "salving thy amiss"; excusing thy sins (which are) more than their sins are.'

9. For to thy *sensual* fault I bring in *sense* = understanding, discernment, appreciation. Cf. *Comedy of Errors*, II. i. 22, where 'Men' by contrast to the brute creation are:—

> 'Indued with intellectual sense and souls';

and *Love's Labour's Lost*, V. ii. 258:—

> 'Cutting a smaller hair than may be seen,
> Above the sense of sense; so sensible
> Seemeth their conference.'

There is, also, a play on the opposite meaning of 'sense,' akin to that of 'sensual.' Cf. *Measure for Measure*, I. iv. 59:—

> 'A man whose blood
> Is very snow-broth; one who never feels
> The wanton stings and motions of the *sense*,
> But doth rebate and blunt his natural edge
> With profits of the *mind*, *study* and fast.'

Sense is *sence* in Q. Malone suggested *incense*; but 'No English writer ever accented the substantive *incense* on the last syllable.'—Steevens.

10. *Thy adverse party is thy Advocate*:—Dowden conjectures '"thy adverse party *as* thy advocate" = sense, against which he has offended, brought in *as* his advocate?' But Advocate, with a capital, and the sequence of the next line, in which the Poet himself 'commences a lawful plea,' confirm the Q. text and indicate 'thy Advocate' = the Poet.

XXXVI. 5. *But one respect* = 'perfect similarity,' Tyler. Dowden, commenting on 'my bewailed grief,' l. 10, conjectures that the passage may mean:—'I may not claim you as a friend, lest my relation to the dark woman—now a matter of grief—should convict you of faithlessness in friendship.' There is much of probability in this gloss and, if it be accepted; then ll. 5, 6:—

'In our two lives there is *but one respect*
Though in our lives a separable spite':—

may also allude to the same situation. 'Respect' in that case must be taken to retain much of its first meaning, akin to the first meaning of 'regard' = 'looking towards' one object. Cf. *Comedy of Errors*, IV. iv. 44.:—

'Respice finem; respect your end.'

6. *separable* = separating, Malone.

9. *ever more* S. Walker conj., 'ever-more' Q., 'evermore' Cambridge.

13, 14:—These lines are repeated in xcvi.

XXXVII. 7. *Intituled in their parts, do crownéd sit.* 'Intitled...sit' Q. and Kelmscott. Malone (Capell MS.) substituted 'thy' for 'their,' adding:—'*Entitled*, thus, means, I think, *ennobled*.' He is followed by Bell, Dowden, Tyler, Cambridge. Tyler explains:—'The various endowments of the Poet's Friend are spoken of as though each were a monarch reigning in its own domain with just title. The word *crowned* describes their pre-eminence.' I retain 'their,' and suggest that *Intitled*—a contraction formed according to the poet's usage from *Intituled—parts*, and *crowned* may all three be explained by reference to contemporary terms of Heraldry. Cf. note on *Lucrece*, 57-72. Guillim (*A Display of Heraldrie*, 1610) has a table of the science. The skill of Armoury is divided into

(i) *Accidents* and (ii) *Parts*; and, without pursuing all the sub-heads under *Parts*, I may sum them up, generally, by saying that *Parts* = the technical term for the places in a shield on which armorial devices are borne. In the long heraldic passage of *Lucrece* we read, 55-58:—

> 'When Beautie bosted blushes, in despight
> Vertue would staine that ore (= *or*) with silver white.
> But Beautie in that white *entituléd*
> From Venus doves, doth challenge that fair *field*.'

Guillim passes at the end of his work from the *Escocheon*, with its *fields* and *charges* and *colours*, to ornaments exteriorly annexed to any *Coate-Armour*:—the *Crest* or *Timber, Wreath, Mantle, Helme,* etc., which, with the shield, make up the *Atchievement*. After dealing with the *Wreath* and *Cap of Dignity*, he goes on to 'other sorts of *Crownes*.' And it appears that *Crownes* had a place in the *Atchievements* even of knights:—'As in this *Atchievement* you may observe a *Wreath* or *Torce* interposed between the *mantle* and the *crest*, so in this next ensuing example you shall finde the like interposition of a *Crowne*. This *Atchievement* belongeth to the Right Worshipfull *Sir John Scudamore*' (2nd Ed.). I take it, therefore, that the passage = Be it beauty, birth or wealth or wit which is displayed—as in an *achievement* beneath the *Crown, charges* are blazoned each in its *part of the coat-armour*—'I make my love ingrafted to this store,' l. 8 = 'your worth and truth,' l. 4, and so 'by a part of all your glory live,' viz. by your worth and truth, making no account of the rest of your glory = your beauty, birth, wealth, and wit.

I am confirmed in my conjecture that the Poet drew on his knowledge of Heraldry to express the contrast between his Friend's worth and truth, which were for him alone, and his other glorious qualities displayed, as in an *achievement*, to the world at large, by a strange similarity between a passage in Guillim's chapter (1st Ed.) on achievements and ll. 4-8 of this Sonnet.—Speaking of '*noble families*: whose first raisers were honoured for their good services with *titles of dignity*, as *badges* of their *worth*,' he goes on:—'if their *offspring* vaunt of their *linage* or *titular dignity*, and want their *vertues*, they are but like base servingmen, who carry on their sleeves the *badge* of some *Noble Family*, yet are themselves but *ignoble persons*. In which respect *Aristotle* discoursing of nobility, makes foure parts thereof; the 1 of *Riches*, the 2 of *Bloud*, the 3 of *Learning*, the 4 of *Vertue*.' The comparison of *titular dignity* with *badges*, and the citation of four *parts* of nobility which, with the substitution of *Beauty* for *Vertue*, *are* the four parts in the sonnet, constitute a remarkable coincidence between Shakespeare's heraldic lore and Guillim's. This citation was a tag familiar to the learned in Heraldry—Ferne has it in *The Glorie of Generositie*, 1586—and, therefore, to Shakespeare, who plays on two senses of the word 'parts,' both germane to that science. Some such classification is alluded to by Henry Constable in his *Diana* (1594), Sonnet x.:—

> 'Heralds at arms do three perfections quote,
> To wit, most *fair*, most *rich*, most *glittering*;
> So, when those three concur within one thing,
> Needs must that thing, of honour, be a note.
> Lately I did behold a fair rich coat....'

i.e. the arms of *Rich*, who married Penelope Devereux, Sidney's Stella.

On the other side it is fair to set *Love's Labour's Lost*, V. ii. 822:—

> 'If this thou do deny, let our hands part
> Neither *intitled* in the other's heart':—

where 'intitled' smacks of Law, from 'title' = the instrument which is evidence of a right of ownership. I was, at first, disposed to accept a like interpretation of 'Intitled in their *parts*,' comparing *parts* with 'of the first part...of the second part' in legal instruments. But this interpretation will not include *crowned*.

9. *So then I am not lame*:—Cf. 'made lame by Fortune's dearest spite,' l. 2. 'Lame' is here, obviously, metaphorical, arising out of the illustration drawn, ll. 1-2, from a 'decrepit father,' who takes delight in 'his active child.' In lxxxix. 3:—

> 'Speak of my *lameness* and I straight will *halt*':—

follows (as an illustration of some imputed delinquency) upon:—

'Say that thou didst forsake me for some fault,
And I will comment upon that offence':—

and the Sonnet goes on:—

'Thou canst not, love, disgrace me half so ill
To set a form upon desiréd change,
As I'll myself disgrace.'

And here, also, 'made lame,' 'I am not lame,' follows an allusion in the preceding number to some disgrace which, whether deservedly or not, has overtaken the Poet:—

'So shall these blots that do with me remain...
Lest my bewailed guilt should do thee shame....'

10. *Whilst that this shadow doth such substance give*:— Shakespeare frequently contrasts 'shadow' and 'substance.' He takes the two terms from the philosophy of his day and uses them for poetical effect, as modern essayists take terms from modern philosophy, e.g. objective and subjective, and use them in criticism:—

'Love like a shadow flies when substance love pursues.'
Merry Wives of Windsor, II. ii. 215.

'The substance of my praise doth wrong this shadow
In underprizing it, so far this shadow
Doth limp behind the substance....'
Merchant of Venice, III. ii. 128.

'Each substance of a grief hath twenty shadows.'
Richard II., II. ii. 14.

'I am but shadow of myself!
You are deceived, my substance is not here.'
1 *Henry VI.*, II. iii. 50.

'That are the substance
Of that great shadow I did represent.'—2 *Henry VI.*, I. i. 14.

'Grief has so wrought on him
He takes false shadows for true substances.'
Titus Andronicus, III. ii. 80.

'Dreams indeed are ambition, for the very substance of the ambitious is merely the shadow of a dream.'—*Hamlet*, II. ii. 265.

'Shadow' and 'reflexion' were used by renaissance Platonists as alternative metaphors in expounding Plato's doctrine that Beauty which we see is the copy of an eternal pattern—Giordano Bruno had discoursed in Paris *De Umbris Idearum*:—or, rather, they use 'shadow' where we should use 'reflexion':—

'Let us clime up the stayers, which at the lowermost stepp have the *shadowe* of sensual beawty, to the high mansion place where the heavenlye, amiable and right beawtye dwelleth.'—Hoby, *The Fourth Booke of the Courtyer*, 1561.

> 'But, mindfull still of your first countries sight,
> Doe still preserve your first informéd grace
> Whose *shadow* yet shynes in your beauteous face.'
>
> Spenser's *Hymne in Honour of Beautie.*

'In the glorious lights of heaven we perceive a *shadow* of his divine countenance.'—Raleigh.

In these examples there is no meaning of 'shade,' but only of 'reflexion.' So does Shakespeare employ 'shadow,' even apart from any philosophical significance, to mean only the 'projection of likeness,' and not the obscuring of light: sometimes simply, e.g. *Venus and Adonis*, 162:—

> 'Narcissus so himself himself forsook
> And died to kiss his *shadow* in the brook':

sometimes metaphorically; of paintings, e.g. *Lucrece*, l. 1457:—

> 'On this sad shadow Lucrece spends her eyes':—

that is, on the picture of Helen; of actors, 'The best in this kind are but shadows' (*A Midsummer Night's Dream*, V. i. 213); of a son as the reflexion of his father's likeness, 'Thy mother's son! Like enough, and thy father's shadow' (2 *Henry IV*., III. ii. 137). But he also uses the term, here and elsewhere in the *Sonnets*, with less, or with more, approximation to the metaphysic use from which it was borrowed:—

> 'Then thou, whose shadow shadows doth make bright,
> How would thy shadow's form form happy show
> To the clear day.'—xliii. 5-7.
>
> 'What is your substance, whereof are you made,
> That millions of strange shadows on you tend?
> Since every one hath, every one, one shade,

And you, but one, can every shadow lend....
The one doth shadow of your beauty show....'—liii. 1-4, 10.

'Why should poor Beauty indirectly seek
Roses of shadow, since his rose is true?'—lxvii. 7, 8.

'And you away
As with your shadow I with these did play.'—xcviii. 13, 14;

i.e. with the lily and the rose.

Drayton, whose Sonnets offer so many perplexing points of comparison with Shakespeare's, has one 'To the Shadow' (Amour 21, ed. 1594: Sonnet xiii., ed. 1619). He addresses the Shadow in it: since all else, 'letters, lines, the diamond, metals, paper and ink,' etc., are subject to change and decay. But not so the Shadow whilst the light endures:—

'O sweetest Shadow, how thou serv'st my turn!
Which still shalt be, as long as there is sun....
That everything whence shadow doth proceed,
May in his shadow, my Love's story read.'

Here the poetical use of this term borrowed from philosophy is anigmatical as anywhere in the *Sonnets*.

XXXVIII. 2. *breathe, that* Ewing, breath that Q.

XXXIX. 7, 8. *That by this separation I may give*
That due to thee which thou deserv'st alone:—

Separation justifies the poet's praise of the Friend, which was not justified whilst their dear love was undivided, ll. 5, 6; for to praise him then was for the Poet to praise himself, l. 3, since they were one, the Friend being all the better part of the Poet, l. 1.

12. *Which time and thoughts so sweetly dost deceive* Q.:—Malone substituted 'doth deceive,' and has been generally followed. The sense would then be:—'O absence, what a torment wouldst thou prove, were it not that thy sour leisure gave sweet leave to entertain the time with thoughts of love, *which* (i.e. love) *doth deceive time and thoughts so sweetly.*' Malone, to make sense, explains *deceive* = beguile. This may serve for *time*, but hardly for *thoughts*. I retain the Q. text, for the construction in the second person singular, which begins with the apostrophe to *absence* in l. 9, recurs, with *absence*

again as the subject, in l. 13, *And that thou teachest.* It is, therefore, I think, rightly maintained in l. 12 'dost deceive,' where the ellipsis of a 'thou' presents no difficulty, being immediately supplemented by 'And that thou' of l. 13. In ll. 1-8 the poet argues that, the Friend being the better part of himself, l. 2, his 'own self,' l. 3, he cannot praise him because thus he would be praising himself, l. 4. For this let them be divided, l. 5, that by *separation*, l. 7, he may give 'that due' = praise, to the Friend who alone is entitled to it, l. 8. Here follows the apostrophe to *absence*, or *separation*:—What a torment wouldst thou prove, were it not thy sour leisure gave *sweet* leave to entertain the *time with thoughts* of love, l. 11, *which* (i.e. which same) time and thoughts (of love) thou (absence) dost so sweetly (cf. 'sweet leave,' l. 9) *deceive*! *Deceive* here does not mean to 'mislead'—a sense which Malone repudiates for 'beguile'—but 'to cause to fail in fulfilment or realization' (*Imp. Dict.*), to defraud, defeat, undo, make vain. For kindred uses of this word cf. *Troilus and Cressida*, V. iii. 90:—

'Thou dost thyself and all our Troy deceive':—

where Cassandra tells Hector that if he neglects her warnings he will undo himself and his country; and *Macbeth*, I. ii. 63:—

'No more that thane of Cawdor shall deceive
Our bosom interest.'

Absence gives a sweet opportunity for passing away time with thoughts of love, but, though sweetly, still, by its very nature, it does defraud and make vain time and these thoughts of love.

XL. 1. *all*; all. Q.

5, 6. *Then if for my love, thou my love receivest* = If in place of my love for you, you accept the woman I love, l. 5 (cf. xlii. 9), I cannot blame thee, for thou usest my love, l. 6. Here the Poet plays on the two meanings of 'love' given in the preceding line.

7. *But yet be blam'd, if thou this selfe deceauest*:—Thus in Q. Modern editions have 'thyself' for 'this self.' Dowden explains:—'Yet you are to blame if you deceive yourself by an unlawful union while you refuse legal wedlock.' Tyler:—'Mr. W.H., it is suggested, may be committing a fraud on himself.'

This is no more satisfactory than the Q. text, which I retain since it will bear a meaning.

The Sonnet was evidently written at the same time and on the same theme—the theft of the Poet's mistress by his Friend—as the one which precedes and the two which follow it. 'This self' = the Poet, must, therefore, be interpreted in connexion with the identity of himself and the Friend stated in xxxix. 1-4, and re-stated in xlii. 13, 14:—

> 'But here's the joy, my friend and I are one,
> Sweet flattery, then she loves but me alone':—

a couplet which concludes the whole matter of the four. And note that, when the same matter is re-handled in the Second Series (cxxvii.-clii.), the same identity is urged:—

> 'And *my next self* thou harder hast engrossed.'—cxxxiii. 6.
> 'Think *all but one*, and *me* in that *one Will*.'—cxxxv. 14.

'This self' = the Poet, in l. 7 is distinguished from 'thy self' = the Friend of l. 8; and this distinction of two persons who are one self is in harmony with the conceit which runs through the four numbers. 'Deceivest,' l. 7, as in xxxix. 12 = defraud, undo.

8. *By wilful taste of what thy self refusest*:—This, the last line of the quatrain must be read in the light of the three lines which precede it. For here, in accordance with Shakespeare's usual practice, the quatrain is one, both as a measure of verse and in grammatical construction. 'Of what' refers back, grammatically, to 'my love' in l. 6. But there 'my love' is ambiguous (*supra*), holding implicitly the two meanings of the phrase exhibited in l. 5, where the first 'my love' = the Poet's love for the Friend, and the second = the Poet's mistress. The sense of the quatrain is:—Then if, in place of *my love* for you, you prefer *my mistress*, I cannot blame you, for each of these, in a sense, is *my love*, and that you are free to use, since mine is made yours and yours mine by the identity of our two selves in one. But yet you are to blame if, of the two, you defraud this, my self, by wilfully tasting *my love* = my mistress, while you, the other self, refuse *my love* = my love for you.

XLI. 8. *he have* Q., she have Malone (Tyrwhitt conj.):—The Q. reading is more subtile in sense and more musical in sound.

XLII. *That thou hast her,* etc.:—Closes Group C. Cf. cxxxiii.

9. *my love* = the Poet's mistress. Cf. the second *my love* in xl. 5.

12. *lay on me this cross*:—

> 'To him that bears the strong offence's cross.'—xxxiv. 12.
> 'A torment thrice three-fold thus to be crossed.'—cxxxiii. 8.

XLIII. 1. *When most I wink* = when most I close my eyes, viz. when I sleep. The word bears no meaning of brevity or alternation with opening:—

> 'To the perpetual wink for aye might put
> This ancient morsel.'—*Tempest*, II. i. 285.
> 'And I will wink; so shall the day seem night.'
> *Venus and Adonis*, 121.
>
> 'They are not blind, but they *wink*.'—Tillotson.

2. *unrespected* = unheeded, with a play on the first sense = unseen.

4. *And darkly bright, are bright in dark directed*:—'*Darkly bright*' echoes l. 1, repeating the statement that the Poet's eyes *see best when closed*. '*Are bright in dark directed*' is contrasted against l. 2, when the eyes, though seeing in the day, take no heed, for it states that when *in dark directed*, they *are bright*, viz. heedful. The sense is—'My eyes see best when they are most firmly closed, for all the day, though they view things, they do not heed them; but when I sleep they look on thee in dreams, and, seeing although closed, in the dark they heed that on which they are fixed.'

5. *Then thou, whose shadow shadows doth make bright*:—See Note on xxxvii. 10.

11. *thy Malone*, their Q.

XLIV. 11. *But that, so much of earth and water wrought*:—In the next Sonnet the Poet explains that of the four elements which compose him, Fire and Air are absent with his Friend, leaving him with but the heavier two, 'so much of earth and water wrought':—

> 'Does not our life consist of the four elements.'
> *Twelfth Night*, II. iii. 10.

> 'The dull elements of earth and water never appear in him.'
> *Henry V.*, III. vii. 23.

> 'I am fire and air; my other elements I give to baser life.'
> *Antony and Cleopatra*, V. ii. 292.

13. *naught*, naughts Q.

14. But *heavy tears, badges of either's woe*:—That is of earth and water, by their weight and moisture.

XLV. *The other two, slight air*, etc.:—Connected with the preceding sonnet.

4. *present-absent*, hyphened by Malone.

9. *life's*, *liues* Q.

12. *thy* Malone (Capell MS.), their Q.

XLVI. Conceits of the *eye* and *heart* are in the convention of Elizabethan sonneteering. Cf. Watson's *Tears of Fancie*, Sonnets 19, 20, 1593; Henry Constable's *Diana*, Third Decade, Sonnet 9; Sixth Decade, Sonnet 7, 1594; Drayton's *Idea*, 1619, Sonnet 33, a rewritten version of Amour 33, Edition 1594.

3. 8. 13. 14. *thy* Malone (Capell MS.), their Q.

9. *to side this title* Q.:—To adjudge this title to one or the other side, viz. to the eye or to the heart which are at mortal war, the eye being the defendant in an action brought by the heart to recover its title to the 'picture's sight' or 'fair appearance' of the Friend. Sewell (Ed. Q) suggested 'cide.'

10. *quest* = a jury of inquest, here 'impanneled' to try the case. Cf. *Richard III.*, I. iv. 189:—

> 'What lawful quest have given their verdict up
> Unto the frowning judge.'

12. *moiety* = portion.

XLVII. *Betwixt mine eye and heart,* etc.:—Connected with the preceding sonnet.

10. *art* Malone (Capell MS.), are Q.

XLVIII. *How careful was I*, etc.:—Connected with the preceding sonnet.

11. *Within the gentle closure of my breast*:—Cf. *Venus and Adonis*, l. 782:—

'Into the quiet closure of my breast.'

XLIX. 4. *advised respects*:—Cf. 'reasons of settled gravity,' l. 8; 'lawful reasons,' l. 12. The metaphor of this Sonnet is drawn from the law. The Poet imagines an *audit* at which the love of his Friend for him shall discharge all its obligations.

10. *desert*, desart Q.:—Rhyming with part.

11. *And this my hand against myself uprear*:—The Poet will give evidence on oath, lifting his hand, but against himself and in confirmation of the 'lawful reasons' urged by his Friend.

13. *thou hast the strength of law* = thou hast the law on thy side.

14. *Since why to love* = since why you should love me.

L. 3. *Doth teach that ease and that repose to say*:—The end of his journey, which the Poet seeks, makes the ease and repose natural to it, to say, 'Thus far the miles are measured from thy friend,' l. 4. First marked as a quotation by Malone.

LI. Connected with the preceding sonnet.

4. *posting*:—To post is to travel without pausing by the use of fresh horses taken at certain stations or posts, hence to travel rapidly. Cf. Milton:—

'And *post* o'er land and ocean without rest.'

6. *swift extremity* = 'the extreme of swiftness' (Tyler).

8. *In wingéd speed no motion shall I know*:—The whole expression of his line is hyperbolical. 'I shall perceive no progression in winged speed' is an extravagant development of the conditional, 'I should spur, though mounted on the wind,' in the preceding line.

10. *perfect'st* perfects Q.

11. *Shall neigh, no dull flesh in his fiery race*:—Shall neigh as a spirited horse neighs. A 'race' of colts was a sporting term of the time (Madden)—akin to our 'bevy' of quails, 'wisp' of snipe, 'herd' of deer.

14. *to go* = to walk step by step, or leisurely. Cf. *Two Gentlemen of Verona*, III. i. 388:—

'Thou must *run* to him; for thou hast staid so long that *going* will scarce serve the turn.'

> 'A foot...serveth to three purposes...to go, to runne, and to stand till...sometimes swift, sometimes slow...or peradventure steddy.'
>
> *Arte of English Poesie*, 1589.

Perhaps, also, with the second sense, *Give him leave to go* = 'dismiss him' (Tyler).

LII. 8. *carcanet*, carconet Q.

9. *So is the time that keeps you as my chest*:—Cf. lxv. 10:—

> 'Where, alack,
> Shall Time's best jewel from Time's *chest* lie hid?'

LIII. *What is your substance*, etc.:—Cf. Note on xxxvii. 10, Note V., and Introduction, p. cxviii.-cxxiii.

LIV. *O, how much more doth beauty*, etc.:—Connected with the preceding sonnet.

5. *Canker-blooms*. Dowden, Tyler, Bell explain, 'blossoms of the dog-rose,' following Malone:—'The *canker* is the *canker-rose* or *dog-rose*.' The rose and the canker are opposed in like manner in *Much Ado About Nothing*:—'I had rather be a *canker* in a hedge than a *rose* in his grace.' Steevens comments:—'Shakespeare had not yet begun to observe the productions of nature with accuracy, or his eyes would have convinced him that the cynorhodon is by no means of as deep a colour as the *rose*. But what has truth or nature to do with sonnets?' But, *pace* Steevens, the Poet here, as elsewhere in the *Sonnets*, meant a blossom eaten by canker. The image is used five times to illustrate one of the leading themes:—

> 'And loathsome canker lives in sweetest bud.'—xxxv. 5.
> 'For canker vice the sweetest buds doth love.'—lxx. 7.
> 'Which like a canker in the fragrant Rose.'—xcv. 2.
> 'In pride of all his growth
> A vengeful canker eat him up to death.'—xcix. 13.

Cf. also *Venus and Adonis*, 656:—

> 'This canker that eats up Love's tender spring.'
> 'In the sweetest bud
> The eating canker dwells....'
>
> *Two Gentlemen of Verona*, I. i. 43.

'The most forward bud
Is eaten by the canker ere it blow.'—*Ibid.*", I. i. 46.

'Some to kill cankers in the musk-rose buds.'
Midsummer Night's Dream, II. ii. 3.

'Now will canker sorrow eat my bud.'—*King John*, III. iv. 82.

'O, that this good blossom could be kept from cankers.'
2 *Henry IV.*, II. ii. 102.

'Hath not thy rose a canker, Somerset?'
1 *Henry VI.*, II. iv. 68.

'Full soon the canker death eats up that plant.'
Romeo and Juliet, II. iii. 30.

So far as I know, 'canker' is used by Shakespeare for the 'dog-rose' or wild briar only twice (*Much Ado About Nothing*, I. iii. 28 and 1 *Henry IV.*, I. iii. 176).

14. *vade*. Cf. *Passionate Pilgrim*:—

'Sweet rose, fair flower, untimely pluck'd, soon *vaded*.'

14. *my*, Malone (Capell MS.); by Q.

LV. *Not marble, nor the gilded*, etc.:—Tyler has traced a remarkable similarity between this Sonnet and a passage in Meres' *Palladis Tamia*, registered September 7, 1598. See Note III. (4).

1. *monuments* Malone, monument Q.

9. *enmity*, emnity Q.

13. *Till the judgment that yourself arise*:—'Till the decree of the judgment-day that you arise from the dead.'—Dowden. Cf. 'the ending doom' of l. 12.

LVI. *Sweet love, renew thy force*, etc.:—Opens Group D (lvi.-lxxiv.). This Sonnet seems written in immediate anticipation of an absence voluntarily imposed by the Friend.

9-12. The image is obscure. Perhaps it contains an allusion to the story of *Hero and Leander*. Marlowe's two sestiads were published in 1598.

9. *Int rim*, Intrim Q.

13. *Or*, Malone, suggested to him by Tyrwhitt; As Q.; Else, Palgrave.

LVII. 5. *world-without-end*, hyphened by Ewing (Capell MS). Dowden explains:—'The tedious hour that seems as if it would never end.' So, *Love's Labour's Lost*, V. ii. 799:—

'A time methinks, too short
To make a world-without-end bargain in.'

13. *Will*, thus in Q. Cf. cxxxv., cxxxvi., cxliii.

LVIII. 6. *Th' imprison'd absence of your liberty* = the absence which, arising out of your liberty, is as imprisonment to me.

7. *And patience, tame to sufferance, bide each check*, Ewing; 'And patience tame, to sufferance bide each check, Q.

LIX. *If there be nothing new,* etc.:—See Introduction, p. cxxvi.

6. *hundred*, hundreth Q.

8. *character*, carrecter Q.

11. *whe'r*, where Q.; '*whether* we are mended, or *where* better they.' Cf. *Venus and Adonis*, 304:—

'And *where* he runne, or flie, they know not *whether*.'

LX. 1. *pebbled*, pibled Q.

5. *Nativity, once in the main of light*. Dowden explains:—'The entrance of a child into the world at birth is an entrance into the main or ocean of light; the image is suggested by l. 1, where our minutes are compared to waves.' *Main* may possibly echo the sea imagery of the first quatrain, but this and the two next lines have primarily and essentially an astrological significance. *Nativity* is a term of Astrology denoting the moment of a child's birth in relation to the scheme or figure of the heavens, particularly of the Twelve Houses, at that moment, and it is employed by Shakespeare, almost invariably, with this connotation:—

'My nativity was under Ursa Major.'—*Lear*, I. ii. 140.

'Thou hast as chiding a nativity
As fire, air, water, earth, and heaven can make,
To herald thee from the womb.'—*Pericles*, III. i. 32.

'At my nativity
The front of heaven was full of fiery shapes.'
1 *Henry IV.*, III. i. 13.

The 'crooked eclipses' of l. 7 derive also from astrology:—

> 'The mortal Moon hath her eclipse endured
> And the sad Augurs mock their own presage.'
> Sonnet cvii. 5, 6.

'Crooked' = malign. Cf. *Two Gentlemen of Verona*, IV. i. 22:—

> 'If crooked Fortune had not thwarted me';

and 'crooked malice,' *Henry VIII*, V. iii. 44.

Shakespeare uses the word 'main' elsewhere for the principal portion or embodiment of that which follows it in the genitive case:—'our main of power' (*Troilus and Cressida*, II. iii. 273); 'the main of Poland' (*Hamlet*, IV. iv. 15); and *Merchant of Venice*, V. i. 97:—

> 'As doth an inland brook
> Into the main of waters.'

Main indeed came thus to mean the ocean as distinguished from lesser waters, and the 'mainland' as distinguished from islands:—'In 1589 we turned challengers, and invaded the *main* of Spain.'—Bacon. And here, though possibly with a secondary echo of the sea-image from the first quatrain, *main of light* means the hollow sphere of the universe filled with light as conceived in Shakespeare's day. Life beginning at a point in time within the shining sphere of the Heavens, whose aspect is charged with its fate, crawls to maturity only to be thwarted by their fateful powers, and time despoils the worth of his gift.

13. *times in hope* = 'future times,' Dowden.

LXI. 3. *broken*:—An assonantal rhyme with 'open,' l. 1. Cf. cxx. 9-11, '...remembred...tendred.'

4. *While shadows like to thee do mock my sight*:—Cf. xliii. 11, 12:—

> 'When in dead night thy fair imperfect shade
> Through heavy sleep on sightless eyes doth stay!'

8. *tenure* Q.; tenour Malone (Capell MS.):—Cf. *Lucrece*, 1310.

LXII. 7, 8:—And my definition of my worth is such that, according to it, I excel all other men in all kiwis of worth.

10. *Beated*:—'The regular participle, from the verb *to beat*, may be right. We had in a former sonnet "weather-beaten

face." In *King Henry V.* we find *casted*, and in *Macbeth thrusted.*'—Malone. He also suggests 'bated.' Cf. *Merchant of Venice*, III. iii. 32:—

> 'These griefs and losses have so *bated* me,
> That I shall hardly spare a pound of flesh
> To-morrow.'

Dowden, retaining 'beated,' points out a possible connexion between 'bated,' from 'to bate,' a process of leather-dressing, and 'tann'd,' 'tand,' in Q.

11, 12. *self-love...self-loving*, hyphened by Gildon.

13, 14. See Introduction, p. cxviii.

LXIII. 2. *crush'd*, chrusht Q.

LXIV. 10. *Or state itself confounded to decay*:—'State' = condition in the abstract; that which is cognised in all things, conceived by the mind only inasmuch as they are conditioned. Cf. cxxiv. 1:—

> 'If my dear love were but the child of state,'

where the Poet argues that his love is unconditioned and eternal.

13. *This thought is as a death, which*:—Which = 'inasmuch as it' cannot choose, etc.

LXV. 6. *wrackful*, Ewing substituted wreckfull. Cf. cxxvi. 5:—

> 'Nature, Sovereign mistress over wrack';

and *Macbeth*, V. v. 51:—

> 'Blow, wind! come, wrack!
> At least we'll die with harness on our back.'

10. *Shall Time's best jewel from Time's cheat lie hid*:—Theobald suggested 'Time's quest.' But cf. lii. 9:—

> 'So is the time that keeps you as my chest.'

12. *of beauty* Malone, '*or beautie*' Q., 'o'er beauty' Capell MS., 'on beauty' Gildon.

LXVI. *Tired with all these*, etc.:—In this Sonnet only some of the personifications have capitals in Q.: Nothing, Folly (Doctor-like), Truth, Simplicitie, Captaine ill. I follow the Kelmscott in generalising the practice.

8. *disabled*; dishabited, Bayne conj. (*Notes and Queries*, 1887); discomforted, Anon. conj. (*Ibid.*).

LXVII. 4. *lace*:—I.e. embellish itself. So, in *Romeo and Juliet*, III. v. 8:—

> 'What envious streaks
> Do *lace* the severing clouds.'—Steevens.

The ornament was called lace from its likeness to netting, from French *lacs*, O. Fr. *laz*, Latin *laqueus*, originally a noose, and thus toils or a *net* used in hunting, into which the stag or boar was driven:—

> 'Comment Vulcanus espia
> Sa femme, et moult fort la lia
> Dun *laz* avec Marz, ce me semble
> Quant couchiés les trouva ensemble.'
> *Roman de la Rose*, ll. 14445-49.

'That day that I was tangled in the lace.'—Surrey.

Lace in the sixteenth century was, often, of gold or silver threads applied in a large diagonal pattern, sometimes with a pearl at each intersection, upon a silk or satin foundation. It appears in many portraits, notably in those of Henry viii. and Francois I. The Poet, when he uses the verb 'to lace,' had this embellishment in his mind rather than what we now call lace:—

> 'Cloth o' gold, and cuts, and *laced* with silver,
> Set with pearls.'—*Much Ado About Nothing*, III. iv. 20.

> 'Here lay Duncan
> His silver skin laced with his golden blood.'
> *Macbeth*, II. iii. 118.

The ornaments on an English officer's tunic are still called 'gold lace.'

5-8. *false-painting...Roses of shadow, since his Rose is true.* An allusion, perhaps primarily, to the imitation of the Friend's beauty by the use of cosmetics among his companions, but, as I submit, also and with deeper intention, to the 'false art' of other 'eternizers,' viz. the Rival Poets. See Introduction, pp. cxxiv.-cxxvi. Cf. xxi. 1-3, etc.:—

> 'So is it not with me as with that Muse
> Stirr'd by a painted beauty to his verse
> Who heaven itself for ornament doth use,' etc.

'To shew false Art what beauty was of yore.'—lxviii. 14.

'Yet when they have devized
What strainéd touches Rhetoric can lend,
Thou truly fair wert truly sympathized
In true plain words by thy true-telling friend;
And their gross *painting* might be better used
Where cheeks need blood; in thee it is abused.'—lxxxii. 9-14.

'I never saw that you did *painting* need,
And therefore to your fair no *painting* sea.'—lxxxiii. 1, 2.

'Who is it that says most? which can say more
Than this rich praise, that you alone are you?...' lxxxiv., 1, 2.

'My tongue-tied Muse in manners holds her still,
While comments of your praise, richly compiled,
Reserve their character with golden quill
And precious phrase by all the Muses filed.'—lxxxv. 1-4.

Note that in *Love's Labour's Lost* our poet compares 'praise' to 'painting' (Act II. i. 13, 14):—

'My beauty, though but mean,
Needs not the *painted* flourish of your praise';

and in Act IV. iii. he runs on from this illustration:—

'Lend me the flourish of all gentle thoughts,—
Fie, *painted* rhetoric! O, she needs it not....'

to a direct allusion to the use of cosmetics:—

'O, if in black my lady's brows be deck'd,
It mourns that *painting* and usurping hair
Should ravish doters with a false aspect.'

That is to say, he uses the term *painting* precisely with that double sense which I attribute to it here.

6. *dead seeing* = dead semblance.

7. *Beauty*:—Thus with a capital in the Kelmscott. I retain the capital here, and in 'Nature' (Cambridge), l. 9, believing that poor Beauty is, not 'beauty indifferent and imperfect' (Tyler), but abstract Beauty personified and called 'poor,' as abstract Nature personified is stated to be 'beggar'd,' and with 'no exchequer now but his,' ll. 10, 11.

12. *proud of many*:—Proud of the multiplicity of life with an appearance of beauty, possesses true beauty only in him.

LXVIII. 1. *map*:—Cf. *Richard II*., V. i. 12.:—'Thou map of honour.' 'In thy face I see The map of honour.'—2 *Henry VI*., III. i. 203. 'Thou map of woe.'—*Titus Andronicus*, III. ii. 12. Illustrations are frequently drawn from a 'map' by Elizabethan writers, owing to the interest aroused by voyages to the New World Cf. *Twelfth Night*, III. ii. 85:—

'He does smile his face into more lines than is in the new map with the augmentation of the Indies.'

> 'Age rules my lines with wrinkles in my face;
> Where, in the Map of all my Misery.'
> Drayton, *Idea*, xliv. (1619, first published 1599).

3. *borne*, borne Q.:—Modern spelling restricts the Poet's play on this word:—he employs it to mean 'borne,' but also to suggest 'born,' with an echo of 'lived and died' in the preceding line.

5. *golden tresses*. Cf. Surrey:—

> 'Her golden tresses cladde alway with blacke.'

7. *second*, scond Q.

10. *Without all ornament*:—Cf. Bassanio's long tirade against 'ornament' (*Merchant of Venice*, III. iii. 73-100):—

> 'So may the outward shows be least themselves:
> The world is still deceived with ornament,' etc.

LXIX. 3. *due* Tyrwhitt, end Q.:—'The letters that compose the word due were probably transposed at the press, and the *u* inverted.'

4. *commend*, Commend Q.

5. *Thy* Malone, 1780 (Capell MS.); Their Q.

14. *soil*, solye Q.:—'As the verb "to soil" is not uncommon in old English, meaning "to solve," as, for example: "This question could not one of theim soile" (Udal's *Erasmus*, Luke, fol. 154 *b*), so the substantive "soil" may be used in the sense of "solution." The play upon words thus suggested is in the author's manner.'—*Cambridge*. Cf. 'Assoil' for 'absolve,' meaning (1) to solve, 'to *assoil* this seeming difficulty' (Waterland); (2) to pronounce absolution:—

'To some bishop we will wend,
Of all the sins that we have done,
To be *assoiled* at his hand.'—*Percy Reliques*.

'The solve,' Malone; 'the sole,' Steevens; 'the foil,' Caldecott.

LXX. 6. *Thy*, Their Q. *Woo'd of Time*, woo'd of time Q. Tyler refers this to 'slander' in l. 5.:—'Slander coming under the soothing influence of time will show thy worth to be greater.' Dowden, referring the phrase to the Friend, accepts Steevens' argument that 'of time' = 'of the times,' giving Steevens' quotation from Ben Jonson's *Every Man out of his Humour*, 'O, how I hate the monstrousness of time.' It should, however, be noted that 'Asper' in the same prologue has, 'I'll strip the ragged follies of the Time.... They shall see the Time's deformity.... Do not I know the Time's condition?' I suggest that 'time' here, as elsewhere in *The Sonnets* = not 'the time' or 'the times' but, 'Time,' personified. Cf. cxvii. 6, 'And given to Time your own dear-purchas'd right,' and the Note on that line, in which the remaining examples are collected. The sense is:—'If only you be virtuous, slander doth but approve your worth the greater, since you are woo'd by Time (= wooed and not yet won by Time, an object still for Time's solicitation), for you are in your "pure unstained prime," and "canker-vice loves the sweetest buds."' Malone's correspondent 'C.' (probably Capell) suggested 'wood oftime' (1780) and 'wood of time' (1790), referring the last to slander and explaining 'wood' = mad. Other conjectures have been 'void of crime,' Malone (withdrawn); 'weigh'd of time,' Delius; 'woo'd of crime,' Staunton.

8. *unstainéd*, unstayined Q.

10-12. *...charged...enlarged*, charg'd...inlarged Q. Enlarged = let loose. In Ireland the stag to be hunted is still said to be enlarged when let out of its cart.

LXXI. 4. *vilest* Gildon, vildest Q.

LXXII. 9. *false*, falce Q.

12. *And live no more to shame nor me nor you*. Here, as else-where, the poet uses terms of moral censure when delivering an artistic judgment. The next two lines prove that the 'shame'

is for the *verses* he brings forth. Thus 'of me untrue,' l. 10, must mean, at least in part:—of me whose poetry is imperfect. Unless, indeed, untrue be an adverb = untruly and qualifying 'speak well.'

LXXIII. 4. *Bare ruin'd*, edition 1640; Bare rn'wd Q.:—This most beautiful image was nearer and more vivid when many great abbeys, opened to the weather within the memory of men living, were beginning to be ruins ere they were forgotten as 'chantries, where the sad and solemn priests sing.'

LXXIV. *But be contented*, etc.:—Closes Group D.

1. *contented: when* Malone, contented when Q.

3. *some interest* = some revenue of fame falling in, year by year, after my death. Thus tears are 'sorrow's interest' (*Lucrece*, 1797, and Sonnet xxxi. 7).

8. *My spirit is thine, the better part of me*:—Cf. Drayton's *Idea*, xliv. (1619, first published 1599):

> 'Ensuing Ages yet my Rhymes shall cherish
> Where I entombed my *better part* shall save.'

11. *The coward conquest of a wretch's knife*:—Some discover a reference here to an actual wound suffered by the poet. But it is, I think, metaphorical: the destruction of the body by death and its subsequent corruption is a squalid tragedy.

12. *rememberéd* Sewell, remembred Q. There is little authority for the emendation. The verb is, almost invariably, *remembre* in the writings of Shakespeare and his contemporaries. If so, the line is defective; cf. lxvi. 8, 'disabled.'

13, 14. *The worth of that* (= the body) *is that which it contains* (= the spirit). *And that is this* (= the poet's verse).

LXXV. 2. *sweet-season'd*, hyphened by Malone. Seasoned = seasonable.

3. *peace of you* = 'peace of possessing your love,' in antithesis to 'strife.'

6. *Doubting the filching age will steal his treasure.*

The note struck here, and in the nut sonnet, with its reminiscence of xxxii., seems prelusive to Group E, lxxviii.-

lxxxvi. But that the theme is dropped in lxxvii., lxxxv. and lxxvi. might be included in that Group.

LXXVI. 3, 4. *Why with the time do I not glance aside*
To new-found methods and to compounds strange?

Cf. xxxii. 4-8:—

'These poor rude lines of thy deceaséd Lover:
Compare them with the bett'ring of the time,
And though they be outstripp'd by every pen,
Reserve them for my love, not for their rhyme,
Exceeded by the height of happier men';

and cxxv. 5-7:—

'Have I not seen dwellers on form and favour
Lose all, and more, by paying too much rent
For *compound sweet*.'

7. *tell* Malone (Capell MS.), fel. Q. *f* and *t* are very similar in the type (1609). *Spell* Nicholson, conj.

LXXVII. *Thy glass will show thee,* etc.:—'Probably this sonnet was designed to accompany a present of a book consisting of blank paper.'—Steevens. 'This conjecture seems to me very probable. We learn from the 122nd Sonnet that Shakespeare received a *table-book* from his friend.'—Malone. Dowden conjectures that the Poet began a new MS. with Sonnet lxxv., and 'knowing that his Friend was favouring a rival,' ceased writing after this sonnet, inviting his Friend to fill up the blank pages. Tyler rejects this view. Whether the book was wholly, or partially blank, the sense is clear:—viz., that the Friend is to set down the reflections suggested by his glass and dial, on the blank pages of a book sent him by the Poet: l. 13, 'These offices, so oft as thou wilt look,' i.e. in your glass or at your dial; l. 14, 'Shall profit thee and much enrich thy book.'

1. *wear* Sewell, were Q.

2. *minutes*, mynuits Q.

3. *The*, These (Capell MS.) and Malone conj.

10. *blanks* Theobald, blacks Q.

13, 14. Ewing's edition, by a strange error, substituted the final couplet of cviii.

LXXVIII. *So oft have I invoked thee*, etc.:—Opens Group E, lxxviii.-lxxxvi.; cf. xxxii.

3. *As every* Alien *pen hath got my use* = not my manner of writing or style, but my habit of praising you in verse. Note that more Rival Poets than one are referred to:—l. 11, 'In others' works thou dost but mend the style.'

6. *fly*, flie Q.:—Dowden states, 'The Quarto has *flee*.' This, according to *Cambridge*, is true of the copy in the Bridgewater Library.

7. *learned's,* learneds Q.

10. *born*, borne Q.

LXXIX 4. '*another place*':—some one Rival is singled out.

LXXX. 7. *saucy* Gildon, sawsie Q.

11. *wreck'd*, wrackt Q.

LXXXI. 9-14. The present Countess of Pembroke states (*Pall Mall Magazine*, October 1897) that these lines, with 'ever' for 'even' in l. 14, are found written in 'seventeenth-century character on an old parchment, pasted on the back of a panel bearing a small painting of William, third Earl of Pembroke, and beneath them the following words:—

"William, Earl Pembroke, died suddenly April 10, 1630. When his body was opened in order to be embalmed, he was observed (on the incision being made) *to lift up his hand*. This circumstance may be depended upon as fact, having been related by a member of the family, and was considered by the faculty to afford strong presumptive evidence that the distemper of which he died was apoplexy."'

I am indebted to Lord Pembroke for the information that a letter, now unfortunately mislaid, existed at Wilton from Lady Pembroke to her son, the third Earl, telling him to bring James I. over from Salisbury to witness a representation of *As You Like It*. The letter contained the words:—'We have the man Shakespeare with us.' Since the lock of Queen Elizabeth's hair, to be seen at Wilton, was once similarly mislaid, it is to be hoped that this letter may also be brought to light. Lord Pembroke has no doubt but that Shakespeare was often at Wilton, and he adds that a good statue of him stands in Holbein's Porch, indicating that the tradition of his connexion with Wilton is of old standing. There is at Wilton a copy of *Poems of Lord Pembroke* (the 3rd Earl) and *Sir Benjamin Rudyard.*

13. *pen*, Pen in Q. = poetry or style. See Note V.

14. *Where breath most breathes, even in the mouths of men*:—In Shakespeare's day the *breath* was all but identified with the spirit, and the mouth, consequently, is held in special honour by platonic writers. In Hoby's *Courtyer*, iv. (1561), kissing is defended on the ground of the sanctity attaching to the mouth as the gateway of the soul.

LXXXII. 3. *dedicated words*:—'This may only mean *devoted words,* but probably has reference to the words of some dedication prefixed to a book.'—Dowden. Tyler agrees. 'Dedicate' is a word often used by Shakespeare, and always in its ordinary sense. It bears it here, but refers, as I think, to the body of the book—the praises dedicated to their object—and not merely to the prefixed dedication.

5-14; *Thou art as fair*, etc.:—Cf. xxi., xxxii., lxvii., lxviii., lxxv., lxxvi., the whole of this Group, lxxviii.-lxxxi., and cxxv.

8. *time-bettering*, hyphened by Gildon.

11. *sympathized*, matched with congruity, harmonised. Cf. *Love's Labour's Lost*, III. i. 52:—

> *Arm.* 'Fetch hither the swain; he must carry me a letter.
> *Moth.* A message well sympathized; a horse to be ambassador for an ass.'

> 'True sorrow then is feelingly sufficed
> When with like semblance it is sympathized.'
> —*Lucrece*, 1113.

12. *true-telling*:—Hyphened by Sewell (ed. 1).

LXXXIII. 1, 2. *painting* = high-flown poetical praise. Cf. lxxxv. 3, 4:—

> 'Comments of your praise, richly compiled,
> And precious phrase by all the Muses filed.'

2. *your fair* = your beauty. Cf. *Venus and Adonis*, 1086:—

> 'Sun and sharp air
> Lurk'd like two thieves, to rob him of his fair.'

> 'Neither in inward worth nor outward fair.'—Sonnet xvi. 11.

7. *modern* = 'common' or 'trite,' Malone. But the ordinary sense is intended. In the *Sonnets* the poet constantly contrasts Modernity unfavourably with Antiquity. Cf. lix.:—

> 'Show me your image in some antique book.
>
> 'In him those holy antique hours are seen.'—lxviii.
>
> 'I see their antique pen would have expresséd
> Even such beauty as you master now.'—cvi.
>
> 'But makes antiquity for aye his page.—cviii.

LXXXIV. 1, 2. ...*most?...you?* pointed by Malone;...most, ...you, Q.

4. *grew.* grew? Staunton conj. (Alten, 1874). But the sense is that 'the store,' l. 3 = the whole wealth of Beauty, which should show your parallel, is enclosed in you.

5. *pen*, Pen Q. = Poet.

8. *story*, Q. story, Cambridge (1866). Cambridge (1893) reverts to the punctuation of the Quarto.

14. *Being fond on praise, which makes your praises worse*:—Cf. *A Midsummer Night's Dream*, II. i. 226:—

> 'That he may prove
> More fond *on* her than she upon her love.'

Tyler explains, 'By which "your praise," the praise due to you, is really lessened and deteriorated.' But, in view of the general contention of the Group—that 'precious phrase by all the Muses filed' (lxxxv. 4) is an injury to the Truth of the Friend's Beauty—may it not mean that the Friend, by his indiscriminate patronage of 'eternizers,' encourages the production of meretricious verse?

LXXXV. 3. *Reserve their character*:—The *u*, for *v*, in Reserve is inverted in Q. The phrase has been generally considered unintelligible. Reserve = preserve, Malone. 'But what does preserve their character mean?'—Dowden. Tyler accepts an anon. conj. 'rehearse' for 'reserve,' and suggests 'thy' for 'their,' explaining 'character' = 'face.' But in view of the general drift of the Group the meaning is not obscure. *Reserve their character* = preserve or treasure up their style by labouring it preciously, with a secondary suggestion of fastidious restraint.

The sense goes on, 'with golden quill and precious phrase by all the Muses filed,' and, l. 8, 'In polish'd form of well-refinéd pen': cf. the '*strained touches*' of *Rhetoric* (lxxxii.), the *painting* of lxxxii. and lxxxiii.; also, the 'false painting' of lxvii. 5, and *false Art* of lxviii. Reserve is often used by Shakespeare for *preserve*. Cf. *Pericles*, IV. i. 40:—'reserve that excellent complexion.' That *character* = style, is confirmed by its being printed with a capital in Q. See Note V., and cf. Pen; thus in Q., lxxxi. 13, and lxxxiv. 5.

14. *speaking in effect*, i.e. in 'love to you,' l. 11.

LXXXVI. 2. (*all-too-precious*), (all-to-precious) Q. The Cambridge omits the hyphens in citing Q. and attributes them to Ewing. As they are in Q. I retain them.

7. *compeers*, compiers Q. This, and the whole passage 5-10, shows that the Rival boasted of inspiration from the mighty dead. See Note IV. on Rival Poets.

LXXXVII. *Farewell! thou art too dear*, etc.:—Opens Group F., lxxxvii.-xcvi.

4. *determinate* = expired. 'The term is used in legal conveyancing' (Malone). Cf. other technical terms of law in this Sonnet: charter, bonds, granting, patent (l. 8) = a grant by letters patent.

11. *misprision*, mistaking, from O. Fr. *mesprise*, a mistake; *mesprendre*, to mistake. Cf. *Much Ado About Nothing*, IV. i. 187:—

> *Friar*. 'There is some strange *misprision* in the princes
> *Bene*. ...if their wisdoms be *misled* in this...'

The Guide into Tongues (1617) gives:—'*Misprision* signifieth in our Common Law, neglect, or negligence, or oversight. As for example Misprision of Treason, is a neglect, or light account shewed of treason committed, by not revealing it when we know it to be committed. Misprision signifieth also a mistaking.'

LXXXVIII. 1. *disposed*, dispode Q.

8. *shaft*, shall Q.

12. *double-vantage*:—Hyphened by Malone.

LXXXIX. 3. See Note on xxxvii. 9.

7. *disgrace*: disgrace, Q.

8. *I will acquaintance strangle and look strange*. Cf. Drayton, *Idea*, lxi. (first published 1619):—

'And when we meet at any time again
Be it not seen in either of our brows
That we one jot of former love retain.'

XC. 4. *after-loss*:—Hyphened by Sewell.

13. *strains* = kinds, with the sense, also, of comparative degrees (O. Eng. streen = stock, race). Cf. *The fine strains of honour* (Coriolanus, V. iii. 149); *Or swell my thought to any strain of pride* (2 *Henry IV*., IV. v. 171). The poet, perhaps, plays here, as often, on the identity of this word with the other *strain* (O. Fr. *estraindre* = to strain), suggesting the *strain* imposed by woes on the sufferer. Tyler holds that it may also involve 'the idea of extension or lengthening.'

XCI. 2. *bodies'*, bodies Q., body's Cambridge, Tyler, Dowden. But cf. l. 3, *garments*.

4. Hawkes...Hounds...Horse, all with capitals in Q. See Note V. on the Typography of Quarto 1609. '*Horse*. Probably the plural meaning *horses*.'—Dowden. He cites:—

'Another tell him of his hounds and horse.'
Taming of the Shrew, Induction.

But *horse* is not merely a plural. The capitals show that all three words are generalised, and that they stand for the establishments and pursuits of Hawking, Hunting, and the Manege. We still write of a man 'taking the Hounds,' and of the 'Master of the Horse.'

9. *better*, bitter Q.

11. Hawkes...Horses in Q.

XCII. 13. *what's*, whats Q.

XCIII. 8. *strange*. Q.; strange, Cambridge. I retain the punctuation of Q. in the first two quatrains, substituting (—) for (,) after 'change,' l. 6.

13. *Eve's*, Eaves Q.:—See Note V. on the Typography of the Quarto 1609.

XCIV. *They that have power to hurt*, etc.:—This Sonnet is a limb of the continuous argument embodied in Group F. (lxxxvii.-xcvi.), and, so read, is not obscure. The Friend, as described in the preceding number, has a face of which the beauty is a constant expression of love, so that, whatever his thoughts may be, his looks can tell only of sweetness. But this beauty becomes the type of temptation if it be not a true index of virtue. Continuing, in xciv. the Poet develops the ambiguity of the theme. He first puts the case of those who, with an outward beauty that is the engine of temptation, are themselves cold and not easily tempted. They are the owners and controllers of their beauty; but, putting the alternative case, those whose beauty, not only tempts but also, leads them into temptation, are but dispensers of it. As an enem of the first the Poet takes a flower which is sweet to the world around it, although it blossoms and dies to itself, self-contained and unregarding: as an emblem of the second, such a flower if it be infected with a canker. Then it is more noisome than a weed.

In the next Sonnet the Poet, dwelling on the 'ill reports' that affect the Friend's good name, notes that his beauty can still turn censure into 'a kind of praise,' but warns him not to abuse this privilege. And in the next, after elaborating this theme of the privilege of beauty, he reverts to the theme, initiated in xciii., of the Friend's changeless Mask of Beauty, and implores him not to abuse the advantage which it confers.

14. *Lilies that fester smell far worse than weeds*:—This line occurs in *King Edward III.*, a play first printed in 1596. See Note III. on the Date of the Sonnets' Composition.

XCVI. 9, 10. Lambs...Wolfe...Lambe in Q. They are types used as in a fable. See Note V. on the Typography of the Quarto. Printed without capitals, the question might well be addressed to any farmer.

11. *mightst*, mighst Q.

13-14. The couplet is repeated from xxxvi.

XCVII. *How like a Winter hath my absence been*, etc.—The break between this and the preceding sonnet seems the most marked in the First Series.

1. Winter in Q.

5. *this time removed* = this time of absence or seclusion. Cf. *Measure for Measure*, I. iii. 8:—

'How I have ever loved the life *removed*.'

6. *The*, And Capell MS., Then Isaac conj.

teeming = pregnant. Cf. 'The childing autumn' (*Midsummer Night's Dream*, II. i. 111).

7. *the prime* = Spring (Dowden), or, rather, the climax of Nature's activity (in the Spring). Cf. *As You Like It*, V. iii. 33:—

'For love is crowned with the *prime*
In spring time.'

'Like little frosts that sometime threat the spring,
To add a more rejoicing to the *prime*.'—*Lucrece*, 331-32.

10. *hope of orphans*, Orphans Q. = 'hope of leaving posthumous offspring' (Tyler).

XCVIII. *From you have I been absent in the spring*, etc.:— The last Sonnet was evidently written after an absence in late summer and autumn; this one after an absence in April. See Note III. on the Date of the Sonnets' Composition.

1-4. *...spring...trim...thing...him*:—The assonance between the two rhyme-sounds, usually a blemish, is here an effect of art. The quick treble repetition of short *i*-sounds seems to have suggested Spring to the Elizabethans. Cf. *As You Like It*, V. iii.:—

'In the spring time, the only pretty ring time,
When birds do sing, hey ding a ding, ding:
Sweet lovers love the spring.'

'Spring, the sweet spring, is the year's pleasant king;
Then blooms each thing, then maids dance in a ring,
Cold doth not sting, the pretty birds do sing,
Cuckoo, jug jug, pu we, to witta woo.'
Thomas Nash's *Summer's Last Will and Testament*, 1600.

2. *proud-pied* = 'gorgeously variegated' (Schmidt). Cf. *Love's Labour's Lost*, V. ii. 904:—

'Daisies pied and violets blue.'

4. *Heavy Saturn, Saturne in* Q.:—See Note V. on Typography of the Quarto. The planet Saturn 'is melancholy...author of solitariness...in labour patient, in arguing or disputing grave... in all manner of actions austere.'—*An Introduction to Astrology by William Lilly*, 1647.

9-10. *Lily's* (Lillies Q.)...Rose in Q.:—(See Note V. on Typography.)

12-14. *pattern...shadow*:—See Note on xxxvii. 10, and Introduction, pp. cxviii.-cxxiii.

XCIX. *The forward violet,* etc.:—Connected with the preceding Sonnet.

7. *And buds of marjoram had stol'n thy hair*:—Dowden cites Suckling's *Tragedy of Brennoralt*, IV. i.:—

'Hair curling, and cover'd like buds of marjoram;
Part tied in negligence, part loosely flowing':—

and adds Mr. Hart's suggestion 'that the marjoram has stolen, not colour but *perfume* from the young man's hair.' *The Guide into Tongues* quotes Gerard:—'plant a est odorata tota,' and the clean, aromatic scent of this sweet-herb counted, no doubt, for something in suggesting the simile, but the quotation from Suckling gives the more direct clue. The illustration is, primarily, from the fresh, close-leaved spike of marjoram with the crisp bunch of little buds at its summit. Cf. *Two Noble Kinsmen*:—

'His head's yellow,
Hard hayr'd, and curl'd, thicke twind, like ivy-tops,
Not to undoe with thunder....'

9. *one*, our Q.

13. *canker*:—See Note, liv. 5.

These flower-sonnets are in a mode imitated from Petrarch, which overran Europe in the sixteenth century. The Pleïade worked it vigorously and then attacked it, as Shakespeare attacks it in xxi., and again in cxxx. Du Bellay, who attacked it fifty years earlier:—

'Noz bons Ayeulx, qui cest art demenoient,
Pour en parler, Pétrarque n'apprenoient,
Ains franchement leur Dame entretenoient

Sans fard, ou couverture
Mais aussi tost qu'Amour s'est faict sçavant.'

Why, then:—

'De voz beautez, ce n'est que tout fin or,
Perles, crystal, marbre, et ivoyre encor,
Et tout l'honneur de l'Indique thresor,
Fleurs, lis, œillets, et roses':—

is equally inconsistent. Neither the Pleïade nor the Elizabethans could altogether forswear 'Enam'ling with pied flowers their thoughts of gold' (Sidney).

C. *Where art thou, Muse, that thou forget'st so long*:—Opens Group G., c.-cxxv. See Introduction, pp. cxiii.-cxv., cxxvii.-cxxx.

9. *resty*, restive Malone; adopted by Tyler, with the gloss: '*restive* may be taken here as equivalent to *uneasy*.' But the sense is exactly opposite. 'Resty' or 'restive' was a term of manege applied to a horse exhibiting the vice now called 'jibbing.' In a book by 'maister Blundevill of Newton Flatman, in Norffolke' (1597), the following 'correction to be used against restiveness' is recommended:—'Let a footman stand behind you with a shrewd cat tied at the one end of a long pole, with her bellie upward, so that she may have hir mouth and claws at libertie; and when your horse doth staie or goe backward let him thrust the cat between his thighs, sometimes by the rump...and let the footman and all the standers-by threaten the horse with a terrible noise, and you shall see it will make him goe as you will have him; and on so doing be ready to make much of him. Also the shrill crie of a hedgehog being strait tied by the foot under the horse's tail is a reminder of like force, which was proved by maister Vincentio Respino, a Neapolitan, who corrected by this means an old *restive* horse of the King's in such sort, as he had much ado afterwards to keep him from the contrarie vice of running away.'—*Spectator*, 15th August 1891.

CI. 6-8. '*Truth needs no colour*, etc.:—First printed as a quotation by Malone.

6. '*Truth needs no colour with his colour fix'd*:—*Fix* is here a term of paintings = to congeal, to deprive of volatility. Cf. *Winter's Tale*, V. iii. 47:—

> 'The statue is but newly fix'd, the colour's
> Not dry....'

The Poet plays on the word *colour*, which, in the first instance, means defence, extenuation. Cf. 1 *Henry VI.*, II. iv. 43:—

> 'I ove no *colours*, and without all *colour*
> Of base insinuating flattery
> I pluck this white rose....'

Here, as elsewhere throughout the Sonnets, the poet may allude, in a secondary sense, to the truth = constancy of the Friend, but primarily he deals with the philosophic theory of the *Truth of Beauty* (see Introduction), e.g., l. 2, *truth in beauty dyed*; l. 3, *truth and beauty on my love depends*; l. 6, *Truth...with his colour fix'd* = embodied in his beauty; l. 7, *beauty's truth*.

CII. 1. *strengthen'd*, strengthned Q.

7. *Philomell* in Q. See Note V. on the Typography of the Quarto 1609.

8. *his* Q., Kelmscott, Tyler, her Housman (*Collection of English Sonnets*, 1835).

11. *bough* Gildon, bow Q.

CIII. 13. *sit*, fit Delius conj. But Shakespeare uses this verb with a sense frequently comparable to that of the noun *seat*. Cf. xxxvii. 7:—

> 'Entitled in their parts do crownéd sit.'
>
> 'Within his thought her heavenly image sits,
> And in the self-same seat sits Collatine.'—*Lucrece*, 288-89.

CIV. 5. *Autumne* in Q. See Note V. on Typography.

9. *dial-hand*, Dyall hand Q.

CV. 1. *idolatry*, Idolatry Q.

2. *idol*, Idoll Q.

1-4. His love is not idolatry since he worships only at one shrine. There is a liturgical suggestion in 'since all alike my *songs and praises* be, To one, of one....'

6, 7. *Constant...constancy*. There may be a slight play on the words: *constant* = fixed, *constancy* = the quality of fixedness, but perhaps with a secondary allusion to constancy in love.

8. *difference* = accidents, differentiæ. The poet lays terms of logic under contribution. This points to a philosophic drift, or suggestion, which should be noted. In ci. and elsewhere he has identified *Truth* with *Beauty* in the person of the Friend; and here, his 'three themes in one'—(l. 13), viz. 'Fair, kind, and true...which three, till now, never kept seat in one'—are, after all, nothing else than the three primal categories of philosophy—the Good, the Beautiful, and the True.

CVI. 1. *chronicle*, Chronicle Q.

7. *pen*, Pen Q. = art of Poetry. See Note V. on the Typography of the Quarto 1609.

11. *divining*, devining Q., foreseeing, as one foresees who practices divination. Cf. Milton:—

> 'Yet oft his heart *divine* of something ill
> Misgave him.'

12. *still* Q., skill Malone (Tyrwhitt conj. and Capell MS.). This emendation has been universally adopted, but it puts the sense of the last six lines out of focus. They suggest a sharp antithesis by their sound which, however, with this emendation, they blur by their sense. In ll. 1-8 the Poet defers, here as elsewhere, to the artistic excellence of the antique presentment of beauty; cf.:—lix. 'Shew me your image in some *antique* book'; lxviii. 'In him those holy *antique* hours are seen'; cviii. 'But makes *antiquity* for aye his page.' In these passages, and here, he assumes that the Ideal is, as we say, the Classic, the type determined long since by a tradition of great artists. The Quarto reads, 'They had not *still* enough your worth to sing'; although they *could* write—could, indeed, 'blazon sweet beauty's best'—*still* they lacked something essential, viz. the model which we can behold and wonder at, 'but lack tongues to praise.' They had the 'tongues,' but lacked the model; we have the model, but not their excellence in the art of description. Tyrwhitt's emendation, by denying the antients' 'skill,' defeats the antithesis of the passage and counters Shakespeare's general view of their excellence in Art.

CVII. *Not mine own fears*, etc.:—This Sonnet is obscure unless it be read as a limb of the sustained attack on Time (c.-cxxv.), which culminates in a denial of its reality (cxxiii.-iv.). The sense seems to be.:—ll. 1-4, 'Not mine own fears (expressed in civ.), nor the whole world's prophetic expectation of things to come—(suggested by 'divining eyes' of cvi.) implying, as it does, that they are to come in place of the things that are—can limit the continuation of my love, which, in common with all things, seems, but only seems, subject to limitation. Ll. 5-8 have been held to refer, by Massey and Minto, to the death of Elizabeth; by Tyler, to the Rebellion of Essex. I doubt both explanations, and it suffices for the sense that they do point to some crisis, in Nature or Politics, which excited an apprehension not justified by the event. So, the poet goes on (ll. 9-14), 'does my love *now* look fresh in this most balmy time'—(Tyler suggests that the sonnet may have been written in spring or summer)—and, reverting to the theme of immortality conferred by his verse, Death makes submission to the victory of his verse.

12. *dull and speechless tribes* = those who, being unable to write immortal verse, are voiceless after death.

14. *crests*:—I.e. on mortuary achievements.

CVIII. 3. ...*new*...*now* Q...*new*...*new* Malone. The emendation is unnecessary. There are two ideas:—(1) What *new* thing can be said, which has not been said; (2) What can be said *now*, to-day, when I am taking up my pen again, a practice once abandoned.

5, 6. *but yet, like prayers divine, I must each day say o'er the very same*. Cf. the liturgical suggestion of cv. 3, 'Since all alike my *songs and praises be*, To one, of one....'

7, 8. *Counting no old thing old, thou mine, I thine,*
Even as when first I hallow'd thy fair name:—

Cf. 'Our love was new...when I was wont to greet it with my lays' (cii.). This was some three years earlier (civ.), and even then the Poet had touched this theme tentatively: then as now—given the identity of himself with his friend, 'Thou mine, I thine'—he counted 'no old thing old'; not even his own face 'chopp'd with tann'd *antiquity*' (lxii.), since

> ''Tis thee (*my self*) that for myself I praise,
> Painting my *age* with beauty of thy days.'

The primary sense begins at this point to be doubled by a larger philosophic sense. The obvious meaning—that neither the Poet's 'songs and praises,' though 'all alike' (cv.), nor the beauty of the Friend, though it 'steals away,' can ever be old (civ.)—is stated in terms so wide as to embrace a mystical suggestion that this, which is true of the Friend's beauty and of the Poet's devotion, is also true universally. Eternal Love (l. 9), in 'love's fresh case,' as differentiated by accident, is unaffected by age. So, in cv., the Poet, when 'one thing expressing leaves out difference,' because he is singing that which is 'constant in a wondrous excellence' = a thing miraculously abstracted from the scheme of Time and Change. This Sonnet is an integral part of the whole 'satire to decay' (c.-cxxv.), the machinery of which consists in a retrospect over the inward moods and outward chances that have befallen to the Poet and the Friend during three years. But these actual experiences serve for texts to an esoteric doctrine which affirms the eternity of Love and denies the reality of Time.

12. *But makes antiquity for age his page*:—I am convinced that the Poet does *not* refer to any change in the outward beauty of the Friend. He has just declared (civ.), 'as you were'—i.e. three years earlier—'such seems your beauty still.' He is arguing, indeed, *from* the constancy of his own love, and *from* the incidents of the last three years; but in ll. 9-14 he advances from these premises to a general statement, given in sonorous terms:—that Eternal Love in its successive embodiments, each conditioned by accident, transcends the 'injury of age.' And when he says that Eternal Love makes *antiquity* his page for ever, he associates with the theme, that the Friend can never seem old to him (civ.), the more esoteric theme of cv., that the 'praise of ladies dead and lovely knights'—the 'blazon of sweet beauty's best,' by the '*antique* pen' of earlier generations—is but a 'prophecy prefiguring' the beauty now embodied in the Friend. Thus—in the apparent immutableness of the Friend's beauty; and, more largely, in the antique preshadowing of this incarnation of an eternal type by writers, long dead, describing

beautiful men and women long dead—does the Poet come to find (l. 13) the first conception of love originating 'where time and outward form would show it dead.'

This closes the exordium (c.-cviii.) of the whole attack on the power of Time and Dacay (c.-cxxv.). Then, in cix.-cxiv. the poet illustrates his thesis by reviewing and explaining away the appearances of change in his love. In cxv., cxvi. he reverts to the thesis of the exordium. In cxvii.-cxxii. he continues the review of, and apology for, his apparent inconstancy. In cxxii., coming to one instance of such apparent inconstancy, he puts in his defence for having given to another a book of tables, given to him by the Friend, and makes it serve for a transition to the peroration of the whole argument (cxxiii., cxxiv.) in which by comparison with the eternity and the changelessness of Love he denies the reality of Time.

CX. 2. *a motley* = a jester, or fool:—Cf. 'A motley fool' (*As You Like It, passim*).

4. *Made old offences of affections new* = 'enduring *offences*' (Tyler).

6. *Askance*, asconce Q.

7. *blenches* = swervings to one side, as when a horse shies. Cf. *Measure for Measure*, IV. v. 5:—

'Sometimes you do *blench* from this to that.'

9. *have...have*, save...have Malone (Tyrwhitt conj.). The emendation is unnecessary.

12. *A God in line to whom I am confined.*—'This line seems to be a reminiscence of the thoughts expressed in cv. and to refer to the First Commandment.'—Dowden. I agree, and, if it be so, the reference to heaven in l. 13 may be in the nature of a saving clause.

CXI. 1. *with* Gildon, wish Q.

10. *eisel*, Eysell Q., vinegar (Anglo-Saxon *eisile*). Cf. Chaucer, 'Eisell strong and egre.' Steevens quotes *A Merry Geste of the Frere and the Boye*:—

'God that dyed for us all
And dranke both eysell and gall.'

'Vinegar is esteemed very efficacious in preventing the communication of the plague and other contagious distempers.'—Malone.

CXII. 5. *All the world* Q.

8, 11, 12. *...wrong: ...are:—...dispense—*. In Q. wrong,... are:...dispence. Excepting the change of punctuation (—for.) after 'dispense,' I take the Quarto reading. The of Q. does not necessarily close the sense grammatically, but, if the text be not corrupt, it indicates an emphatic pause, begetting expectation. This is indicated, also, by the opening of l. 12—'Make how.' But the text of ll. 13, 14, in Q:—

> 'You are so strongly in my purpose bred,
> That all the world besides me thinkes y' are dead':—

has been generally considered corrupt. And the first step in emendation, taken by Malone (1780, Capell MS. and Steevens conj.) was, l. 14, to alter 'me thinks' into 'methinks'—'That all the world besides methinks....' That being done it follows that: (1) 'besides' must now refer back to 'you' in l. 13; (2) the rest of the line, 'y' are dead,' must give the proposition of which 'All the world besides' is the subject. Malone and subsequent Editors (save Mr. F.S. Ellis in the Kelmscott, who reproduces the Quarto reading without comment) have attacked the problem in this shape: seeking to find in 'y' are dead,' or some emendation of those words, a proposition which agrees in sense with the subject, 'All the world besides (you).' Malone (1780) cuts the knot by omitting 'y'—'That all the world besides methinks are dead' = You are so strongly in my purpose bred that every one else seems dead to me. The Cambridge accepts this reading, although Malone himself rejected it (in 1790), and printed, 'That all the world besides methinks they are dead. Dyce (1857) and Dowden accept this with an elision, 'methinks they're dead': Dowden explaining the Q. by saying, 'y' = th' = they.' To sum up:—If the first emendation, 'methinks' for 'me thinks,' be accepted, then the second, in some form or other, must also be accepted to make sense. But why was the first, which entails the second, made? Not—and this is crucial—to make sense of a passage which, as printed in Q., is non-sense; but, because the emendators reject the sense which it bears, when so printed, as improbable. That sense is unexpected, even startling:—Every one, except myself, thinks that you are dead. Is it impossible that Shakespeare should have meant this? If not impossible, the alterations in the text, unrewarded by any signal addition to the meaning of the sonnet, can hardly be defended. Now the couplet, as emended, *adds* nothing to the meaning: it merely repeats one half of the meaning of l. 7, 'none else to me...alive.' That, indeed, was the evident object of Malone's emendation: having rejected the sense of the couplet as it stood, he altered it to suit the sense of the second quatrain. Shakespeare has some weak couplets, but none which merely repeats—or, as here, repeats less completely—an idea already completely set forth. And he can scarce have echoed the second quatrain feebly after a third quatrain intervening with a strong *crescendo* of emphasis—'In so profound abysm I throw all care'—and a further, and more emphatic, appeal for attention—'Mark how with my neglect I do dispense.' He creates an expectation of some startling declaration. In Q. we get one. Not only is the Friend 'All the world' to the Poet (l. 5)—every one else dead to the Poet and he dead to every one (l. 7)—but, and he begs us to 'mark bow' he dispenses with his neglect at the hands of the world, the Friend is so in his 'purpose bred' = so thoroughly kneaded into the intention of his being, that he too shares the Poet's case: him also the world holds for dead. The Sonnet is hyperbolical throughout, and its *crescendo* movement prepares us for a last extravagance of hyperbole. Is this, the straightforward meaning of Q., too startling? I think not. Shakespeare often uses hyperbole to enforce the closeness of the relation between the Friend and himself. He declares that their identities are merged in one, and, sometimes, he draws a fantastic result from this fanciful identification. In xlii., after lamenting the injury done him by the Friend in robbing him of the woman he 'loved dearly,' he writes, 'But here's the joy, my friend and I are one'; and draws the deduction, 'Sweet flattery, then she loves but me alone.' In cxxxiii.; written on the same theme, he calls the Friend his 'next self'; and draws the deduction that any one who imprisons his own heart must also, perforce, imprison the Friend's heart which is within it. In lxii. he conceives his own beauty to be perfect until his glass undeceives him; and, in the couplet, he resolves the error: it arises from his Friend's identity with him:—

> ''Tis thee (my self) that for myself I praise
> Painting my age with beauty of thy days.'

In all four Sonnets the movement of the quatrains leads up to a climax in the couplet: in all four, the sense of the couplet tallies with the climax of its sound, giving a sudden and fantastic resolution of accumulated difficulties.

CXIII. 3. *part his function,* perhaps = 'share his function with the mind'; but more probably, depart, abandon. Cf. *Richard II.*, III. i. 3:—

> 'Since presently your souls must part your bodies.'

The distinction of sense and the similarity of sound—'doth *part* his function and is partly blind'—are in Shakespeare's manner.

6. *latch* Malone, lack Q. He explains, 'to *latch* formerly signified to *lay hold of*. So, in *Macbeth*:—

> "But I have words,
> That should be howl'd out in the desert air,
> Where hearing should not latch them."'

'Latch' in Old English meant a 'cross-bow'; also a 'snare,' akin perhaps to 'leash,' French *laisse*.

10. *favour* is countenance, Malone.

14. *My most true mind thus maketh mine untrue*. 'Untrue' is a substantive. Cf. *Measure for Measure*, II. iv. 170:—

> 'Say what you can my false o'erweighs your true.'

But there is also a phonetic suggestion of 'mine' = m' eyne = my eyes.

CXIV. 2. *this flattery*:—In immediate sequence to the preceding Sonnet, 'this flattery' = this false presentment of other shapes in your more pleasing shape, as the truth is improved for a 'monarch's' ear.

4. *Alchemy*, *Alcumie* Q. The sense of the passage is this:—Or is my eye truthful, and has your love taught it to transmute, as base metals are transmuted by Alchemists into gold.

10. *most kingly*:—Reverting to the image of a 'monarch' and 'flattery,' l. 2.

11. '*greeing* Gildon, greeing Q.

13, 14. *If it be poison'd, 'tis the lesser sin,*

That mine eye loves it and doth first begin:—

The imagery changes a third time, and instances, after the Flatterer and the Alchemist, the Taster to a King.

CXV. 5. *million'd*, milliond Q. Million Gildon:—But Q. is right, as we say 'doubled,' 'decupled,' 'centupled.'

9. *Time's*, times Q.:—Tyler has 'Time's' and the analogy to 'Time's fool' (Q.) in the next sonnet is obvious.

10. *'Now I love you best.'* Printed as a quotation by Malone.

13, 14. *Love is a Babe, then might I not say so,*

To give full growth to that which still doth grow.

'babe' in modern editions, but the reference is, obviously, to Cupid the God of Love.

14. *grow*. Q. and Tyler; grow? Gildon, Cambridge, Dowden, Bell. The emendation defeats the sense of the whole Sonnet. The *ictus* or stress on 'not,' l. 13—(cf. the *ictus* on 'then' and 'now' in l. 10)—shows that the couplet *refutes* the argument of the third quatrain: it is a contradiction, not a reiterated interrogative. The Poet asks, 'Might I not *then*'—in those early days, 'fearing time's tyranny,' say '*Now* I love you best'? And he answers in the negative:—'Love is a Babe; then might I *not* say so....'

CXVI. *Let me not to the marriage of true minds*, etc.:—The index number of this Sonnet is printed '119' in Q. for '116.'

Having opened his attack on Time (c.-cviii.), explained his apparent inconstancy (cix.-cxii.), and asserted his absorption in the Friend (cxiii.-cxiv.), in cxv. the Poet reverted to his main theme, 'Time's tyranny,' l. 10, and in this sonnet he develops it:—'Love's not Time's fool,' l. 9.

4. *Or bends with the remover to remove*; cf. xxv. 13, 14 :—

'Then happy I that love, and am beloved,
Where I may not remove, nor be removed.'

5. *mark* = sea-mark. Cf. *Coriolanus*, V. iii. 74:—

> 'Like a great sea-mark, standing every flaw
> And saving those that eye thee.'

7. *It is the star to every wandering bark*:—The kindred image of a star by which ships steer.

8. *whose worth's unknown*:—A mystical assertion that, as the unknown worth and occult influence of a star is in excess of the practical service it affords to mariners, so has Love an eternal value immeasurably superior to the accidents of Time. S. Walker suggested 'North's,' which does not add to the sense and destroys the alliterated stresses on 'Ẃandering...ẃorth.' Cf. Drayton, *Idea*, (1619), Sonnet xliii., which first appears in that edition:—

> 'So doth the ploughman gaze the wandering star,
> And only rest contented with the light;
> That never learned what constellations are,
> Beyond the bent of his unknowing sight.

CXVII. *Accuse me thus,* etc.:—The poet takes up again his extenuation of apparent inconstancy.

5. *been*, binne Q.

6. *And given to Time*, time Q.:—'To society, to the world, or, given away to temporary occasion what is your property, and therefore an heirloom for Eternity.'—Dowden. 'Given to *them*,' Staunton conj. But 'Time' is the personified object of the whole argument (c.-cxxv.), and appears as such in the two preceding Sonnets: 'Time's tyranny,' 'Love's not Time's fool.' When the peroration is reached (cxxiii. 1) the Poet apostrophises this personal object of his attack, and arraigns him:—'No, Time thou shalt not boast....' Cf. 'the fools of Time' (cxxiv. 13). The *Sonnets* must be read in the light of contemporary verse. *E.g.* Drayton (*Idea*, lv., 1619), writes:—

> 'With so pure love as Time, should never boast.'

The major theme of the whole First Series is the defeat of Time, by Breed, by Fame, and by Love. Cf. v. 6:

> 'For never-resting Time leads summer on.'
>
> xii. 13. 'And nothing 'gainst Time's scythe can make defence
> Save breed, to brave him....'

xv. 13. 'And all in war with Time for love of you.'

xvi. 2. 'Make war upon this bloody tyrant, Time.'

xix. 13, 14. 'Yet do thy worst, old Time: despite thy wrong,
My love shall in my verse ever live young.'

lx. 9. 'Time doth transfix the flourish set on youth.'

lxiv. 1, 12. 'When I have seen by Time's fell hand defacéd...
That Time will come and take my love away.'

And this major theme—the defeat of Time—is restated in the last movement, as in a symphony, with greater emphasis:—

c. 10-13. 'If Time have any wrinkle graven there,
If any, be a *Satire* to decay,
And make Time's spoils despiséd every where.
Give my love fame faster than Time wastes life.'

cviii. 13. 'Finding the first conceit of love there bred
Where Time and outward form would show it dead.'

cxxiii. 1, 14. 'No! Time, thou shalt not boast that do change...
I will be true, despite thy scythe and thee.'

cxxiv. 3, 13. 'As subject to Time's love or to Time's hate...
To this I witness call the fools of Time.

Let me illustrate the contemporary vogue of these attacks on Time, once more, from an address to Guillim by John Davies of Hereford:—

'Thy matchlesse Art,
Incites my Muse to raise her Armes of power,
With princes to lay open thy desert,
To make it all-devouring Time devoure.'

7. *That I have hoisted sail to all the winds*:—Cf. the image of a 'wandering bark' which, in the preceding Sonnet, immediately precedes the reflexion, 'Love's not Time's fool.'

11. *Bring me within the level of your frown,*
But shoot not at me.

'Level' = effective range, here; elsewhere, generally = aim. Cf. *A Lover's Complaint*, 22, 23:—

'Sometimes her levell'd eyes their carriage ride,
As they did battery to the spheres above.'

Malone quotes from *Winter's Tale* (II. iii. 6):—'Out of the blank and level of my aim':—where 'blank' = the *white* centre of an archer's target, whence 'point-blank.'

CXVIII. *Like as, to make our appetites more keen*, etc.:—This Sonnet, developing the sense of the last couplet, continues the apology for apparent inconstancy.

12. *rank of goodness*:—Dowden cites 2 *King Henry IV.*, IV, i. 64:—

> 'To diet *rank* minds sick of happiness,
> And purge the obstructions which begin to stop
> Our very veins of life.'

CXIX. *What potions have I drunk*, etc.:—The apology continues.

1. *Siren, Syren* Q. See Note V. on Typography of the Quarto, and Note II. on *Lucrece.*

2. *Limbecks*, Lymbecks Q. = alembics.

7. *spheres* Spheares Q.; *fitted*:—'how have my eyes started from their hollows in the fever-*fits* of my disease' (Dowden), who cites *Hamlet*, I. v. 17:—

> 'Make thy two eyes, like stare, start from their spheres.'

But 'Fit' sometimes = a sudden emission. Cf. Coleridge:—

> 'A tongue of light, a *fit* of flame.'

CXX. 4. *nerves*, Nerves Q.

6. *time*, Time Q.

10, 12. *rememb'red...tend'red*:—A defective rhyme. Cf. lx.

1, 3:—'open...broken.'

10. *rememb'red* = 'reminded, an active verb governing *sense* in l. 11.'—Dowden. I agree; and, that being so, 'our night of woe' clearly refers to some one occasion of great sorrow, well-known to the Friend and to the Poet, which the Friend '*once*' caused by his 'crime,' (l. 8), but for which he '*soon* tendered' the fitting salve.

13. *But that, your trespass*, But that your trespass Q. and modern Editions. I place a comma after 'that' to show that it is a demonstrative pronoun, referring back to 'your crime,' and forward to 'your trespass.' The rhythm, apart from the sense,

shows that it is not a conjunction, for, unless it be stressed, the line collapses.

CXXI. 2. *When not to be* = when not to be vile. I retain the comma of Q. which makes this clear.

3, 4. And the lawful pleasure lost, which is judged vile from the point of view of others and not from any sense of shame on our part.

7. *frailer spies*:—Cf. cxxv. 13, 'Hence, thou suborn'd *Informer*.'

8. *in their wills* = according to their wishes.

9. *level* = aim. Cf. Note on cxvii. 11.

11. *bevel* = 'Crooked; a term used only, I believe, by masons and joiners.'—Steevens. The sense is rather 'oblique' than 'crooked.'

CXXII. 1. *thy tables* = a book of tables, note-book, memorandum. Cf. Bacon, *New Atlantis*:—'he drew forth a little scroll of parchment (somewhat yellower than our parchment, and shining like the leaves of writing tables, but otherwise soft and flexible).'

2. *Full character'd with lasting memory* = Filled up with the notes of lasting memory. Cf. *Hamlet*, I. v. 97-103:—

'Remember thee!
Yea, from the *table* of my *memory*
I'll wipe away all trivial fond *records*,
All saws of books, all forms, all *pressures* past,
That youth and observation *copied* there;
And thy commandments all alone shall live
Within the *book* and *volume* of my *brain*.'

'And these few precepts in thy *memory*
See thou *character*...'—*Hamlet*, I. iii. 57.

8, 9, 10. *record...poor retention...tallies...score*:—Cf. the attack on Time's *dates, records* and *registers* in the next sonnet.

13. *adjunct*:—Sir Henry Wotton uses this word of a colleague with the sense of an 'assistant':—

'An *adjunct* of singular experience and trust.'

CXXIII. 1. *No! Time, thou shalt not boast*:—See Note on cxvii. 6. This apostrophe opens the peroration to the poet's attack on Time. See Introduction, p. cxxvii.-cxxx.

4. *They are but dressings of a former right*:—but repetitions of antenatal experience. See Introduction. 'sight:' in Q. The apostrophe is sustained throughout the sonnet.

7. *borne* Q.:—That is, bourne or limit.

8. *told* = reckoned. 'told:' in Q.

9-12. The Poet here denies the reality of Time and of his effects.

CXXIV. 1. *state* = accident; an effect of Time. See Introduction.

2. *It might for Fortune's bastard be unfather'd,* i.e. It might be disinherited in favour of any other effect of Time and Chance.

3. *Time's...Time's*, times...times in Q. But the personification is obvious.

5. *accident* :—A term of metaphysics. Cf. l. 1, 'state.'

9. *Heretic*, Heriticke Q. See Note V. on Typography of the Quarto 1609, and Note II. on *Lucrece*.

13. *the fools of Time,* time Q. But the personification is sustained. Cf. cxvi. 9, 'Love's not Time's fool.'

14. *Which die for goodness, who have lived for crime*:—Who are so much the dupes of Time that they attach importance to the mere order of sequence in which events occur, and believe that a death-bed repentance can cancel a life of crime.

CXXV. *Were't aught to me*, etc.:—This Sonnet is obscure. See Introduction, pp. cxxx.-cxxxii., and Note IV. on Rival Poets.

1. *I bore the canopy*:—A metaphor leading up to the next line. The word 'canopy' may contain an allusion to some one of the many allegories current among the cultivated court circle of that day. Contemporary letters offer examples of such allusions to allegories, to anecdotes from the ancients, to heraldic conceits, and to Platonic catch-words, which are no less obscure than the like allusions in Shakespeare's verse. In a letter from Francis Beaumont to Anne Fytton, Mary's sister, you

read:—'In which conceite of myne (if I did amisse for dutiful love is ever full of fearfull care) your owne preatie stoarie of the Canopy, and myne of Timantes for covering affectiones with curtaines may be my all sufficient warrant.'—(*Gossip from a Muniment Room*, London, 1897.)

2. *With my extern the outward honouring*:—That is, honouring outward beauty with public praise (cf. lxix. 5); but, as I hold, with a larger philosophic suggestion, in the manner of the time, and in pursuance of the argument in the two preceding Sonnets, viz. that the Poet's love is esoteric and eternal. Cf. Chapman's *Peristeros, or the Male Turtle* (1601):—

> 'Nought lasts that doth to outward worth contend
> All love in smooth brows born is tomb'd in wrinkles....
> And Time and Change (that all things else devours
> But truth eternized in a constant heart).'

See Note IV. on Rival Poets.

3, 4. *Or laid great bases for eternity*
Which proves more short than waste or ruining?

Proves Q., Tyler; *Prove Dowden*, Cambridge. In an obscure sonnet it is safest to preserve the Q. text so long as it yields sense. The sense here seems to be:—'or ostentatiously claimed an eternity for my panegyrics' which *eternity* proves short-lived as "waste or ruining."' Cf. Drayton's proud claim, *Idea*, xliv. (1619, first published in 1599):—

> 'Ensuing Ages yet my Rhymes shall cherish....'

his contempt of other versifiers, *Idea*, xliii. (1619, first published in that year):—

> 'Why should your fair eyes, with such sovereign grace
> Disperse their rays on every vulgar spirit...
> Would God! I were as ignorant as they!
> When I am made unhappy by my skill!'

5-7. *Have I not seen dwellers on form and favour*
Lose all, and more, by paying too much rent
For compound sweet; foregoing simple savour,

I preserve the punctuation of Q., emphasised, as it is, by a capital after the semicolon—'sweet; Forgiving.' Modern Editions give '...rent, ...sweet foregoing....' But the 'dwellers on form and favour' are 'eternizers' with their 'extern the outward honouring' to secure 'eternity' by their public panegyrics of outward beauty. Cf. lxxxv. 8:—'In polished *form* of well-refinéd pen.' The 'compound sweet' for which they pay too much rent is, I submit, their 'couplement of proud compare,' xxi.; their 'false painting,' lxvii.; 'false art,' lxviii.; 'strainéd touches,' lxxxii.; 'comments of praise richly compiled...golden quill' and 'well-refinéd pen,' lxxxv.—such merits, for example, as Drayton gloried in. For these laboured tributes to outward beauty they forego the 'simple savour,' i.e. the simple appreciation of true affection, and are 'pitiful thrivers, in their gazing spent.'

9, 10. *No, let me be obsequious in thy heart,*
And take thou my oblation, poor but free.

Cf. Drayton's *Idea*, liv. (1619)[1]:—

'Receive the incense which I offer here,
By my strong faith ascending to thy fame!
My zeal, my hope, my vows, my praise, my prayer,
My soul's *oblations* to thy sacred Name!'

Our Poet pays in the Friend's 'heart,' an oblation which is 'poor,' i.e., not '*precious*' and '*refinéd*' and '*filed*'; and which is 'free,' i.e. voluntarily offered with no ulterior design on eternal Fame for the author.

11. *Which is not mix'd with seconds*:—See Introduction, p. cxxxii. Seconds, I submit = 'assistants,' 'colleagues,' or, at least, other poets similarly engaged in conquering 'Eternity' by laboured 'Petrarchizing.' Our Poet goes on to say that his 'oblation...knows no *art*. But mutual render, only me for thee.' Cf. xxxii.:—

'O, then vouchsafe me but this loving thought;
"Had my friend's Muse grown with this growing age,
A dearer birth than this his love had brought,
To march in ranks of better equipage:
But since he died *and Poets better prove,*
Theirs for *their style* I'll read, his for *his love*."'

13. '*Hence thou suborn'd* Informer' Q.:—See Introduction, p. cxxxii., and Note V. on Typography of the Quarto 1609.

1. This sonnet occurs in the earlier editions.

The Poet's attitude towards other writers, expressed here and elsewhere, is rendered intelligible by the knowledge that there did exist a fraternity of poets who affected 'learning' and 'art,' and who praised each other for their merits, whilst they poured contempt on the 'unlearned' and 'artless.'

CXXVI. This is not a Sonnet but an Envoy to the First Series written in six couplets. In Q. two sets of parentheses follow l. 12, as if to indicate that two lines are wanting.

2. *Dost hold Time's fickle glass, his sickle, hour;* in Q. 'Doest hould times fickle glass, his sickle, hower.' Many emendations have been suggested:—*tickle hour*, Kinnear conj.; *fickle hower*, Lintott; *sickle-hour*, Hudson 1881 (S. Walker conj.); *fickle mower*, Bullock conj.; *fickle hour*, Kinnear conj. The *Cambridge* has a note (v.): 'Capell in his copy of Lintott's edition has corrected "hower" to "hoar," leaving "fickle." Doubtless he intended to read "sickle hoar."' But 'hower,' rhyming with 'power,' can scarce be a misprint for 'hoar.'

12. *Quietus*:—The technical term for an acquittance given to an accountant, or official charged with the administration of funds; from the phrase *quietus est* in such documents. Thus:—'Th accompt of John Tayler and John Shakspeyr,'—the poet's father—'Chamburlens, made the xth day of January,' 1564, is thus acquitted: "Et sic *quieti sunt*, Johannes Tayler et Johannes Shakspeyr."—Halliwell-Phillipps, *Outlines*, II. 224.

CXXVII. *In the old age black was not counted fair*, etc.:—This Sonnet opens the Second Series, where the poet addresses his mistress, or comments on the wrong she has done him. Most of the numbers were evidently written at the same time as the numbers of Group C. (xxxiii.-xlii.), and on the same theme.

2. *were*, weare Q.

4. Beauty in Q. See Note V. on Typography of the Quarto 1609.

7. *Beauty*, beauty Q.; *bower*, boure Q.

9. *Mistress' eyes...raven,* Mistersse eyes...Raven Q.

9, 10. *...eyes...eyes*:—Many emendations have been suggested: *...eyes...hairs*, Capell MS.; *hairs...eyes*, Hudson 1881 (S. Walker and Delius conj.); *brows...eyes*, Editors Globe ed.

(Staunton and Bræ conj.); *eyes...brows*, Staunton conj.; *hairs ...brows*, Kinnear conj. But no emendation is necessary. 'Her eyes so *suited*' makes an additional proposition about the 'eyes' which leads up to 'and they mourners seem.' Cf. *Hamlet*, I. ii. 78, 'customary *suits* of solemn black,' and *Ibid.*, 86, 'the trappings and the *suits* of woe.'

11. *At such who, not born fair, no beauty lack*:—That is, such who supply the defects of Nature with Art. The theme of this sonnet is handled by Biron in *Love's Labour's Lost*, IV. iii, e.g.:—

> 'O, if in black my lady's brow be deck'd,
> It mourns that painting and usurping hair
> Should ravish doters with a false aspect;
> And therefore is she born to make black fair.'

Tyler compares, also, Sidney's *Astrophel and Stella*, Sonnet VII.:—

> 'That, whereas blacke seemes beautie's contrary,
> She even in blacke doth make all beauties flow.'

CXXVIII. 5. *envý*, envie Q., accented on the second syllable. Cf. Ben Jonson, *Poetaster*, Prologue:—

> *'Their moods he rather pities than enviés.'*

This is an example of a licence then permitted, viz. the 'wrong ranging the accent of a sillable. ...as to say,...*eńdure* for *endufe.*'—*Arte of Poesie*, 1589.

5. *jacks*, Iacks Q.

CXXIX. 1. Spirit in Q.:—See Note V. on the Typography of the Quarto 1609.

1, 2. Tyler cites:—'It hath been observed by the ancients that much use of Venus doth dim the sight...the cause of dimness of sight...is the expense of spirits.'—Bacon, *Nat. Hist.* (Ed. Spedding, ii. 555, 556).

9. *Mad*, made Q.; *pursuit*, pursut Q.

11. *A bliss in proof, and proved, a very woe*, A blisse in proof and proud and very wo Q.:—'The Quarto is here evidently corrupt'—Malone. But the corruption is not very extensive: 'proud' stands naturally for 'proved' with, as always, 'u' for 'v' and, as frequently, no apostrophe to mark the omission of

a mute 'e'—e.g. *proposed* in the next line. 'A' may well have been mistaken for the symbol of 'and.'

CXXX. *Mistress...Sun...Roses...Music.* See Note V. on the Typography of the Quarto 1609, and Note III. on *Lucrece.*

2. *Coral*, Currall Q.

CXXXI. 1. *so as thou art:*—That is, as described in the preceding Sonnets.

4. *jewel*, Iewell Q.

5. *Yet in good faith some say that thee behold* Q.:—Generally punctuated, 'Yet, in good faith.' But this suggests that 'in good faith' may be an expletive of the author, whereas, of course, it is his tribute to the good faith of his mistress's detractors. He goes on, 'To say they err, I dare not be so bold.'

CXXXII. 2. *torments*, Ed. 1640, which is obviously right. Q. has 'torment.'

5. *Sun of Heaven:*—I preserve the capitals of Q. throughout this Sonnet. See Note V. on Typography of the Quarto 1609, and Note III. on *Lucrece.*

6. *the East*, th' East Q.

9. *mourning eyes:*—There is a play on the word, referring back to 'morning sun' of l. 5.

CXXXIII. 6. *my next self:*—That is, the Friend.

8. *A torment thrice threefold thus to be crosséd:*—Cf. xlii., written at the same time on the same theme:—

'If I lose thee, my loss is my love's gain,
And losing her, my friend hath found that loss;
Both find each other, and I lose both twain,
And both for my sake lay on me this *cross.*'

9-14:—Prison my heart in your bosom; but then let my heart be bail for and, so liberate, my Friend's heart. Whoever keeps me, let me keep him; then, you cannot use rigour to him since he will be in my gaol = my heart. And yet you will; for, since I am imprisoned in you, I am in your power, and consequently my Friend also, since he is imprisoned in me.

CXXXIV. 1. *he is thine:*—Because in the preceding Sonnet 'I, being pent in thee, Perforce am thine, and all that is in me.'

2. *And I myself am mortgaged*:—Because (*Ibid.*) I am ready to go bail for my friend.

3. *that other mine*:—The Friend, in pursuance of the theme of identity. Cf. 'my next self' (*Ibid.*).

7. *He learn'd but surety-like to write for me*:—This suggests that the Friend came under the fascination of the poet's mistress in discharging some office of kindness or civility to her on the poet's behalf. Cf. l. 11:—'And sue a friend came' = that became 'debtor for my sake.'

9. *The statute*:— '*Statute* has here its legal signification, that of a security or obligation for money.'—Malone.

12. *unkind abuse* = abuse of his good-nature, which has turned out ill for him. The metaphor of this, and other sonnets, is reminiscent of the straits to which the poet's father reduced himself and his friends who went surety for him to the baker. See Introduction, p. xx.

CXXXV. The capitals and italics of Q. are retained throughout this sonnet.

1. *Will*, a play on 'will' = desire and 'Will,' which we learn, from this and other numbers, to have been the name of both the Poet and his Friend.

2. And *Will* too, boote, and *Will* in over-plus, Q. Some find in this line a suggestion of three persons with the name of 'Will,' and conjecture that the Dark Lady had a husband with that name. But this interpretation is not needed. *Will* in l. 1 stands for 'desire' and the name of the Friend; l. 2 adds the name of the Poet, and then states that this addition is also an excess. It must, however, be mentioned that the Fytton letters, published by Lady Newdigate-Newdegate (*Gossip from a Muniment Room*, 1897), show that Sir William Knollys, to whose charge Mary Fytton was entrusted by her father, fell in love with her before, and continued in love with her after, she became Will Herbert's mistress. The chief difficulty in accepting Mr. Tyler's identification of Mary Fytton with Shakespeare's Dark Lady lies in the late date—1607—of Mary Fytton's marriage. For, if the words of clii. 3—'In act thy bed-vow broke'—indicate that the Dark Lady was married, the identification of the two

would necessitate a date later than 1607 for the composition of that Sonnet and Group C. (xxxii.-xlii.).

4-8. 'Will' is used for desire throughout, now of the Dark Lady, and, again, of the Poet.

5-7. *...spatious...gracious*, another example of 'wrong ranging the accent of a sillable,' which, it so happens, is given in the *Arte of Poesie*: 'as to say...gratious for grátious.'

13. *Let no unkind, no fair beseechers kill:*—'But perhaps the line ought to be printed thus: "Let no unkind 'No' fair beseechers kill," i.e. "let no unkind refusal kill fair beseechers."'—Dowden. But the rhythm, clearly indicated by a comma after 'no' in Q., would be shattered by this emendation. *Kill*, skill (Rossetti conj.). Tyler, commenting on this and the ensuing Sonnet, cites a similar play on 'Will' = desire, and 'Will' = William, in the dedication by John Davies, in his *Select Second Husband for Sir Thomas Overbury's Wife, now a Matchless Widow* (1606), curiously enough, to 'William, Earle of Pembroke." He cites also Davies' epigram addressed to Shakespeare:—

> 'Some say, good *Will* (which I, in sport, do sing),
> Hadst thou not plaid some kingly parts in sport....'

CXXXVI. 8. *Among a number one is reckon'd none*:—A contention put forward by arithmeticians in Shakespeare's day. See Note on VIII. 14: '*Thou single will prove none.*'

CXXXVII. 4. *Yet what the best is, take the worst to be*:—That is, take the worst = your appearance, to be what the best is. The preceding line, 'They know what beauty is, see where it lies,' suggests the Friend in whom the poet recognised the Type of Ideal Beauty. But this recognition could not preserve him from loving a woman whom he compares to 'the bay where all men ride' (l. 6), to 'the wide world's common place' (l. 10), and to a 'false plague' (l. 14).

9, 10. *...several plot...common place*:—Dowden cites from Halliwell:—'Fields that were enclosed were called *severals*, in opposition to *commons*, the former belonging to individuals, the others to the inhabitants generally.'

13, 14. *In things right true my heart and eyes have erréd*
And to this false plague are they now transferréd:—

The Poet contrasts his 'erring' from constancy to the Friend with his infatuation for the Dark Lady. Cf. xxxvi. 10, written at the same time:—

> 'Lest my bewailéd guilt should do thee shame....'

CXXXVIII. 12. *to have years told*, t' have yeares told Q. *Told* = reckoned. This Sonnet is the first number of *The Passionate Pilgrim* (1599) with certain variations:—

> 4. 'Unskilful in the world's false *forgeries*.'
>
> 8-14. 'Outfacing faults in love with love's ill rest.
> But wherefore says my love that she is young?
> And wherefore say not I that I am old!
> O, love's best habit is a soothing tongue,
> And age, in love, loves not to have years told.
> Therefore I'll lie with love, and love with me,
> Since that our faults in love thus smother'd be.'

These variations, with the unlikely repetition of 'tongue' as a rhyme in the third quatrain, after it had served in the second, confirm the view that Shakespeare's numbers in *The Passionate Pilgrim* were pirated, perhaps from recollection only.

CXL. 4. *pity-wanting*:—Hyphened by Gildon.

7. *sick-men.*:—I retain the hyphen of Q., as it is needed by the rhythm.

11. *ill-wresting*:—Hyphened by Lintott.

12. *mad slanderers by mad ears believéd be*:—The line may hold a reference to the Poet's own case. Cf. cxii.:—

> 'Your love and pity doth th' impression fill,
> Which *vulgar scandal* stamp'd upon my brow.'
>
> ''Tis better to be vile than vile esteemed,
> When not to be, receives reproach of being.'—cxxi.

CXLI. 9. *my five wits*:—'"The wits," Dr. Johnson observes, "seem to have been reckoned five, by analogy to the five senses, or the five inlets of ideas. *Wit* in our author's time was the general term for the intellectual power." From Stephen Hawes' poem called *Graunde Amour* and *La Bell Pucel*, 1554, ch. 24, it appears that the five wits were "common wit, imagination, fantasy, estimation, and memory."'—Malone.

my five senses:—These the Poet has described, ll. 1-8. Cf. Chapman's *Ovid's Banquet of Sense*, in which he deals with *'Auditus, olfactus, visus, gustus, tactus,'* and Drayton's *Idea*, xxix. (1619), where the same theme is handled (published first in 1599).

11. *Who leaves unsway'd the likeness of a man*:—I agree with Tyler in understanding the passage to mean:—'My five wits and five senses cannot dissuade my heart, that is but one against ten, from serving thee. And my heart, which they cannot *dissuade*, leaves them *unsway'd*.' The 'likeness of a man' = the five wits and five senses.

14. *pain*:—In its first meaning of 'penalty, punishment' (French *peine*, Latin *pœna*).

CXLII. 2. *Hate of my sin, grounded on sinful loving*:—That is, hate of my sin, grounded on *your* sinful love of others. You hate my love, not because it is sinful, but because you love, sinfully, elsewhere. This is evident from the remainder of the Sonnet, where the Poet argues that his state does not merit reproof from lips which have 'seal'd false bonds of love as oft' as his own, and asks, 'Be it lawful I love thee as thou lov'st *those*.'

7. *And seal'd false bonds of love as oft as mine*:—Cf. *Measure for Measure*, IV, i. 6:—

> 'Take, O take those *lips* away,
> That so sweetly were *forsworn*....
> But my kisses bring again, bring again;
> *Seals of love*, but sealed in vain, sealed in vain.'

8. *others' beds' revénues*, others beds revenues Q., bed-revenues Capell MS.

11, 12. *...pity...pity,* (1) = compassion; (2) = ground or subject for compassion. Cf. *Othello*, IV. i. 206, 'But the pity of it, Iago.'

13. *If thou dost seek to have what thou dost hide*:—That is, if you seek love from another, which you withhold from me. This Sonnet is the last of four written in an unbroken chain—the sense and even the phrasing of the concluding lines in each being taken up in the opening lines of the next.

CXLIII. *Lo, as a careful housewife*, etc.:—This Sonnet, also, belongs to the unbroken chain of the preceding four. It opens with an illustration in ll. 1-8, and its application ll. 9-12. But the couplet does but restate the sense of cxlii. 11-14.

13. *Will* = the Friend.

CXLIV. *Two loves I have*, etc.:—This Sonnet appears with certain variations in *The Passionate Pilgrim* (1599), viz. l. 2, 'that like' for 'which like'; ll. 3-4, 'My better...My worser,' for 'The better...the worser'; l. 6, 'side'—evidently the correct reading—for 'sight' Q.; l. 8, 'fair' for 'fowle'; l. 9, 'feend' for 'finde'; l. 11, 'to me' for 'from me'; l. 13, 'the truth I shall not' for 'yet this shal I nere.'

The 1640 *Sonnets* prints *The Passionate Pilgrim* version. Fleay, Dowden, and others compare Drayton's *Idea*, xx. (first published as xxii. in 1599):—

> 'An evil Spirit (your Beauty) haunts me still
> Wherewith, alas, I have been long possest;
> Which ceaseth not to attempt me to each ill....
> Thus am I still provoked to every evil,
> By this good-wicked Spirit, sweet Angel-Devil.'

The likeness is but of phrasing, for Drayton refers only to one person, and if, as I believe, the Second Series was written at the same time as Group C. (xxxiii.-xlii.)—perhaps in 1598 or the early part of 1599—Drayton's sonnet seems just such a superficial plagiarism as are his later sonnets, published first in 1619, of Shakespeare's numbers in the later Groups. See Note IV. on the Rival Poets, and Note on Shakespeare's cxvi. 5-8.

2. *suggest* = tempt. Cf. Note on *Lucrece*, l. 37.

6. *side* P.P., sight Q.

9. *fiend*, finde Q. The 'e' has evidently been misplaced.

CXLV. This Sonnet is in octosyllabic verse, with an unpleasing assonance between the rhyme-sounds of the first quatrain, and but little in it that recalls Shakespeare's hand save:—

> 'That follow'd it as gentle day
> Doth follow night....'

7. *doom*, dome Q., doome edition 1640.

13. I...*threw*, 'I hate—away from hate she flew,' Steevens conj. But the sense is better in the Q. reading.

CXLVI. 2. *My sinful earth these rebel powers array*. This is Massey's emendation of an obviously corrupt passage in Q.:—

> 'Poor soule the center of my sinfull earth,
> My sinfull earth these rebell powres that thee array.'

It has the merit of *adding* nothing to the text, and of restoring euphony to one of the finest among Shakespeare's Sonnets. There is warrant for repeating the last words of a preceding line. E.g. in cxlii. 1, 2:—

> 'Love is my sin, and thy dear virtue *hate*,
> Hate of my sin....'

in xc. 1, 2:—

> 'Then hate me when then wilt; if ever, *now*;
> *Now*, while the world....'

In *Venus and Adonis*, 963-64:—

> 'Both crystals, where they view'd each other's sorrow,
> Sorrow that friendly sighs sought still to dry....'

So, too, for the parenthetical development in the second line of a term used in the first, e.g. cxi.:—

> 'O, for my sake do you with Fortune chide,
> The guilty goddess of my harmful deeds,
> That did not better....'

and cxv.:—

> 'Those lines that I before have writ do lie,
> Even those that said I could not love you dearer.'

Many other emendations have been suggested:—*Fool'd by those rebel*, Malone. *Starv'd by the rebel,* Steevens. *Fool'd by these rebel*, Dyce. *Thrall to these rebel*, Anon. *Press'd by*, Dowden. *Foil'd by*, Palgrave. *Hemm'd with*, Furnivall. *My sense these rebel*, Bullock. *Slave of these*, Cartwright. *Leagu'd with these rebel*, A.E. Bræ, adopted by Dr. Ingleby in 'the Soul arayed,' p. 15. *Why Feel'st, Tyler.*

array:—'"Array" here does not only mean dress. I think it also signifies that in the flesh these rebel powers set their battle in array against the soul.'—Massey. Dowden adds, 'There is no doubt the word "aray" or "array" was used in this sense by Elizabethan writers, and Shakespeare, in *The Taming of the Shrew*, III. ii. and IV. i., uses "raied," though nowhere "aray," except perhaps here in this or a kindred sense.' There may well, as so often in the *Sonnets*, be double meaning in the word. *Array* = (1) beleaguer, afflict = (2) adorn. Dowden also cites *Lucrece*, ll. 722-728, and notes the close juxtaposition of *siege and livery* in Sonnet ii. An association of the ideas of a 'siege' and of 'outward embellishment' does, certainly, seem suggested. And the next two lines:—

> 'Why dost thou pine within and suffer dearth,
> Painting thy *outward walls* so costly gay?'

recall Macbeth:—

> 'Hang out our banners on the *outward walls*.'

8. *...charge?...end?* Q.: a good example of careful punctuation in Q.

10. *aggravate* = increase, pile up; *thy* Q., my Lintott. 'Malone says that the original copy and all the subsequent impressions read "my" instead of "thy." The copies of the 1609 Edition in the Bodleian—one of which belonged to Malone himself—in the Bridge-water Library, and in the Capell Collection, as well as Steevens' reprint, have "thy."'—*Cambridge*, Note x.

13, 14. *...Death...Death*, death...death Q.

CXLVII. I retain the capitals of Q. See Note V. on the Typography of the Quarto 1609, and Note III. on *Lucrece*.

7, 8. *and I desperate now approve*
Desire is death, which Physic did except.

Q. has a comma after 'approve,' but this raises no grammatical presumption. (See Note V. on the Typography of the Quarto 1609.) The sense is:—'I, being in despair, now recognise that desire to be fatal which took exception to the teaching of Physic.'

9. *Past cure I am, now Reason is past care*:—'So in *Love's Labour's Lost*, V. ii. 28:—

> "Great *reason*; for *past cure* is still *past care*."

It was a proverbial saying'—like 'Fast bind, fast find; A proverb never stale in thrifty mind' (*Merchant of Venice*, II. v.

54).—'See Holland's *Leaguer*, a pamphlet published in 1632: "She has got this *adage* in her mouth; *Things past cure, past care*."'—Malone.

CXLVIII. 1. *O me*! Q. has the note of exclamation. *Love*, love Q.

8, 9. *Love's eye is not so true as all men's: no,*
How can it! O, how can Love's eye be true.

This exquisite piece of punctuation in Q. (see Note V. on Typography of the Quarto 1609) has been frequently destroyed by emendation: *all men's: no*. S. Walker conj., *all men's 'No,'* Editors Globe ed. (Lettsom conj.), taking *eye* as a pun on *'Ay.'* Any change in the Q. punctuation destroys the rhetorical force of the two heavy stresses, the second heavier than the first, on '*...can...can*' in l. 9.

CXLIX. 2. *partake,* pertake Q.:—'*I.e.* take part with thee against myself.'—Steevens. 'A *partaker* was in Shakespeare's time the term for an *associate* or *confederate* in any business.'—Malone. Dowden cites '*your partaker,* Pole,' i.e. partisan, 1 *Henry VI.*, II. iv. 100. *The Guide into Tongues* (1617), gives:—'Partaker, vide Partner.'

3, 4. *when I forgot*
Am of myself all tyrant for thy sake?

I retain the punctuation of Q. Malone put '*all tyrant, for thy sake*? That is, for the sake of *thee*, thou tyrant.' Dowden also refers *all tyrant*, as an apostrophe, to the Dark Lady. But the Q. reading is, almost certainly, correct; and the plain sense is:—'I forget myself, a tyrant to myself for your sake.'

10. *That is so proud thy service to despise*:—That is, what *merit* of mine is so proud as to despise the state of slavery to you.

13, 14. A conceit on the Poet's blindness, due to his love, which furnished matter for a conceit in the couplet to the preceding sonnet. The next number continues to work on the same theme, proving that the three numbers were written at one time.

CL. Cf. l. 2 with ll. 11 and 12 of CXLIX., l. 3 with ll. 1 and 2 of CXLVIII.

CLI. A piece of amatorious argument: the reference to 'conscience' in ll. 1, 2, 13 suggests that it was written in reply to an appeal, probably playful, addressed to the Poet's conscience. That appeal, if made, and whether playful or serious, was in any case not seriously entertained.

6. *gross,* grose Q.

10. *prize: proud,* prize, proud Q.

CLII. *In loving thee thou know'st I am forsworn,* etc.:—A similar piece of playful debate. L. 11, *And, to enlighten thee, gave eyes to blindness*, connects this Sonnet closely with cxlvii., cxlviii., cxlix., cl., in which continuous discourse is resumed between the Poet and his mistress after the break, indicated by cxliv., where the Poet comments, in suspense, on the infidelity of his mistress with his Friend; cxlv., in octosyllabic verse, and cxlvi., with its grave appeal to his soul. Before the break, the Poet doubts whether his Mistress have not altogether abandoned him; after the break, it is clear that she has again taken him into her favour: cxlix. 'Canst thou, O Cruel! say I love thee not'; cli. 'Then, gentle cheater, urge not my amiss'; and here, l. 2, 'But thou art *twice forsworn*, to me *love swearing*.' This reference to a double infidelity—l. 3, 'In act thy bed-vow broke and *new faith torn*' and l. 5, 'But why of *two oaths*' breach do I accuse thee'—shows that the Dark Lady, who had broken her bed-vow, soon also broke off her 'new faith' with the Friend. The numbers of the Second Series were written at the same time as Group C. (xxxiii.-xlii.), and on the same theme. That Group is but episodical in the First Series: and if, as I have suggested (Note on cxx. 9)—'O that our night of woe might have remembered,' i.e. reminded 'my deepest sense, how hard true sorrow hits,' refers back to some one occasion of sorrow on which the Friend 'soon...tendered the humble salve,' then it seems probable, from the tenor of the two main discourses of the Second Series, that the Friend, after an explanation from the Poet, so acted as to lead the Dark Lady to break off her 'new faith' and to enter on a *reintegratio amoris* with the customary argument that it was her lover, and not she, who had been remiss in love:—

'Canst thou, O Cruel, say I love thee not?'

The Second Series ends with this Sonnet, for the next two are but exercises on a Renaissance convention. It is important, let me repeat, to remember that the numbers of this Series rank chronologically with the numbers xxxiii.-xlii., and that, like them, they are early as well as episodical, and in the main playful, with but little, by comparison to the later groups, of grave speculation and ethereal beauty. The Poet's love for the Dark Lady may have been well over some three years before he took up his pen to write a 'Satire to Decay' (c.-cxxv.).

11. *And, to enlighten thee, gave eyes to blindness*:—That is, to shed a more favourable light on thee, I. shut my eyes.

13. *perjured I,* periured eye Q. This may be correct, with a play on the two words '...I...eye,' since it follows on l. 12 'made them (= eyes) swear against the thing they see.'

CLIII. 'This and the following sonnet are composed of the very same thoughts differently versified. They seem to have been early essays of the poet, who perhaps had not determined which he should prefer.'—Malone. Dowden and Tyler note that Herr Hertzberg (*Jahrbuch der Deutschen Shakespeare-Gesellschaft*, 1878, pp. 158-162) has tracked the conceit developed in these two sonnets 'to a poem in the Anthology by Marianus, written, as he thinks likely, in the fifth century after Christ. The Epigram is ix. 627 of the Palatine Anthology' (Tyler).

6. *Dateless* = eternal. Cf. xxx. 6, 'death's dateless night.'

11. *bath*:—'Query, whether we should read Bath (i.e. the city of that name). The following words seem to authorize it'—Steevens.

14. *eyes,* eye Q. This line offers an example of the use of stops in Q. to indicate the duration of a rhythmical pause:—

'Where *Cupid* got new fire; my mistres eye.'

CLIV. I retain the capitals of Q. (see Note V. on Typography of the Quarto 1609), except for *legions* (Legions Q.), and *well* (Well Q.).

A LOVER'S COMPLAINT

I. *The Text.*—The text, as in the case of the Sonnets, has been founded on the facsimile by Charles Praetorius, from the Museum copy of the First Quarto, 1609, and the same rules have been observed in editing it.

II. *Notes on the Text.*

7. *Storming her world with sorrow's wind and rain*:—Her world = herself, as a microcosm. Cf. *King Lear*, III. i. 11:—

> 'Strives in his little *world* of man to out-scorn
> The to-and-fro-conflicting *wind and rain*.'

Sorrowes, wind and raine in Q.

14. *lattice*, lettice Q. Cf. Sonnet III. 11, 12:—

> 'So thou through *windows* of thine age shalt see
> Despite of wrinkles this thy golden time.'

15. *napkin*, Napkin Q.

18. *That season'd woe had pelleted in tears*:—'*Pellet* was the ancient culinary term for a *forced meat ball*, a well-known *seasoning*.'—Steevens.

22. *Sometimes her levell'd eyes their carriage ride; levelled* = aimed, as guns on their *carriages*. Cf. the Note on Sonnet cxvii. 11.

28. *commix'd*, commxit Q.

31. *sheav'd*, sheu'd Q.

36. *maund* = a hand-basket. *The Guide into Tongues gives*:—'a maunde or great basket, a Lat. manus, a hand, quod manu gestari soleat.' Cf. Bishop Hall's *Virgidemiarum*, lib. v.:—

> 'Or many maunds-full of his mellow fruite':—

and Dekker, *Jests to Make You Merry*:—

> 'In her maund, a basket which
> She bears upon her arm':—

and Herrick:—

> 'There, filling maunds with cowslips, you
> Shall find your Amaryllis.'

37. *bedded jet,* bedded Iet Q., 'beaded' Sewell, Cambridge:— But 'bedded' is probably right = imbedded and descriptive of

the actual condition in which jet is found. Cf. *Tempest*, I. ii. 252:—

> 'Therefore my son i' the ooze is bedded.'

41. *let*, lets Q.

45. *posied*, Posied Q., i.e. bearing some loving inscription; cf.:—

> 'Is this a prologue, or the posy of a ring.'—*Hamlet*, III. ii. 162.

46. *sepulchres*, Sepulchers Q.

48. *sleided*, separated or parted into threads, as weavers prepare for their sley, slay or reed. Cf. *Pericles*, iv., Gower, 21:—

> 'Be't when she weaved the sleided silk
> With fingers long, small, white as milk.'

Pericles, a play which, though not included in the first two Folios, shows unmistakable marks of Shakespeare's hand, was first published in Quarto in the same year—1609—as *The Sennets* and *The Lover's Complaint.*

48. *feat*, feate Q., i.e. featly, delicately. Cf. *Tempest*, I. ii. 380:—'Foot it featly heare and there'; and *Winter's Tale*, IV. iv. 176:—'She dances featly.'

49. *Enswathed and seal'd to curious secrecy*. 'Anciently the ends of a piece of narrow ribbon were placed under the *seals* of letters, to connect them more closely.'—Steevens. 'Florio's Italian and English Dialogues, entitled his *Second Frutes*, 1591, confirm Mr, Steevens's observation. In p. 89, a person who is supposed to have just written a letter, calls for "some wax, some *sealing thread*, his dust-box and his seal."'—Malone.

51. *gave to tear*, gave to teare Q. and Kelmscott. Apparently = 'made a motion as if to tear,' ''gan to tear,' Malone, Cambridge.

58. *ruffle* = flaunting commotion. 'In Sherwood's *French and English Dictionary*, at the end of Cotgrave's *Dictionary*, *ruffle* and *hurliburly* are synonymous. Again, in Camden's *Remaines*, 1605:—"then there was a nobleman merrily conceited and riotously given, that...came ruffling into court in a new suit."'—Malone.

60. *hours observéd as they flew*:—Malone closes the parenthesis after 'hours,' and refers the sequel to the torn fragments of paper. But it refers to the hours observed by the 'blusterer,' who was also a philosopher of life.

61. *this afflicted fancy* = the love-sick lady.

64. *grained bat*, greyned bat Q.; 'staff in which the grain of the wood was visible; cf.:—"my grained ash"—*Coriolanus*, IV. v. 114.'—Steevens. 'Where go you with *bats* and clubs.'—*Ibid.* I. i. 57. *The Guide into Tongues* gives:—'a Bat, or clubbe. Vi. Batte, Clubbe, or Staffe.'

65. *comely-distant*, hyphened by Malone.

73. *judgment*, Iudgement Q.

84. *Deified* Q.

87. *hurls*, purls. *Boswell, conj.*

88. *to do will aptly find* = will readily find people to do it.

91. *sawn* Q., seen: an irregular past participle. 'Sown,' Boswell, conj. and Bell; 'drawn,' Lettsom, conj.

93. *phœnix,* perhaps = incomparable, or appertaining to a state of transition. The Phœnix was a type of the nonpareil and of transmutation which engaged the attention of the age. Mandeville had lifted that rare bird from Pliny; King James versified Mandeville's description in 1585, and Shakespeare, Jonson, Chapman, Marston, Drayton, Daniel, all wrote on the Phœnix. Vere, Earl of Oxford, and Sir William Herbert were contributors to a book of verses called *The Phœnix Nest* (London, 1593).

94. *Termless* = youthful.

96. *Yet show'd his visage* = yet his visage show'd. *cost* = display.

112. *Or he his manege by th' well doing steed*; Or he his mannad'g, by' th wel doing Steed, Q. The 'rounds, bounds, course' and 'stop' of l. 109 are terms of the manege or riding-school *Mannad'ge*, manage in Malone and modern Editions is, manege, i.e. horsemanship, *haute école*: and the sense: whether the horse by him (= thanks to his rider's horsemanship) *became his deed* (= exhibited the feats of the manege with ease and

grace), or he his manege (= or whether the rider controlled the horse with grace) by th' well doing steed (= thanks to the horse's training).

116. *In himself not in his case* = not in his conditions, here in the sense of accessories. Shakespeare frequently uses *case* in its metaphysical sense. Cf. Sonnet cviii. 9:—'In Love's fresh case.'

118. *Can for additions*:—Sewell suggested 'came.' But 'can' is here used in its pre-auxiliary sense = to be effective in a pursuit. Cf. *Hamlet*, IV. vii. 85:—

'I have seen myself, and served against the French
And they *can* well on horseback.'

The sense is:—All accessories, made fairer by falling to him, *count* for additions to his perfection, yet their designed fitness did not make up the sum of his grace, but each of them was graced by him.

126. *Craft of will* = faculty of influencing others. The next stanza (127-133) is somewhat obscure. In Q. it runs:—

127. That hee didde in the general bosome raigne
128. Of young, of old, and sexes both inchanted,
129. To dwel with him in thoughts, or to remaine
130. In personal duty, following where he haunted,
131. Consent's bewitcht, ere he desire have granted,
132. And dialogu'd for him what he would say,
133. Askt their own wils and made their wils obey.

In such cases it is safest to abide, as nearly as possible, by the punctuation of Q. I take out the comma at the end of line 128, for in that place it need have no grammatical significance (see Note V. on *The Sonnets*); I substitute a colon for a comma at the end of line 130, and insert a comma after 'And' in line 132. The sense is then:—

126. Catching all passions by his faculty for influencing others:
127. So that he reigned generally in the hearts
128. Of young and old and enchanted both sexes

129. To dwell with him in imagination when absent, or to stay with him
130. In personal attendance, following him in his haunts:
131. Consents bewitched by his grace, have conceded his wish ere he expressed it,
132. And, put through question and answer on his behalf, as if he had himself held speech,
133. Have made his requests to their own wills and made their wills comply with them.

The insertion of a comma after 'And,' l. 132, my only drastic emendation, is justified, I submit, by the fact that the passage cannot be construed unless 'dialogued' be taken for a past participle passive. Shakespeare uses the word as a verb. Cf. *Timon of Athens*, II. ii. 52:—

'How dost, fool? Dost dialogue with thy shadow?'

137. *labouring*. 'Labour' would make better sense.

140. *owe* = own. *landlord*, Land-lord Q.

144. *and was my own fee-simple*:—'Had an absolute power over myself; as large as a tenant in fee has over his estate.'—Malone. *The Guide into Tongues* (1617) gives:—Fee-simple = 'that, whereof wee are seized in these generall words: To us and our heires for ever.'

Not in part, (not in part) Q., i.e. not in part-ownership.

154-55. '*the foil Of this false jewell* (Iewell Q.):—That is, his previous conquests were as the foil, or thin leaf of metal, placed behind stones by jewellers to make them appear transparent or to give them a particular colour.

157-58. *Or forced examples 'gainst her own content*
To put the by-past perils in her way?':—

Or insisted on the examples which tell against her own (apparent) happiness in order to hinder herself from pursuing it by realising the past dangers of others.

164. *forbid*, ed. of 1640; 'forbod' Q. *seem* Gildon; seemes Q.

171. *orchards*, Orchards Q.

173. *Knew vows were ever brokers to defiling*. 'A broker formerly signified a pander.'—Malone. Cf. *Hamlet*, I. iii. 137:—

'Do not believe his *vows*; for they are *brokers*,
Mere implorators of unholy suits.'

174. *characters*, Characters.

176. *city*, City Q.

182. *vow* Q, woo Dyce 1857 (Capell MS. and Collier conj.).

185. '*acture*' = action Malone, Bell. But perhaps the word was coined, on the model of 'facture,' to express, here, the 'mere nature of action' abstracted from other ideas, e.g. of 'intention,' which are most often associated with 'action.' A blunter, but somewhat analogous distinction, is drawn between the ideas expressed by the two adjectives 'visual' and 'visible.' And our Poet was given to distinctions which have proved too fine for preservation in common speech. 'My offences' in l. 183, and 'their reproach' in l. 189, seem both to mean illegitimate children, the fruit of relations in which 'neither party; is true or kind. Such witnesses, therefore, raise no presumption that love has been given, or vowed.

192. *to th'*, to th, Q., where the apostrophe has evidently been let drop.

193. *charméd*, Charmed Q.

198. *Of palid pearls and rubies red as blood*, Of palyd pearles and rubies red as blood Q., palid ed. 1640. This beautiful line has too long been injured by Malone's emendation 'paled.'

204. *talents*, tallents Q. 'These *lockets*, consisting of hair platted, and set in gold.'—Malone. 'There was no such term applied expressly to lockets.'—Bell. Shakespeare uses the word twice for an *accomplishment*; twelve times in its original sense of a sum or weight of Greek currency, all in *Timon of Athens*; and once, as perhaps here, for a precious possession. Cf. *Cymbeline*, I. vi. 79:—

'In you, which I account his beyond all *talents*' (tallents in First Folio).

205. *impleach'd*, intertwined as in a fence of pleached wattle. Cf. *Much Ado About Nothing*, III. i. 7:—

'Bid her steal into the *pleached* bower.'

210. *nature*, Nature Q. = occult properties. Cf. 'invised (= *invisible*) properties,' l. 212. *quality*:, quality. Q., but the full

stop is not grammatical, for the sense runs on into the next stanza, which gives the matter of the 'deep-brain'd sonnets,' amplifying the nature of these stones, till each 'with wit well blazon'd smiled or made some moan,' l. 217.

211. '*the Diamond,—*', the Diamond? Q.

215. *blend* = blended.

219. *pensiv'd*, pensiu'd Q., pensive Hudson 1881 (Lettsom, conj.).

221. *render;—*, render: Q.

224. *Since I their altar, you enpatron me*, Since I their Aultar, you en patrone me Q., enpatrone ed. 1640. The sense is:—Since I being the altar on which they are offered, you are the patron in whose name that altar was erected. Cf. *Lear*, I. i. 144:—

> 'Whom I have ever honour'd as my king,
> Loved as my father, as my master followed,
> As my great *patron* thought on in my prayers.'

225. Oh then advance (of yours) that phraseless hand Q., phraseless = ineffable, beyond the compass of praise.

228. *Hollowed* Q., which may be right, i.e. 'carved' of the 'similes, locks intertwined with metal and gems blazon'd with wit'; hallowed, Sewell, Cambridge, Bell, Kelmscott.

229. *What me your minister for you obeys*:—That which serves under me as your steward and representative.

234. *Which late her noble suit in court did shun*:—'Who lately retired from the solicitation of her noble admirers.'—Malone.

234. *Whose rarest havings made the blossoms dote*:—'Whose accomplishments were so extraordinary that the flower of the young nobility were passionately enamoured of her.'—Malone.

236. *of richest coate* = of highest lineage (blazoned on their coat-armour).

240. *strives*? strives, Q.

241. *Playing the place which did no form receive*, Place Q.:—This is obscure. I am disposed to think it merely a metaphysical conceit, in the author's manner, with the meaning:

'making oneself as it were without form or void.' If so, it would be an ancient and laboured equivalent for the modern and vulgar colloquialism, making oneself scarce. Some confirmation of this gloss may be found in l. 245:—

'And makes her *absence* valiant, not her might.'

Many emendations have been suggested. *Planing,* Capell MS. *Paling,* Malone, with the gloss, 'securing within the pale of a cloister that heart which had never received the impression of love.' *Salving...harm receive*, Lettsom, conj. *Painting*, Anon. *Flying*, Bullock, conj. *Playning*, Orson, conj.

242. *unconstrainéd*, unconstraind Q.

251-52. *...immured...procured* Gildon, enur'd...procure Q.:—The corruption of the text is not so extensive as it appears. *Enur'd* evidently, with but *n* for *m*, was *emur'd*; the apostrophe for a mute 'e' is in accordance with the invariable practice of Q., and *emured* stands for immured (*Love's Labour's Lost*, III. i. 118) in *all* the Quartos and in the First Folio.

Now, to tempt all, liberty, now to tempt all liberty Q.:—The sense is:—She sought the cloister to avoid temptation, and now has procured her liberty to tempt all (= to prove the whole experience of love). Gildon has 'now, to tempt (= to seduce), all liberty procured.'

258. *congest*, 'collect together' Bell.

260. *Sun, Sunne* Q., Variorum 1821, Bell, Kelmscott:—The metaphor is not far-fetched—a very sun of sanctity—and 'Sunne' can scarce be a misprint for 'nun' (Malone, conj.; Capell MS.; Dyce, 1857; Cambridge).

261. *Who disciplin'd, ay, dieted in grace*, Dyce 1857 (Capell MS. and Malone, conj.), Cambridge, Kelmscott '*Who disciplin'd I dieted in grace*' Q., *and dieted*, Malone, Bell. 'Ay' was frequently spelt 'I.' Cf. Drayton's *Idea* (1619), v. 1:—

'Nothing but "No!" and "I!" and "I!" and "No!"'

273. *aloes, Alloes*, with capital and italics, Q. See Note V. on *The Sonnets.*

280. *prefer and undertake* = put forward and guarantee.

281-82. *dismount...levell'd.* Cf. l. 22, for the same image of a gun aimed on its carriage.

290. *but with*, i.e. with but.

293. *o cleft effect*, or cleft Q. = O double effect.

297. *doff'd* = doff'd.

303. *cautels*, Cautills Q. 'Insidious purposes,' Malone, who cites *Hamlet*, I. iii. 15:—

'Perhaps he loves you now;—
And now no soil of *cautel* doth besmirch
The virtue of his will.'

The Guide into Tongues (1617) gives:—Cautell = 'a crafty way to deceive.'

305. *swounding* Cambridge, sounding Q.:—An older form of the same word.

308. *swound*, sound Q.

309. *in his level*, within his range of deadly fire:—Cf. ll. 22, 281-82, and Sonnet cxvii, 11.

316. *Grace* Cambridge, Variorum, Kelmscott; *grace* Q.

329. *maid, Maide* Q.